HEALTH MATTERS

UNIVERSITY OF
GLOUCESTERSHIRE
at Cheltenham and Gloucester

HEALTH MATTERS

A sociology of illness, prevention and care

Edited by

ALAN PETERSEN &
CHARLES WADDELL

OPEN UNIVERSITY PRESS
Buckingham

Open University Press
Celtic Court
22 Ballmoor
Buckingham
MK18 1XW

Email: enquiries@openup.co.uk
World wide web: http://www.openup.co.uk

First published 1998

A catalogue record of this book is available from the British Library

ISBN 0 335 20260 8 (pbk)
ISBN 0 335 20261 6 (hbk)

Printed and bound in Singapore.

Contents

Preface

Health Sociology textbooks inform us through the exploration of sociological issues in health, illness, disease, injury and disability, and the way these things are distributed, experienced and treated. They tell us about the social nature of these health matters which are profoundly social in cause and consequence; in experience and treatment; in prevention, distribution and biases. Today's health matters are not fixed entities but are part and parcel of how we live with each of them. As such, they can be changed, or improved upon, so that we can all live more healthy lives.

We put this book together in the same vein—to inform you about the social nature of health matters, but we have used a particular approach which each contributor to this book shares. All involved in this book want to convey to readers—students, health care providers, the interested public—that health does matter. Health matters in at least two ways.

Health matters to sociologists. A multiplicity of reasons motivate people to come into health sociology—interests, career potential, great lecturers. But one reason we stay in this field is because we want to improve the health of people: to care for that fragile ecology of body, mind and spirit through which we share life with each other. Health sociologists strive to cultivate the social ecology of the whole person— body, mind and spirit—as the person interacts with others.

Health matters, also, to you. The healthier you are in body, mind and spirit the richer your life; the richer your life, the more you have to share with each other. There is far too much unnecessary suffering in the world. Morbidity and mortality are inevitable, but much morbidity and premature mortality is socially avoidable. What is more, that which cannot be avoided can be better handled socially than we handle it at present. As the contributors to this book make clear, even in sickness and even unto death, we could live more healthy lives.

We have divided this book into four parts: sociology matters, experience matters, care matters, and prevention matters. However, as you will soon discover, these divisions are largely heuristic. Many of the chapters could be placed in more than one part as topics are highly interrelated. A short introduction precedes each part, serving not only to introduce the respective chapters but also to place them within a larger sociological literature.

In our selection of contributors we have endeavoured to convey a sense of the breadth of work currently being undertaken in the sociology of health in the United Kingdom, Australia and New Zealand, particularly in relation to inequalities in health and illness, health care and prevention. We recognise, however, that we could never adequately represent the diverse theoretical and empirical contributions of health sociologists.

We hope that you find this book useful, and that it helps stimulate further thinking and research.

Alan Petersen, Perth
& Charles Waddell, Rome

ACKNOWLEDGEMENTS

We thank all our contributors for agreeing to be part of this project. We are grateful to Judy Waters who commissioned the book, and to Elizabeth Weiss for her editorial assistance. We also wish to acknowledge the support of our colleagues at Murdoch University and the University of Western Australia.

We dedicate this book to Ros and Greg.

Contributors

Waqar Ahmad is Senior Lecturer and Director of the Ethnicity and Social Policy Research Unit at the University of Bradford, UK.

Gillian Bendelow is Lecturer in Health and Social Policy in the Department of Applied Social Studies, University of Warwick, Coventry, UK.

David Buchbinder is Associate Professor in the School of Communication and Cultural Studies, Curtin University of Technology, Western Australia.

Robin Bunton is Principal Lecturer in Social Policy and Co-Director of the Centre for Social and Policy Research at the University of Teesside, UK.

Roger Burrows is a sociologist and currently the Assistant Director of the Centre for Housing Policy in the Department of Social Policy and Social Work, University of York, UK.

James Chisholm is Senior Lecturer in Medical Anthropology and Anatomy at the University of Western Australia.

Valerie Clifford is Senior Lecturer of Higher Education Development at the University of Otago, New Zealand.

Ann Daniel is Professor of Sociology at the University of New South Wales.

Deirdre Davies is a postgraduate sociologist at Murdoch University, Western Australia.

Nick Fox is Senior Lecturer in Sociology at the University of Sheffield, UK.

Dennis Gray is Associate Professor of Drug and Alcohol Abuse at Curtin University of Technology, Western Australia.

Gillian Hatt is Lecturer in Social and Cultural Studies at Edith Cowan University, Western Australia.

Saras Henderson is Lecturer in the School of Nursing at Curtin University of Technology, Western Australia.

Lesley Jones is Senior Research Fellow in the Ethnicity and Social Policy Research Unit, University of Bradford, UK.

Allan Kellehear is Foundation Professor of Palliative Care at La Trobe University, Victoria.

Deborah Lupton is Associate Professor in Cultural Studies and Cultural Policy in the School of Social Sciences and Liberal Studies, Charles Sturt University, Bathurst, New South Wales.

Beverley McNamara is a postgraduate sociologist/anthropologist at the University of Western Australia.

Lenore Manderson is Professor of Anthropology in International and Tropical Health, University of Queensland.

Julie Mulvany is Senior Lecturer in Mental Health in the School of Social and Behavioural Sciences, Swinburne University of Technology, Melbourne.

Sarah Nettleton is Lecturer in Social Policy in the Department of Social Policy and Social Work, University of York, UK.

Alan Petersen is Senior Lecturer in Sociology at Murdoch University, Western Australia.

Pat Pridmore is Lecturer in the Institute of Education, University of London.

Sherry Saggers is Senior Lecturer in Social and Cultural Studies at Edith Cowan University, Western Australia.

Wendy Seymour is Senior Lecturer in the School of Social Work and Social Policy at the University of South Australia.

Stephanie Short is Senior Lecturer in Health Services at the University of New South Wales.

Charles Waddell is Honorary Research Fellow at the University of Western Australia; and *Scholastic* at Beda College, Rome.

Catherine Waldby lectures in the Communication and Cultural Studies program at Murdoch University, Western Australia.

Simon J. Williams is Lecturer and Warwick Research Fellow in the Department of Sociology, University of Warwick, UK.

PART 1

Sociology matters

The need to examine the social context of differences in health status is a widely accepted tenet nowadays. Health is not purely a matter of individual physiology, and health care does not simply equate with medical care undertaken in hospitals. The biomedical model of health—which views the body as a machine, disconnected from social environments—has been substantially questioned. Sociologists, acutely aware of the social structuring of life experiences, have been at the forefront of efforts to place the study of 'the social' at the centre of the analysis of health and health care. Most sociologists see themselves as contributing, at least in small measure, to the amelioration of the suffering that is seen to be at least in part socially produced. Equipped with a strong social consciousness and the appropriate social research methods, many, if not most, have set about uncovering the 'facts' of health disadvantage, in a relatively disinterested way, in order to lay the groundwork for health justice. Increasingly, however, the question of what counts as 'fact' and what counts as 'fiction' has been debated. Recent trends in social thought have undermined some of sociologists' cherished beliefs about their subject matter. Under the influence of postmodernism and poststructuralism, in particular, many scholars have begun to interrogate basic categories and concepts. The meanings of terms such as 'social justice', 'equality', 'participation', 'freedom', and 'identity', so often taken for granted in so-called modernist sociology, are now being vigorously debated throughout the social sciences and humanities, leading us to ask: exactly what is 'a just sociology of health'?

The chapters in this section present some of the diverse theoretical perspectives brought to the study of health inequalities and health justice. Together, they reflect broader theoretical debates regarding the question of what counts as knowledge. Many contemporary arguments

3

in sociology concern the issue of faith in realism. Realists believe in the ability of sociology to know all there is to know, without doubt; that is, to gain unmediated access to the objective 'truth'. For them, the overriding problem is how to 'get at the facts', and so social research often becomes preoccupied with questions of method: who to question, what to ask, how to analyse. Some scholars, however, reject the ideal of realism, or the notion of a single, transparent 'truth'. From this perspective, what we take to be 'reality' is a construction, and there is no direct access to an objective world 'out there' that is independent of our own subjective world. In its extreme versions, 'anti-realism' often leads to 'defeatism' involving the repudiation of the distinction between fictional and nonfictional accounts of the world (Stones 1996, pp. 13–22). Much work in the sociology of health, including these chapters, reflects the ongoing tensions between, and attempts to reconcile, these two major contending positions.

The sociology of health and illness is an ever-changing field, characterised by the emergence of new topics and perspectives, and new ways of approaching questions of knowledge. It currently encompasses such areas as the analysis of illness experience, health care practices, gender and health, ethnicity and health, ageing experience, sexuality, and public health and health promotion. It is an area undergoing constant re-definition in line with changes in broader theoretical foci and changing practical concerns. This makes the sociological study of health inequalities an interesting and challenging undertaking. What seemed to be an important theoretical and practical problem only yesterday is now likely to be considered passé. The question of what constitutes 'a just sociology of health', then, depends not only on whom one asks, but also *when* one asks. Rather than risk foreclosing debate on what 'a just sociology of health' is, or might be, in this text we have tried to convey a sense of how sociologists themselves currently deal with this question in their own work.

Sociology is not just abstract theory, but rather involves ongoing efforts to bring a theoretical understanding to important practical and policy issues of the day. The sociology of health, perhaps more than any other area of sociology, is known for its focus on practical concerns and for its close connections with the policy-making process. Although the sociology of health is an area that has been criticised for its lack of theory, it is perhaps more accurate to say that researchers often fail to make explicit the kind of knowledge that they are producing, and to consider fully the political and practical implications of their theories. Explicitly and implicitly, researchers are constantly grappling with the problem of matching theory and practice. Regardless of one's conception of 'a just sociology of health', theory matters a great deal in what counts as 'fact'—a point that is underlined by most of the contributors to this volume. But, as will become evident, some writers are more explicitly concerned with theory: with questioning dominant sociological 'ways of seeing' and with developing a more 'reflexive' sociology of health.

It is important, we believe, that sociology remains reflexive. A reflexive sociology is one which involves the constant questioning of *all* categories and concepts. Sociology is, above all, a critical discipline. Sociologists should seek to interrogate that which is taken for granted, including their own theories and methods. This has not always been in evidence in the practice of sociologists. Keen to prove that sociology is a science, sociologists have often overlooked the creative possibilities for studying 'the social'. Recent work in the social sciences and humanities, however, has helped recast thinking about the 'social', and the associated dualisms of individual/society, nature/culture, and mind/body. The idea of the autonomous, rational individual who is 'socialised' and constrained by 'society', which has been, and still is, central to much sociology, is being re-thought by scholars working in diverse fields of thought. This does not necessarily mean that the concepts of individual and society have been totally abandoned, or that there has been an abrupt and total shift in theoretical paradigms. However, the grand narratives of Western modernity—particularly the idea of social progress through rational understanding and the application of rational knowledge—are being opened to scrutiny as never before, creating possibilities for re-thinking 'the social'. Sociology of health cannot remain immune to these developments. As evidence of the impact of these changes on the broader discipline of sociology, Marxism as a theory and practice is in steep decline, and the fundamental premises of feminism are being questioned (see, e.g. Grant 1993). We are also witnessing the emergence of a body of 'queer theory' which, among other things, has drawn attention to the role of sociology in the 'normalisation' of socio-sexual arrangements (Seidman 1996). These developments have exposed the fallacy that one can produce a disinterested sociological knowledge, unaffected by relations of power. A reflexive sociology, we believe, should be attuned to questions of value, and to the political implications of adhering to particular 'ways of seeing'.

Nick Fox and Robin Bunton are two of our contributors who explicitly question the categories and concepts of modernist thought and, in the process, point to new directions in the sociological study of health inequalities and health justice. In Chapter 1, Fox reflects upon the applications of postmodern social theory to the analysis of health and medicine. In his view, the ethics and politics of the postmodernist position are about 'becoming' rather than being, and about diversity, multiplicity, relationship and giving. Biomedicine and modernist human sciences seek to persuade us to a particular perspective on the human subject through the concepts of health and illness. The dominant biomedical discourse defines 'health' simply as an absence of illness, thereby denying alternative claims about the body and restricting possibilities for *becoming other*. Drawing on the work of the French philosophers Gilles Deleuze and Félix Guattari, Fox proposes the concepts of *arche-health*, 'an unfolding which is much more than "health"', and of *nomads*, which are 'subjectivities resisting and refusing discourse, not patients but impatients'. One of the features of the turn towards postmodernism, seen clearly in this analysis, is the shift in the conception of the operations of power. Rather than focusing on macro structures of power, such as the dynamics of class (seen in Marxism) or of 'patriarchy' (as in feminism), the focus is on *micropolitics*, that is, 'the minute workings of discourse within human interactions'. As Fox argues, postmodernism points to a new ontology and politics, and a radically different understanding of 'health' and 'health care' from that of conventional, modernist sociology.

In Chapter 2, Robin Bunton questions the value of adherence to any single guiding policy principle such as 'inequalities in health'. In his view, the study of inequalities in health is located within a modernist welfare state policy paradigm which is increasingly problematic. A number of assumptions—such as the assumption that social policy can ameliorate problems generated by conflicts of class society, that nation states can effectively intervene, and that basic needs (such as health) are identifiable, predictable and universal—have been undermined by developments over the last twenty-five years or more. Among these are the emergence of self-help and social movements, increasing criticisms of singular definitions of need, changes in employment patterns, and the growth of 'post-Fordist' forms of organisation. A transformation in the way we have come to understand 'the social' points to the need for an updated sociology—one with a more complex understanding of possibilities for bringing about change. As Bunton explains, in this context, the work of Michel Foucault, and his followers, finds useful application. In his chapter, he employs a Foucauldian governmentality perspective to examine new emphases in health care, particularly the consumerist ethos and the development of flexible health care delivery systems, and spells out the implications for the discussion of inequalities.

The final three chapters in this section—by Stephanie Short, Simon Williams, and James Chisholm, respectively—problematise 'health' and embodiment in very different ways, but each poses important questions for the development of 'a just sociology of health'. Biomedicine presents a view of 'the body' as abstracted from particular social and historical contexts and lived experience, and is premised upon the power of experts to define problems. Biomedical knowledge and practice involve the separation of mind from body, culture from nature, society from biology, and subject from object. It is an area in which faith in realism reigns supreme. However, the biological reductionism and certainty of scientific medical knowledge have been challenged by various forms of social constructionism, including poststructuralism. In Chapter 3, Short examines the impact of social constructionism on health research conducted by Australian consumers, and more specifically, research conducted under the now-defunct Consumers' Health Research and Development Program. She addresses the question of 'whether the consumer research projects accepted uncritically, excluded from critical scrutiny, or critically reconstructed medical knowledge of biophysical reality'. More specifically, she asks: were the research projects conducted under the aegis of the above Program able to integrate the patient's/consumer's (subjective) perspective with the biomedical (objective) perspective? The chapter is based upon an analysis of filed materials and correspondence for each of the seventy-five projects funded over the period of the Program, 1987 to 1992. As Short discovered, social constructionism has indeed had an impact on the consumer's perspective—a finding which is perhaps not so surprising when one discovers that sociologists have had a direct role both in setting up the research funding program and in devising the guidelines for applicants!

In Chapter 4, Williams presents another challenge to the subject/object and mind/body dualisms in his discussion of the emotions. The study of the emotions has been long neglected by mainstream sociology, but has recently made an appearance in the sociology of health and illness. Although sociologists have recently 'discovered' 'the body', they have tended to focus on issues of regulation and representation, rather than on lived experience. In this chapter, Williams discusses various approaches to the emotions—ranging from 'organismic' to 'social constructionist' perspectives—and spells out the significance of the sociology of emotions for the 'problem' of human embodiment. He then explores the relevance of the emotions for the analysis of health inequalities and 'redistributive justice', particularly in light of the increasing pre-eminence of psychosocial factors in the aetiology and social patterning of contemporary Western disease. In Williams' view, the 'mindful', emotionally expressive body provides 'a potentially fruitful future direction of research within the sociology of health and illness'.

Finally, in Chapter 5, Chisholm argues that we are on the verge of revolution in medical epistemology, involving the exploration of how modern evolutionary theory might augment established ways of knowing. At the core of evolutionary medicine is evolutionary theory and the idea of natural selection, originally developed by Charles Darwin in the nineteenth century. As Chisholm explains, 'the fundamental assumption of evolutionary medicine is that this theory can help guide us to a better, more therapeutic understanding of ourselves and our diseases'. Evolutionary theory is presently out of vogue in sociology—despite its continuing appearance in some 'functionalist' models of society—and sociologists are likely to bristle at the suggestion of an evolutionary perspective on health and disease. However, according to Chisholm, evolutionary theory has been given a bad name by Social Darwinism. It has important implications for therapy because its primary focus now is on the interactions between the organism and environment that effect the emergence of individual differences in adaptability. Evolutionary theory challenges much contemporary thinking about 'health' and 'good health' because natural selection favours reproductive capacity, not health. Thus, if environments are not conducive to reproduction, people are unlikely to allocate scarce resources to improving their own health or that of their children. Chisholm presents a number of interesting case studies to illustrate his arguments. His analysis leads him to advocate public health policies which seek to reduce environmental risk and uncertainty, both subjective and objective.

REFERENCES

Grant, J. 1993 *Fundamental Feminism: Contesting the Core Concepts of Feminist Theory* Routledge, London
Seidman, S. ed. 1996 *Queer Theory/Sociology* Blackwell, Cambridge, Massachusetts
Stones, R. 1996 *Sociological Reasoning: Towards a Past-Modern Sociology* Macmillan, Houndmills

1 Postmodernism and 'health'

Nick J. Fox

In this chapter I reflect upon what postmodern social theory brings to an exploration of health and medicine. The ethics and politics of this position (at least as I shall explore them) are about 'becoming' rather than being, about diversification and multiplicity, about relationship and giving (Fox 1993). The promise of postmodernism thus lies in its emphasis on openness, diversity and freedom.

This is a promise to open up the discourses that fabricate our bodies and our health and illnesses. The discourses of biomedicine and its collaborators in the modernist human sciences seek to territorialise us as 'organisms'—bodies-with-organs (Deleuze & Guatarri 1984), doomed to face the ministrations of these disciplines: to 'health', 'beauty', to a 'full and active life', to patience in the face of the failure of senses and memory, to *be*, never again to become other. I shall speak not of a health fabricated by the body-with-organs, but of *arche-health*, an unfolding which is much more than 'health', which cannot be spoken because to speak it would inscribe it, and of *nomads*, subjectivities resisting and refusing discourse, not patients but impatients.

To attempt to set out any kind of a program for a postmodern perspective on health is perhaps questionable, given the commitments to open-endedness, difference and fragmentation which postmodern writers espouse (Baudrillard 1988; Hutcheon 1987). So in setting an agenda for this chapter, I shall constrain myself to the proposition that postmodern social theory asks us to reflect upon our assumptions about the world, and our representation of it and its contents. In relation to questions of health and illness, this means that the enterprise of postmodern exploration is concerned with what could be expressed as *the politics of health-talk*. This phrase implies an interest in the construction of the world in *discourse* (the systems of concepts which create 'knowledge' about objects and/or people), and its conse-quences for power, control and authority. Foucault (1980) called this association of knowledge and power *power/knowledge*.

The postmodern approach focuses on the *micropolitics* of such outworkings of power and authority rather than the macro-structures of a society. It looks closely (and uses the approach of *deconstruction*) at the movements of difference and deferral within discourses and their claims to truth. This leads to a general scepticism about the commonsensical notions of social structuring, organisation and conti-nuity of the world, and a new interest in what is repressed and unconscious, in addition to the rational and articulated. Finally, the politics of this kind of postmodern perspective is *intertextual*. This means that in seeking ways to resist power, we look at the interplay of *power/knowledge* texts (with texts here meaning not only writing, but any kind of meaningful systems of communication or behaviour), asking questions of a text, and seeking its construction in order to subvert it.

Later in the chapter I will offer an example of how this way of thinking provides new reflections on a current issue in health: the concern with 'health-promotion'. Before that, I want to explore the theorising of the body in postmodernism, and how that leads to a new perspective upon 'health'.

UNSETTLING THE BODY AND HEALTH

Michel Foucault's book *The Birth of the Clinic* (1976) documents the construction of a new way of thinking about the body and health in the period since the Enlightenment (the period of *modernity*, in which science and rationality are applied as ways to fully know the world around us, and ourselves). In the opening pages of that book, he describes the great changes between the eighteenth and nineteenth centuries in how and what those who explored the interior of the body saw. Something which at one point in history was made visible by power/knowledge in one way, would appear quite differently under a different regime of knowledge, even when the observers claimed a continuity of discipline (in this case, anatomy). New disciplines within medical science—physiology, embryology, immunology—have since vied to fabricate the body authentically, to speak the truth about it. More recently, psychology and sociology have had an impact, with some of their concepts incorporated in medical discourse, as a biopsychosocial model of medicine transforms the early biomedical body (Armstrong 1987).

In a medical model, *health* is defined in terms of its opposite, often through operational definitions concerning time in hospital, days off sick and so on (Doyal 1981, p. 241). Outside medical discourse however, health is rarely defined so simply as an absence of illness. The World Health Organization (WHO 1985) speaks of health as a state of 'complete physical, mental and social well-being', while Wright (1982) suggests an anthropological phenomenology of 'what it is to function as a human', with illness—somewhat paradoxically— defined as circumstances of a failure to function which continues to be seen as human. Canguilhem (1989) sees health and illness as positive and negative biological values, and Kelly and Charlton call it a 'neutral idea relating to non-pathological physical functioning and the fulfilment of ordinary social roles' (Kelly & Charlton 1995, p. 83). Illness is a 'notion of increasing dependency' for de Swaan (1990, p. 220), and Sedgewick identified illnesses as socially constructed definitions of natural circumstances which precipitate death or a failure to function within certain norms (1982, p. 30). For Sacks' patients, the 'health' supplied to Parkinsonism patients by L-Dopa was an awakening (Sacks 1991).

All these definitions (be they medical or sociological) have a politics associated with them; all try to persuade us to a particular perspective on the person who is healthy or ill. The writings of Oliver Sacks on the variety of human experiences of health and illness which he has encountered as a neurologist suggest the problems associated with acting on any of these definitions of health. Just as the body is contested in the different discourses of the medic, the lover and the beautician (among many others), so 'health' turns out to be a similarly moveable feast. Many of Sacks' patients rejected a definition of their condition as illness, and saw what a doctor might have called 'health' as undesirable. A man with Tourette's syndrome considered his medication as destructive of his personality, while an old lady who heard music from her youth considered silence as a great emotional loss (Sacks 1985).

The Peter Greenaway film *The Pillow Book* concerns the relationship between body, writing and power, as the central figure inscribes her lovers with texts which together construct them and herself within a story of love and hate. Similarly, the postmodern theorists Gilles Deleuze and Félix Guattari suggest (1984, 1988) that we need to understand the body not in medical, physical terms, but as a 'philosophical' surface upon which are inscribed a range of knowledgeabilities (texts of power/knowledge), only one of which is the knowledgeability called biomedicine, which constructs the body as a 'natural' organism—whose functioning is called 'health' and dysfunction, 'illness'. The apparent physicality of our bodies is a consequence of such systems of knowledge, not a prior or essential character. Our bodies can be constructed (and are so constructed) by a myriad of other discourses, including those of the social sciences. Deleuze and Guattari call this 'philosophical' body the body-without-organs (henceforth BwO).

This is not simply a replication of a mind/body dualism, of a physical body whose behaviours and demeanour are disciplined through internalisations of cultural ideals of belief, taste, judgements and choice, codes of morality, and knowledge. For the postmodern position does not assume a prior self which reads culture on to a body. Rather, the inscription of the BwO *is* the self, subjectivity.

To give an example, a reaction to a diagnosis of a chronic incurable illness may be a sense of great loss. The diagnosis inscribes the body, cutting across previous subjectivity or sense-of-self. Now this subjectivity is challenged, the subject responds with grief and sadness, fabricating cognitions, emotions and patterns of behaviour to inform and pad out this new self. The subject's sadness may be read (and misread) by others in demeanour and in interaction, reinforcing or refining the subject. New bodily strategies are adopted (self-care, risk reduction or perhaps abandonment), through which the subject in turn is reconstituted and reread (see de Swaan 1990; Kleinman 1988). Butler emphasises the active character of this process, referring to the 'performative acts' by which identity is constructed (Butler 1990, p. 139).

This idea of the BwO sums up the very different conception of the body in postmodern theory, and reminds us that we are not speaking of the representation of the body-with-organs (the 'organism') which has constituted the medical body of the modern era. Nor are we speaking of the body as it is vaguely conceptualised in modernist social science. The body, we are reminded (Giddens 1984) takes up space and cannot be superimposed on other physical entities. It moves through a 'life course', and the 'biographical body conception' is both subjective and constrained by this unidirectional and finite temporality (Bury 1991, p. 453). In contrast, the BwO is not constrained in space and time: not because it is imaginary or symbolic, but because it cannot 'know' these concepts in some privileged way.

Of course it becomes subject to spatial and temporal constraint, but this is the outcome of inscription. But what is it which is inscribed upon the BwO, and which leads to this construction of identity? Poststructuralists and postmoderns such as Foucault, Deleuze and Guattari implicate *power/knowledge* mentioned earlier, the sets of authoritative claims to know who we are and how we should behave which comprise the systems of thought of the social world in which we live. These discourses or *regimes of truth* imprint the BwO, creating subjects who are constrained by these claims about the way the world is and what it is to be a human being.

Biomedicine is such a powerful discourse in the West, describing the body in terms of function as related to form. When functioning adequately (according to norms set by the discourse), it is in a state of 'health', deviations are defined as 'illness', to be treated and perhaps cured by those expert in the discipline of biomedicine—doctors. The discourse serves those who control it, by giving them authority, and denying alternative claims about the body. Thus, historically, the medical profession excluded other regimes of truth which rivalled their own, leading to much enhanced power and authority for those who possessed the rights to practise biomedicine. Only recently have 'complementary' theories of health and illness become strong enough (or perhaps it is because of doubts about biomedicine and its claims to cure) to offer a possible alternative system of treatment, and to have the validity of that system acknowledged, both popularly, and to an extent, by the medical profession itself.

Yet biomedicine is just one discipline of the modern era, among others including the law, the various psychotherapies and the social sciences. For Foucault (who is the author of many analyses of such disciplinary regimes), modern civilisation is a 'project' which relentlessly writes the body, transforming it entirely into a cultural object (Butler 1990, pp. 129–130). There is no escape: even 'liberating' movements contribute to this writing. For example, twentieth-century sexual 'liberation' from 'repression' is not liberation at all, but the domination and subjection of the body in a normalising discourse on sexuality and desire. Any theory of resistance is merely a further discourse on power and knowledge, creating a new subjectivity. The result of Foucault's analysis seems like a human being devoid of any capacity to resist or to mobilise resources for resisting power/knowledge (Fox 1997; Lash 1991). However, Deleuze and Guattari's theory of the BwO tries to recognise the possibility of resistance, and they consider the BwO as a contested realm. This is where I turn in the next section.

DIFFERENTIATION, NOMADISM AND *ARCHE-HEALTH*

I said earlier in this chapter that the politics of postmodernism was a *micropolitics*. This means that we seek the achievement of power and authority not in social structures, but in the minute workings of discourse within human interactions. Understanding this micropolitics and how to resist it was at the heart of Deleuze and Guattari's project, which they came (1986) to describe as a *nomadology*.

In this perspective, discourse is not something which is *done* to the BwO, but is a process in which the BwO is active, making sense and creating a sense-of-selfhood. The patternings of the BwO by the wide variety of knowledgeabilities in the social world mean that no single discourse is necessarily able to become dominant. The surface of the BwO, and thus subjectivity, is highly contested, fragmented and involved in a fluctuating struggle for the body. Biomedicine may be persuasive, but we are subjected to rival discourses too, and it is the *reading* rather than the *writing* which is of significance. Such rivalries are everywhere, and I have documented the struggles between different medical specialties (Fox 1992), education professionals (Fox 1995a) and mental health therapists (Lewis & Fox forthcoming). Let me offer an example from some research on constructions of health among anaesthetists and surgeons during in-patient surgery (Fox 1994).

In this research, I found that surgeons and anaesthetists used different and potentially opposing discourses on their patients while undergoing surgical procedures. Surgeons constituted their patient within a framework of their disease, while anaesthetists were concerned with their 'fitness', that is, their capacity to undergo the rigours of surgery and recover. Both specialists depended upon the other for their work, yet their perspectives on the patient mean that, while surgeons wanted to do as radical a job as possible to ensure disease is removed or reduced, anaesthetists wanted surgeons to exercise caution, so as to avoid placing too much physiological stress upon the patient's resource of fitness. These opposing views were played out in the actual practices of the surgical operation, in what one anaesthetist described as a 'love–hate' relationship, with both parties acknowledging the authority of the other, while seeking to limit or resist it.

Surgeons seemed to have the advantage in this rivalry most of the time. When an elderly patient was inadequately anaesthetised to enable surgery to proceed, the anaesthetist was wrong-footed and had to compromise the fitness of the patient more than he wished. But when a neurosurgical patient suffered a haemorrhage as a consequence of the surgical procedure, it was the anaesthetist who took command, organising a second emergency operation to remove the haematoma. The surgeon's authority was seriously compromised, and it was instructive to see him standing at the rear of the operating theatre, passive and without apparent moral authority over the situation. So the ongoing process of inscription which results from interactions in the social world opens up possibilities for resistance. The unforeseen accident in the operating theatre tips the balance of power/knowledge in the favour of a discourse emphasising patient fitness, giving an anaesthetist a small window of opportunity to break free of the dominant surgical discourse (to become *nomadic*, if you will). The inscription of surgical discourse is reread, enabling new possibilities for the anaesthetist's sense-of-self. This reading is intrinsically political, because

> the reclaiming of the body, desire, the subject . . . [is] a first step against the prevailing forms of domination. And further steps are possible as soon as it is understood that the social order of capitalism is only one of a myriad possibilities, and that its cohesive force is present everywhere as the manifestations of constrained and twisted desiring machines. (Boyne & Lash 1984, p. 156)

This is the relevance of the postmodern position, which is not relativistic or theoretical. In its commitment to resisting discourse, it possesses an unequivocal ethics and politics of engagement with the social world.

Let me be absolutely clear here. In this example, I am not elevating the anaesthetic discourse 'above' the surgical, or vice versa. When I talk about a window of opportunity for the anaesthetist in this example, I am not talking about imposing a new discourse, but about breaking free from discourse altogether, if only for a moment. This postmodern understanding of contestation of the BwO cannot be concerned simply with enhancing 'health' or limiting 'illness', because all definitions of health and illness turn out to be varieties of power/knowledge which seek to persuade us to a version of truth about what is good and what is bad.

Because differentiation, a breaking free, a moment of nomadic subjectivity are necessarily 'in the eyes of the beholder' and not objective, it is hard to show what might constitute such moments. I can offer two brief instances which exemplify what I am getting at. First, in de Swaan's (1990) description of life on a terminal cancer ward:

> To patients it means much when doctors and nurses know how to handle their wounds competently and without fear. The nurse patiently washing a dilapidated patient, changing his clothes, is also the only one who dares touch him without disgust or fear, who quietly and competently

handles the body which so torments and frightens the patient . . . [and who] knows how to deal skilfully with the wounds and lumps, in doing so liberating the patients for the moment from their isolation. (de Swaan 1990, p. 48)

Such simple actions may displace the discourses of medicine, and the inscriptions of fear and anger which have constructed a dying person's sense-of-self, yet these actions are open-ended, and do not attempt to be a fresh discourse on liberation or empowerment which tells the other *how* to be more free or more sexy or more something else, and of course in doing so, closes down the possibilities, making the other an appendage of the discourse. It does not say what something is, or is not: it allows, for a moment at least, a thing to become multiple, to be both something and another thing and another. Bunting offers us a further example of such opening-up, in

a family working with a child with special health needs. As the family members work with the child and with one another, each moves beyond the self and the present reality to the possibles that unfold . . . The family's health is the movement toward and the expression of these possibles as they are chosen and lived. (Bunting 1993, p. 14)

These examples show first, the possibility for a subjectivity freed from discourse, and second, a politics of the body not grounded in a narrow notion of health. To explore this further, I want briefly to introduce two notions here. The first is the *nomad*: an icon for a postmodern politics; the second is *arche-health*.

Nomadology, argue Deleuze and Guattari, is the response of the dispossessed to those who wield power through their discourses on the human condition. The nomad does not put down roots, or manipulate her environment to suit her needs and wishes. She does not seek control, she takes what is on offer, assimilates it, and moves on. She is at war with the forces which would territorialise her, the rationalism which values the stable, the static and the instrumentalism of matching actions to goals (Deleuze & Guattari 1986). Civilisation, norms, taste, social distinctions mean nothing to her: she is at one with her environment, yet never part of it. She is a warrior without a strategy (Deleuze & Guattari 1986; Plant 1993). The nomad is a refusenik, rejecting the 'territorialisations' of her subjectivity which discourse seeks to impose. Her silence is eloquence, her passivity is an act of resistance, her politics of non-engagement in the political and legal apparatus of the state have the power of Gandhi, Christ.

It is hard to be a nomad; in fact there *are* no nomads, there is only nomadism—it is a process, not an identity. Nomadism is about becoming other, and one never finally becomes other, rather, we lurch from one identity to another. Deleuze and Guattari (1988, p. 11) see nomadism as 'rhizomatic', a growth which is branching and diversifying, refusing to follow a single line of development.

To explore nomadology in matters concerning 'health' and 'illness', I coined the term *arche-health* (Fox 1993) to suggest a radically different conception of human potential. *Arche-health* is a becoming-other, a freeing of the BwO from discourse, a nomadic subjectivity. It is not intended to suggest a natural, essential or in any way prior kind of health, upon which the other healths are superimposed, it is not supposed to be a rival concept, indeed the reason for using this rather strange term is its homage to Derrida's (1976, p. 56) notion of *arche-writing*, which is not writing but that which supplied the possibility of writing, that is, the system of difference upon which language is based. Similarly, *arche-health*:

- Is the *becoming* of the organism which made it possible for the first time to speak of health or illness.
- Is present, in the sense that a trace of it is carried, in every discourse on health, however and with whatever *logos* that discourse has constituted itself.
- Can never become the object of scientific investigation, without falling back into discourse on health/illness. It is not the outcome of deconstruction of these discourses, it *is* deconstruction: difference and becoming.
- Is multiple in its effects. As difference, it is meaningless to speak of its unity or its division.

Every BwO has an *arche-health*, which is its *becoming other*. Whereas health and illness constrain the BwO by their discourses, *arche-health* is the refusal of and resistance to this discourse. Your, or my, *arche-health* may be more or less developed, depending how territorialised our subjectivities are by the discourses of medicine and the social sciences. It is the path towards the BwO, one which is a life-long journey:

> You never reach the Body-without-Organs, you can't reach it, you are forever attaining it, it is a limit . . . But you're already on it, scurrying like a vermin, groping like a blind person, or running like a lunatic: desert travels and nomad of the steppes. On it we sleep, live our waking lives, fight—fight and are fought—seek our place, experience untold happiness and fabulous defeats: on it we penetrate and are penetrated: on it we love. (Deleuze & Guattari 1988, p. 150)

The ethics and politics of *arche-health* are deconstructive, reminding us to ask hard questions of the modernist disciplines which inscribe us into subjectivity through their conceptions of, and preoccupations with, 'health' and 'illness'. *Arche-health* refuses to be reduced to language and discourse. Perhaps it is easiest to understand as the play of pure difference, which, as soon as it becomes a text, ceases to be *arche-health*. Yet that does not mean that its trace cannot be discerned, it can be encouraged and enhanced in settings of caring. I cannot tell you how to achieve *arche-health* or even that there is one *arche-health*. But we can open up the possibilities for a politics of *arche-health*, through the deconstruction of discourses on health and illness, from wherever they derive, and an ethics of *arche-health*, which offers difference in place of identity, and generosity in place of control. In the final section, I will offer one such deconstruction.

POSTMODERN REFLECTIONS ON HEALTH PROMOTION

What does a commitment to the becoming subject, the *arche-health* of the *nomad*, mean for a practical issue of concern to social theorists of health—so-called 'health promotion'? For example, in Sheffield, UK, a project entitled 'Heart of Our City' has been concerned with addressing issues around coronary heart disease (CHD) in some inner-city areas. While identifying some of the 'causes' of CHD related to poverty and other social conditions, the emphasis in terms of its interventions is aimed at changing individual behaviour: reducing levels of smoking, of intake of cholesterol and saturated fats, encouraging exercise, reducing stress and also promoting medical check-ups to identify early signs of CHD (Heart of Our City n.d.). This program is in many ways typical of a large number of interventions in health promotion which target at the level of individual prevention, and in particular focus on changing behaviour away from higher risk towards lower risk behaviour.

Initial questions of such a program might include: Whose voice is being heard in the discourse on lifestyle? What authority is being spoken here, what body of expertise is being cited, what are the conditions of promulgation of these messages through and by which we are asked to accept the authenticity of the discourse? Answering these questions begins to identify the kinds of power/knowledge involved. In this particular case, both medical and community development discourses seem important in defining the objectives and the criteria for outcomes.

These questions lead to a more fundamental deconstruction of what is involved in 'health promotion'. The term situates the individual person in an interesting way. What is being promoted? The answer might be: a healthy person. But it is not promoting personhood, or people in general, but the 'healthiness' which a person carries with them. Health promotion is forced to delimit some attributes as concerned with 'health'. The delimitation may be very wide—to incorporate mood, sexuality, security and such like; or it may be much more narrow. Feasibly the delimiting will involve attribution of those behaviours (the lifestyle) which are involved in 'health'. However, such a behaviourist interpretation may be problematic if the intervention seeks to influence lifestyle. Glassner (1989) has argued that discourses on health and fitness requires a thinking subject, capable of agency. So there is a double movement here. First, a notion of some things as delimitable as 'health', secondly, a subjectivity situated in relation to this health. There is a dissociation between the person and their health: in this perspective, subjects have the potential to rationally act to influence their health. On the other hand, 'health' has the potential to radically affect the subject—who, though separate, depends upon it for survival. This dissociation provides the potential for victim-blaming: the person is both victim of their health turned nasty, but also the agency responsible for this state of affairs. It is a dissociation, incidentally, with which modernist sociology has colluded, in its continued mind/body separation.

It would be possible to continue the deconstructions which are involved in an intervention, and no doubt collecting commentaries from people involved might provide further material in the play of intertextuality. For example, we could examine the issues raised by this comment from a family doctor surveyed by the project: 'I'm sure it's very useful but the problem that I see is that it's getting the wrong people, the ones not at risk. The people at risk don't seem interested.' (Heart of Our City 1992, p. 26)

I shall look briefly at one further element, the characterisation of the *contact* between the health promoter and the 'promotee'. This contact occurs in a 'preventive' context, and hence does not necessarily have the same discourse as curative/caring contact. Szasz and Hollender (1956) would probably put this contact within the realm of 'mutual participation', where a professional helps clients to help themselves, supposedly within an adult-to-adult relationship. The extent to which such a relationship can be mutual, as opposed to constraining and based on a professional discourse, will depend upon a number of factors, including:

• The context and personnel involved. Non-clinical personnel can take on many aspects of promotion, avoiding moves towards the dependency of the clinician/client contact.

- An emphasis on choice, responsibility and calculability of costs and benefits will tend to open up the interaction, while inputs which introduce fear, or dwell on the technicalities of the disease and/or the intervention will constrain it within a discourse on biomedicine.
- Whether the intervention draws upon other discourses, such as that of 'the family'. Targeting mothers as the primary agents involved in ensuring a healthy diet constructs them as 'responsible' and potentially culpable (Graham 1979).

These elements also suggest the conditions of resistance to the inscriptions which a health promotion of lifestyle might entail. The opportunities for relationships of generosity, and the challenge of professionalising discourses of care would need to be assessed in making judgements on the ethical–political involvement. On the basis of these deconstructions, the question becomes how to act with an appropriate *lightness of care* (White 1991). Such a response would entail at least: an emphasis which would act very locally, as opposed to more indiscriminate or totalising interventions; programs which enable people to make active decisions about the lives they lead; a celebration of diversity in the target population, rather than a perspective which sees individuals as deviates from some norm of behaviour; involvements which take advantage of spaces in routines and lives to explore new possibilities for activities and identity; and programs which do not detract from the humanity of those who are clients, for example, by an overblown emphasis on 'being healthy' as opposed to 'becoming this or that'.

CONCLUSION

I hope this example has indicated the potential of a postmodern analysis and commitment to a radically different kind of 'health' in the becoming-other nomadology of *arche-health*. Perhaps it is necessary to reflect on these different ideas of health in terms of ethical engagement with others. Modernism and humanism have, in their pursuit of rationality, relativised moral codes (Bauman 1989; Caputo 1993), yet White argues (1991) that the underlying and unacknowledged ethics of modernism is a *will to mastery*. This can be seen in the emphasis in modern medicine upon the heroic, where the attempt to succeed has sometimes come to be held in greater esteem than any possible benefits of action (Fox 1994; Knowles 1977). At the root of any such claim to justify intervention is the *responsibility to act* (White 1991); theories and codes of professional conduct underpin such active engagement—potentially regardless of outcome or impact. White goes on to connect postmodern ethics with a rival *responsibility to otherness*. The latter is the rejection of a will to mastery, and the substitution of an identity-seeking discourse with a celebration of what is other, different and diverse. White suggests that the 'mood' of such a postmodern ethos might be one of 'grieving delight': grief as our response to suffering, delight in the diversity of our humanity (White 1991, p. 129).

A responsibility to otherness leads us to reflect on human potential and its failing, and of what constitutes the 'health care' which engages with this potential. The objective of care in this perspective is to do with becoming and possibilities, about resistance to discourse, and a generosity towards otherness. It is a process which offers promise, rather than fulfilling it, offers possibility in place of certainty, multiplicity in place of repetition, difference in place of identity. It is the *gift* which expects no recognition (Fox 1995b).

REFERENCES

Armstrong, D. 1987 'Theoretical tensions in biopsychosocial medicine' *Social Science & Medicine* vol. 25, pp. 1213–18
Baudrillard, J. 1988 *Selected Writings* Polity, Cambridge
Bauman, Z. 1989 *Postmodern Ethics* Blackwell, Oxford
Bunting, S. 1993 *Rosemarie Parse: Theory of Health as Human Becoming* Sage, Newbury Park, CA
Bury, M.R. 1991 'The sociology of chronic illness' *Sociology of Health & Illness* vol. 13, pp. 451–68
Butler, J. 1990 *Gender Trouble* Routledge, London
Canguilhem, G. 1989 *The Normal and the Pathological* Zone Books, New York
Caputo, J.D. 1993 *Against Ethics* Indiana University Press, Bloomington, Indiana
Deleuze, G. & Guattari, F. 1984 *Anti-Oedipus: Capitalism and Schizophrenia* Athlone, London
——1986 *Nomadology. The War Machine* Semiotext(e), New York
——1988 *A Thousand Plateaus* Athlone, London
Derrida, J. 1976 *Of Grammatology* Johns Hopkins University Press, Baltimore, MD
de Swaan, A. 1990 *The Management of Normality* Routledge, London
Doyal, L. 1981 'A matter of life and death: Medicine, health and statistics' in *Demystifying Social Statistics* eds J. Irvine, I. Miles & J. Evans, Pluto Press, London
Foucault, M. 1976 *The Birth of the Clinic* Tavistock, London
——1980 'Truth and power' in *Power/knowledge* ed. C. Gordon, Harvester Press, Brighton
Fox, N.J. 1992 *The Social Meaning of Surgery* Open University Press, Buckingham
——1993 *Postmodernism, Sociology and Health* Open University Press, Buckingham

——1994 'Anaesthetists, the discourse on patient fitness and the organisation of surgery' *Sociology of Health & Illness* vol. 16, pp. 1–18

——1995a 'Professional models of school absence associated with home responsibilities' *British Journal of Sociology of Education* vol. 16, pp. 221–42

——1995b 'Postmodern perspectives on care: The vigil and the gift' *Critical Social Policy* vol. 15, pp. 107–25

——1997 'Is there life after Foucault? Texts, frames and differends' in *Foucault, Health and Medicine* eds A. Petersen & R. Bunton, Routledge, London

Giddens, A. 1984 *The Constitution of Society* Cambridge University Press, Cambridge

Glassner, B. 1989 'Fitness and the postmodern self' *Journal of Health and Social Behaviour* vol. 30, pp. 180–91

Graham, H. 1979 'Prevention and health: every mother's business' in *The Sociology of the Family* ed. C. Harris, Keele University Press, Keele

Heart of Our City, no date *Report* Heart of Our City, Sheffield, UK

——1992 *Heart Health Promotion in General Practice* Heart of Our City, Sheffield, UK

Hutcheon, L. 1987 *The Politics of Postmodernism* Routledge, London

Kelly, M. & Charlton, B. 1995 'The modern and the postmodern in health promotion' in *The Sociology of Health Promotion* eds R. Bunton, S. Nettleton & R. Burrows, Routledge, London

Kleinman, A. 1988 *The illness narratives* Basic Books, New York

Knowles, J. 1977 *Doing Better and Feeling Worse* Norton, New York

Lash, S. 1991 'Genealogy and the body: Foucault/Deleuze/Nietzsche' in *The Body* eds M. Featherstone, M. Hepworth & B.S. Turner, Sage, London

Lewis, S. & Fox, N.J., forthcoming 'The social origins of "depression"' *Social Science & Medicine*

Plant, S. 1993 'Nomads and revolutionaries' *Journal of the British Society for Phenomenology* vol. 24, pp. 88–101.

Sacks, O. 1985 *The Man Who Mistook his Wife for a Hat* Picador, London

——1991 *Awakenings* Picador, London

Sedgewick, P. 1982 *Psychopolitics* Pluto, London

Szasz, T. & Hollender, M. 1956 'A contribution to the philosophy of medicine: The basic models of the doctor–patient relationship' *Archives of Internal Medicine* vol. 97, pp. 585–92

White, S. 1991 *Political theory and postmodernism* Cambridge University Press, Cambridge

World Health Organization 1985 *Targets for health for all* WHO, Geneva

Wright, W. 1982 *The social logic of health* Rutgers University Press, New Brunswick

2 Inequalities in late-modern health care

Robin Bunton

Discussion of inequalities in health necessarily deal with visions, utopian and distopian, which offer ways to reduce or eradicate unacceptable levels of inequity. Yet, available visions offered by social scientists often appear predictable and familiar, and relate sometimes nostalgically to a welfarist policy discourse rather than the contemporary policy context. Some recent work has focused upon 'doing something' about inequalities as opposed to studying further the nature of the inequalities. The calls for agenda and action in this work repeat statements made over a century ago by reformers and social activists.

This chapter examines some of the features of the study of inequalities in health and situates it within a modernist universal welfare state policy paradigm. It argues that such approaches, though laudable, are unlikely to engage the current 'policy-making' community and do not deal adequately with a number of important features of contemporary globalised post-industrial capitalism. It goes on to argue that health and the social and welfare relations surrounding health care have undergone considerable transformation and reconceptualisation which render single guiding policy principles such as inequalities in health problematic. Moreover, the importance of 'other' knowledges in the field of health and health policy have resulted in more diverse values guiding health policy.

'THE POINT IS TO CHANGE IT'

A recent review of policy in the UK concluded that 'the time is long overdue' and that 'now is a good time to start' advocating policies that will redress inequalities in health. It suggests that '[m]uch more work will be required to engender political will before the prospect of

23

equity in health can be transformed from a distant aspiration if not a tangible achievement' (Benzeval et al. 1995). This report is one of a number of recent studies which have focused on the effectiveness of work attempting to tackle inequalities in health, as opposed to more and more erudite analyses of why gross inequalities persist (Benzeval et al. 1995; Bunton et al. 1995). While this shift in focus is to be welcomed, there has never been any shortage of suggestions for social policy to redress inequalities. Another recent UK statement from the Association for Public Health (1997) reiterates a number of familiar calls for action from Government to implement national policies, in time for a New Labour Government. The consistency in the content of these statements is perhaps more remarkable than their frequency.

The Benzeval article is perhaps typical of the reviews of the policy options which have called for 'wide-ranging and radical reshaping of economic and social policies' (1995, p. 140). Approaches mentioned in recent statements are not drastically different from those appearing in the 1980 UK Black Report seventeen years earlier. Approaches to housing, income maintenance, the access to care in the NHS, and smoking cessation run alongside reappraisals of tax benefits and subsidies, education, employment and childcare policies (the latter being the focus of Black's recommendations also). Whitehead (1995), provides a useful and wide-ranging summary of the range of possible interventions targeted: general socioeconomic, cultural and environmental conditions, living and working conditions, social and community influences, and individual lifestyle factors. The Benzeval et al. (1995) collection reports on a UK conference which concluded that no strategy to tackle health inequalities will be worthy of the name if it is not committed to 'reducing unemployment'. It also focused on the physical environment, other social and economic influences such as income and wealth, the quality of social relations and social support, the barriers to adopting healthier lifestyles, and access to appropriate and effective health and social services. There are not many surprises here. Another UK report limited its focus to particular positivist proof of institutional level interventions (Centre for Reviews and Disseminations 1995). These attempts to analyse, 'what works', however, have tended to frame the question in 'modernist' welfarist discourse.

HEALTH, SOCIAL POLICY AND POST-INDUSTRIAL SOCIETY

The analysis of social policy process has become increasingly important in contemporary health care, especially due to an increased emphasis on the enhancement or promotion of health rather than simply the treatment of illness. Yet at the same time the possibilities for coherent social policy are being increasingly restricted and our conceptions of social policy have undergone considerable change.

The idea of 'Social policy' or an engineered society is eminently a 'modernist' one, based upon universal, basic needs and collective means of meeting them (Ginsberg 1998; Williams 1992). It assumes a number of things about the world that have recently been subject to radical questioning. The notion of an 'inherent' opposition between capitalism and national and social cohesion has been fundamental to social policy analysis along with the idea that the tension between the two can be managed through social policy design. It had been assumed that the conflicts of class society could be overcome by ameliorative social measures and that the nation state could control 'society' through the influence of policy. Basic needs (such as health) were viewed as predictable and universal and the full-time employment of breadwinner(s) allowed welfare collectivity. The state could underwrite social citizenship juridically and financially and deliver services on a local, non-profit-making basis (Ginsberg 1998). Several of these assumptions have been called into question by developments in the last twenty-five years or more. The 'run-away' world with which we are now faced cannot be acted upon with the certainty of previous decades. Even the possibility of policy defined as 'a long-term, continuously used standing decision by which more specific proposals are judged for acceptability' (Blum 1981), must be questioned when behavioural consistency and routinisation in social life becomes problematic.

In such circumstances the opposition between capital and social need has been lost. Neo-liberalism is now the nearest approximation to a universal theme in world affairs. A number of contra assumptions can be put forward as characterising this more uncertain policy environment (Ginsberg 1998). First, the nation state has lost some of its supremacy which restricts the capability of governments to influence healthy public policies. Cross-national political units such as the EC now determine policies on, say, cigarette advertising and liquor sales which override national governments' concerns (Harrison 1989; Powell 1989). The strength of multinationals has meant that employment flows are very different in this period and economic activity is paced by the agendas of others. Secondly, universal needs in health and welfare are not so universal any more. Growth in self-help and social movements, as well as the market and consumer, is placing emphasis on personal choice and individual determination of need.

There has been increased criticism of singular definitions of need and their tendency to reproduce primarily white, male, heterosexist and disablist needs (Williams 1992). 'New voices' have emphasised difference and pluralism in relation to need which has rendered discussion of disadvantage and rights to welfare more complex. The assumption of 'one community of fate' has disappeared. Thirdly, employment patterns have changed fundamentally and we are no longer in a position to expect to work for most of our lives or to have one career, and some groups might expect long periods of unemployment. It follows that state finance to underwrite social citizenship is more precarious. Finally, increasing organisational change has stressed the need to work in smaller, more independent units, tailored to more local needs and to more diverse needs. This suits a post-bureaucratic logic and also a post-Fordist form of organisation.

Fundamental to the above changes is a transformation in what we understand by the 'social'. The 'social' was something over which we expected the nation state to have some type of control. In the latter part of the twentieth century the nature of the social has been disputed. New ways of 'understanding, classifying and acting upon the subjects of government' have emerged as well as, 'a new relation between the ways in which they [subjects] are governed by others and the ways in which they govern themselves' (Rose 1993). The distaste for the social displayed by Margaret Thatcher and others relates to a fundamental retreat from the idea of universal provision across the social, which has had continuing consequences in a period of 'anti-' or post-social policy (Squires 1990). Anti- or post-social policy would appear to replace social concerns with those of global economic freedom, a sectoral rather than national economic focus, increasingly more localised state intervention such as community focus, and individualised risk and insurance approaches that stress privatised service provision and promote an 'enterprising self'. In short, social life has been transformed and in order to understand any social policy today we need to account for considerations of 'what is to be done', for inequalities in health must take account of transformations in policy and the social. At a theoretical level, the role of 'modernist' approaches to social transformation has been questioned by Lash and Urry, who ask: 'Who reads Marx anymore? After the decade of leveraged buyouts, global concern for the ozone layer and above all the collapse of communism in "eastern Europe", is there any writer now more dated, more of a "dinosaur" than Marx?' (1994, p. 1).

The 1980s put paid to any assumptions that the unfolding contradictions of industrial capitalism were about to engender societal transformation. Another Marx is drawn upon in their analysis which helps address the changes of the millenium which rely on a less overly structuralist conception of social processes of capitalism. Reflexive human subjectivity and the processes of 'reflexive modernisation' feature in this account and Lash and Urry examine the rapid and varied flows of objects and subjects through time and space, offering updated analytical tools for understanding the processes of contemporary 'disorganised capital'. The analysis of the 'economies of signs and space' they present explain not simply disturbing tendencies to meaninglessness, homogenisation, abstraction and the destruction of the subject, but also offer prospects for recasting work and leisure and reconstituting the community and subjectivity to suit the heterogeneity and complexities of contemporary everyday life. Such sociology, I would argue, provides a much needed updated analytic framework from which to conceive the policy options concerning issues relating to health inequalities. On the one hand, it provides a more complex understanding of the possibilities for developing strategies to bring about change. On the other hand, it provides insight into the important processes surrounding reflexivity and individualisation, particularly the increased importance of the flows of information and more diverse forms of knowlege that form a part of contemporary health care. It should be understood that this change refers to something more than an analysis of a new policy environment. It refers also to new ways of experiencing health and illness.

LATE-MODERN HEALTH

Contemporary health care systems have been subject to considerable restructuring and transformation, not simply in the ways that services themselves are organised (in a shift from Fordist or post-Fordist principles, for example) but also in the ways in which health is conceived, achieved and delivered. Health promotion is increasingly central to contemporary health policy concerns (Bunton et al. 1995; Lupton 1995; Petersen & Lupton 1996). Newer strategies for health involve not just health care systems that draw on a singular medical knowledge base, they draw upon and produce 'active citzenship' through the participation of communities outside the usual health care systems. Such regimes typically privilege public health and design decentred, preventative, non-institutional, non-specialist, low-cost, and risk reduction oriented responses (Armstrong 1983; Bunton & Burrows 1995). These strategies configure subjects who engage more actively and flexibly in managing and producing their health across time and space (Arney & Bergan 1984). Increasingly, health is becoming de-differentiated and diffuse, entering all sectors of social and cultural life (O'Brian 1995). We might typify health care systems as existing within a tension between two organising priniciples involving new forms of governance on the one hand, and new forms of expression and reflexivity on the other. In contemporary health we can see evidence of an emerging rationality of governance which relies on the play of new, more fluid forms of consumption.

With a focus on governance we can see that some features of contemporary health care might be typified as neo- or advanced liberal in their focus (Bunton 1997). According to Rose (1993), advanced liberalism, as it developed in Germany in the post-war period and in the Anglo Saxon World, has three distinct features: a new relationship between expertise and politics, a pluralisation of technologies, and a new specification of the subject. Contemporary health care systems attempt to adopt the first of these principles by building new relationships between the medical professions and the state. More recently, states have exercised critical budgetary scrutiny of medical practice, involving monetary calculation, accountancy and audit. They have rendered medical expertise more governable by eradicating the uncertainty of medical 'truth claims' that have previously generated the need for health care. An apparent redistribution of power has been achieved by handing over decisions to consumers and reducing the ability of professionals to define needs.

The market principle has increasingly been used, in the UK and in Australia, for example, to organise and distribute services and to regulate expertise in the delivery of health care. Led by 'new right' thinking in the UK, the Griffiths Report (Department of Health and Social Security 1983) is typical of this thinking, and moved away from a consensus-led approach involving teams of doctors, nurses and administrators, towards a system of commercial business management borrowed from the commercial sector and involving the principles of an 'internal market' (Cox 1991; Harrison et al. 1990; Hunter 1991). Increased use of private contractors in health care delivery threatened professional clinical autonomy (Gabe et al. 1994), though this new system was still heavily reliant upon self-governing professional power. Physicians work alongside managers to align clinical 'truth' with economic rationality.

A second feature of neo- or advanced liberal rationality apparent in contemporary health care regimes involves a pluralisation of technologies. Social technologies of the welfare state appear to have been increasingly detached from centralised regulation and given over to various autonomised agencies. Again, Western and Antipodean health care systems have seen a noticeable pluralisation in health intervention technologies and a shift in the temporal and spatial location of care. This shift is nicely encapsulated in the title of the UK Government's policy document of the mid-1970s: *Prevention and Health: Everybody's Business* (DHSS 1976). Around this time a series of internationally influential policy statements emerged redefining the responsibilities of governments towards health care. The Canadian Ministerial report by Lalonde (1974) directed attention to the influences over health that were far beyond the reaches of government and the provision of health care—the environment, lifestyle, and the bio-structure. WHO programs at that time were working to develop strategies to respond to the 'new social, political, economic and environmental challenges' facing nation states by redesigning health policy and health infrastructures (WHO 1991). Health promotion and the 'new public health' introduced and expanded both the agenda and the range of sites of intervention in which to promote health, including the public policy arena, the environment, and the community (WHO 1986). Health was now an issue of intersectoral collaboration and personal skill development and required the reorientation of health services. Perhaps the best known of WHO initiatives, *Health for All 2000* (1985), has attempted to identify new sites of concern— healthy cities, healthy schools, and healthy workplaces (Davies & Kelly 1993). Finally, neo-liberalism or advanced liberalism specifies a subject of government under which risk management is privatised and in which the client becomes a customer. O'Malley (1992) has described the ways in which citizens are increasingly obliged to adopt a calculative and 'prudent' personal relationship to risk and danger. Social work or physician-based care gives way to the self-help group and the helpline, and citizens take on a new authority of their own. Power effects under this style of governance are different from those experienced under liberalism. People do not possess or seize power. Modern citizens largely are agents of their own government (Hacking 1986; Rose 1989).

Neo-liberal health care strategies draw centrally upon risk analysis. Risk allows a flexible and diverse approach to the production of health. The phenomenal rise of risk analysis can in part be attributed to its appropriateness as a rationale of governance. Castel, echoing Foucault's concerns with the 'dangerous individual' (Foucault 1988), has suggested that we can identify a shift in health (and social) care regimes based upon 'dangerousness' to those based upon 'risk' (Castel

1991). Newer strategies dissolve notions of subjects or concrete individuals and replace them with a combination of *factors* of risk. Interventions are no longer simply a matter of face-to-face contact between the professional and client. Rather, professionals are concerned with the *flow of populations* and a range of abstract factors deemed liable to produce risk in general. The system of care for the ill is being transformed into a system for monitoring the health and welfare of populations. Epidemiological survey data under the regime of risk becomes the main strategy of the health professional and the dispensary becomes the focus of a new extended medical gaze (Armstrong 1983). New modes of surveillance, aided by technological advances, make the calculation of probabilities of 'systematic pre-detection' more and more sophisticated. Populations are managed on the basis of profiles of factors such as their age, social class, occupation, gender, relationships, locality, lifestyle and consumption; and interventions take more diverse forms.

Risk management has entered more consciously into government policy statements on health such as that made in the UK's *Health of the Nation* document (Department of Health 1992a), which has drawn heavily upon international health promotion discourse in constructing a strategy on risk. In this statement, and supporting documentation, it stresses population and risk claiming: 'Two basic approaches can be taken to the promotion of good health, the population approach and the high risk approach. The most effective programme combines both approaches' (Department of Health 1992b, p. 33). This document outlines risk factor targets such as the reduction in cigarette smoking, saturated fatty acid intake, and the number of people who are obese.

Health risk discourse has become dominant in the study of social aspects of health and public health, and health promotion in particular, and has received some critical attention in recent years with reference to its regulatory or disciplinary potential (Baum 1993; Bunton 1992; Gillick 1984; Greco 1993; Lupton 1995; Petersen 1996; Petersen & Lupton 1996; Stevenson & Burke 1991). Risk also relates to reconfiguring of the subject in new health strategies.

The regulation of risk allows population strategies but also individualising foci. Although a collective concept (Ewald 1991), in health promotion discourse risk has been made 'internal' and an individual quality. This contrast with the 'external', environmental risk is highlighted in the work of Beck and Douglas (cited in Lupton 1995). 'Risk takers' become demonised as new 'sinners' (Douglas 1984). Smokers in public, drink drivers, or those practising unsafe sex are subject to public scrutiny and judgement. Forms of group identification, exclusion, marginalisation and regulation are practised, defining some 'at risk', some as 'Self' and some as 'Other' (Figlio 1989). The modernist science of epidemiology constructs insiders and outsiders. Risk management individualises and privatises health concerns in ways that coincide with a broader individualising process. Risk profiling and the rational calculation of personal conduct have received critical attention in some recent sociology. Giddens has made much of the monitoring and management of the self as a project as a feature of reflexive modernisation (Giddens 1991). Modernity, he argues, confronts the individual with complex and diverse choices as a result of the entry of global and abstract systems into more and more daily concerns. Social relationships are increasingly lifted out from the immediacy of tradition or Gemeinschaft and rearticulated in other times and spaces. Expert systems, such as medicine, provide a means of judgement that outstrip and supersede relationships based upon trust. Everyday life is becoming saturated with expert knowledge which advises us on what food to eat, what exercise to take, from routine health education through to more in-depth therapy. Self-realisation takes place through more reflexive consideration of lifestyle options and *life planning*. The 'search for self-identity' becomes understandable in such circumstances and the self as a project can be understood as a balance between opportunity and risk. Through risk profiling, neo-liberal subjects construct enterprising, calculating and prudent selves (Rose 1993). Subjectivity is accomplished through such discourse and health becomes, at least in part, the responsibility of citizens. It is in recognition of this phenomena that accusations of 'healthism' (Crawford 1980) and 'bodyism' (Dutton 1995) have emerged. The pursuit of the ideals of health, fitness, youthfulness and beauty have taken place as a particular moral form. Gillick (1984) has pointed out that the incentives for such self-care have come from a number of quarters including sport, leisure industries and a more general economic rationale. The emergence of employee assistance programs, stress management courses and reduced insurance premiums for those with healthier lifestyles are clear examples of this encouragement.

Self-care and self-help have long since run alongside medical expertise, often in response to discontent and scepticism regarding the efficacy of professional medicine (Kickbusch 1989). Under late-modern regimes of health care, however, there has been a deliberate attempt to marry 'mainstream' health care with self-help and relevant social movements such as the environment and the women's health movement (Stevenson & Burke 1991). Coupled with a rise in consumerism, the self-help movements have been written into some recent policy statements such as the UK's *Patient's Charter* and the WHO Sundsvall Statement on health and the environment (cited in Department of Health 1991, and WHO 1985). Though often seen as successful challenges to modern medicine (Kelleher et al. 1994) these developments may be seen as strategies for producing the enterprising, healthy citizen.

We can, then, conceive of a number of recent changes in health care as echoing features of transformations in governmental techniques and rationalities associated with advanced liberalism and a new understanding of the social. A parallel shift in organisation, however, relates to increased choice, expressiveness and individualising of health relating to the consumption of health.

In contemporary consumer culture, health, like other goods, tends to become a 'free floating signifier' which has implications for the assumption of identity. Increasingly, aspects of health identity, consumption and lifestyle are interwoven, as shopping, promotion, advertising and design focus on the consumer as a self-determining agent. A dazzling and 'carnivalesque' style of consumption has been characteristic of recent decades such that the familiar social categories of class, gender and race are being deconstructed or even distorted (Featherstone 1991, 1995). Studies of consumption have stressed the way in which an expansion in commodity production affects the cultural sphere and generates new cultural forms and new identities. In the health sphere the growth in 'health-related' goods and services is influenced by a market logic which produces both new products and new, more discerning, health conscious consumers. The prominence of health-related consumption has implications for health identity which is no longer fixed in relatively stable 'sick roles' but becomes a ubiquitous aspect of the consumption of health and an aspect of embodied existence (Bunton & Burrows 1995). In conditions of consumer culture the body as a sign system becomes central to the consumption of identity (Featherstone 1991; Shilling 1993). Contemporary health consumption can tell us much about the nature of lifestyle formation and new forms of class identity. The 'new middle classes', for example, may be forging new signs of social distinction (Burrows & Nettleton 1994; Savage et al. 1992). While forms of class identity may be reproduced, however, there may also be evidence of a more playful and creative consumption pattern and a more fluid health identity associated with postmodernity (Bunton 1997). This fluidity in some ways runs counter to surveillance and micro-disciplinary regulations imposed by risk technologies of governance outlined above.

In summary, contemporary health care systems have been subject to a number of changes typified by a shift towards a neo- or advanced liberal rationality that specifies new relationships between the state and professional knowledge, a more plural set of policy interventions and a new configuration of the healthy citizen. This new rationality relies upon risk calculation and management as a technology of governance. Alongside these changes a parallel and interrelated organising principle is emerging which highlights choice, self-expression and even playfulness focused upon the body. The influence of consumer culture has produced an 'aesthetisation of health' as a more general aesthetisation of everyday life (Featherstone 1991). These newer health strategies and their tendencies towards a more 'free floating' value of health have a number of implications for the discussion of inequalities.

SOME IMPLICATIONS FOR HEALTH INEQUALITIES

One implication of newer health strategies is that they generate increased diversity in health care and in health care knowledge. There is some evidence of a breakdown in the biomedical 'grand narrative' in the newer discourses on health promotion in which the 'other' voices of the community, of women, of black people and of the subjects of health care is being heard and the older medical disciplines are being questioned and adapted (Kelly & Charlton 1995; Krieger & Zierler 1997; Watt & Rodmell 1993). Turner (1992) has documented a noticeable shift in the medical curriculum in a similar direction. Such a shift confronts the concept universality in health care with diversity and difference in health care. This confrontation is similar to that found in other areas of social policy (Williams 1992). A distrust of a 'false universalism' has been demonstrated by largely 'bottom up' critiques mentioned above, focusing upon gender, race, disability, age and sexuality (Spicker 1994). Such critiques have called for more varied values of health and more varied health knowledges. While there has been some move to take gender, race and other inequalities more seriously in debates on health inequalities, they remain largely rooted in a modernist framework of class inequalities, and fail to acknowledge the fundamental challenge posed by newer forms of diverse health values to existing epidemiological, biomedical discourse. A disciplinary bias is indicative of this problem. Though social science is central to the field of study, the social scientists involved are predominantly those with a quantitative perspective and the research

methods rely on the social survey and often help reproduce the
categories and social distinctions such as race that support fixed
modern identities (Lupton 1997; Petersen & Lupton 1996).

In short, debates on inequalities in health are centred on a single
knowledge base which provides a singular measure by which to judge
health care systems. In this sense the terms we use to describe the
field reproduce and support a singular perspective. Klein has pointed
out that the term inequalities presumes a prima facie case for social
concern and moral outrage (Klein 1988). Indeed the shift in the UK
towards the term's health variations by both the Department of Health
and the Economic and Social Research Council is an acknowledgement of the disappearance of the universalist appeal. By including
new knowledges and 'the voice of the other', the new strategies of
health would appear to disrupt this singular focus by providing alternative knowledges and health values.

A second implication of recent strategies for health relates to
increased reflexivity in relation to health and risk. The argument
above is in some ways similar to Menzel's critique of 'medical egalitarianism' and the possibility and morality of reducing inequalities in
health. Menzel appears to be arguing from a position of the limits
such policies impose on 'rational choice' (Menzel 1992). I do not argue
here in support of the assumption of an autonomous acting individual
but, rather, want to observe that a new, more reflexive health subjectivity has emerged which reduces the possibilities for a universalist
interventionist strategy to redress inequalities. The project of self
draws more on individualised actions and judgements in relation to
risk. This reflexiveness results from existence within a 'risk society' in
which threats are posed by scientific knowledge itself (Beck 1992). In
a contradictory manner, the new health citizen is likely to be more
immersed in health discourses while, simultaneously, more sceptical of
it. The frequency of challenges to medical authority is typical of such
radical reflexivity. Moreover, dispute over seemingly universal issues
of risk are subject to dispute and negotiation by different sectors. The
conflict over the risk of BSE between European states is indicative of
such dispute (Wynne 1996). Reflexivity is likely to create increased
resistance to overarching universalist policy on inequalities.

A final implication of recent approaches to health is the likelihood of misrecognition of a new species of health policy statements.
Some newer statements on inequalities in health have familiar features
but are quite distinct from previous modernist programs. One reason
inequalities in health have remained on the political agenda in Europe
and Australia throughout the late 1970s is because the focus has been

subtly changed. *Health for All 2000* statements, for example, secured signatures from some neo-conservative governments throughout the 1980s. In view of the retreat from centralist welfare policies characteristic of this period this might seem surprising, as might the 'idealism' associated with the HFA movement. This anomaly can be understood by considering the broader shifts occurring in health policy at this time which privileged public health.

In public health terms it makes sense to reduce inequalities, as Vågerö notes (1995), not in pursuit of social justice but in the name of national efficiency. It makes sense for national governments to reduce inequalities in health because this will improve the health of the population in general. This is the basis of the World Bank's recent support for redressing health inequalities (The World Bank 1993). Health is an economic as well as social and personal resource. This type of public support for reducing inequalities is quite different from the more familiar social justice motivated approaches familiar to modernist approaches to health and welfare. European statements on *Health for All 2000*, for example, call for wide ranging mechanisms and a commitment to 'reducing the differences': 'By the year 2000, the actual differences in health status between countries and between groups within countries should be reduced by at least 25%, by improving the level of health of disadvantaged nations and groups.' (WHO 1986, p. 24.) Earlier it states that, 'Health for all implies equity', and that people should be given a positive sense of health so that they can make full use of their capacities. Reduction in inequity in the cause of the pursuit of health is not an end in itself. Alongside targets for reduction of inequity it calls for participation of communities, multisectoral cooperation and health promotion as the only effective way to secure the prerequisites for health. At the heart of this statement, then, there would appear to be contradictory elements: on the one hand, a medically calculated measure of health differences and, on the other, a suggestion that non-medical empowerment might be the way forward, a means of listening to 'other' knowledge communities. Such policy statements call for international collaboration and global action on public health and inequality. The commitment to address inequalities is only one of many public health targets, however, and other principles of health promotion conflict with centralised attempts to reduce inequalities, such as the commitment to community participation and empowerment which highlights self-governance and diversity. This tension means that health inequalities are unlikely to be as high on the agenda as they were in, say, the UK in 1948.

CONCLUSION

I have argued here that the debate on the inequalities in health has failed to engage with some recent sociology and social policy which has increasingly stressed the difficulties faced by national health and welfare strategy. Global, economic and cultural changes have had a profound effect on welfare which has made the pursuit of national policy objectives along the lines of modernist universalist thinking highly problematic. Newer social policy problematics have addressed issues of diversity and difference, consumer choice and flexible delivery systems as well as the need for transnational policy-making. By failing to engage centrally with these issues much of the inequalities in health literature will remain unappealing to policy-makers and will not provide useful guides to action. This literature will not engage with the more complex issues of how to implement policy under conditions of post-industrial capitalism or 'reflexive modernisation', in which global flows of goods, people and information play an increasingly important role. In such a 'runaway world', the nation state is less able to underwrite social citizenship judically and financially and has less ability to control and influence health and other policy. It seems increasingly unlikely that state-centred approaches addressing inequalities in health will come up with solutions.

If the implementation of health policy is increasingly problematic when viewed from previous paradigms of welfare, however, it is also unlikely to match an environment in which new health care strategies play an increasingly important role. The privileging of public health and health promotion in such strategies has several profound implications for the social relations of welfare which substantially change the experience of health and stresses more heterogenous health values. The existence of these new strategies of 'late-modern' health creates a number of difficulties for any approach to addressing inequalities in health that relies on a singular notion of health based upon biomedical knowledge systems.

Working with a different rationale appropriate to neo-liberalism and to a world in which consumption has become an important organising principle, new relations of welfare have developed in the health field which are changing the nature of the relationship between the state and professionals in which the nature of clinical truth has been allied to principles of economic accountancy and discipline. Increasingly pluralised interventions are being devised and generated which call for collective, multisectoral action to promote health. Risk is increasingly being used as a technology of governance aimed at population flows rather than dangerous individuals. The promotion of active citizenship is supported by a 'moral imperative' to instil the duty of self-managed risk. We are witnessing the emergence of a health strategy which gravitates against state-centred regulation and fundamentally questions the singular medical authority on which the inequalities policy debate is based. From a perspective on governance we can identify critical features that are profoundly influenced by neo-liberal market mechanisms. At one level, we can analyse these developments as new forms of personal and moral imperative. At another level, we can see that there are elements of play and a freeing-up of health values. The increased importance of consumption on the experience of health, lifestyle and identity is generating diverse health values, as health becomes increasingly implicated in the processes of reflexive self-formation.

In such circumstances we are not likely to deal with inequalities in health through what might be considered 'modernist' policy strategies. The diminished state will not be able to implement them, health care strategies will not prioritise them and highly reflexive enterprising subjects will not choose them. At best we might hope for alleviation of some of the worst excesses of inequality among the economically disadvantaged. At the very least we might find it necessary to face up to the fact that some of the newer health policy statements such as *Health for All 2000* cannot centrally address inequalities and are of a different nature from older more familiar Fabian socialist ideals. Arguing such a position is not necessarily being pessimistic. It is merely recognising that the era in which it was possible to hold a singular value of health in policy is now over and newer conceptions of health and welfare are now in existence.

REFERENCES

Armstrong, D. 1983 *Political Anatomy of the Body: Medical Knowledge in Britain in the Twentieth Century* Cambridge University Press, Cambridge
——1993a 'From clinical gaze to a regime of total health' in *Health and Wellbeing: A Reader* eds A. Beattie, M. Gott, L. Jones & L. Sidell, Macmillan, London
——1993b 'Public health spaces and the fabrication of identity' *Sociology* vol. 27, no. 3, pp. 393–410
Arney, W.R. & Bergen, B. 1984 *Medicine and the Management of Living: Taming the Last Great Beast* Chicago Press, London
Ashton, J. & Seymour, H. 1988 *The New Public Health* Open University Press, Milton Keynes
Baggot, R. 1991 'Looking forward to the past? The politics of public health' *Journal of Social Policy* vol. 20, no. 2, pp. 191–213

Baum, F. 1990 'The new public health: Force for change or reaction?' *Health Promotion International* vol. 5, no. 2, pp. 145–50

——1993 'Healthy cities and change: Social movement or bureaucratic tool?' *Health Promotion International* vol. 8, no. 1, pp. 31–40

Beck, U. 1992 *Risk Society: Towards a New Modernity* Sage, London

Benzeval, M., Judge, K. & Whitehead, M. (eds) 1995 *Tackling Inequalities in Health: An Agenda for Action* Kings Fund, London

Blum, H. 1981 *Planning for Health: Generics for the Eighties* Human Sciences, New York

Bunton, R. 1992 'More than a woolly jumper: Health promotion as social regulation' *Critical Public Health* vol. 3, no. 2, pp. 4–11

——1997 'Popular health, advanced liberalism and *Good Housekeeping* magazine', in *Foucault, Health and Medicine* eds A. Petersen & R. Bunton, Routledge, London

Bunton, R. & Burrows, R. 1995 'Consumption and health in the "epidemiological" clinic of late modern medicine' in *The Sociology of Health Promotion* eds R. Bunton, S. Nettleton & R. Burrows, Routledge, London

Bunton, R., Burrows, R., Gillen, K. & Muncer, S. 1994 *Interventions to Promote Health in Economically Deprived Areas: A Review of the Literature* Northern Regional Health Authority, Newcastle

Bunton, R., Nettleton, S. & Burrows, R. (eds) 1995 *The Sociology of Health Promotion* Routledge, New York

Burrows, R. & Nettleton, S. 1994 'Going against the grain: An analysis of smoking and "heavy" drinking amongst the British middle classes' paper presented to the British Sociological Association Medical Sociology Group Annual Conference, University of York, September

Carter, J. (ed.) 1998 *Postmodernity and the Fragmentation of Welfare: A Contemporary Social Policy* Routledge, London

Castel, R. 1991 'From dangerousness to risk' in *The Foucault Effect: Studies in Governmentality* eds G. Burchell, C. Gordon & P. Miller, Harvester Wheatsheaf, London

Centre for Reviews and Disseminations 1995 *Review of the Research on the Effectiveness of Health Service Interventions to Reduce Variations in Health* CRD Report 3 Part 1 University of York, York

Cox, D. 1991 'Health service management—a sociological view: Griffiths and the negotiated order of the hospital' in *The Sociology of the Health Service* eds J. Gabe, M. Calnan & M. Bury, Routledge, London

Crawford, R. 1980 'Healthism and the medicalization of everyday life' *International Journal of Health Services* vol. 10, no. 3, pp. 365–88

Department of Health 1991 *The Health of the Nation* Consultative document HMSO, London

——1992a *The Health of the Nation: A Strategy for Health in England* HMSO, London

——1992b *The Health of the Nation . . . and You* HMSO, London

——1993 *Working Together for Better Health* HMSO, London

Department of Health and Social Security (DHSS) 1976 *Prevention and Health: Everybody's Business* HMSO, London

——1983 *NHS Management Enquiry (Griffiths Report)* HMSO, London

Douglas, M. 1984 *Purity and Danger: An Analysis of the Concepts of Pollution and Taboo* Ark, London

Dutton, K. 1995 *The Perfectible Body: The Western Ideal of Physical Development* Cassell, London

Ewald, F. 1991 'Insurance and risk' in *The Foucault Effect: Studies in Governmentality* eds G. Burchell, C. Gordon & P. Miller, Harvester Wheatsheaf, London

Featherstone, M. 1991 *Consumer Culture and Postmodernism* Sage, London
——1995 *Undoing Culture: Globalization, Postmodernism and Identity* Sage, London
Figlio, K. 1989 'Unconscious aspects of health and the public sphere' in *Crisis of the Self: Further Essays in Psychoanalysis and Politics* ed. B. Richards, Free Association Books, London
Foucault, M. 1988 'The dangerous individual' in *Michel Foucault: Politics, Philosophy, Culture* ed. L.D. Kritzman, Routledge, New York
Gabe, J., Calnan, M. & Bury, M. (eds) 1991 *The Sociology of the Health Service* Routledge, London
Gabe, J., Kelleher, D. & Williams, G. 1994 *Challenging Medicine* Routledge, London
Giddens, A. 1990 *The Consequences of Modernity* Polity, Cambridge
——1991 *Modernity and Self-Identity: Self and Society in the Late Modern Age* Polity, Cambridge
Gillick, M.R. 1984 'Health promotion, jogging, and the pursuit of the moral life' *Journal of Health, Politics, Policy and Law* vol. 9, no. 3, pp. 369–84
Ginsberg, N. 1998 'Postmodernity and social Europe' in *Postmodernity and Fragmentation of Welfare: A Contemporary Social Policy* ed. J. Carter, Routledge, London
Greco, M. 1993 'Psychosomatic subjects and the "duty to be well": Personal agency within medical rationality' *Economy and Society* vol. 22, no. 3, pp. 357–72
Hacking, I. 1986 'Making up people' in *Reconstructing Individualism: Autonomy, Individuality, and The Self in Western Thought* eds T. Heller, M. Sosna & D. Wellberg, Stanford University Press, Stanford
Harrison, I. 1989 'The information component' in *Controlling Legal Addictions* eds D. Robinson, D. Maynard & R. Chester, Macmillan, Basingstoke
Harrison, S., Hunter, D. & Pollitt, C. 1990 *The Dynamics of British Health Policy* Unwin Hyman, London
HMSO 1991 *The Health of the Nation: A Consultative Document for Health in England* HMSO, London
Hunter, D. 1991 'Managing medicine: a response to "the crisis"' *Social Science and Medicine* no. 32, pp. 441–49
Kelleher, D., Gabe, J. & Williams, G. 1994 'Understanding medical dominance in the modern world' in J. Gabe, D. Kelleher & G. Williams *Challenging Medicine* Routledge, London
Kelly, M. & Charlton, B. 1995 'The modern and the postmodern in health promotion' in *The Sociology of Health Promotion* eds R. Bunton, S. Nettleton & R. Burrows, Routledge, New York
Kelly, M.P., Davies, J.K. & Charlton, B.G. 1993 'Healthy cities: A modern problem or a post-modern solution' in *Healthy Cities: Research and Practice* eds J. Davies & M. Kelly, Routledge, London
Kickbusch, I. 1986 'Health promotion: A global perspective' *Canadian Journal of Public Health* vol. 77, no. 5, pp. 321–26
——1989 'Self-care in health promotion' *Social Science and Medicine* no. 29, pp. 125–30
Klein, R. 1988 'Acceptable inequalities' *Acceptable Inequalities?* ed. D.J. Green, IEA Health Unit, London
Kreiger, N. & Zierler, S. 1997 'Accounting for the health of women' *Critical Public Health* vol. 7, nos 1 & 2, pp. 38–49
Lalonde, M. 1974 *A New Perspective on the Health of Canadians* Information Canada, Ottawa
Lash, S. & Urry, J. 1994 *Economies of Signs and Space* Sage, London
Liedekerken, P.C., Jonkers, R. et al. 1990 *Effectiveness of Health Education* Dutch Health

Education Centre, Van Gorcum Utrecht/Uitgeverij voor Gezondheudsbevaderry, BV Asseen, Netherlands

Lupton, D. 1994 *Medicine as Culture: Illness, Disease and the Body in Western Societies* Sage, London

——1995 *The Imperative of Health: Public Health and the Regulated Body* Sage, London

——1997 'Epidemiology as a sociocultural practice' *Critical Public Health* vol. 7, nos 1 & 2, pp. 28–37

Lyotard, J.F. 1984 *The Post-Modern Condition: A Report on Knowledge* trans. G. Bennington, B. Mascum, Manchester University Press, Manchester

McKinlay, J.B. 1993 'The promotion of health through planned sociopolitical change: Challenges for research and policy' *Soc Sci Med* vol. 36, no. 2, pp. 109–17

Menzel, P. 1992 'Equality, autonomy, and efficiency: What health care system should we have?' *Journal of Medicine and Philosophy* no. 17, pp. 33–57

O'Brien, M. 1995 'Health and lifestyle: A critical mess? Notes on the dedifferentiation of health' in *The Sociology of Health Promotion* eds R. Bunton, S. Nettleton & R. Burrows, Routledge, New York

O'Malley, P. 1992 'Risk, power and crime prevention' *Economy and Society* vol. 21, no. 3, pp. 252–75

Petersen, A. 1996 'The "healthy" city, expertise, and the regulation of space' *Health & Place* vol. 2, no. 3, pp. 157–65

Petersen, A. & Lupton, D. 1996 *The New Public Health: Health and Self in the Age of Risk* Allen & Unwin, Sydney

Powell, M. 1989 'Tax harmonisation in the European Community' in *Controlling Legal Addictions* eds D. Robinson, D. Maynard & R. Chester, Macmillan, Basingstoke

Rose, N. 1989 *Governing the Soul: The Shaping of the Private Self* Routledge, London

——1993 'Government, authority and expertise in advanced liberalism' *Economy and Society* vol. 22, no. 3, pp. 283–98

Savage, M., Barlow, J., Dickens, P. & Fielding, T. 1992 *Property, Bureaucracy and Culture: Middle Class Foundation in Contemporary Britain* Routledge, London

Shilling, C. 1993 *The Body and Social Theory* Sage, London

Spicker, P. 1994 'Understanding particularism' *Critical Social Policy: A Reader* ed. D. Taylor, Sage, London, pp. 220–33

Squires, P. 1990 *Anti-Social Policy: Welfare Ideology and the Disciplinary State* Harvester Wheatsheaf, London

Stevenson, H.M. & Burke, M. 1991 'Bureaucratic logic in new social movement clothing: The limits of health promotion research' *Health Promotion International* no. 6, pp. 281–96

Turner, B.S. 1992 'The interdisciplinary curriculum: From social medicine to postmodernism' in *Regulating Bodies: Essays in Medical Sociology* ed. B.S. Turner, Routledge, London

Vågerö, D. 1995 'Health inequalities as policy issues—Reflections on ethics, policy and public health' *Sociology of Health and Illness* vol. 17, no. 1, pp. 1–19

Watt, A. & Rodmell, S. 1993 'Community involvement in health promotion: progress or panacea?' in *Health and Well Being: A Reader* eds A. Beattie, M. Gott, L. Jones & M. Sidell, Macmillan, in association with the Open University, Basingstoke

Whitehead, M. 1995 'Tackling inequalities: a review of policy initiatives' in *Tackling Inequalities in Health: An Agenda For Action* eds M. Benzeval, K. Judge & M. Whitehead, Kings Fund, London

Williams, F. 1992 'Somewhere over the rainbow: Universality and diversity in social policy' in *Social Policy Review* no. 4, eds N. Manning & R. Page, Social Policy Association, Canterbury

Williams, G. & Popay, J. 1994 'Lay knowledge and the privilege of experience' in *Challenging Medicine* eds J. Gabe, D. Kelleher & G. Williams, Routledge, London

World Bank 1993 *World Development Report 1993: Investing in Health* Oxford University Press, Oxford

World Health Organization (WHO) 1985a *Health for All 2000: Targets for Europe* WHO, Copenhagen

——1985 *Targets for Health For All, 2000* WHO, Copenhagen

——1986 'Health promotion: Ottawa Charter for Health Promotion' *Health Promotion* vol. 1, no. 4, pp. 1–5

——1991 *To Create Supportive Environments for Health: The Sundsvall Handbook* WHO, Geneva

Wynne, B. 1996 'May the sheep safely graze' in *Risk, Environment and Modernity* eds S. Lash, B. Szerszynski & B. Wynne, Sage, London

3 Consumer reconstructions of medical knowledge in Australia

Stephanie D. Short

This chapter seeks to describe and analyse the reconstructions of medical knowledge undertaken by health consumer groups with the support of the Consumers' Health Forum of Australia. The Consumers' Health Forum Research and Development Program has been selected as the substantive focus for this study as it supported research and development projects managed and conducted by health consumer groups. It is unique in the world in that respect. The Consumers' Health Forum has grown considerably in terms of both resources and expertise since its inception in 1987, however, the Research and Development Program was not re-funded after 1992. In this chapter I focus on the consumer research supported by the Program within the context of contemporary sociological debates about the implications of 'social constructionism' (Chodorow 1995; Craib 1997; Giddens 1991; Popay & Williams 1996; Short 1994, 1996). The chapter is centrally concerned with the question of whether the challenge to the certainty of scientific medical knowledge contained in 'social constructionism' and related poststructuralist trends is evident in health research conducted by consumers. As Prior (1994, p. 263) noted:

> The problem with social constructionism, however, is that like that of the genie let loose from the bottle—once introduced into the world it cannot be easily contained. What is more, the genie can turn just as easily on its liberator as it does on its assumed natural enemies.

Theoretically, I examine whether the consumer research projects accepted uncritically, excluded from critical scrutiny, or critically reconstructed medical knowledge of biophysical reality (Short 1991,

p. 337). That is, my critical sociological analysis of these research projects will examine whether the research conducted under the Consumers' Health Forum Research and Development Program integrated knowledge of the subject (the patient experience) with the object (biomedical knowledge) worlds.

At the empirical level the chapter focuses on the seventy-five research projects funded by the Consumers' Health Forum of Australia over the six-year funding period 1986/7 to 1991/2. Research projects were conducted by a geographically dispersed range of groups, including the Kimberley Aboriginal Medical Service, Better Hearing Australia (Tasmania), and the Ingham Women's Resource Centre in Queensland. In addition, the projects led to a diverse and creative mixture of outputs, including books (Henderson et al. 1991; McDonald 1992), videos, photographs and unpublished reports (Arthritic Women's Task Force, 1988; Brisbane Women's Health Centre, 1989). And, although the areas of interest varied widely—from environmental pollution, through hydrotherapy and massage to schizophrenia—there is no doubt that the single most popular issue was women's health. Indeed, over a third of the seventy-five projects explicitly focused on women's health concerns.

In 1994 I received permission from the Consumers' Health Forum to copy and analyse the contents of the files and correspondence relevant to the Program for research purposes. I turn now to examine the genealogy of this unique research program, that is, the social conditions which made the birth of the Program possible.[1]

THE CONSUMER RESEARCH DEVELOPMENT FUNDING PROGRAM

In 1985 'The Swinging Door' report on community participation in the Commonwealth Department of Health's activities recommended that the Government allocate funds to community organisations to research the information needs of their constituency and to carry out 'participatory/social action research'. Then, in the following year, the *Report of the Better Health Commission* recommended '. . . that a national community development fund should be established to assist in, and educate local communities about participation and advocacy projects' (Commonwealth Department of Health 1986, p. 75). In 1987, the Consumers' Health Forum of Australia had as part of its foundation budget a small fund ($60 000 p.a.) earmarked for grants to consumer and community groups for research and development projects. This Grants Program had an important and unique role in research funding in Australia, and indeed internationally, as the funds enabled consumer and community groups to initiate and carry out their own projects—not to have research done about them by an expert, but for the groups to undertake the activities themselves, defined in their terms and by their assessment of perceived needs and information gaps. 'This tiny fund, . . . represented almost the entire monies available for consumer and community controlled research projects' (CHF Communication to Commonwealth Department of Health 24 May 1989).

Information about the Grants Program pointed to ' . . . the significance of these grants, in terms of community control', and correspondence associated with the Grants Program indicated that its educative potential may have outweighed the amount of monies allocated to it. Between 1987 and 1989 the Committee administering the CHF Grants Program was chaired by a sociologist, Yoland Wadsworth, a well known advocate for participatory or action research (Wadsworth 1984, 1988, 1989), and when Wadsworth resigned from the Committee, in 1991, I accepted an invitation to join the Grants Committee, renamed the Consumer Research Development Funding Committee, which funded consumer research projects for two more years.

The Consumers' Health Forum Research Funding Program aimed to fund only those applications which especially demonstrated and furthered a consumer perspective. The Information Kit which provided 'guidelines to applicants' to the Consumer Research Development Funding Program specified that it aimed '. . . to promote action oriented research which is consumer based and managed, and thus relevant to the concerns of health care consumers' (Consumers' Health Forum 1992, p. 1). The application form asked applicants to specify how consumers would be involved in the management of the project, and groups representing professional, government or commercial interests were not eligible to apply. It was, however, acceptable for consumer groups to seek assistance from another group in carrying out its project; the project remained eligible if it was managed and initiated by consumers and genuinely oriented to consumers. Criteria used to assess projects included the extent of active consumer management of and participation in the project; the extent to which the project enhanced consumers' access to information and knowledge; and the extent to which a project would create a 'voice' for a group of consumers (Consumers' Health Forum 1992, p. 2). The centrality of research to the work of the Forum is illustrated in the following excerpt from correspondence from the Forum to the Commonwealth Department of Health (24 May 1989):

The CHF was established to strengthen the 'voice' of the consumer and community sector in health policy decision making. We believe that a strong consumer voice is one which grounds its arguments in research. For this to be possible, consumers must have access to the resources and education necessary to undertake research work which is of a high quality, as well as community controlled and community based.

Funding for the Consumers' Health Forum Research Funding Program ceased in 1992, after the review of the Community Organisations' Support Program (COSP), under which the Consumers' Health Forum was funded (House of Representatives Standing Committee on Community Affairs 1991). This review recommended the application of stricter public sector accountability requirements to the administration of the Consumers' Health Forum, and other organisations funded under the Program. This managerialist incursion meant that the Consumers' Health Forum could no longer justify having its own research program, when no other community organisation had one (Short 1998).

THE THEORETICAL CHALLENGE(S) POSED BY CONSUMER HEALTH RESEARCH

While sociologists have often attempted to understand how individual patients reconstruct biomedical concepts in the light of their own illness experiences (Williams 1984; Blaxter, cited in Radley 1993), this chapter attempts to understand how consumer groups reconstruct biomedical knowledge in the light of their shared social experience. Furthermore, as the research projects were completed by consumer groups themselves, rather than sociologists, the Program provides an ideal site for examining the knowledge and attitudes of consumer groups in a direct or unmediated way.

There is a range of theoretical and methodological approaches in the sociology of medical research (Kelly 1994; Pilgrim & Rogers 1994; Prior 1994; Short 1991, 1994). While the work of Parsons (1951, 1977) and others, which shall be referred to as 'medical objectivism',[2] tends to accept uncritically the content of biomedical knowledge about biophysical reality, the work of Freidson (1970, 1989) and other phenomenologically-informed sociologists of medical knowledge tends to exclude the content of biomedical knowledge (about the object world) from critical sociological scrutiny. A third theoretical and

methodological approach, social constructionism, which draws particularly on the ideas of the late philosopher and historian of ideas,
Michel Foucault, focuses on understanding the conditions of possibility
which makes thinking in a particular way possible (Armstrong 1983;
Bury 1986; Foucault 1975; Nettleton 1993; Petersen & Lupton 1996).
In a Foucauldian, or genealogical, analysis one does not seek to explain
the origins of a way of thinking, or discourse. Rather: 'History is the
concrete body of a development, with its moments of intensity, its
lapses, its extended periods of feverish agitation, its fainting spells;
and only a metaphysician would seek its soul in the distant ideality
of the origin' (Foucault 1991, p. 80).

A critical perspective (Figlio 1982; Pilgrim & Rogers 1994; Short
1994), however, which draws particularly on the ideas of critical
theorists (Fraser 1989; Habermas 1978; Marcuse 1964), examines the
uses and limitations of biomedical knowledge from a particular social
position and perspective. This fourth theoretical and methodological
approach lends theoretical support to the reconstruction of health
knowledge within more participatory or democratic research environments.

I now seek to assess the relevance of these four paradigms within
the sociology of medical knowledge: medical objectivism; sociological
subjectivism; social constructionism and critical theory, for understanding the content and context of health consumer knowledge and
research.

CONSUMER RECONSTRUCTIONS OF MEDICAL KNOWLEDGE

Between 1987 and 1992 seventy-five consumer research projects were
funded under the Consumers' Health Forum Research Development
Funding Program, to the total value of A$364 000. Over the six years
of the Program, between nine (1992/3) and seventeen (1989/90)
grants were funded in any single year. When I first gained access to
the files and correspondence relating to the Program in 1993, I was
most impressed with the range of research outputs produced—reports,
pamphlets, videos, photos and books—and the insights about health
and illness which seemed to jump out from the page. In 1994 I read
through the files for each of the seventy-five projects and coded each
one according to whether it had accepted, excluded from critical
scrutiny, ignored or reconstructed the *content* of medical discourses
relevant to the group's concerns. I also recorded details about the
social *context* within which the research projects had been conducted,

and I noted whether the research had been consumer initiated and/or managed.

Methodologically, of the seventy-five projects:

- None of the projects excluded from critical scrutiny or ignored the content of contemporary medical discourses relevant to their concerns.
- Seventy-four projects reconstructed or aimed to reconstruct contemporary medical discourses relevant to their concerns.
- One project accepted uncritically contemporary medical discourse 'about the right food to eat', in a play for school children. As we shall see below, the play reproduced medical terms such as 'gout', 'constipation' and 'diarrhoea' in a script that was supposed to be developed by and for 10–14-year-old schoolchildren.

Thus, none of the projects was compatible with the perspectives of sociological subjectivism or social constructionism, and all but one of the projects exhibited a theoretical orientation consistent with a critical theoretical perspective. Only one project, the school nutrition play, appeared to reproduce uncritically the content of medical discourse relevant to its concerns, which is consistent with the perspective of medical objectivism. Theoretically, one can conclude that the seventy-four consumer reconstructions of health knowledge overcame the epistemological and methodological limitations evident in sociological subjectivism and social constructionism, as they transcended modernist sociology's distinction between knowledge of the subject (the patient's illness experience) and object (medical knowledge of the physical body) worlds. It appears that only one project did not integrate 'objective' knowledge about the body and other biophysical phenomena with 'subjective' knowledge derived from the consumer's perspective. I turn now to describe some of the reconstructions of medical knowledge, before I examine the content and context of the project that reproduced medical discourse relevant to teenage nutrition.

A study entitled 'The effects of bio-medical bias on the health and social status of women with rheumatoid arthritis: Consumer perceptions' (Arthritic Women's Task Force 1988), conducted by a group of women with rheumatoid arthritis, pointed to the failure to find the cause of rheumatoid arthritis, and the failure of much of the health system to deal appropriately and sensitively with the health concerns of women with rheumatoid arthritis. It claimed that the biomedical approach had failed to improve the health and social status of women with rheumatoid arthritis. The study, which was based on interviews with a group of fifty women with rheumatoid arthritis exploring issues of health and social status, concluded that:

> The poor quality of doctor/patient relationships, the coercion used to ensure conformity to the bio-medical model, and the failure to provide adequate information to enable women to make informed decisions regarding their health and treatment options have exacerbated the overall problem of RA and further degraded the social status of these women. (Arthritic Women's Task Force 1988, Summary)

The report criticised the biomedical approach to rheumatoid arthritis most severely and referred to the extent of harm being done by the biomedical bias of RA treatment, the failure to provide emotional support to the women, and the failure to perceive the problem of RA from a feminist perspective. 'It is only by seeing the women isolated in their homes, that the degree of harm can be measured' (Arthritic Women's Task Force 1988, Summary). The study clearly fitted into the category of a study that had critiqued or critically reconstructed medical discourses on rheumatoid arthritis, particularly from a feminist perspective.

The Northcote Self-Help Hydrotherapy and Massage Group received funding in 1987 to collect written material for the first draft of a book which would demonstrate how older people can maintain their independence and manage their own lifestyles. Members of the self-help group conducted interviews with all members of the group, and they collected material from professional health and community workers directly associated with the group. They photographed all aspects of the group's activities and edited the material for presentation to a publisher. The themes identified for the book included positive old age, massage and hydrotherapy, social interaction, death and desertion, and retaining independence. Five years after completion of the project the following letter was received by the Forum from the Group:

> The Northcote Self-Help and Hydrotherapy and Massage Group and I are thrilled to pass on the great news that Penguin Books Australia are publishing the book now titled *Put Your Whole Self In*. The support which the Consumers' Health Forum generously provided for photographic and research materials and expenses certainly helped tremendously in this process and once again we offer our thanks. (M. McDonald communication to CHF, 8 May 1992)

The book, *Put Your Whole Self In*, and the beautiful photographs in it, are a testament to the success of this particular project, and to the strength and integrity of the women who comprise the group

(McDonald 1992). Clearly, this group had not ignored medical discourses on ageing, however, they had supplemented these discourses with knowledge derived from their own experience, and from other sources, and thus supplemented and reconstructed their knowledge about ageing and health.

I turn now to a third project conducted by Congress Alukura, an Aboriginal Women's Organisation based in Alice Springs in Central Australia, where staff have been involved for some years in providing obstetric care to hundreds of Aboriginal women. The Consumers' Health Forum provided Congress Alukura with funds to conduct a consultation on birthing services with Aboriginal women from rural and remote areas. This consultation project was later recognised as being crucial to their success in achieving support from the Aboriginal and Torres Strait Islander Commission (ATSIC) for establishment of an Aboriginal-controlled birthing centre in Alice Springs. I quote from correspondence received by the Forum (4 April 1991):

> The Congress Alukura would like to share some information with the Committee that the years of political lobbying, negotiation, Aboriginal self-determination and tremendous community involvement and participation have now been rewarded. The ATSIC have given approval for the Congress Alukura to purchase land and to construct a new building.

Again, this group, which represented the views of one of the most disadvantaged groups in Australian society, had reconstructed traditional medical discourses on obstetrics in the light of their own experience of 'borning' and on the basis of the Grandmothers' Law.

A feminist study, 'Service Difficulties and Faults: Women's Experience of Menopause', which communicated to me immediately, was conducted by a group of women at the Brisbane Women's Health Centre. The study was based on interviews with women about the menopause. It concluded: 'The problem of women's health is embedded in the position of women in society—many exist in isolation, with little support, and succumb to entrenched attitudes of women's worth and a trivialisation of women's issues.' (Brisbane Women's Health Centre, October 1989, p. 18)

Another project, The Multicultural Women's Health Education Project, was undertaken with support from the Fairfield Community Resource Centre which employed four women with language skills in Laotian, Arabic, Spanish and Italian, trained them to conduct forums where women's health issues could be discussed and information shared, and prepared a report on identified needs. The Project also received support from the New South Wales Department of Education and the Regional Health Promotion Coordinator. The Multicultural Women's Health Project report was accompanied by the following correspondence:

> The funding of this innovative project . . . [has] . . . provided local (Spanish, Arabic, Laotian and Italian-speaking) women with access to information and services in their local area, thus increasing their life choices. We thought you would be interested to know that this project has provided a model for the newly funded Immigrant Women's Health Programme which has been funded by the Western Sydney Area Assistance Scheme. (15 March, 1989)

The Adolescent Parenting Program produced a video on the problems of adolescent pregnancy and parenting. It was produced by women from two support groups, one comprising pregnant adolescents and the other young mothers. In correspondence, the Committee for Adolescent Parenting Program wrote:

> Philosophically, there was a belief that the needs of these young women should be addressed in the context of: societal limitations placed upon the power and control women have over their own lives, the social constructions of femininity and motherhood and how these may restrict women's choices or invalidate their experiences. (Young Parents Program, July 1989, p. 2)

Each of these three projects clearly exhibited a critical feminist perspective towards health knowledge.

In 1987, the first year of the Program, funding was received by the Yean House Community Centre in the Southern Highlands of New South Wales for a 'Theatre in Education' project. The Centre received $3200 to aid in the production of a script on the importance of nutrition among 10–14-year-old children. The Yean House Community Centre proposed liaising with local schools and community health workers and local young people in order to develop the script for a play. The group paid a script writer to develop the script 'Out of the Frying Pan', about the right food to eat, which included the following dialogue:

> Toby: 'My dad's been an invalid since I was a kid. It started in his feet and worked its way up. Gout, clots, constipation, diarrhoea, stones, ulcers, hypertension, diabetes, and then he started getting really sick.'

The medical language in this dialogue indicates that the script writer accepted rather than reconstructed the content of medical discourse on nutrition. The use of technical terms such as 'gout', 'constipation' and 'diarrhoea' is perhaps surprising in a script developed by and for 10–14-year-olds.

Examination of the social context within which the script was written reveals that the Yean House Community Centre commissioned a playwright to write the play. The report on the project reveals that the playwright consulted with community health workers, and then conducted formal discussions with young people, asking them to explain their understanding of nutrition. The second and third drafts of the play were read by the Yean House Committee, and by professional theatre workers, and a reading of the final draft was performed for the Committee on 28 March 1988. Correspondence from the Yean House Committee (10 February 1988) noted: 'The main problem encountered was contact and liaison with students in state schools. This was hampered and delayed by Departmental Policy and red tape.'

Thus, the New South Wales Department of Education bureaucracy was the main factor that inhibited implementation of the original proposal, which required the involvement of children in each stage of the script development. In short, the inflexibility of the school bureaucracy effectively sidetracked the original aims of the project. As children were not fully involved in the process of script development, their knowledge and language is not evident in the script. Instead, the script uncritically reflects medical discourse on diet and nutrition, which is consistent with the paradigm of medical objectivism.

CONCLUSION

Initially, I was most surprised by my findings, and then humbled. I was surprised to find that the research projects had been so sophisticated, epistemologically and methodologically, and humbled to find that the research appeared to overcome or transcend many of the limitations evident in modern sociological research, and identified here as the problems associated with medical objectivism, sociological subjectivism or social constructionism.

This surprise and humility then brought me to attempt to understand *why* the content of the vast majority of the consumer research projects was consistent with a critical sociological perspective towards health research. In examining the social context within which the Program developed, I realised that a researcher with a doctorate in sociology, Richard Mohr, was the consultant responsible for writing 'The Swinging Door' consultancy in 1985 which originally recommended establishment of the Consumers' Health Forum and of a research funding program to encourage and resource research conducted by and for consumer health groups (Commonwealth

Department of Health 1985). Then, I examined the guidelines for applicants to the Consumers' Health Forum Research Funding Program and realised that they were explicit in proposing that only projects which researched the consumer perspective and which were managed by consumers would be funded. Then, it occurred to me that these guidelines were written and developed by the committee chaired by Yoland Wadsworth, a researcher with a doctorate in sociology and a string of publications on action and participatory research. Thus, the findings are not surprising when one considers that sociologists were involved in the establishment of the Consumers' Health Forum, and of the research funding program, and in drafting the research funding guidelines.

While I had expected to find more projects which had adhered to the assumptions of medical objectivism, or perhaps instances of sociological subjectivism, in this study I found instead that the Program overwhelmingly supported research conducted using participatory methodologies consistent with a critical sociological perspective. Only one project, the Yean House play, reproduced the content of medical discourse uncritically.

Moreover, I realise now that numerous projects effectively reproduced sociological discourses, about 'the biomedical model', 'social interaction', 'life choices', 'social constructions of femininity and motherhood', and so on. This insight is significant because I had originally presumed that consumer research provided a way of gaining direct access to what consumers think, in a way that is unmediated by the involvement of sociology and/or sociologists. Perhaps this explains why I was so excited on gaining access to and reading the project reports. I was seeing my own discourse coming back to me, through consumer reconstructions of health knowledge. Thus, consumer health research and sociological research can be viewed as interpenetrating discourses, rather than as separate discourses, as originally envisaged. It is clear now that the 'genie' of social constructionism played a significant part in the birth and development of consumer health research in Australia.

ACKNOWLEDGEMENT

I would like to acknowledge the financial assistance received from the University of New South Wales Faculty of Professional Studies Research Management Committee, and the assistance received from staff in the Secretariat of the Consumers' Health

Forum of Australia. I thank, also, Alan Petersen for his insightful and constructive comments on this chapter.

NOTES

1   See Short (1997) for a more detailed analysis of the rise and demise of this unique research Program.
2   Claus Offe used this term in a seminar, 'Membership Orientation in Compulsory Health Insurance Organisations in Germany' presented to the Social Policy Research Centre at the University of New South Wales, 21 March 1994.

REFERENCES

Armstrong, D. 1983 *The Political Anatomy of the Body* Cambridge University Press, Cambridge
Arthritic Women's Task Force 1988 'The effects of bio-medical bias on the health and social status of women with rheumatoid arthritis: Consumer perceptions' Unpublished report
Brisbane Women's Health Centre 1989 'Service difficulties and faults: Women's experience of menopause', Unpublished report
Bury, M.R. 1986 'Social constructionism and the development of medical sociology' *Sociology of Health and Illness* vol. 8, no. 2, pp. 137–69
Chodorow, N. 1995 'Gender as a personal and cultural construction' *Signs* vol. 20, no. 3, pp. 516–44
Commonwealth Department of Health 1985 *The Review of Community Participation in the Commonwealth Department of Health: 'The Swinging Door'* AGPS, Canberra
——1986 *Report of the Better Health Commission, Volume 1* AGPS, Canberra
Consumers' Health Forum of Australia 1992 *Information Kit: Guidelines to Applicants, Consumer Research Development Funding Program* Consumers' Health Forum of Australia, Canberra
Craib, I. 1997 'Social constructionism as a social psychosis' *Sociology* vol. 31, no. 1, pp. 1–15
Figlio, K. 1982 'How does illness mediate social relations? Workmen's compensation and medico-legal practices 1890–1940' in *The Problem of Medical Knowledge: Examining the Social Construction of Medicine* eds P. Wright & A. Treacher, Edinburgh University Press, Edinburgh
Foucault, M. 1975 *The Birth of the Clinic* Vintage, New York
——1991 'Nietzsche, genealogy, history' in *The Foucault Reader: An Introduction to Foucault's Thought* ed. P. Rabinow, Penguin, London
Fraser, N. 1989 *Unruly Practices: Power, Discourse and Gender in Contemporary Social Theory* Polity, Cambridge
Freidson, E. 1970 *Profession of Medicine: A Study of the Sociology of Applied Knowledge* Dodd Mead, New York
——1989 *Medical Work in America* Yale University Press, New Haven
Giddens, A. 1991 *Modernity and Self-Identity* Polity, Cambridge
Habermas, J. 1978 *Knowledge and Human Interests* Heinemann, London

Henderson, L., Riley, R. & Wood, R. 1991 *Explaining Endometriosis* McCulloch, Melbourne

House of Representatives Standing Committee on Community Affairs 1991 *You have your moments: A report on funding of peak health and community organisations* AGPS, Canberra

Kelly, M. 1994 'Worlds of illness: Biographical and cultural perspectives on health and disease' *Sociology of Health and Illness* vol. 16, no. 1, pp. 122–24

McDonald, M. 1992 *Put Your Whole Self In* Penguin, Ringwood

Marcuse, H. 1964 *One Dimensional Man* Beacon Press, Boston

Nettleton, S. 1993 *Power, Pain and Dentistry* Open University Press, Buckingham

Parsons, T. 1951 *The Social System* Routledge and Kegan Paul, London

——1977 'Value-freedom and objectivity' in *Understanding and Social Inquiry* eds F.R. Dallmayr & T.A. McCarthy, University of Notre Dame Press, Notre Dame

Petersen, A. & Lupton, D. 1996 *The New Public Health: Health and Self Through the Age of Risk* Allen & Unwin, Sydney

Pilgrim, D. & Rogers, A. 1994 'Something old, something new . . . : Sociology and the organisation of psychiatry' *Sociology* vol. 28, no. 2, pp. 521–38

Popay, J. & Williams, G. 1996 'Public health research and lay knowledge' *Social Science and Medicine* vol. 42, no. 5, pp. 759–68

Prior, L. 1994 [Review] Conrad, P. & Schneider, W. 'Deviance and Medicalization: From Badness to Sickness' *Sociology of Health and Illness* vol. 16, no. 2, pp. 263–64

Radley, A. (ed.) 1993 *Worlds of Illness: Biographical and Cultural Perspectives on Health and Disease* Routledge, London

Short, S.D. 1991 'The social application, transmission and production of medical knowledge: A framework for analysis' PhD thesis, University of New South Wales, Sydney

——1994 'Towards the democratization of health research' in *Just Health: Inequalities in Illness, Care and Prevention* eds C. Waddell & A. Petersen, Churchill Livingstone, Melbourne

——1996 'Social reconstructions of health knowledge' *Annual Review of Health Social Sciences* vol. 6, School of Health Services Management, University of New South Wales, Sydney

——1997 'Elective affinities: Research and health policy development' in *Health Policy in Australia* ed. H. Gardner, Oxford University Press, Melbourne

——1998 'Community activism and the health policy process: The case of the Consumers' Health Forum of Australia, 1987–1996' in *Activism and the Policy Process* ed. A. Yeatman, Allen & Unwin, Sydney (in press)

Wadsworth, Y. 1984 *Do it Yourself Social Research* Victorian Council of Social Service and the Melbourne Family Care Organisation, Melbourne

——1988 'Participatory research and development in primary health care by community groups', Report to the National Health and Medical Research Council Public Health Research and Development Committee from the Consumers' Health Forum of Australia, Canberra

——1989 *Consumers Health Forum Grants Programme: First Triennium, 1987–1989. Report of Internal Review* Consumers' Health Forum of Australia, Canberra

Williams, G. 1984 'The genesis of chronic illness: Narrative reconstruction' *Sociology of Health and Illness* vol. 6, no. 2, pp. 175–200

4 Emotions, equity and health

Simon J. Williams

Emotions lie at the juncture of many traditional divisions and debates within Western thought, such as mind/body, culture/nature, society/biology, reason/emotion, object/subject, human/animal, and meaning/cause. Historically, and even to the present day, emotions are seen to be the very antithesis of the detached scientific mind and its quest for 'objectivity', 'truth' and 'wisdom'. Yet emotions, as we shall see below, are not only central to many contemporary debates in mainstream sociological theory: they are also crucially important to the sociology of health and illness, dealing as it does with key aspects of human embodiment such as disease and illness, pain and suffering, sickness, disability and death (Scheper-Hughes & Lock 1987; Turner 1992).

Despite the recent explosion of interest in the body and society (Featherstone et al. 1991; Grosz 1994; Shilling 1993; Turner 1992, 1996) much still remains to be done to 'bring the body back in' in ways which not only satisfactorily resolve the tensions and dilemmas between the biological and the social, nature and culture, reason and emotion but also avoid the pitfalls of previous crude socio-biological explanations (Bendelow & Williams 1998; Williams & Bendelow 1998). To date, much of the sociological discussion has been *about* bodies (i.e. issues of regulation, representation, restraint etc.) rather *from* bodies (i.e. a more phenomenologically grounded emphasis on the body as a lived structure of ongoing experience). More generally, as Benton (1991) has recently argued, a number of contemporary social trends and movements are beginning to pose a significant challenge to seemingly 'settled' and 'ossified' conceptual forms within the social science traditions.

It is this opportunity and challenge which forms the starting point of the present chapter. Having briefly outlined some of the key contemporary issues within the sociology of emotions, including the biology/society debate, I shall then proceed to illustrate the relevance of this newly emerging field for contemporary research in the sociology of health and illness, paying particular attention to the inequalities in health and the social causes of disease debate. Not only does the sociological study of emotions shed important new light on these health-related issues, it also offers us a potentially fruitful way out of formerly rigid dichotomous modes of thinking through a unified conception of the 'mindful', emotionally expressive body as the existential basis of structure and agency, culture and self. It is to these neglected issues that I now turn as a backdrop to the discussion which follows.

THE SOCIOLOGY OF EMOTIONS AND THE 'PROBLEM' OF HUMAN EMBODIMENT

Emotions, as suggested above, lie at the juncture of a number of classical and contemporary debates in sociology including the micro/macro divide, positivism versus anti-positivism, quantitative versus qualitative, prediction versus description, managing versus accounting for emotions, and biosocial versus social constructionist perspectives (Kemper 1990). Central questions here include: Can emotions be isolated, defined, observed and understood as universal 'things' in themselves or as 'social constructs'? Can we can delineate a distinct, autonomous realm of 'measurable' emotions, or are they instead culturally specific products of particular contexts, beliefs and value-systems? How, precisely, given their complexity, are we to relate micro-interactional processes of emotion management to broader macro-structural issues of power and status, conflict and control?

Broadly speaking, approaches to emotions can be conceptualised on a continuum ranging from the 'organismic'[1] at one end to the 'social constructionist' at the other, with 'interactionist' approaches, as the term implies, somewhere in between. In contrast to organismic theories, social constructionist approaches, as the name implies, stress the primarily social as opposed to the biological nature of emotions (Harre 1986; 1991; Jackson 1993). From this perspective, 'emotions are not "inside" bodies, but rather actions we place in our world . . . feelings are *social* . . . constituted and sustained by group processes . . . irreducible to the bodily organism and to the particular individual who feels them' (McCarthy 1989, p. 57). More generally, social constructionists view human emotions as historical products and socially contingent phenomena (Lutz 1988; Stearns 1994; Stearns & Haggarty 1991; Stearns & Stearns 1988). Certainly, the naming of feelings, the situations in which they occur, the display rules associated with them, and their relationship to the self, are all endlessly elaborated across time and through culture. Yet in stressing these issues, social constructionists, like their organismic counterparts, also fall foul of the temptation to overstretch their explanatory frames of reference (i.e. move to the other extreme of the organic–social spectrum). Indeed, a 'purely' constructionist perspective in the sociology of emotions, as Freund rightly argues: 'ignores biological process and presents a disembodied view of human emotions . . . The relationship between body and emotions is not resolved by ignoring the body's relevance or by viewing emotions simply as cognitive products' (1990, p. 455). 'Going beyond' the biological, in short, does not mean ignoring it altogether. Rather, it necessitates a more intricate model than organismic theorists or social constructionists propose of how social and cognitive influences 'join' physiological ones in the genesis of human emotions.

Hochschild, for example, develops an interactionist model, defining emotion as 'bodily co-operation with an image, a thought, a memory—a co-operation of which the individual is aware' (1979, p. 551). In doing so, she joins three theoretical currents. First, from Dewey (1922), Gerth and Mills (1964) and Goffman (1959), she explores what gets 'done' to emotions and how feelings are permeable to what gets done to them. Secondly, from Darwin (1955/[1895]) in the organismic tradition, she is able to posit a sense of what is there, impermeable, to be 'done to' (i.e. a biologically given sense which, in turn, is related to an orientation to action). Finally, through Freud's (1984/[1923]) work on the 'signal' function of human feelings, Hochschild is able to circle back from the organismic to the interactionist tradition, by tracing the way in which social factors influence what we expect and thus what these feelings actually 'signify' (Hochschild 1983, p. 222; Hochschild 1998). From this starting point, Hochschild is able to develop her 'emotion management' perspective; one which enables her to inspect, through the sociological notion of 'The Managed Heart', the increasingly commoditised and commercialised relationship between emotional labour, feeling rules and ideology in advanced capitalist society (Williams 1998).

These differing approaches to emotion, each in their own way, raise deeper philosophical and ontological questions concerning the problematic status of human embodiment as simultaneously both nature and culture. Emotions, as Denzin (1984) argues, are embodied experiences; ones which radiate through the body as a lived structure of ongoing experience and centrally involve self-feelings which constitute the inner core of emotionality. For individuals to understand their own lived emotions, they must experience them socially and reflectively. It is here, according to Denzin, at the intersection between emotions as *embodied* experiences, their socially faceted nature, and their links with feelings of selfhood and personal identity, that a truly sociological perspective and understanding of emotions can most fruitfully be forged.

From this viewpoint—one which is not merely *about* the body but *from* the body—embodiment is neither reducible to representations of the body, to the body as an objectification of power, to the body as a physiological entity, nor to the body as an inalienable centre of individual consciousness (Csordas 1994a, 1994b). Rather, it becomes instead the existential basis of social and cultural life. Moreover, the interactive, relational character of embodied emotional experience offers a way of moving beyond micro-analytic, subjective, internal or individualistic analyses, towards a more 'open-ended horizon' in which embodied agency can be understood not merely as individual but also as 'institution making' (Csordas, 1994a, p. 14; Lyon & Barbalet 1994).

Emotions, in short, are most fruitfully seen as *embodied* existential modes of being; ones which involve an active engagement with the world and an intimate connection with both society and self, structure and agency, health and illness (Bendelow & Williams 1998). Not only do emotions underpin the phenomenological experience of our bodies in health and illness, they also provide the basis for social reciprocity and exchange (compare the notion of 'deep sociality' (Wentworth & Yardley 1994), and the 'link' between personal problems and broader public issues of social structure (Mills 1959). Indeed, to paraphrase Giddens' (1984) structuration theory, structure may fruitfully be seen as both the *medium* and *outcome* of the *emotionally embodied practices* it recursively organises. The emphasis here is on the active, emotionally expressive body as the basis of self, sociality, meaning, and order within the broader socio-cultural realms of everyday life and the 'ritualised' forms of interaction and exchange they involve.

Underpinning these arguments, of course, is a broader critique of the dualist legacies of the past; legacies which, as suggested above, have sought to divorce mind from body, nature from culture, and reason from emotion. Contra centuries of Western thought, emotions and feelings are not 'intruders' into the rationalist (male) citadel, but inextricably enmeshed within its network, giving many subtle shades and textured nuances to cognitive decision-making processes (Damasio

1994). Seen in these terms, the irrational passion for dispassionate rationality is itself wholly unreasonable: a view which not only serves ideological functions but drags attention away from the bodily basis of meaning, imagination and reason (Johnson 1987). It is this notion of the 'mindful' (Scheper-Hughes & Lock 1987), emotionally 'expressive' body (Freund 1990) as a lived reality, one which is active in the interactional contexts of power, conflict and social exchange which, I suggest, strikes at the very heart of these dualities (Williams & Bendelow 1998). Embodiment captures the essential ambiguity of human being as both nature and culture, and the transcendence of duality at the pre-objective level of ongoing lived experience. Here, mind and body, reason and emotion, can only be arbitrarily separated by an act of conscious reflection and objectification.

Having sketched the outlines of these broader debates within the sociology of emotions, together with my own particular position within them, it is to a fuller account of their relevance to the sociology of health and illness that we now turn. In doing so, I hope to further illustrate how emotion provides the 'missing link' between mind and body, experience and representation, structure and agency, macro and micro, public and private, and a host of other dichotomous ways of thinking.

EMOTIONS, EMBODIMENT AND THE PSYCHOSOCIAL
PATHWAYS TO DISEASE

The relevance of emotions to the sociology of health and illness, as I have already suggested, is an axiomatic, yet neglected, fact, spanning a diverse array of issues from the meaning and experience of pain and suffering (Bendelow 1993; Bendelow & Williams 1995a, 1995b), to the gendered division of emotional labour in health care (James 1993, 1992, 1989; Lawler 1991; Olesen & Bone 1998; Page & Meerabeau 1998; Smith 1992; Stacey 1988) and the proliferation of 'psy' and holistic therapies in contemporary Western society. In this chapter, however, I have chosen to concentrate instead on what is perhaps a less well developed, yet equally rich, topic of sociological investigation, namely the 'link' which emotions provide between social structure and health, particularly in the light of recent theories on the psychosocial pathways to disease.

As Wilkinson (1996) has recently argued, the contemporary links between social structure and health draw attention to the fact that psychosocial, rather than material, factors are now the limiting component in the quality of life of developed Western societies. Apparently regardless of the fact that health differences within societies remain so closely wedded to socioeconomic status, once a country has passed a certain level of income—one associated with the 'epidemiological transition' from infectious to chronic degenerative diseases—its whole population can be 'more than twice as rich as another without being any healthier' (Wilkinson 1996, p. 3).

What matters most, it seems, is not so much the direct effects of absolute material living standards as the effects of 'social relativities'. As Wilkinson states:

> The indications that the links are psychosocial make these relationships as important for the real subjective quality of life among modern populations as they are for their health . . . Sources of social stress, poor social networks, low self-esteem, high rates of depression, anxiety, insecurity and loss of a sense of control, all have such a fundamental impact on our experience of life that it is reasonable to wonder whether the effects on the quality of life are not more important than their effects on the length of life. (1996, pp. 5–6)

To talk of psychosocial factors in the aetiology of disease does not, of course, mean that the basic cause of these problems is psychological, or that it can be dealt with in these terms. Rather, as Wilkinson rightly argues, the point in differentiating psychosocial from material pathways is to distinguish the social and economic problems affecting health *indirectly* through various forms of worry, stress, insecurity and vulnerability, from those like environmental pollution that affect health *directly* through wholly material pathways, even if we are totally unaware or unconcerned by them at the cognitive–emotional level (Wilkinson 1996, p. 184).

The upshot of these arguments is clear: having attained a basic minimum standard of living for the vast majority of the population, psychosocial rather than material factors become pre-eminent in the aetiology and social patterning of contemporary Western disease. This, in turn, places emotions centre-stage in aetiological terms, yet to-date they remain a strangely neglected topic and undertheorised aspect of the inequalities debate; particularly as the 'missing link' between structure and agency, mind and body, biology and society.

How, then, are we to theorise this emotionally mediated micro–macro link, and what empirical evidence is there to support these seemingly abstract theoretical contentions? A first clue to these issues is provided by Collins (1981, 1990) who argues, in classically Durkheimian style, that social order and solidarity ultimately rest on collective moral sentiments and commitments which emerge in the course of 'interaction ritual' chains and emotional exchanges at the micro level. Conflict, too, rests on an emotional foundation, involving as it does the mobilisation of sentiments of anger toward carriers of opposing social values and interests. 'Power rituals', for instance, which mainly occur in large-scale organisations, involve interactions structured in terms of 'order-givers' and 'order-takers'. While order-givers derive positive 'emotional energy' from these interactional exchanges, order-takers, on the other hand, frequently experience a loss of emotional interest as a consequence of being neglected and their wishes being ignored. 'Status rituals', in contrast—which are somewhat independent of power-based rituals—involve interactions structured along the lines of membership 'inclusion and exclusion', 'centrality or periphery' of location, and the 'localism or cosmopolitanism' of one's network of interactional associates: divisions which, like power-based rituals, increase or decrease emotional energy respectively (Collins 1981, 1990).

Underpinning these ideas is Collins' suggestion that interaction patterns, and the 'transient emotions' they involve, provide a microfoundation of long-term emotional resources or energies which in turn serve as the basis for further interactions. It is these 'interaction ritual chains'—chains which accumulate across time and space—that provide the macro-structures of social stratification. As Collins states:

> The IR [interaction ritual] chain model . . . proposes that individuals acquire or lose emotional energy in both power and status interactions. Order givers gain EE [emotional energy], order-takers lose it; successful enactment of group membership raises EE, experiencing marginality or exclusion lowers it . . . Interaction rituals are connected in chains over time, with the results of the last interactions (in emotions and symbols) becoming inputs for the next interaction. Thus, EE tends to accumulate (either positively or negatively) over time. (Collins 1990, p. 39)

It is in this way that society 'gets inside' the individual's 'mindful' body. Emotional energy ebbs and flows across a chain of interaction rituals depending on the ups and downs of the individual's experiences of power and status, operating both to 'stably reproduce social structure', and to 'energize the dynamics of conflict and change' (Collins 1990, p. 52).

The implications of these arguments for health have recently been taken up and more fully explored in Freund's (1982, 1988, 1990, 1998) work on the emotionally 'expressive body' as a common ground for the sociology of emotions and health and illness. A central part of understanding human emotions for Freund is to see them as existential 'modes of being' (Buytendijk 1950, 1962, 1974), involving a fusion of physical and psychic states which can be either 'pleasant' or 'unpleasant' in nature. In keeping with Collins' (1990) notion of 'emotional energy', the crucial issue for our purposes is that these differing modes of emotional being are, in effect, different felt ways of feeling *empowered* or *disempowered:* feelings which are very much linked to people's material and psychosocial conditions of existence throughout their embodied biographies. It is here, at this nexus, that:

> 'External' social structural factors such as one's position in different systems of hierarchy or various forms of social control can influence the conditions of our existence, how we respond and apprehend these conditions and our sense of embodied self. These conditions can also affect our physical functioning. (Freund 1990, p. 461)

A person's social position and status will determine the resources they have at their disposal in order to define and protect—through 'status shields' (Hochschild 1983) and various other means—the boundaries of the self and counter the potential for 'invalidation' by powerful and significant others. Being in an extremely powerless social status, in other words, 'increases the likelihood of experiencing "unpleasant" emotionality or emotional modes of being' (Freund 1990, p. 466). Less powerful people, therefore, face a 'structurally in-built handicap' in managing social and emotional information; one which may, in turn, contribute to existential fear, anxiety and neurophysiological perturbation of many different sorts. Since the body is a means of expressing meaning, including socio-cultural meaning, it is not unreasonable to suppose that:

> . . . people might somatically express the conditions of their existence. Pain, for instance, can express a sense of an existence that weighs heavily on one or a sense of powerlessness . . . Cultural factors can shape the language of the body.[2] (Freund 1990, p. 463)

In particular, the 'dramaturgical stress' (Goffman 1959) of social relationships may engender—through the agency of an 'ontologically insecure self' (Laing 1965)—a form of what Freund, borrowing from Kelly (1980), refers to as 'schizokinesis'; one involving a split between what is shown and consciously experienced, and what occurs somatically. Here Freund poses two extremely important questions: first, How 'deep' can the social construction of feelings go?; and secondly, Can emotion work eliminate the responses of an unconsciously knowing body? The implications of his argument seem to suggest that society affects physiological reactivity deep within the recesses of the human body—although, as the concept of schizokinesis implies, the 'mind' may, consciously at least, be unaware of the 'body's' response. As continued emotional and other kinds of distress alter physiological reactivity, neuro-hormonally-related functions such as blood pressure may markedly increase in response to a psychosocial stressor but not be consciously experienced.[3]

Certainly, there is now plenty of empirical evidence which points towards this emotionally mediated, psychosocial link between social structure, disease and disorder: from the 'physiological marks' of unremitting socioeconomic stress to the biological effects (e.g. endocrine and immunological disorders) of status hierarchies among baboons (Sapolsky 1993, 1991) and civil servants (Brunner 1996); and from the (anticipated) consequences of unemployment, job insecurity, and a lack of control over one's working conditions (Karesek & Theorell 1990; Marmot et al. 1991; Mattiasson et al. 1990), to the beneficial effects of social support, both at home and in the community, for health (Berkman 1995; Berkman & Syme 1979; Cohen & Syme 1985; Thoits 1995).

These general findings have been reinforced by research within the life-events paradigm which has documented, with increasing precision, the complex relationship between social factors, cognitive–emotional responses and the onset of a variety of physical and mental conditions. Brown and Harris (1978), for instance, in their classic sociological study, highlight the 'depressogenic' links between provoking agents (i.e. severe life events and long-term difficulties), vulnerability factors (e.g. death of mother before the age of eleven, lack of a close confiding relationship, absence of outside employment, three or more children under the age of fifteen at home), and the onset of clinical depression; a process which works, they suggest, through the ontological agency of 'chronically low self-esteem' and the transition from short-term to more generalised feelings of 'hopelessness'.

Craig (1989), in contrast, demonstrates the importance of goal-frustration, as opposed to the more usual loss or danger associated with severe events and long-term difficulties, in the onset of gastrointestinal disorders, contrasting the lowering of pain thresholds consequent upon emotional distress with changes in gut motility (i.e. abnormalities of the motor activity of the bowel, causing the development of pain). Other studies within the life-events paradigm have demonstrated the increased chances of conditions such as myocardial infarction in those experiencing accumulated work stress over a ten-year period (Neilson et al. 1989): a finding which appears to hold even after controlling for other possible confounding factors such as cigarette smoking and higher alcohol consumption. Perhaps a more subtle illustration of these psychosocial processes, however, concerns Andrews and House's (1989) finding of a link between what they term 'conflict over speaking out' (CSO) events—that is, situations which provide, on the one hand, a challenge to speak out, protest, or complain, and on the other, an unusual constraint upon such outspoken behaviour—and the development of functional dysphonia in women (i.e. a difficulty in vocal production which cannot be explained by way of structural lesions of larynx or by any neurological lesion). In seeking to explicate this intriguing finding, the authors draw attention to the high rate of muscular tension these women experienced in the laryngeal region; a factor which, they suggest, may provide the intervening link between CSO events and functional dysphonia.[4]

Here we return, via these empirical examples, to the manner in which the emotionally expressive body translates broader psychosocial and material conditions of existence, including conflict situations, into the recalcitrant language of disease and disorder.[5] The argument here is for a subtle and sophisticated form of externally 'pliable' or 'socialised' biology rather than socio-biology; one which accords emotional modes of being a central role in linking the health and illness of the existential–phenomenologically embodied agent with wider structures of power and domination, civilisation and control in society. Freund summarises this position in the following terms:

> One's positions, and the roles that accompany them in various systems of social hierarchy, shape the conditions in which one lives. This position influences access to resources. It may also determine the forms of emotional–social control to which one is subject as well as the severity of the impact these controls have on the person . . . Such a process may mean internalising the emotional definitions that others impose on what we are or 'should' be. The physiological aspects of such processes are of interest to those studying emotions. However, these physical aspects may also be seen as examples of ways in which controls are sedimented and fixed in the psycho-soma of the person. Physiological aspects of social activity can also act as a form of feedback that colours the tone of existence. This feedback can *indirectly* serve social control functions. For instance, conditions that create depression . . . construct an emotional mode of being where the motivation to resist is blunted. (1990, p. 470)

It is here, at this existential nexus, that the 'mindful', emotionally 'expressive' body is located: one which is active in the context of power and status, conflict and control. This, in turn, raises broader questions concerning the relationship between emotions, health and 'distributive justice'; an issue to which I shall now turn in the next section of this chapter.

EMOTIONS, HEALTH AND 'DISTRIBUTIVE JUSTICE'

Talk of psychosocial pathways and subtly nuanced emotional responses suggests a complex, multi-factorial picture of disease causation in contemporary Western societies; one involving a considerable degree of individual variability which defies neat and tidy aetiological or epidemiological modelling. On the one hand, we have the 'immutable uncertainties' and 'fateful moments' of everyday life; events from which none of us are immune. On the other hand, however, we must also confront the fact that these very adversities, including the emotionally embodied responses they call forth, are socio-structurally patterned in various ways. Seen in these terms, class structure and the broader political regime impinge on the health of the emotionally expressive body in two main ways: 'First, through the impact they have on the incidence of life-events as such, and second, through the influence they exert on the availability of means and skills needed to cope with an event after it has occurred' (Gerhardt 1979, p. 220).

Most of the class difference in female depression, for example, appears to be due to the fact that working-class women experience more provoking agents and vulnerability factors than their middle-class counterparts (Brown & Harris 1978). This, coupled with the notion of 'conveyor belts' to continuing adversity (Brown & Harris 1989), serves to capture the dialectic between personal troubles and broader public issues of social structure, so central to Mills' (1959) 'sociological imagination'.

To suggest that socioeconomic factors now affect health primarily through indirect psychosocial rather than direct material routes, is not, therefore, to suggest that we concentrate on 'inner' rather than 'external', individual rather than political, issues. Quite the reverse. Far from being 'irrational', feelings of absurdity and alienation, bitterness and resentment, entrapment and despair are often entirely realistic assessments and understandable responses to existing social circumstances. Here, 'inner' and 'outer' worlds meet, and it is from there that the sociologist must go on to build links with the wider cultural, economic and political system (Brown 1977, p. 11). This, in turn, raises broader questions about the relationship between emotions, health and 'distributive justice', about which problems of income distribution and social integration loom large. As Wilkinson's (1996) work clearly demonstrates, it is not the richest but the most egalitarian societies which have the best health: those which foster, through equitable forms of income distribution, a sense of social cohesion and community life in an increasingly 'atomised' society. Income distribution, in other words, alongside all the other factors considered above, is an important determinant of the 'psychosocial welfare' of a society, promoting not only more healthy societies, but also more egalitarian, internally cohesive ones. This, in turn, tells us something very important about how the social fabric is affected by the amount of inequality in a society and its impact on health. Recognition of this fact gives governments an important opportunity to take practical steps to improve, instead of side-step, these pressing matters:

> The importance of knowing that social cohesion is likely to be improved by narrower income differences is that it gives policy-makers a way of improving important aspects of life in our society . . . Because income distribution is powerfully affected by government policy, governments may be able to improve the psychosocial condition and morale of the whole population. (Wilkinson 1996, pp. 184–85)

Emotions, health and distributive justice are therefore intimately related in the developed Western world: a link which constitutes both a challenge and opportunity to governments concerned with the corrosive effects of 'unhealthy societies' and the 'afflictions of inequality'.

ANALYTICAL REFLECTIONS AND CONCLUSION

A central aim of this chapter has been to discuss, albeit in an exploratory fashion, the links between emotions, embodiment and health, using the inequalities debate as a paradigmatic example. As I have argued, the fact that socioeconomic factors now primarily affect health through psychosocial rather than material pathways places emotions centre-stage in the social patterning of disease and disorder in advanced Western societies. In this sense, emotions, as existentially embodied modes of being-in-the-world, provide the 'missing link' between 'personal troubles' and broader 'public issues' of social structure.

Underpinning these arguments is a commitment to fundamentally re-thinking the 'biological' in non-reductionist terms. Biology is not fixed or immutable. Rather, as biologically 'unfinished' creatures, human beings are 'completed' as well as 'depleted' by society and culture. In this respect, adapting Gerhardt's (1979) earlier reconstruction of the life-events approach, it may be useful to distinguish, analytically, between psychoneuroimmunological *adaptation*, psychosocial *coping* and socio-political *praxis*. In the first case, the type of event experienced may be characterised as a disruptive 'change' of some sort, for which psychoneuroimmunological 'arousal control' and the restoration of homeostatic 'balance' (i.e. the teleonomic capacities of the organism) is the most appropriate response. At the second, psychosocial, level of coping, the type of event experienced may be loosely referred to as a 'loss' of some kind (e.g. a death, a cherished idea, an important role etc.), while the appropriate response becomes one of 'meaning construction'. Finally, at the broadest level of socio-political praxis, the type of event experienced may best be described as an (ongoing) difficulty, and the appropriate response one of 'project formation'—which, in turn is linked to the wider economic and political structure of power, rights and privileges within society (Gerhardt 1979, p. 219).

From this viewpoint, different responses of the emotionally expressive body are, as Gerhardt points out, more or less successful, depending on the type of event experienced. In the case of long-term difficulties of a 'public' nature, for example, active changes in the individual's environment—that is, socio-political praxis rather than psychosocial coping via processes of meaning construction—may be the most appropriate response. In contrast, disruptive changes involving no loss but considerable flexibility and endurance may be most effectively overcome through adaptive psychoneuroimmunological processes of 'arousal control' and the re-establishment of homeostatic balance (Gerhardt 1989, p. 215). Discussion of these issues again returns us to broader problems concerning the relationship between emotions, health and distributive justice in contemporary Western societies, including problems of income distribution and social cohesion: issues which need to be at the 'heart' of future policy initiatives in this area.

To conclude, a focus on the 'mindful', emotionally expressive body, provides, I suggest, a potentially fruitful future direction of research within the sociology of health and illness. Whilst I have chosen to focus on the inequalities debate as illustrative of these issues, it is equally clear that emotions are central to a number of other issues within the sociology of health and illness, from human reproduction to the social organisation of health care, and from the ethical dilemmas of high-technology medicine to the growing popularity of holistic therapies and lay reskilling in a socially reflexive age. Emotions, in short, contra Descartes' Enlightenment vision of a 'disembodied' rational world, have truly come of age!

NOTES

1   Organismic theorists include Darwin (1955/[1885]), for whom emotion is an 'archaic remnant' of instinctual bodily gesture, Freud (1984/[1923]) who saw

emotions in 'dammed up' libidinal and 'signal function' terms (e.g. anxiety as the model for all other emotions) and James and Lange (1922), for whom emotion was the brain's conscious reaction to instinctual visceral change.

2   Lynch (1985) makes a similar point in his book *The Language of the Heart: The Human Body in Dialogue.*

3   See also Lyon's (1994) account of the relationship between emotions and respiration.

4   For other examples of this now well-established link between life events and illness—including anxiety, schizophrenia, appendicitis, menstrual disorders, and multiple sclerosis—see Brown and Harris (1989).

5   Perhaps the first person to systematically explore this link was the 'sexual radical' Reich (1983/[1942], 1969/[1951], 1949), whose work on 'character armour' and its translation into 'muscular tension' and rigid bodily posture has now been transformed, via contemporary discourses on stress, from a psychotherapeutic insight into conventionalised wisdom within lay and popular culture.

REFERENCES

Andrews, H. & House, A. 1989 'Functional dysfonia' in *Life Events and Illness* eds G.W. Brown & T.O. Harris, Unwin Hyman, London

Bendelow, G. 1993 'Pain perceptions, gender and emotion' *Sociology of Health and Illness* vol. 15, no. 3, pp. 273–94

Bendelow, G. & Williams, S.J. 1995a 'Transcending the dualisms: Towards a sociology of pain' *Sociology of Health and Illness* vol. 17, no. 2, pp. 139–65

——1995b 'Pain and the mind–body dualism: A sociological approach' *Body & Society* vol. 1, no. 2, pp. 83–103

——1998 (eds) *Emotions in Social Life: Critical Themes and Contemporary Issues* Routledge, London

Benton, T. 1991 'Biology and social science: why the return of the repressed should be given a (cautious) welcome' *Sociology* vol. 25, no. 1, pp. 1–29

Berkman, L.F. 1995 'The role of social relations in health promotion' *Psychosomatic Research* no. 57, pp. 245–54

Berkman, L.F. & Syme, S.L. 1979 'Social networks, host resistance, and mortality: A nine year follow-up of Almeda County residents' *American Journal of Epidemiology* no. 109, pp. 186–204

Brown, G.W. 1977 'Depression: A sociological view' *Maudsley Gazette* Summer, pp. 9–12

Brown, G.W. & Harris, T.O. 1978 *The Social Origins of Depression: A Study of Psychiatric Disorder in Women* Tavistock, London

——1989 *Life Events and Illness* Unwin Hyman, London

Brunner, E. 1996 'The social and biological basis of cardiovascular disease in office workers' in *Health and Social Organisation* eds E. Brunner, D. Blane & R.G. Wilkinson, Routledge, London

Buytendijk, F.J.J. 1950 'The phenomenological approach to the problem of feelings and emotions' in *Feelings and Emotions: The Mooseheart Symposium in Cooperation with the University of Chicago* ed. M.C. Reymert, McGraw-Hill, New York

——1962 *Pain: Its Modes and Functions* trans. Eda O'Shiel, University of Chicago Press, Chicago

Buytendijk, F.J.J. 1974 *Prolegomena to an Anthropological Physiology* Duquesne University Press, Pittsburgh

Cohen, L. & Syme, S.L. (eds) 1985 *Social Support and Health* Academic Press, London

Collins, R. 1981 'On the micro-foundations of macro-sociology' *American Journal of Sociology* no. 86, pp. 984–1014

——1990 'Stratification, emotional energy, and the transient emotions' in *Research Agendas in the Sociology of Emotions* ed. T.J. Kemper, State University of New York Press, New York

Craig, T. 1989 'Abdominal pain' in *Life Events and Illness* eds G.W. Brown & T.O. Harris, Unwin Hyman, London

Csordas, T.J. (ed.) 1994a *Embodiment and Experience: The Existential Ground of Culture and Self* Cambridge University Press, Cambridge

——1994b 'The body as representation and being-in-the-world' in *Embodiment and Experience: The Existential Ground of Culture and Self* ed. T.J. Csordas, Cambridge University Press, Cambridge

Damasio, A. 1994 *Descarte's Error* Papermac, London

Darwin, C. 1955/[1895] *The Expression of Emotions in Man and Animals* Philosophical Library, New York

Denzin, N.K. 1984 *On Understanding Emotion* Josey Bass, San Francisco

Dewey, J. 1922 *Human Nature and Conduct: An Introduction to Social Psychology* Holt, New York

Featherstone, M., Hepworth, M. & Turner, B.S. (eds) 1991 *The Body: Social Process and Cultural Theory* Sage, London

Freud, S. 1984/[1923] 'The ego and the id' in *On Metapsychology* ed. S. Freud, Penguin, Harmondsworth

Freund, P. 1982 *The Civilized Body: Social Control, Domination and Health* Temple University Press, Philadelphia PA

——1988 'Understanding socialized human nature' *Theory and Society* no. 17, pp. 839–64

——1990 'The expressive body: A common ground for the sociology of emotions and health and illness' *Sociology of Health and Illness* vol. 12, no. 4, pp. 452–77

——1998 'Social performances and their discontents: Reflections on the biosocial psychology of role-playing' in *Emotions in Social Life: Critical Themes and Contemporary Issues* eds G. Bendelow & S.J. Williams, Routledge, London

Gerhardt, U. 1979 'Coping as social action: Theoretical reconstruction of the life-events approach' *Sociology of Health and Illness* no. 1, pp. 195–225

Gerth, H. & Mills, C. Wright 1964 *Character and Social Structure: The Psychology of Social Institutions* Harcourt, Brace and World, New York

Giddens, A. 1984 *The Constitution of Society* Polity, Cambridge

Goffman, E. 1959 *The Presentation of Everyday Life* Doubleday Anchor, New York

Grosz, E. 1994 *Volatile Bodies* Indiana University, Bloomington and Indianapolis

Harre, R.M. (ed.) 1986 *The Social Construction of Emotions* Basil Blackwell, New York

——1991 *Physical Being: A Theory of Corporeal Psychology* Blackwell, Oxford

Hochschild, A. 1979 'Emotion work, feeling rules and social structure' *American Journal of Sociology*, no. 85, pp. 551–75

——1983 *The Managed Heart: The Commercialisation of Human Feeling* University of California Press, Berkeley, CA

——1998 'Emotions as a way of seeing: The case of love' in *Emotions in Social Life: Critical Themes and Contemporary Issues* eds G. Bendelow & S.J. Williams, Routledge, London

Jackson, S. 1993 'Even sociologists fall in love: An exploration of the sociology of emotions' *Sociology* vol. 27, no. 2, pp. 201–20

James, N. 1989 'Emotional labour: Skill and work in the social regulation of feelings' *The Sociological Review* no. 37, pp. 15–42

——1992 'Care = organisation + physical labour + emotional labour' *Sociology of Health and Illness* vol. 14, no. 4, pp. 488–509

——1993 'Divisions of emotional labour: The case of cancer and disclosure' in *Emotion and Organizations* ed. S. Fineman, Sage, London

James, W. & Lange, C. 1922 *The Emotions* Wilkins and Wilkins, Baltimore

Johnson, M. 1987 *The Body in the Mind: The Bodily Basis of Meaning, Imagination and Reason* University of Chicago Press, Chicago

Karesek, R. & Theorell, T. 1990 *Healthy Work: Stress, Productivity and the Reconstruction of Working Life* Basic Books, New York

Kelly, D. 1980 *Anxiety and Emotions* Charles C. Thomas Publishers, Springfield, ILL

Kemper, T.J. 1990 'Themes and variations in the sociology of emotions' in *Research Agendas in the Sociology of Emotions* ed. T.J. Kemper, State University of New York Press, New York

Laing, R.D. 1965 *The Divided Self* Penguin, Harmondsworth

Lawler, J. 1991 *Behind the Screens: Nursing, Somology and the Problem of the Body* Churchill Livingstone, London

Lutz, C.A. 1988 *Unnatural Emotions: Everyday Sentiments on a Micronesian Atoll and their Challenge to Western Theory* University of Chicago Press, Chicago

Lynch, J. 1985 *The Langauge of the Heart: The Human Body in Dialogue* Basic Books, New York

Lyon, M. 1994 'Emotion as mediator of somatic and social processes: The example of respiration' in *Social Perspectives on Emotion* eds W.M. Wentworth & J. Ryan, JAI Press Inc., Greenwich, CT

Lyon, M. & Barbalet, J. 1994 'Society's body: Emotion and the "somatization" of social theory' in *Embodiment and Experience: The Existential Ground of Culture and Self* ed. T.J. Csordas, Cambridge University Press, Cambridge

McCarthy, E. Doyle 1989 'Emotions are social things: An essay in the sociology of emotions' in *The Sociology of Emotions: Original Essays and Research Papers* eds D.D. Franks & E. Doyle McCarthy, JAI Press Inc., Greenwich, CT

Marmot, M., Davey Smith, G., Stansfield, S., Patel, C., North, F. & Head, J. 1991 'Health inequalities among British civil servants: The Whitehall II study' *Lancet* no. 337, pp. 1387–93

Mattiasson, I., Lingarde, F., Nilsson, J.A. & Theorell, T. 1990 'Threat of unemployment and cardiovascular risk factors: longitudinal study of quality of sleep and serum cholesterol concentrations in men threatened with redundancy' *British Medical Journal* no. 301, pp. 461–66

Mills, C. Wright. 1959 *The Sociological Imagination* Oxford University Press, New York

Neilson, E., Brown, G.W. & Marmot, M. 1989 'Myocardial infarction' in *Life Events and Illness* eds G.W. Brown & T.O. Harris, Unwin Hyman, London

Oleson, V. & Bone, D. 1998 'Emotional dynamics in changing institutional contexts' in *Emotions in Social Life: Critical Themes and Contemporary Issues* eds G. Bendelow & S.J. Williams, Routledge, London

Page, S. & Meerabeau, L. 1998 'Drama and dignity: Nurses' accounts of cardiopulmonary resuscitation and death' in *Emotions in Social Life: Critical Themes and Contemporary Issues* eds G. Bendelow & S.J. Williams, Routledge, London

Reich, W. 1949 *Character Analysis* Farrar, Straus and Giroux, New York

Reich 1969/[1951] *The Sexual Revolution* 4th rev. edn, trans. T.P. Wolfe, Vision Press Ltd, London

——1983/[1942] *The Function of the Orgasm* trans. V.F. Carfagno, Souvenir Press, London

Sapolsky, R.M. 1991 'Poverty's remains' *The Sciences* no. 31, pp. 8–10

——1993 'Endocrinology alfresco: Psychoendocrine studies of wild baboons' *Recent Progress in Hormone Research* no. 48, pp. 437–68

Scheper-Hughes, N. & Lock, M. 1987 'The mindful body: A prolegomenon to future work in medical anthropology' *Medical Anthropology Quarterly* vol. 1, no. 1, pp. 6–41

Shilling, C. 1993 *The Body in Social Theory* Sage, London

Smith, P. 1992 *The Emotional Labour of Nursing* Macmillan Educational Books, Basingstoke

Stacey, M. 1988 *The Sociology of Health and Healing* Routledge, London

Stearns, P.N. 1994 *American Cool: Constructing a Twentieth Century American Style* New York University Press, New York

Stearns, P.N. & Haggarty, T. 1991 'The role of fear: Transitions in American emotional standards for children, 1850–1950' *The American Historical Review* no. 96, pp. 63–94

Stearns, C.Z. & Stearns, P.N. 1988 *Emotions and Social Change* Holmes and Meier, New York

Thoits, P. 1995 'Stress, coping, and social support processes: Where are we? What next?' *Journal of Health and Social Behaviour* Extra issue, pp. 53–79

Turner, B.S. 1992 *Regulating Bodies: Essays in Medical Sociology* Routledge, London

——1996 *The Body and Society* 2nd edn, Sage, London

Wentworth, W.M. & Yardley, D. 1994 'Deep sociality: A bioevolutionary perspective on the sociology of emotions' in *Social Perspectives on Emotion* eds W.M. Wentworth & J. Ryan, JAI Press Inc., Greenwich, Connecticut/London

Wilkinson, R.G. 1996 *Unhealthy Societies: The Afflictions of Inequality* Routledge, London

Williams S.J. 1998 'Arlie Russell Hochschild' in *Key Sociological Thinkers* ed. R. Stones, Macmillan, London

Williams S.J. & Bendelow G.A. 1998 *Embodying Sociology: Critical Perspectives on the Dualist Legacies* Polity, Cambridge

5 Evolutionary medicine

James S. Chisholm

> There is, I assure you, a medical art for the soul. It is philosophy, whose aid need not be sought, as in bodily diseases, from outside ourselves. We must endeavour with all our resources and all our strength to become capable of doctoring ourselves.
>
> Cicero (106–43 BC)

Western medicine is on the verge of a revolution—a revolution in epistemology.[1] From its beginning on the bedrock of scientific induction and reductionism, Western medicine is now poised to take the radical philosophical step of exploring how modern evolutionary theory might augment these venerable ways of knowing. We are thus at 'the dawn of Darwinian medicine', as two of the authors of this revolution, evolutionary biologist George C. Williams and physician Randolph Nesse (1991), recently put it. While our long history of wondrous medical breakthroughs may have inured us to the idea of 'yet another' revolution in medicine, my goal in this chapter is to describe Darwinian or evolutionary medicine and to suggest that it is indeed revolutionary and does indeed have important implications for the way we think about health and disease—and indeed, about the therapeutic role of science itself (specifically evolutionary theory).

I will begin with a quick sketch of evolutionary medicine. In this initial overview I will examine its core concept, adaptation by natural selection, and review a few already-classic examples of the novel therapeutic insights that are being achieved via this concept. However, so that you can fully appreciate how and why an evolutionary perspective in medicine really is new and significant, and especially why it justifies the implications that I will draw from it later in the chapter,

I will then describe in somewhat greater detail the core principles of evolutionary ecology that in my opinion give evolutionary medicine its most powerful epistemological foundation. After showing how these principles give rise to and justify evolutionary medicine broadly, I will argue that they also take it in the direction of *preventive* evolutionary medicine or 'evolutionary public health' (Chisholm 1995).

EVOLUTIONARY MEDICINE

At the heart of evolutionary medicine, of course, is evolutionary theory—Darwin's theory of adaptation by natural selection. The fundamental assumption of evolutionary medicine is that this theory can help guide us to a better, more therapeutic understanding of ourselves and our diseases. Because of the long (and, sad to say, continuing) misuse of evolutionary theory by Social Darwinists, however, many social scientists and physicians are uncomfortable with this assumption. Given the real harm that has been done in the name of evolutionary theory, they fear that all evolutionary perspectives on humankind are the same, united by their inherent genetic determinism and insensitivity to historical contingencies—especially those affecting inequalities associated with race, class, and gender. In fact, as I will argue below, evolutionary theory has important implications for therapy precisely because its primary focus now is on the organism–environment interactions that affect the emergence of individual differences in adaptability. For this reason modern evolutionary ecology and life history theory are *inherently nondeterministic*.[2]

Western medicine has traditionally been based on *induction* (the patient building up of general principles about health and disease from innumerable observations of the molecules, cells, tissues, organs and behaviour of healthy and unhealthy people in particular environments) and *reductionism* (explaining health or illness in terms of [i.e. reducing it to] the nature or condition of people's behaviour, organs, tissues, cells, and molecules in particular environments). From the perspective of evolutionary medicine all of this is necessary for effective therapy (intervention and prevention) but not sufficient, *because both human beings and their illnesses have evolutionary histories*. Evolutionary theory enables us to go beyond standard induction and reductionism because it provides a powerful basis for explaining in principle why particular organisms and diseases exist and how they came to be the way they are. Evolutionary medicine is about exploring the implications for therapy of *understanding the processes of adaptation*

that produce the evolutionary histories that culminate in a particular
person, presenting with a particular complaint, at a particular place
and time. On this view, anyone presenting for treatment should be
viewed not only as a unique person with a unique developmental and
medical history, nor only as a representative of a particular culture or
social group with its own unique cultural and medical history, *but also
as a member of the human species, with its own unique evolutionary and
disease histories.* Evolutionary medicine is fundamentally based on the
premise that evolutionary theory—our only scientific theory of life—
makes it not only possible, but indeed necessary and thus responsible
to use that theory to generate therapeutically relevant insights.

Pathology or adaptation?

The insight that diseases, as part of life, have their own evolutionary
histories is what makes the evolutionary perspective in medicine
unique and valuable. Evolutionary history is the immensely long
history of individual differences in the reproductive success of all
organisms that ever lived. This history is the product of all the reasons
why some individuals 'transmit' more copies of their genes to future
generations via their descendants than others who have fewer or no
descendants, and so pass on fewer or no copies of their genes. The
reason that we (descendants, all of us) exist, is that each and every
one of our direct ancestors (back to the beginning of life) stayed alive,
grew and developed, and ultimately produced and reared offspring.

All of this takes work, however. Staying alive, growing and
developing, and producing and rearing offspring is the work of life,
and in life work is done only by adaptations. Adaptations are complex
assemblies of interacting molecules, cells, tissues, organs, and
behaviours (and among humans, beliefs and values) known as organisms. Organisms possess—indeed they *are*—adaptations for doing the
work of life. The work of life, however, cannot be done in the abstract
or in a vacuum. Adaptations are thus always for doing the universal
work of life (surviving, growing, reproducing etc.), but they are
actually adaptive *only in specific local environments.* Adaptations are
always to certain more-or-less specific environments. The essence of
evolutionary theory is the assumption or working hypothesis that the
traits we see are ultimately explainable in terms of the process of
adaptation by natural selection to more-or-less specific environmental
challenges or problems. The essence of evolutionary medicine, therefore, is evolutionary theory's fundamental assumption that *every* trait
that we observe—even pathological ones—is a product or by-product

of the process of adaptation by natural selection in some particular environment. While it is certainly true that the adaptationist approach, as this is called, can be misused (e.g. Gould & Lewontin 1979), and while we don't *really* believe that every trait is adaptive, the *assumption* of adaptation—evolutionary theory's 'default assumption' (as Dennett (1995, pp. 213) put it)—has proved itself an immensely useful place to start. Nor is there any longer any serious doubt about either its fundamental logical and evidential legitimacy or its efficacy and generativity (e.g. Dennett 1995; Parker & Maynard Smith 1990; Plotkin 1994). Further, as we shall now see, the assumption of adaptation has important therapeutic implications for the way we think about health and disease.

For a straightforward example, consider Williams and Nesse's (1991; Nesse & Williams 1995) observations about two of the body's most common responses to infection; elevated body temperature (fever) and the sequestering of iron. Whereas the standard view has long been that both are symptoms of *disease*, the emerging evolutionary view is that they are evidence instead of the operation of an evolved *pathogen defence mechanism*. The distinction here between pathology and adaptation (i.e. disease and defence against disease) is the one made by Nesse (1991) between 'defect' (disease) and 'defence'. When fever is viewed as part of a disease, it makes sense to prescribe analgesics to bring it down. However, when viewed as part of an evolved defence mechanism (for mobilising white blood cells to fight infection and inhibit bacterial growth) the optimal therapeutic strategy may be watchful waiting. Prolonged high fever can cause its own damage, of course, but in many cases it may make sense to encourage the body's natural defence mechanisms, for by artificially lowering body temperature one may inadvertently prolong the disease to which the elevated temperature is the adaptive response (Doran et al. 1989). Likewise, just as temperature goes up during infection, iron levels usually drop, as iron becomes more tightly bound to protein and is removed from circulation by (i.e. sequestered in) the liver. When depressed haemoglobin is viewed as part of a disease, it makes sense to prescribe iron supplements to raise it. From an evolutionary medical perspective, however, the optimal therapeutic strategy may again be watchful waiting, for sequestering iron in the liver means that bacteria and parasites cannot so readily use it for their own survival, growth, and reproduction. Again, while prolonged low haemoglobin levels can themselves cause problems, the too-early prescription of iron supplements may prolong the disease to which the low haemoglobin levels are an adaptive response (Weinberg 1984).

Although neither of these researchers used evolutionary theory to arrive at their conclusions (i.e. they worked inductively), adding evolutionary theory to medicine enables us to explain in principle *why* elevated body temperature and iron sequestration exist—as adaptations for defence. Bringing an evolutionary perspective to medicine compels us always (1) to question our assumptions about normality and pathology, (2) to recognise that such questions have important therapeutic implications, and (3) to accept that it is impossible to define normality and pathology usefully without specifying a particular environment (including its history).

For example, while pathogens and parasites have been a constant presence throughout human evolution (and long before), the increasingly crowded, complex, and competitive industrial environments that we have created for ourselves (mostly in the past few hundred years) bear little resemblance to the environments in which our ancestors evolved for millions of years[3]—yet biologically we may differ from them scarcely at all. To avoid confusing 'defect' and 'defence' in modern humans, therefore, it is especially important to keep in mind the possibility that what looks like pathology today might in fact have been adaptive in some ancestral environment. More than anything else, this simple fact of evolutionary ecology is helping evolutionarily-minded health scientists to re-think their assumptions about pathology and to develop novel therapies.

Evolutionary biologists have devised two ways to go about reconstructing ancestral environments: through so-called 'referential' and 'strategic' modelling (e.g. Tooby & DeVore 1987). Referential modelling uses some *objectively real* phenomenon to represent, stand for, or 'reference' the unknown evolutionary past. For example, a fossil bone, an early stone tool, or the behaviour of modern day chimpanzees may serve to stand for or refer to—that is, to 'model'—some aspect of our evolutionary history. In strategic modelling, on the other hand, the elements of the model are not real, objective phenomena (or better, they do not *refer to* real, objective phenomena), but instead mental images that refer to the conceptual elements of evolutionary theory (e.g. 'number of offspring', 'average age at first birth', or 'probability of survival to age x') whose relationships are logically and analytically specified—for example, by *ifs* and *thens*. The two approaches are not at all mutually exclusive, of course, but it is important to distinguish between them because it is the strategic approach that really *uses* evolutionary theory—as the basis for making predictions (i.e. generating *ifs*). Given the paucity of the fossil record, and the fact that behaviour never fossilises, strategic modelling has emerged as a powerful tool for reconstructing our past. This is because the more we actually find in nature the *thens* that our *ifs* led us to believe we would find, the more confident we can be that our model of nature that prompted us to think of these *ifs* in the first place is a good one (i.e. a reasonable representation of how the process of natural selection worked in ancestral environments).[4]

We now have several already-classic examples of how evolutionary biology helps us reconsider the nature of human pathology. I begin with four brief examples based on reconstructions of ancestral environments that were derived from relatively narrow referential models. After examining the core principles of evolutionary ecology that in my opinion give evolutionary medicine its most powerful epistemological rationale, I then focus on just a single example, but one derived from a sweeping strategic model based on these principles.

Women's reproductive cancers

On the now-standard assumption that the subsistence patterns and social organisations of modern hunter–gatherers are not unlike those of 99 per cent of all humans who ever existed (e.g. Lee 1979), the physician Boyd Eaton (Eaton et al. 1994) proposed that changes in the reproductive patterns of women in industrial societies place them at increased risk of breast and ovarian cancers. The reason, according to Eaton, is that women in industrial societies experience earlier menarche (first menstruation), later first birth, fewer births, shorter breastfeeding (if any), and later menopause. One consequence is that hunter–gatherer women ovulate much less frequently than women in industrial societies. Eaton and his colleagues (1994) estimate that in affluent industrial societies the average woman ovulates 450 times during her life, compared to only 160 times for hunter–gatherer women. During the first five years after the onset of menarche, breast tissue may be vulnerable to carcinogens because of the high rate of proliferation of epithelial cells. Eaton et al. speculate that when pregnancy and lactation follow quickly after menarche they slow the rate of epithelial cell proliferation in breast tissue, thereby providing protection against breast cancers. Similarly, there is empirical evidence of a link between the number of ovulations a woman has experienced in her lifetime and her risk of ovarian cancer. The mechanism may be that ovulation damages the ovarian epithelium and thereby exposes it to higher hormone levels.

The therapeutic lesson from this example is the possibility that the ancestral demographic and developmental–socio-sexual conditions to which the reproductive physiology and endocrinology of modern women seem to be adapted was one which tended to *prevent* the development of certain kinds of cancer. Since modern industrial environments seem to lack the features that may have protected our female ancestors from reproductive cancers, an evolutionarily-informed modern therapy might aim to protect women (and not just their children) by encouraging breastfeeding, or, perhaps for women at highest risk, by using hormone interventions to mimic at least the endocrine component of the ancestral protective factors (if not the actual developmental–socio-sexual events and conditions that were the source of the hormones that offered the original protection).

Pregnancy sickness

Despite the fact that some pathologies are indeed common, for evo-lutionary-minded health scientists common pathologies nonetheless raise a red flag, for they invite the question—if pathologies represent adaptive failure, and are thus selected against, how can a pathology that is common actually be pathological? This is the question (derived from evolutionary theory's 'default assumption' of adaptation) that motivated Margie Profet's (1992) reconsideration of 'pregnancy sick-ness' (nausea during pregnancy) as part of a complex adaptive response to environmental toxins (poisons). Noting (1) that such toxins can constitute a severe chemical threat to the body, (2) that there is a cluster of nerve cells in the brain stem which constantly screen for such toxins, causing defensive nausea and vomiting when any are found,[5] and (3) that the developing foetus may be especially vulnerable to environmental toxins in the first trimester, when its major organs are forming (i.e. during organogenesis), she wondered if some preg-nancy sickness might represent an evolved mechanism for protecting the developing foetus from toxins ingested by the mother.

There are two observations that are at least consistent with Profet's evolutionary model. The first is that 'morning sickness' is in fact most common during the first trimester, when the growing foetus is especially vulnerable to environmental perturbations. The second is that spontaneous abortions are three times more common among women who suffer little or no nausea during pregnancy compared to women who suffer more extreme nausea. Although additional work is obviously required to rule out other interpretations (e.g. different toxin levels), one possibility is that women who suffer little or no pregnancy sickness are less sensitive to environmental toxins, and so consume more of them, which increases the risk of foetal abnormalities and spontaneous abortion. If Profet's model turns out to be accurate, it has a novel therapeutic implication, namely, that the *absence* of pregnancy sickness is not necessarily a sign of health. Indeed, for women living in highly toxic environments the absence of morning sickness might itself constitute a symptom of their impaired sensitivity to toxins, and so indicate careful diet monitoring.

Infant colic

To have produced us, their descendants, each of our direct ancestors had first to survive as infants before they could grow and develop and ultimately bear and rear their own children. In other words, the ancestral environment to which we are adapted is not just that of our adult ancestors, but that of our infant and juvenile ancestors as well. This insight led the paediatrician Ronald Barr (1990, in press; Barr et al. 1991) to the idea that infant colic, or 'excessive' crying, is not a disease of infancy, but rather an evolved response of healthy infants to hunger and insecurity—which only becomes problematical in the 'unnatural' social environment of prolonged maternal separation and/or limited maternal responsiveness.

Also operating on the common assumption that the lifestyles of modern hunter–gatherers are not dissimilar to those of 99 per cent of all humans who ever existed, Barr compared the crying patterns of infants in Western industrial societies (USA and Holland) with those of !Kung San infants of the Kalahari desert. He found that despite the huge differences in the physical and social environments of infancy in these societies, in each one infants showed an increase in the frequency of crying up to a peak at about six weeks, then a gradual decrease through the twelfth week. Where the infants differed dramatically, however, was in the duration of their crying, with the crying bouts of Western infants lasting twice as long as those of the !Kung infants (Barr et al. 1991).

The reason that Western infants have such long bouts of crying, Barr argues, is that Western parents respond more slowly and less often to infant crying—partly because Western infants are more often physically separated from their parents (e.g. in their own bedrooms) and partly because of a widespread cultural belief that children should not be 'spoiled'. !Kung infants, on the other hand, are almost never out of body contact with mother and !Kung mothers generally respond immediately to signs of infant upset. Barr concludes that the environments to which our ancestors were adapted as infants included patterns of mother–child interaction not unlike those of the !Kung. Under such conditions crying is fundamentally healthy, for the rapidity, frequency, and sensitivity of adult responses to crying virtually guarantees that 'excessive' crying will not occur. The therapeutic lesson from this evolutionary reinterpretation of pathology is that colic is not a disease, or if it is, that it is not a disease of infants but rather of modern Western societies. Seeing the dysfunction in the child's relationship to its environment rather than in the child himself raises the possibility that education about the nature of infant crying and the role of culture in childcare practices may be an effective treatment.

Sudden infant death syndrome

Another important reinterpretation of pathology based on reconstructions of the environment of evolutionary adaptedness of infants is that of the anthropologist Jim McKenna (1986, in press; McKenna et al. 1990, 1994), who argues that, like 'excessive crying,' sudden infant death syndrome (SIDS) may be in part a disease of civilisation. Noting that solitary sleeping for infants is a relatively recent practice in Western industrial societies, and limited almost exclusively to such societies, McKenna's premise is that during human evolution infants surely slept with their mothers, as they do in most hunter–gatherer societies today and as is the case in all non-human primates. Therefore, he reasoned, infants may be adapted to survive, grow, and develop in a sleep environment that is different from that which we in the industrial West ordinarily provide.

To test predictions from this evolutionary model of infant sleep, McKenna and his colleagues undertook the first laboratory studies of mother–infant co-sleeping. Comparing the micro-environments of co-sleeping and solitary-sleeping infants, they found that the co-sleepers were exposed to a rich variety of stimuli that the latter simply did not experience: maternal breathing and heart sounds, heat, odour, and body movements. As a consequence of this abundance of social stimuli, co-sleeping infants were aroused from deep sleep significantly more often than infants sleeping alone. Because failure to rouse from deep sleep (e.g. in response to hypoxia) is implicated in SIDS, McKenna argued, co-sleeping probably prevented many cases of SIDS during human evolution and probably reduces vulnerability to SIDS today.

One obvious therapeutic implication of McKenna's evolutionary model is that parents of children at risk for SIDS might consider taking them into the parental bed. However, not all parents want small, squirming, waking babies in bed with them. For such parents an alternative therapeutic implication of McKenna's model is that if they choose to sleep alone, they might consider other means to supply their infants with the stimuli that in our evolutionary past probably helped prevent children from spending too much time in the deepest stages of sleep. McKenna's insights are important, for they force us to re-think assumptions not only about where it is 'normal' for children to sleep, but about the relationship between culture and health as well as evolution and health. While the risk of SIDS is blessedly low, and most children do well regardless of where their parents place them at night, in an absence of an evolutionary perspective on SIDS there would be no particular reason ever to compare the micro-environments of solitary- and co-sleeping infants. The difference between them would thus remain as it was before, simply arbitrary, a matter purely of tradition or taste—which McKenna's work suggests is not entirely the case.

PRINCIPLES OF EVOLUTIONARY ECOLOGY

I turn now to the principles of evolutionary ecology that in my opinion give evolutionary medicine its strongest epistemological justification and move it in the direction of 'evolutionary public health'. (For precision's sake, these principles actually come from a branch of evolutionary ecology known as life history theory. For accessible introductions to this exciting, burgeoning field, see Charnov and Berrigan 1993; Chisholm 1993, 1995, 1996; Hill 1993; Worthman 1993.)

Work and resources

According to the laws of evolution, to be alive is to have ancestors who were themselves once alive. To have left descendants (us) each of our direct ancestors had to survive, grow and develop, and ultimately bear and rear children who also remained alive, grew and developed, and produced children. This of course takes work, for according to the Second Law of Thermodynamics, entropy (disorganisation, dissipation, decay) tends to increase. Therefore, in order for life to arise, to become more widespread and complex over time, and for each of our ancestors to fend off their own personal decay long enough to reproduce, work had to be done.

This is the work of life: acquiring the resources that are required to survive, grow and develop, and reproduce. At a minimum, such resources include energy, nutrients, safety, information, and time.

Energy and nutrients are required to maintain organismic structure and function. Safety is a statistical or actuarial resource; it is what you need to avoid dying before you can reproduce (i.e. produce and/or rear children). If you persist in risky activities like hang-gliding, childbirth, or gang violence the probability of your early death goes up. Information is a resource in the sense that it can be used to obtain energy and nutrients and to ward off danger. Finally, time is a resource, for all work takes time to complete.

What makes things interesting is that all of these resources are limited. While occasionally some individuals (especially of our species, in our time) have access to more energy and nutrients than they can possibly use, the vast majority do not, and starvation puts an upper limit on all populations. In any event, safety is always limited, in the sense that no environment is absolutely without risk. Information is always limited in the sense that no environment is absolutely predictable; no organism ever has perfect, full knowledge of every aspect of its environment. Finally, time is always limited, in two senses. First, time is limited in the sense that there are always occasions when it is impossible to do two things at once (i.e. opportunity costs). Secondly, time is limited in the sense that all sexually reproducing organisms have a genetically determined 'maximum life potential' or lifespan.

Life then, takes work, and work takes resources, which are always limited. But what makes things *really* interesting is that while resources are always limited, natural selection always favours *more* life; or better, traits that are associated with *greater* fitness or *higher* reproductive success. This is because what matters in evolution is not passing on just *many* copies of your genes into subsequent generations, but *more* copies than other individuals in your population who are carrying different genes. Selection, in other words, does not favour traits associated with reproductive success per se, but with *greater* reproductive success. Fitness is intrinsically a relative concept. What this means is that at the very heart of life itself there is an inherent, inescapable tension between ends (never-ending selection for traits associated with greater fitness) and means (forever limited resources).

The principle of allocation

This inherent tension between the ends and means of life is where biology (the work of life) meets physics (the origin and nature of work) and where life history theory's principle of allocation originates. 'If you wanna live, you gotta eat' is how Daniel Dennett (1995, p. 128) expressed this idea. But if you wanna live and wanna grow and develop and wanna have babies you gotta eat more and keep on eating so your babies can eat too. But what if there is no more food—or time to eat it? Then you gotta decide what to do: continue living, continue growing, or have babies. Can you do all three? If there isn't enough food or time to do all three what's the best thing to do? Because there can never be sufficient resources (energy, safety, time etc.) to meet natural selection's never-ending demand for greater fitness (more descendants), something has to give. Because the Second Law of Thermodynamics takes precedence over the Laws of Evolution, the only thing that can give is one or more of the components of fitness: survival, growth and development, and the production of offspring (which raises their quantity) and their rearing (which raises their quality). So, given limited resources, if you decide to have more babies they can *only* be of lower quality (e.g. smaller, weaker), or you *must* sacrifice your own health or lifespan to produce them, or you have *no choice* but to start having them earlier, which reduces the time available for you to grow and develop, thereby perhaps making you smaller, or less well-educated.

Thus we have *trade-offs*. A trade-off occurs when an increase in one thing entails a decrease in another. When resources are limited, those allocated to the work of staying alive, for example, cannot be used as well to grow bigger. Or when scarce resources are allocated to producing large numbers of children, each one can't help but receive less than they would had there been fewer mouths to feed. The logical/physical impossibility of reconciling the conflicting ends and means of life is the rationale for the principle of allocation: we expect (assume) that natural selection will tend to favour traits (adaptations) that allocate limited resources among the different components of fitness (survival, growth and development, and the production and rearing of offspring) in the way that results in the most descendants (and *not* in just the next generation). See Chisholm 1996; Kaplan 1994.

CONCLUSION: EVOLUTIONARY PUBLIC HEALTH

If the above is a reasonable model of natural selection, then it has important implications for understanding health and disease. It means that people, like all other forms of life, are not evolved to maximise health, well-being or lifespan, but to have descendants. It means that health is not the 'goal' of life and that health is not always the best measure of adaptation. It means that if people find themselves in environments that threaten their capacity to produce descendants we should not be surprised to find that they do not always allocate their limited resources to improving their own health, well-being or lifespan—or even that of their own children, for there is a growing consensus that when our ancestors encountered stressful conditions (i.e. conditions of chronic environmental risk and uncertainty), the best way for them to leave descendants may have been to reproduce early and/or often, thereby increasing the probability of producing at least some descendants before they themselves died (e.g. Borgerhoff Mulder 1992; Charnov & Berrigan 1993; Chisholm 1993, 1995, 1996; Hill 1993; Kaplan 1994). It is widely believed today that early and/or frequent childbearing *causes* or exacerbates pathology, and often it does. However, there is increasing reason to believe that during our evolutionary history such reproductive patterns may have been an adaptive *response to* the high levels of risk and uncertainty that were themselves caused by, or a sign of, high levels of pathology (social as well as physical or natural).

The lesson from modern evolutionary ecology is that we expect human reproductive behaviour to be at least partly contingent on the availability and distribution of certain critical limited resources. In particular, we expect that when people lack the resources to limit environmental risk and uncertainty they may be likely to grow and come to behave (most of the time probably quite unconsciously) in ways associated with early and/or frequent reproduction—*even at the cost of decreased health, well-being, and shortened lives*. From an evolutionary perspective this makes sense. Natural selection favours reproductive capacity, not health. What good is health if the amount of environmental risk and uncertainty that one faces means that one is unlikely to live to enjoy it? Or start having descendants? Again, health is not life's goal. It can and should be ours, however. A public health policy informed by evolutionary ecology would therefore work to improve health, well-being, and longevity by reducing environmental risk and uncertainty, both subjective and objective.

As we have seen, from the perspective of modern evolutionary ecology, health is in part contingent on the extent to which modern environments are like those in which we evolved. More particularly, because all organisms evolved to maximise number of descendants, not health or lifespan, health is importantly contingent on the ways that the distribution of resources affected our ancestors' reproductive success. From both comparative studies and strategic modelling it is now apparent that a major influence on human reproduction has been environmental risk and uncertainty. Therefore, just as evolutionary physicians might suggest to parents of colicky babies that they take them into their bed, so too might evolutionary community health workers seek to improve health by reducing perceived and actual environmental risk and uncertainty. One way to reduce environmental risk and uncertainty—ultimately, perhaps the only way—is to increase people's control over their own affairs. Evolutionary physicians would thus surely agree with the World Health Organization's definition of health promotion as 'the process of enabling people to increase control over their lives' (WHO 1987, p. 200; see also Nussbaum 1995; Rissel 1994; Sen 1993; Wiley 1992). By affirming the central role of human rights in the well-being of all people, evolutionary ecology leads evolutionary medicine in the direction of evolutionary public health and policy. Thus, as Cicero and the Hellenistic philosophers knew (Nussbaum 1994), philosophy itself (i.e. knowledge) and politics (the allocation of resources) are really medicine (healing, therapy) carried on by other means.

NOTES

1   'The theory or science of the method or grounds of knowledge' (*Shorter Oxford English Dictionary*).

2   Some of the worst misuse of evolutionary theory has been in attempts to justify discrimination against racial minorities and women. For clear statements of how modern evolutionary theory supports human rights and nondiscrimination see Kohn (1995) on scientific anti-racism, and Gowaty (1997) and Smuts (1992, 1995) on scientific feminism.

3   John Bowlby, the child psychiatrist, coined the phrase, the 'environment of evolutionary adaptedness' (now usually just 'EEA') (1969, p. 50) to refer to this environment.

4   As Pierre Ryckmans expressed this idea in the 1996 Australian Broadcasting Corporation's annual Boyer Lecture Series, 'The saying "to see is to believe" must be reversed: to believe [to assume, to hypothesise, to predict] is to see' (1996, p. 13). Charles Darwin was getting at the same thing when he wrote (to Alfred Russel Wallace, on 22 December 1857), 'I am a firm believer that without speculation there is no good and original observation' (Burkhardt 1996, p. 183).

5   The chemoreceptor trigger zone of the *area postrema*.

REFERENCES

Barr, R.G. 1990 'The early crying paradox: A modest proposal' *Human Nature* vol. 1, no. 4, pp. 355–89
——in press 'Infant crying behavior and colic: An interpretation in evolution perspective'

in *Evolutionary Medicine* eds W. Trevathan, J.J. McKenna & E.O. Smith, Oxford University Press, Oxford

Barr, R.G., Bakeman, R., Konner, M. & Adamson, L. 1991 'Crying in !Kung infants: A test of the cultural specificity hypothesis' *Developmental Medicine and Child Neurology* vol. 33, pp. 601–10

Borgerhoff Mulder, M. 1992 'Reproductive decisions' in *Evolutionary Ecology and Human Behavior* eds E.A. Smith & B. Winterhalder, Aldine de Gruyter, New York

Bowlby, J. 1969 *Attachment. Attachment and Loss, vol. 1* Basic Books, New York

Burkhardt, F. (ed.) 1996 *Charles Darwin's Letters: A Selection: 1825–1859* Cambridge University Press, Cambridge

Charnov, R.L. & Berrigan, D. 1993 'Why do female primates have such long lifespans and so few babies? or Life in the slow lane' *Evolutionary Anthropology* vol. 1, pp. 191–94

Chisholm, J.S. 1993 'Death, hope, and sex: Life history theory and the development of reproductive strategies' *Current Anthropology* vol. 34, no. 1, pp. 1–24

——1995 'Life history theory and life style choice: Implications for Darwinian medicine' in *Perspectives in Human Biology* vol 1, eds L.H. Schmitt & L. Freedman, pp. 19–26

——1996 'The evolutionary ecology of attachment organization' *Human Nature* vol. 7, no. 1, pp. 1–37

Dennett, D. 1995 *Darwin's Dangerous Idea: Evolution and the Meanings of Life* Simon & Schuster, New York

Doran, T.E., De Angelis, C., Baumgardner, R.A. & Mellits, E.D. 1989 'Acetominophen: More harm than good for chicken pox?' *Journal of Pediatrics* vol. 114, pp. 1045–48

Eaton, S.B., Pike, M.C., Short, R.V. et al. 1994 'Women's reproductive cancers in evolutionary context' *The Quarterly Review of Biology* vol. 69, no. 3, pp. 353–66

Gould, S.J. & Lewontin, R. 1979 'The Spandrels of San Marcos and the Panglossian paradigm: A critique of the adaptationist program' *Proceedings of the Royal Society of London* vol. 205, pp. 581–98

Gowaty, P. (ed.) 1997 *Feminism and Evolutionary Biology: Boundaries, Intersections, and Frontiers* Chapman and Hall, London

Hill, K. 1993 'Life history theory and evolutionary anthropology' *Evolutionary Anthropology* vol. 2, no. 3, pp. 78–88

Kaplan, H. 1994 'Evolutionary and wealth flows theories of fertility: Empirical tests and new models' *Population and Development Review* vol. 20, no. 4, pp. 753–91

Kohn, M. 1995 *The Race Gallery: The Return of Racial Science* Jonathan Cape, London

Lee, R.B. 1979 *The !Kung San: Men, Women, and Work in a Foraging Society* Cambridge University Press, Cambridge

McKenna, J.J. 1986 'An anthropological perspective on the sudden infant death syndrome (SIDS): The role of parental breathing cues and speech breathing adaptations' *Medical Anthropology* vol. 10, pp. 9–53

——in press 'Mutual physiological regulatory effects during bedsharing in mother–infant pairs: Evolutionary pediatrics and implications for SIDS' in *Evolutionary Medicine* eds W. Trevathan, J.J. McKenna & E.O. Smith, Oxford University Press, Oxford

McKenna, J.J. & Mosko, S. 1994 'Sleep and arousal, synchrony, and independence, among mothers and infants sleeping apart and together (same bed): An experiment in evolutionary medicine' *Acta Paediatrica Supplement* vol. 397, pp. 94–102

McKenna, J.J., Mosko, S., Dungy, C. & McAninch, J. 1990 'Sleep and arousal patterns of co-sleeping human mother–infant pairs: A preliminary physiological study with implications for the study of sudden infant death syndrome (SIDS)' *American Journal of Physical Anthropology* vol. 83, pp. 331–47

Nesse, R.M. 1991 'What good is feeling bad?' *The Sciences* Nov./Dec., pp. 30–37

Nesse, R.M. & Williams, G.C. 1995 *Evolution and Healing: The New Science of Darwinian Medicine* Weidenfeld and Nicolson, London (Originally published as *Why We Get Sick: The New Science of Darwinian Medicine* Times Books/Random House, New York, 1994)

Nussbaum, M.C. 1994 *The Therapy of Desire: Theory and Practice in Hellenistic Ethics* Princeton University Press, Princeton

——1995 'Human capabilities, female human beings' in *Women, Culture, and Development: A Study of Human Capabilities* eds M.C. Nussbaum & J. Glover, Clarendon Press, Oxford

Parker, G. & Maynard Smith, J. 1990 'Optimality theory in evolutionary biology' *Nature* vol. 348, pp. 27–33

Plotkin, H.C. 1994 *Darwin Machines and the Nature of Knowledge* Harvard University Press, Cambridge, MA (Originally published in Great Britain by Penguin 1993)

Profet, M. 1992 'Pregnancy sickness as adaptation: A deterrent to maternal ingestion of teratogens' in *The Adapted Mind: Evolutionary Psychology and the Generation of Culture* eds J.H. Barkow, L. Cosmides & J. Tooby, Oxford University Press, Oxford

Rissel, C. 1994 'Empowerment: The holy grail of health promotion?' *Health Promotion International* vol. 9, pp. 39–47

Ryckmans, P. 1996 'The signature of humanity' *The Australian*, Tuesday 12 November 1996, p. 13

Sen, A. 1993 'Capability and well-being' in *The Quality of Life* eds M. Nussbaum & A. Sen, Clarendon Press, Oxford

Smuts, B. 1992 'Male aggression against women: An evolutionary perspective' *Human Nature* no. 3, pp. 1–44

——1995 'The evolutionary origins of patriarchy' *Human Nature* vol. 6, no. 1, pp. 1–32

Tooby, J. & DeVore, I. 1987 'The reconstruction of hominid behavioral evolution through strategic modelling' in *The Evolution of Human Behavior: Primate Models* ed. W.G. Kinzey, State University of New York Press, Albany

Williams, G.C. & Nesse, R.M. 1991 'The dawn of Darwinian medicine' *The Quarterly Review of Biology* vol. 66, no. 1, pp. 1–22

Weinberg, E.D. 1984 'Iron withholding: A defence against infection and neoplasia' *Physiological Review* vol. 64, pp. 65–102

World Health Organization 1987 'Ottawa charter for health promotion' *Pan-American Health Organization Bulletin* vol. 21, no. 2, pp. 200–04

Wiley, A. 1992 'Adaptation and the biocultural paradigm in medical anthropology: A critical review' *Medical Anthropology Quarterly* vol. 6, no. 3, pp. 216–36

Worthman, C. 1993 'Bio-cultural interactions in human development' in *Juvenile Primates: Life History, Development and Behavior* eds M. Pereira & L. Fairbanks, Oxford University Press, New York

PART 2

Experience matters

The chapters in Part 2 examine people's diverse experiences of health and illness. They highlight inequalities and other injustices in health experience as measured by incidences of disease and reported illness and by access to, and use of, health services; they examine the perspectives of people who occupy particular social categories—children, women who are considered to be overweight, those who are incontinent, and those who are dying. Sociology offers a vast number of perspectives on inequalities and injustices in the experience of health and illness, and the chapters here present a few. However, despite differences in perspective, sociologists of health and illness tend to share a common criticism of biomedicine's tendency to neglect key aspects of experience. The main focus of biomedicine, it is pointed out, is the biophysical body, viewed in isolation from social contexts and without reference to personal and social meanings. Insofar as issues of health inequalities and health justice enter biomedical thinking at all, the predominant concerns have been with access and equity in relation to existing medical care practices. Thus, questions asked have included: How can we increase access to new medical technologies? How can we improve the standard of medical care among the poor? What policies will encourage doctors to practise in remote areas? There has been relatively little appreciation of how social relations shape the material reality of disease, definitions of sickness, and experiences of illness. In our view, a reflexive, 'just sociology of health' should be concerned with examining the limitations and implications of biomedicine—and its realist approach to understanding 'the body's' make-up, functioning, and dis-ease—while presenting us with insights into the diverse experiences of health and illness.

The following chapters examine 'health' and 'illness' as *social* realities. That is, they take as their starting point the assumption that

these categories are social products and are mediated by social relations. Many, if not most, sociologists of health and illness subscribe
to some version of social constructionism, which suggests that what
we take to be reality (e.g. 'the body', 'health', 'illness') is shaped,
constrained and even fabricated by society. When applied to the
analysis of 'the body', the social constructionist view offers important
insights into how bodies are affected by power relations, enter into
social definitions of the self, and function as social symbols. Unfortunately, those working within this perspective often overlook the
corporeality of bodies, and render invisible the thinking, acting, and
feeling subject (Shilling 1993, p. 99). For sociology, which deals so
centrally with the 'social construction of reality', this is a far from
satisfactory situation. Although not all the following chapters explicitly problematise 'the body' of biomedical discourse, by foregrounding
the social structuring of experience, all at least implicitly question the
biomedical approach to health and illness.

Lenore Manderson in Chapter 6, and Waqar Ahmad and Lesley
Jones in Chapter 7, present macro views on health inequalities,
showing how experiences of health and illness are shaped by cultural
and social circumstances. More specifically, they highlight the importance of socioeconomic status and gender, and minority ethnic status,
respectively, on health experiences. In Chapter 6, Manderson
examines some of the health costs of development, discusses the
limitations of health services within so-called developing countries,
and points to the ways in which gender and poverty affect health
outcomes and health care. Improvements in health in most developing
countries have been linked to socioeconomic development and the
expansion of medical services and public health programs. However,
as Manderson points out, both on a global level and within particular
countries, improvements have been uneven, with health services often
emphasising curative medicine to deal with the 'lifestyle' diseases of
the growing, but still relatively small (on a global level), wealthy
population. Many people continue to experience poor living and
working conditions that adversely affect their health; a problem that
is compounded by inequitable access to health services, and inappropriate health policies. Gender differences in risk of infection, in
experience of illness, and in the quality of care are particularly evident,
argues Manderson, reflecting differences in women's and men's different roles in economic production and in biological, domestic and
social reproduction. In conclusion, Manderson argues that the relationship between health and development is a complicated one,
necessitating a number of strategies for addressing inequalities in health;

for example, the implementation of specific mechanisms for monitoring programs and measuring the benefits of investment and development, increased intersectoral programs for development, and greater government commitment to reducing poverty and inequality.

In Chapter 7, Waqar Ahmad and Lesley Jones examine the health, health care and social context of minority ethnic people's lives in Britain. Broad characterisations of the health status of people in 'developed' and 'developing' countries run the risk of masking significant inequalities in experiences in health and illness, and in access to appropriate services, *within* countries. As Ahmad and Jones point out, racism remains a feature of life for the many and diverse ethnic minorities in Britain (and elsewhere), a fact that is increasingly concealed by the use of the language of culture. Racism has been evident in policies which aim to promote cultural change in minority ethnic communities while affecting only a marginal shift in health policy or practice. However, there are some encouraging developments in policy, for example, recognition of the need for cultural sensitivity, and respect for religious values of all users in a number of government policies, charters and codes of practice. This chapter exposes the limitations and politics of the dominant epidemiological approach to ethnicity and health; presents and critiques a number of explanations of health inequalities; and examines evidence on inequalities in quality of care, access, and use of services. The conclusion is that, despite some improved recognition of minority health needs at the policy level, this has occurred during a period of weakened local democracy, and minority ethnic groups continue to be marginalised in most walks of life (housing, employment, education, immigration), which is manifest in their experiences of health and illness and in their access to state welfare.

The final four chapters—by Gillian Bendelow and Pat Pridmore, Deirdre Davies, Wendy Seymour, and Bev McNamara—focus on how people portray their own experiences of health and illness. The chapters reflect some of the diverse approaches currently employed by health sociologists—the use of drawings (Bendelow and Pridmore), interviews (Davies and Seymour) and ethnographic fieldwork (McNamara). Taking subjective experience as the focus for analysis, they implicitly question the objectivism and reductionism of the biomedical approach, especially the tendency to focus on 'the body' isolated from 'the mind' and from social contexts. In Chapter 8, Bendelow and Pridmore report the findings of research which employs a 'child-centred' approach to health and illness experience; that is, one which employs children's drawings as data. The idea of using children's pictures, in conjunction with writing or dialogue, to explore the health beliefs of young children which inform their health behaviours and influence their health status, offers an alternative to more traditional 'top-down' approaches employing adult categories, classifications and taxonomies. It is seen as a way of empowering children, by both allowing them the opportunity to express their experiences in their own terms while learning from their participation in the process. In this chapter, Bendelow and Pridmore draw on material from two case studies—one involving 9–10-year-olds in southeast England; the other, 9–10-year-olds in Botswana—in order to empirically demonstrate the quality and sophistication of the data collected in this way. This chapter discusses the findings of these studies and argues the benefits of the approach and its applications in diverse cultural contexts. Although, as is pointed out, the technique is still being developed and is in need of careful and sensitive adaptation, it can provide an effective tool in improving the relevance and effectiveness of educational interventions and in overcoming problems of design and delivery of more traditional health education programs.

In Chapter 9, Davies questions the assumed relationship between health and weight: that is, to be 'overweight' is to be 'unhealthy'. Adopting a Foucauldian perspective, she examines how the discourse of weight control serves to regulate bodies, especially women's bodies, and how this affects the subjectivity of those who are deemed to be overweight. She describes the techniques used for categorising bodies, such as height/weight tables and body-size measurements such as the waist-to-hip ratio, and for establishing norms of body weight. Like Ahmad and Jones, above, Davies exposes the practical and political implications of epidemiology, which is seen to play a central role in constructing knowledge about the factors of risk and about the dangers of being 'overweight' or 'obese'. As she shows, arguments about what constitutes a 'risk factor' and 'overweight' are left silenced in health promotion literature and health advice columns of weight control magazines and books on dieting, reflecting the conviction of their authors of the link between being 'overweight' and being 'unhealthy'. Such messages tend to 'blame the victim', who is viewed as irresponsible in not appropriately managing their own body and, hence, their 'risk' of ill health. In this context, it is difficult to conceive of a person considered to be overweight being able to speak of being in good health. However, as Davies shows through her interview data, women employ their own 'lay epidemiology' which presents a view of their own health that is often at odds with what the experts proclaim.

In Chapter 10, Seymour examines the issue of bodily incontinence, as it is phenomenally experienced and in relation to the social body. Her chapter is based on an empirical study involving twenty-four people with varying degrees of bodily paralysis affecting basic physiological processes and sensations, including loss of bowel and bladder control. It describes these people's experiences of 'living in a leaky body', particularly the challenges of successful body management in a society which highly values training and control of the body and care for the self as aspects of adult status and responsible citizenship. For most of these people, the experience of incontinence is a 'constant attack on the embodied self', and participation in bladder and bowel retraining in rehabilitation units, which aim to condition the bladder and bowel to empty at convenient times and in convenient places, involves feelings of shame, much like that experienced by young children during the process of toilet training. Seymour describes how her respondents engage with the regimes of bodily surveillance and disciplines that are required of those who are incontinent in order to avoid untoward leakage of bodily fluids, and spells out the implications for concepts of self. In her view, leaky bodies—whether they be those of women, the old or the sick—are seen to endanger society and its categories. They threaten rational control and the idea of what bodies are and should do. As such, they provide the site for innovative and creative opportunities for conceptualising embodiment.

Finally, in Chapter 11, McNamara examines how the terminally ill person's experience of dying is shaped by socio-cultural factors. Dying is not just a biological fact, but is also a social process which involves negotiations around the meanings and circumstances of dying. This chapter critically examines the notion of the 'good death', especially in light of social constraints on the decision-making capacities of the terminally ill person in the last days of their life. According to current health rhetoric, patients should be 'empowered' to participate in decisions that affect them, for example in relation to life-prolonging medical treatments and issues of pain control. (On the concept of patient participation, see also Chapter 17 by Saras Henderson and Chapter 18 by Allan Kellehear, in the following Part.) However, as McNamara points out, there are a number of factors which constrain individual choice, leading her to suggest that perhaps most deaths are merely 'good enough'. In advanced industrialised societies these include: cultural concepts of individualism and the idea that the patient should participate in health and medical decisions; the terminally ill person's altered conceptions of self which affect their capacity for autonomous decision-making; the individual's social location (e.g. age, place of residence, social position vis-à-vis attending health professionals) and the broader structural context (e.g. policies which may prioritise either social support or high technology curative treatments); 'biomedical culture'; and the individual's 'local moral culture' (e.g. religious and cultural beliefs). In order to advance individual empowerment in decision-making at the end of life, McNamara concludes, there is a need for more research into the social and embodied experience of dying.

REFERENCE

Shilling, C. 1993 The Body and Social Theory Sage, London

6 Health matters in developing economies

Lenore Manderson

In 1993, the World Development Report, *Investing in Health* (World Bank 1993), was published. Its major premise was that investment in development was compromised by ill health, and development strategies would only succeed if efforts were also made to improve people's health. Related policy documents such as the Asian Development Bank's report on *Health, Population and Development in Asia and the Pacific* (1991) and more recently, *Investing in Health Research and Development* (World Health Organization 1996) also emphasise the *economic* need—this, rather than humanitarian concerns, is reckoned to appeal most to bankers—for health justice.

In essence, economists have argued, health may be expected to improve with economic development. But without good health, economic development is slow or impeded. Workers are absent or inefficient; primary producers are unable to meet production targets; children perform poorly in school and so are unable to meet new workforce needs; women are unable to participate fully in the economy because of time lost as a result of their own ill health and time spent caring for others; the costs of curative services are crippling. Further preventable diseases continue to be transmitted, and even people already advantaged by economic development programs are at risk of infection and disease. The burden of illness however is with the poor. Their health is the focus of this chapter.

The arguments above are made primarily by and for economists. They are, however, issues which need to be addressed by other social scientists, who too often have avoided or been excluded from policy debates and so have had little access to or influence on those with the financial and political means to bring about change. In this

97

chapter, I describe some of the health costs of development, discuss the limitations of health services within developing countries, and draw attention to the ways in which gender and poverty compound disadvantages in health outcomes and health care.

ECONOMIC DEVELOPMENT AND HEALTH INEQUALITY

Changes in health in most developing countries have occurred in the past twenty years due to socioeconomic development, and the expansion of medical services and public health programs. Basic public health interventions such as immunisation, water and sanitation, and maternal and child health programs have reduced morbidity and mortality from infectious disease. Yet in Africa especially, in parts of Asia and Latin America, and among indigenous communities in the richest countries, there are still communities without even basic health services. In these communities, children continue to die in unacceptably high numbers from malaria, measles, diarrhoeal disease, and respiratory infections; women from complications of pregnancy and childbirth as well as HIV/AIDS. Table 1 shows this dramatically, by contrasting the health outcomes worldwide. The figures highlight the health transition—the shift of the burden of mortality from infectious to 'lifestyle' diseases (Caldwell et al. 1990, pp. xi–xix). The structural shift from subsistence production to cash crops, increasing industrialisation and urbanisation, improved education, increased expenditure on and improvements in health services, and rising wealth has—Table 1 suggests—led to a shift from communicable diseases, parasitic diseases, diarrhoeal disease and respiratory infections, and injuries and accidents, to non-communicable diseases such as cardiovascular disease and malignancies. Sedentary lifestyles, dietary changes, smoking, and changes in places and conditions of employment have affected morbidity and mortality. In response, governments have increasingly emphasised curative medicine, often introducing expensive and sophisticated technology accessible only to a minority of wealthy urban dwellers.

While some people have become increasingly wealthy in developing countries with structural change, material conditions and health outcomes have changed little for the majority of the world's population. For example, the shift from subsistence production to cash-cropping has meant for farmers loss of land, forcing them to accept poorly-paid employment in agribusiness, extractive industries (mining, logging), manufacturing industry, and tourism. Working conditions

Table 1. Burden of disease by region and the three main groups of causes, 1990 (per 1000 population)

Demographic region and age group	Communicable disease and maternal and perinatal causes	Noncommunicable diseases	Injuries
	Rate	Rate	Rate
Sub-Saharan Africa	408.7	111.4	5.35
India	173.9	138.9	31.4
China	44.9	103.0	29.7
Other Asia and islands	125.7	103.9	29.3
Latin America and the Caribbean	97.7	99.2	34.8
Middle Eastern crescent	146.1	103.2	37.3
Former socialist economies of Europe (FSE)	14.5	125.7	27.9
Established market economies (EME)	11.4	92.0	13.9
World	118.5	109.2	30.9

Source: World Bank 1993, p. 220

and pay are poor. The construction industry provides young men in northeast Thailand with employment opportunities, for example, but not care to prevent accidents or infection:

> Observations of one site indicated that workers had hard hats that were often defective, they occasionally wore them back to front, and did not tighten the straps properly. Others wore cotton cloth on their heads for sun protection. Footwear was what they could afford: slip-ons, sandshoes, rubber boots, and so on. None were observed wearing boots as specified under the Labour Laws. The steel bar workers, masonry workers and pulley operators worked manually, without appropriate gloves. Few welders wore eye protection. The environmental conditions were poor, with indiscriminate storage of waste materials such as cut-offs of steel, metal, bricks and timber. The workers' camp, located on site, was dirty and overcrowded, and lacked adequate hygiene and sanitation facilities and quality water supply. (Hameed et al. 1995)

Here, people are no less at risk of infectious disease and are exposed to new hazards also. Women and children too have moved from working on family plots to employment under poor conditions for low wages, making jewellery, sewing clothes, selling snack foods on footpaths, or working in the expanding sex industries of the capitals:

Many hundreds of men and women, most in their late teens or early twenties, are employed as gemworkers in northeast Thailand villages. Men are almost entirely employed as better-paid cutters and grinders of cubic zirconia, used to manufacture costume jewellery. The women work as polishers. The stone is first cut into planes, strips and small pieces. This work is intensive and demands considerable concentration to avoid injury, as cutters hold gem pieces only a few millimetres in their fingers and cut with the rotating blade of an unguarded electric saw. Grinding is tiring and involves the use of hot caustic soda for cleaning. The commonest source of injury is among polishers, however, through lacerations and bruising from broken belts on the polishing machine, hair and clothing being caught in the spindle, and dust in eyes. Most people worked around 13 hours a day, 6 days a week. (Cooper et al. 1991, pp. 41–48, 62, 67–82)

Women's involvement in paid work has a major impact on child health, both in terms of sustained breastfeeding and the nutritional status of older children (Popkin & Solon 1976; Popkin et al. 1982). Poor women in urban areas are not able to take their infants to work, nor are they given time off work to prepare food. Childcare facilities are rare, and young children are left to be cared for by children who are only marginally older. Women's wages are low relative to men's, and large numbers of households in urban areas are headed by single mothers. Children also enter the workforce at very young ages. The national labour force survey in Bangladesh, 1990–1991, for example, estimated that 46 per cent of boys and 36 per cent of girls were working at 10–14 years of age (Bissell & Sobhan 1996). In rural areas, this was primarily in housework and agriculture, but a large number were employed in non-agricultural occupations such as sales and weaving. In urban areas, children from around five years of age are employed in occupations such as sales, domestic service, waste collection, producing jewellery in small informal factories, shoes, lockmaking and book-binding, electronics, the garment industry, and so on (Bissell & Sobhan 1996; Stalker 1996). Unknown numbers work as sex workers, porters, and brick-breakers:

Amina is a 10-year-old brick-breaker. She works alongside her mother and sister on a construction site where they receive 30 taka [c. US 75 cents] for each hundred bricks they break into small pieces. Sometimes, the hammer slips, or the brick breaks in unexpected ways. If their hands or fingers hurt too much they go collecting waste paper instead. (Stalker 1996, p. 11)

Increasing incidence of 'lifestyle' diseases has often occurred while the incidence of infectious disease has remained constant and, in many places, increased. Malaria, filariasis and dengue, for instance, are all increasing rather than declining in incidence in both urban and rural environments where the combination of vector habitat and behaviour (mosquitoes), poor infrastructure and social practice is ideal for transmission. Dengue increases with urbanisation, for example, because household items (jars of water, buckets, and so on) are ideal for breeding; because dry waste management is inadequate and so garbage tips are especially ideal for mosquito breeding; and new waste products (e.g. used car tyres), once discarded, provide new breeding sites.

The following quote describes the environment of young male refugees from Burundi, who work as tailors in Dar es Salaam, the capital of Tanzania, living in shared crowded conditions in rooms at the back of the shops and working six days a week, 10–12 hours a day. The description of the city reflects the kinds of conditions in many cities in the developing world:

> The physical condition of Dar es Salaam affects all its residents. Most roads in the city are in abysmal condition, making garbage collection infrequent at best. Fumes from burning garbage and dust from passing traffic drift into the tailors' shops throughout the hot, soggy days. Electric power is sporadic. In rainy seasons the roadways become waterways, whose interlaced ponds fill with garbage and spawn malarial mosquitoes. Tailors often work while nursing illnesses. (Sommers 1993, pp. 16–17)

Rural development often also increases transmission of disease. The best documented—since the 1920s with the building of the Aswan Dam in Egypt—is the effect of dams and artificial lakes on the transmission of schistosomiasis (Huang & Manderson 1992; Rubin & Warren 1968; Stanley & Alpers 1975). Similarly, the opening up of forest land and expansion of agriculture and mining increased malaria transmission by increasing the exposure of non-immune populations to infection, and introducing infected individuals to areas with both the vector and non-infected populations. Changes to the environment have led too to increased breeding sites: heavy trucks carrying lumber from logging activities—widespread in tropical countries—leave furrows in roads which create ideal pools for vector breeding of *Anopheles darlingi* in the Amazon (Sawyer 1993) and *Anopheles punctulatus* in the Solomon Islands (Kemp & Gilles 1988).

Biery-Hamilton (1993, pp. 92–98) provides a chilling account of the impact of the construction of the Tucurui Hydroelectric Dam in the Amazon River of Brazil on the environment, economy and social relations. Changes in land tenure, means of production, and employment, and broader economic and demographic changes, have all affected people's health; streams used for drinking water and bathing are polluted by waste from sawmills and mercury used for gold mining, industrial waste and raw sewage; the atmosphere is often dense with smoke from the mills and from burning-off prior to planting crops; people report increasing allergies and respiratory problems, alcoholism and drug abuse.

Urbanisation affects social structure, social organisation, and dependency patterns within households, as well as the economic basis and material well-being of people who constitute those households, and their mental and physical health (Brockerhoff 1995; Harpham 1994). Peri-urban and urban squatter settlements and slums are often intensely crowded, with both social and health problems: substance abuse, sexually transmissible diseases, deaths from violence, 'lifestyle' diseases, high levels of stress, and malnutrition and infectious disease due to poor infrastructure, lack of potable water, and poor sanitation—see, for example, Scheper-Hughes' (1994) extraordinary account of a less urbanised area of Brazil. Tanner and Harpham (1995, p. 39) observe that 'recent arrivals in cities often have high unemployment rates and a few individuals may have to support many people of similar age', and stress the importance of understanding changes in social relations as well as material conditions to understand the determinants of health status and to identify appropriate interventions (Tanner & Harpham 1995; see also Harpham et al. 1988).

Economic difficulties continue as countries expand economically, shift production bases, restructure their administrations, and review government versus private roles in social welfare, health and well-being. These processes have increased with structural adjustment (Mburu 1989). Diseases of poor hygiene, crowding and poverty continue to be primary causes of mortality in the world's poorest countries and among the poorest communities—rural and urban—in all countries. Bacterial, parasitic and viral infections may be transmitted as a result of poor hygiene. Diarrhoeal disease, hepatitis A, schistosomiasis and opisthorciasis, for example, can all be reduced through the introduction of latrines, breakdown of waste material, handwashing, and/or related food safety and hygiene interventions. Attitudes towards waste material, handwashing and other hygiene habits all vary culturally but also as a result of the socioeconomic status of the community, the division of labour, and ideas of risk of infection and cleanliness, and there is still little investment in providing the mass of people with simple, safe and acceptable latrines.

The use of human waste (excreta) in agriculture has been a common practice in China for centuries. Traditional methods of excreta disposal include both dry methods (where faeces are covered with dirt or ash) and wet methods (pit latrines), in association with or separate from animals depending on local ecological and cultural factors. The major purpose is to conserve waste to use in agriculture as a fertiliser and a soil conditioner, although this waste is often supplemented with chemical fertilisers. In some provinces, too, latrines are constructed over ponds so that waste can be used as fish feed. The use of latrine wastes in agriculture and aquaculture contributes to the prevalence of sanitation-related disease in poor provinces, including diarrhoeal diseases, viral hepatitis, typhoid, paratyphoid, dysentery and parasites such as ascaris and hookworm. The answer is not to discourage use of waste, however, given the valuable resource it represents in areas where agricultural production is intense or where people are dependent upon crops and/or fish farms for their livelihoods, where the purchase of alternatives (commercial fish food, fertiliser) is an unnecessary market intrusion, and where alternative waste disposal would be an even greater problem (Manderson & Blumenthal, fieldnotes, 1992).[1]

ORGANISATION AND ACCESSIBILITY OF HEALTH SERVICES

Financing, staff resources and logistics affect government capacity to provide health services. However, a wide range of factors affecting accessibility need to be addressed for available services to be used appropriately and effectively (Timyan et al. 1993). In most poor countries, a two-tiered system exists. This provides the wealthy with sophisticated, expensive privately or government-funded curative services, while the poor continue to be provided with rudimentary primary health care characterised by poor quality services, long waiting hours, and inadequate drugs and other technologies (Hull & Hull 1995). Poor and isolated populations who live long distances from the nearest fixed health post are further disadvantaged, as they lack transport to reach the post for routine or emergency care, and cash resources to cover transport and the service of prescribed drugs. Lack of money is the major factor inhibiting early and appropriate treatment of life-threatening diseases such as pneumonia in Bohol, the Philippines, resulting in continued high mortality among infants and small children (Carpenter et al. 1996; Simon et al. 1996):

> There are always problems in the ward. Often patients can't afford to pay for the medicines, saline drips, needles and so on, so we only ask them to pay on discharge and to leave us any supplies they won't use. For example, this morning one patient left us her medicines so we could start them on a new admission, and sometimes we give donations or

suggest to the mother that she go to the radio to ask for help. She'll be
interviewed on the radio and people will bring money here. (Manderson,
fieldnotes, 1993)

The control of the production, distribution and marketing of
pharmaceuticals by multinational drug companies affects the delivery
of medications worldwide; the choice, cost and availability of various
drugs; trends toward over- and inappropriate prescriptions; non-
compliance with prescriptions; self-medication; and overuse of drugs.
Drug companies supply drugs to doctors and pharmacists directly. This
makes it difficult for governments to implement essential drugs programs and promote generic drugs, ensure cheap and regular supplies
of essential drugs, and prevent irrational use through polypharmacy
(e.g. by the prescription of two, three or four drugs, often similar in
clinical effect). Market manipulation has often been exacerbated
following decentralisation of services (as in the Philippines), where
the structure and organisation of health services at the peripheral level
is only loosely controlled and the supply of pharmaceuticals is poorly
regulated. As a result, pharmaceutical companies have continued to
market their products in ways that have a direct effect on prescribing
practices, the availability and promotion of drugs in pharmacies, and
consumer expectations and behaviour (van der Geest & Whyte 1988;
Kanji et al. 1992). Decentralisation of health services and increased
pressure for local government financing has also resulted in disruption
of programs, increasing local inequity and exacerbating problems at
the periphery in terms of finance, staff, supervision and training, and
resources.

Health policies often result in conflicts between the government
health sector and its consumers, and in contradictions regarding the
use and need for private medical services and community participation
in public health services. Again, Philippines data indicate that the
poorest people often use private rather than public services because
of flexibility of services, with credit facilities available so that people
can receive medical advice and drugs when needed (Simon et al.
1996).

GENDER AND THE HOUSEHOLD PRODUCTION OF HEALTH

With the exception of disease and death related to reproduction,
differences in morbidity and mortality between men and women (see
Table 2) reflect not so much sex differences in the biology of disease,
but the mediation of disease through cultural and social circumstance.

Table 2. **Burden of four major diseases by age of incidence and sex, 1990 (millions of disability-adjusted life years)**

Disease and sex	Age (years)					
	0–4	5–14	15–44	45–59	60+	Total
Diarrhoea						
Male	42.1	4.6	2.8	0.4	0.2	50.2
Female	40.7	4.8	2.8	0.4	0.3	48.9
Worm infection						
Male	0.2	10.6	1.6	0.5	0.1	13.1
Female	0.1	9.2	0.9	0.5	0.1	10.9
Tuberculosis						
Male	1.2	3.1	13.4	6.2	2.6	26.5
Female	1.3	3.8	10.9	2.8	1.2	20.0
Ischaemic heart disease						
Male	0.1	0.1	3.6	8.1	13.1	25.0
Female	<0.05	<0.05	1.2	3.2	13.0	17.5

Source: World Bank 1993, p. 28

Being female or male affects the risk of infection, the social experience of illness, and care and outcome.

Women are active both in economic production and in biological, domestic and social reproduction. They participate in the production of food and goods necessary to maintain health, maintain the domestic environment and undertake the everyday work of feeding household members. In addition, they bear and rear children, care for the sick, and provide information to others to prevent and treat illness and maintain good health. In these multiple capacities women are often targeted in various health interventions.

Local ecological, environmental, economic and cultural factors, including the sexual division of labour and the 'sexual division of responsibility' (Rathgeber 1990, p. 499), influence exposure to infection and risk of disease. In this respect there is no clear direction of sex bias. Depending on the sexual division of labour and the extent of seclusion or mobility of women, either one sex or the other might be at greater risk of infection. In communities at risk for schistosomiasis, for instance, where women's contact with water is relatively limited and where men fish and/or work in fields irrigated with snail-infested water, then men are more likely to be infected.

Elsewhere women may be more exposed because they undertake house-hold tasks such as clothes washing, cleaning of kitchen utensils and so on in infected water sources (Huang & Manderson 1992; Parker 1993). Similarly, in areas where filariasis is transmitted, women may be most exposed to infected mosquitoes because of their use of water and the times when this is done (e.g. for clothes washing, bathing of self and children, collection of water for household use).

Yet until relatively recently, women's own health has received low priority. Reproductive health and women's health have been treated in general as if equivalent, with the focus on pregnancy, childbirth and contraception. Health programs have aimed at reducing maternal and infant mortality rates (safe motherhood programs) and meeting family planning needs. In contrast, until recently, other aspects of women's health have been neglected. Maternal and child health, and reproductive and sexual health services tend to be delivered by vertical programs, with the consequence that women are reluctant to present with health problems unrelated to antenatal care or, particularly, their children's health, unless their own health problem seriously impedes their ability to work. Most illnesses are self-limiting, and many problems cause minor disability only, insufficient to prevent women from undertaking their usual tasks (albeit with diminished productivity).

The usual action when ill is to self-medicate, and there are often lengthy delays between first signs of illness and treatment-seeking. Outside treatment might involve presenting to a rural health clinic or hospital, although it might also involve the resources of other healing services in the community—faith healers, herbalists, masseurs, midwives, bone-setters, local pharmacists, and so on. Biomedical care is sought usually only if a local remedy does not work and if there are no signs of improvement.

Gender differences in access to services affect both women's and children's health. Women everywhere are less well-educated than men, and those who have not had formal schooling tend to have limited knowledge of their health, and are unable to diagnose and act appropriately on signs of disease. Women's decisions to take sick children to clinics are complex and relate to their own understanding of the outcome of illness, need for external intervention, their access to funds and transport, age of child, and so on. Hence a mother explained:

> The younger child has a fever and a cold. Has had it for 1 week now. Nothing has been done yet. They are waiting for the father to come back from Kpong and give them some money to take the child to a

clinic. They want to take the child to Battor (a mission hospital in a neighbouring district). (Agyepong et al. 1995, p. 95)

But asked about the process of deciding what to do with a sick child, the mother distinguished between very young and older children; the age of the child affecting her ability to make a diagnosis and act accordingly:

> If the child cannot speak to you and tell you this is the part that is hurting then you have to take the child to hospital for the doctor to identify the problem. If the child can say 'it's my head' or 'my stomach', it means it can be solved here. (Agyepong et al. 1995, p. 101)

Women tend to assess a child's condition on the basis of various subjectively-determined signs (Nichter 1993), including both physical and behavioural changes in the child, which might include lethargy, crying, fever, vomiting, refusal to eat, disinterest in playing etc. (Agyepong & Manderson 1994). Others determine choice of carer on the basis of symptom. Hence Lina explained that she 'always' takes her children to the hospital when they have a cough because they are 'still young', only presenting to the traditional healer when a child has *piang* (also indicated by a cough, but caused by a falling) (Manderson 1993, fieldnotes). By the same criteria, too, women make their own subjective assessments regarding continuation of treatment: Paz stopped her 5-month-old daughter's medication (prescribed for pneumonia) after four days, because 'the child was already feeling fine if I continued the child could have got an overdose' (Manderson 1993, fieldnotes).

Household interventions draw upon the concept of the household production of health. This has resulted in renewed attention on the role of women in the delivery of health care, as a logical component of their roles as wives and mothers. However, the gender implications of this need exploration, and might include the reinforcement of conventional notions of domestic health/household provision of health being the responsibility of women; the attribution of blame to women for poor outcomes of acute episodes of illness; and lack of account of the impact on women of increased responsibility for family health. This is especially so in female-headed households, which are characteristic in transitional economies. Female-headed households are among the poorest in all countries, and the development of innovative ways to deliver health care needs to take this into account. In addition, attention to the household production of health needs to take account of ideological and institutional factors which limit women's access to information and services.

GENDER INEQUALITY AND THE QUALITY OF CARE

The incidence and severity of disease is exacerbated by difficulties people face when attempting to avoid infection or seek treatment. Lack of access to resources to cover transport, service and treatment costs, restrictions on mobility, and availability of time may all discourage women from attending clinics or other health services (Leslie 1992; Mensch 1993). They can also relate to ethnicity, poverty and gender (Timyan et al. 1993). Andrea Whittaker (1996a, 1996b) illustrates this with respect to women's health in northeast Thailand. Interactions between health providers and clients are limited and reflect and reinforce status differences between the two. Health staff are well-educated and salaried; they live in government houses distant from village houses, dress in uniforms, and typically speak central Thai rather than northeast Isaan (Lao). Nursing staff at primary health care stations typically regard Isaan villagers as 'ignorant' and 'uneducated', demonstrated by the villagers' use of village midwives and herbalists, poor clothing, and basic housing and facilities. Health and disease are coupled in class-specific discourse, Whittaker (1996a, p. 83) argues, which treats as synonymous poverty and dirt, cultural marginality and illness.

Other barriers to use of services include hours of operation of facilities; quality of facilities (equipment, space, assurance of privacy in consultations, diagnostic facilities etc.); time spent waiting and time spent in provider/client interaction; quality of interaction; follow-up and continuity of care; and choice and cost of commodities (e.g. of different kinds of contraception), and regularity of supply and quality of commodities (Bruce 1990; Whittaker et al. 1996). In addition, the range of services and number, sex and technical competence of staff influence women's willingness to attend clinics. Regardless of domestic autonomy, for example, women are rarely willing to present to male health workers with sexual health or related problems. Yet in many poor countries, the primary health care worker is male, and constraints on the mobility of women prevent the recruitment of women health workers in order to overcome this difficulty (Rozario 1992, pp. 126–30). In countries where it has been possible to employ women, workers are often unmarried and their marital status provides a new barrier to older married women discussing personal, reproductive and sexual health problems.

Other local structural and institutional factors also influence access to care. For example, in some settings, women who reside with, or are answerable to, their mothers-in-law (or, in parts of Africa, a senior wife) lack power to make decisions, lack access to cash and hold none of their own, and may be punished for poor performance of household tasks. In this environment they may be especially reluctant to discuss their health or seek treatment. Further, the physical effects of infection, particularly those that cause gross disfigurement (such as filariasis, leprosy, oncodermatitis, leishmaniasis), while they may further compromise women's physical health, also carry social costs such as social rejection, isolation and/or divorce (Amazigo 1994), discouraging women from revealing the disease.

As already noted, women tend to present with health problems of their own only if sickness seriously impedes their ability to work. While improved access to health care would not dissolve gender differences in health status, much can be done to ameliorate women's poor health provided they present for care. The development of integrated services covering the wide range of health issues affecting women and children (antenatal and postnatal care, family planning, sexual health, STDs and HIV/AIDS) offers great potential for better health outcomes, although country programs are often reluctant to support this because of the administrative and institutional changes this might involve. Health care provided at the primary level (at rural health posts, midwifery centres, and so on), which elicits information about women's general health when providing treatment for specific reported problems, may help address difficulties relating to reluctance to report.

CONCLUSION

The ability of poor countries to provide and deliver public health and medical care is an ongoing issue, influenced broadly by structural, institutional, political and economic factors and specifically by the organisation of the health care system and its ability to ensure access to services. The distribution and types of diseases are influenced by broad economic and environmental changes, but individual vulnerability to and treatment for infection and disease are affected by equity. This continues to be a problem as poorer countries join industrialised countries in dismantling state services in favour of privatisation, raising questions about balancing private and public, curative and preventive services to ensure continued access to care for those too poor to pay for private services.

As I have suggested in this chapter, the relationship between health and development is complicated. Economic development, in general, in the long term will usually result in improved health for the population, but the ability of a country to invest in economic development is impeded where the health status of the population is poor, and certain development strategies and projects may compromise rather than improve people's health.

A number of implications flow from these points. First, people's health in the context of development projects needs to be monitored and emerging health problems addressed. Specific mechanisms, therefore, need to be put in place for program monitoring, process evaluation, and outcome and impact evaluation, to measure the benefits of investment and development and its value to recipient populations. Secondly, factors inhibiting the delivery of health services to the poor are common to those of other social service sectors, suggesting the value of increased intersectoral programs for development, for example, for agriculture, education, micro-credit facilities and education as well as health. This may be translated both at a government level by developing institutional capability for the delivery of services, and locally by including intersectoral approaches in specific development projects (e.g. integrating health, education and micro-credit projects in major urban redevelopment projects). Finally, there is little evidence from industrialised countries that economic growth alone reduces poverty, as instanced by the high societal and individual costs of productivity-led economic policy and privatisation of social services in countries like the USA. Government commitment to reducing poverty and inequality, and to improving the health and welfare of the poor, needs to be demonstrated in policies, programs and their implementation, not at the level of rhetoric alone.

NOTE

1   Efforts to reduce health risks by composting waste and constructing new latrines were introduced in 1964, but the technology has sometimes been poorly applied. Biogas converters, for example, produce gas for household use from pig and human waste, but waste is not allowed to 'ferment' for a sufficient period to destroy all pathogens before agricultural use.

REFERENCES

Agyepong, I.A. & Manderson, L. 1994 'The diagnosis and management of fever at household level in the Greater Accra Region, Ghana' *Acta Tropica* vol. 58, nos 3/4, pp. 317–30

Agyepong, I.A., Argee, B., Dzikunu, H. & Manderson, L. 1995 'The malaria manual. Guidelines for the rapid assessment of social, economic and cultural aspects of malaria' *Methods for Social and Economic Research in Tropical Areas* no. 2, WHO/TDR, Geneva

Amazigo, U. 1994 'Gender and tropical diseases in Nigeria: A neglected dimension' in *Gender, Health, and Sustainable Development* eds P. Wijeyaratne, L.J. Arsenault, J.H. Roberts & J. Kitts, Proceedings of a workshop held in Nairobi, Kenya, 5–8 October 1993 IDRC, Ottawa, pp. 85–99

Asian Development Bank 1991 *Health, Population and Development in Asia and the Pacific* Asian Development Bank, Manila

Biery-Hamilton, G.M. 1993 'Disruption of a population that did not relocate: The impact of the Tucurui Dam on a riverside community in the Brazilian Amazon' in *Selected Papers on Refugee Issues: II* eds M. Hopkins & N.D. Donnelly, American Anthropological Association, Arlington, VA, pp. 83–104

Bissell, S. & Sobhan, B. 1996 *Child Labour and Education Programming in the Garment Industry in Bangladesh: Experiences and Issues* UNICEF, Dhaka

Brockerhoff, M. 1995 'Child survival in big cities: The disadvantages of migrants' *Social Science and Medicine* vol. 40, no. 10, pp. 1371–83

Bruce, J. 1990 'Fundamental elements of the quality of care: A simple framework' *Studies in Family Planning* vol. 21, no. 2, pp. 61–91

Caldwell, J., Findley, S., Caldwell, P., Santow, G., Cosford, W., Braid, J. & Broers-Freeman, D. (eds) 1990 *What We Know about Health Transition: The Cultural, Social and Behavioural Determinants of Health* Health Transition Series 2, Health Transition Centre, Australian National University, Canberra

Carpenter, H., Manderson, L., Janabi, M., Kalmayem, G., Simon, A. & Waidubu, G. 1996 'The politics of drug distribution in Bohol, the Philippines' *Asian Studies Review* vol. 17, no. 1, pp. 35–52

Cooper, A., Guthridge, S. & Riare, A. 1991 *Occupational health of home workers. A study of homework in two villages in northeast Thailand* unpublished Master of Tropical Health Report, Brisbane, Tropical Health Program, University of Queensland, St Lucia

Hameed, M., Khemanith, P., Michels, D. & Piliwas, L. 1995 *A description of injuries and safety behaviour amongst construction workers in Khon Kaen, Thailand* unpublished Master of Tropical Health Report, Brisbane, Tropical Health Program, University of Queensland, St Lucia

Harpham, T. 1994 'Urbanization and mental health in developing countries: A research role for social scientists, public health professionals and social psychiatrists' *Social Science and Medicine* vol. 39, no. 2, pp. 233–46

Harpham, T., Lusty, T. & Vaughan, P. 1988 *In the Shadow of the City: Community Health and the Urban Poor* Oxford University Press, Oxford

Huang, Y. & Manderson, L. 1992 'Schistosomiasis and the social patterning of infection' *Acta Tropica* no. 51, pp. 175–94

Hull, T.H. & Hull, V.J. 1995 'Health systems in Indonesia and Vietnam: Transitions to uncertain futures' in *Health and Development in Southeast Asia* eds P. Cohen & J. Purcal, Australian Development Studies Network, Canberra, pp. 120–48

Kanji, N., Hardon, A., Harnmeijer, J.W., Mamdani, M. & Walt, G. (eds) 1992 *Drugs Policy in Developing Countries* Zed Books, London & New Jersey

Kemp, M. & Gilles, M. 1988 *The Human Ecology of Logging in the Solomon Islands* unpublished Master of Tropical Health Report, Brisbane, Tropical Health Program, University of Queensland, St Lucia

Leslie, J. 1992 'Women's time and the use of health services' *IDS Bulletin* vol. 23, no. 1, pp. 4–7

Mburu, F.M. 1989 'Non-government organizations in the health field: Collaboration, integration and contrasting aims in Africa' *Social Science and Medicine* vol. 29, no. 5, pp. 591–97

Mensch, B. 1993 'Quality of care: A neglected dimension' in *The Health of Women: A Global Perspective* eds M. Koblinsky, J. Timyan & J. Gay, Westview Press, Boulder, CO, pp. 235–53

Nichter, M. 1993 'Social science lessons from diarrhoea research and their application to ARI' *Human Organisation* no. 52, pp. 53–67

Parker, M. 1993 'Bilharzia and the boys: Questioning common assumptions' *Social Science and Medicine* vol. 37, no. 4, pp. 481–92

Popkin, B., Bilsborrow, R.E. & Akin, J.S. 1982 'Breast-feeding patterns in low-income countries' *Science* no. 218, pp. 1082–93

Popkin, B. & Solon, F.S. 1976 'Income, time, the working mother and child nutriture' *Journal of Tropical Pediatrics and Environmental Child Health* no. 22, pp. 156–66

Rathgeber, E.M. 1990 'WID, WAD, GAD: Trends in research and practice' *The Journal of Developing Areas* no. 24, pp. 489–502

Rozario, S. 1992 *Purity and Communal Boundaries* Allen & Unwin, Sydney

Rubin, N. & Warren, W.N. (eds) 1968 *Dams in Africa: An interdisciplinary study of man-made lakes in Africa* Case Publishers, London

Sawyer, D. 1993 'Economic and social consequences of malaria in new colonization projects in Brazil' *Social Science and Medicine* vol. 37, no. 9, pp. 1131–36

Scheper-Hughes, N. 1994 *Death without Weeping* University of California Press, Berkeley, CA

Simon, A., Janabi, M., Kalmayem, G., Waidubu, G., Galia, E., Pague, L., Manderson, L. & Riley, I. 1996 'Caretakers' management of childhood ARI and the use of antibiotics, Bohol, The Philippines' *Human Organization* vol. 55, no. 1, pp. 76–83

Sommers, M. 1993 'Coping with fear: Burundi refugees and the urban experience in Dar es Salaam, Tanzania' in *Selected Papers on Refugee Issues: II* eds M. Hopkins & N.D. Donnelly, American Anthropological Association, Arlington, VA

Stalker, P. 1996 *Child Labour in Bangladesh. A summary of recent investigations* UNICEF, Bangladesh

Stanley, N.F. & Alpers, M.P. (eds) 1975 *Man-Made Lakes and Human Health* Academic Press, New York

Tanner, M. & Harpham, T. (eds) 1995 *Urban Health in Developing Countries: Progress and Prospects* Earthscan Publications, London

Timyan, J., Brechin, S.J.G., Measham, D.M. & Ogunleye, B. 1993 'Access to care: More than a problem of distance' in *The Health of Women: A Global Perspective* eds M. Koblinsky, J. Timyan & J. Gay, Westview Press, Boulder, CO, pp. 217–34

van der Geest, S. & Whyte, S.R. (eds) 1988 *The Context of Medicines in Developing Countries* Kluwer Academic Publishers, Dordrecht

Whittaker, A. 1996a 'Primary health services in rural Thailand: Problems of translating policy into practice' *Asian Studies Review* vol. 20, no. 1, pp. 68–83

——1996b 'Quality of care for women in Northeast Thailand: Intersections of class, gender, and ethnicity' *Health Care for Women International* no. 17, pp. 435–77

Whittaker, M., Mita, R., Hossain, B. & Koenig, M. 1996 'Evaluating rural Bangladesh: Women's perspectives of quality in family planning services' *Health Care for Women International* no. 17, pp. 393–411

World Bank 1993 *Investing in Health*. *World Development Report Executive Summary* World Bank, Washington DC

World Health Organization 1996 *Investing in Health Research and Development* Report of the Ad Hoc Committee on Health Research Relating to Future Intervention Options, WHO, Geneva

7 Ethnicity, health and health care in Britain

Waqar Ahmad & Lesley Jones

Health and ethnicity now constitutes a major area of research, policy and practice. This chapter offers a rapid summary of this broad field in relation to the United Kingdom. In reviewing relevant policy and research, we are selective and brief. However, indication of where the reader will find more detailed exposition of the points raised is given.

The chapter begins with a discussion of issues around racism and culture. An appreciation of the articulations and impact of racism is important in understanding the lives of minority ethnic communities and their interaction with services. Increasingly, racism is articulated through the language of culture, heritage, belonging and racialised conceptions of identity. Much of the literature on minority ethnic health experiences is epidemiological and skewed towards certain conditions. It also favours particular explanations of ethnic differentials. We examine some of the major debates and evidence in these areas. The final section considers access to health services.

RACISM, CULTURE AND DIFFERENCE

'Racism' is an elusive concept with competing definitions and conceptions across time, disciplines and political persuasions. Part of the confusion also rests in the fact that the term encompasses attitudes, behaviour and outcome. 'Scientific racism', based on notions of the inherent superiority of some 'races' over others—so important in legitimisation of slavery and imperialism—is now largely discredited in biological and social sciences (but see debate on *The Bell Curve*, Herrnstein & Murray 1994; Fraser 1995).

A popular and resilient definition of racism rested on psychological assumptions about an individual being racially prejudiced and having the power to exercise this prejudice to disadvantage members of other racial groups. Such a definition was reassuring in its ability to locate the problem of racism in an individual's damaged psyche or at best ignorance, thus absolving a racist system of any responsibility. Structural and ideological determinants of racism remained irrelevant in this scheme (Mercer 1986). By locating racism in damaged psyches and cultural difference, this approach articulates arguments for tolerance of difference through better understanding of 'other cultures' rather than for equality of treatment, resources or outcomes, or for solutions aimed at institutional levels.

The late 1970s in Britain witnessed a major critique of multiculturalism and the birth of 'anti-racism' emphasising the importance of understanding and challenging historical, ideological and institutional bases of racism. Racist behaviour and thinking was rooted in the history of slavery and imperialism, the ideology of white superiority over other 'races' and cultures, and the institutionalisation of such ideology in the workings of the state and its agencies (e.g. Centre for Contemporary Cultural Studies 1982).

In terms of professions, professional ideology was seen as a major vehicle for articulation, perpetuation and legitimisation of racism. Ideologies turn racist ideas into received wisdom or commonsense; professional ideologies give societal commonsense scientific legitimacy. The concept of racialisation becomes important in the workings of institutional racism. Increasingly, 'ethnicity' and 'culture' are used as euphemisms for biological difference or 'race'; indeed culture, with its asserted association to lineage, history, common heritage and nationalism has become the main vehicle for articulating racism (Husband 1994). As Ahmad (1993, p. 19) has argued, racialisation takes place in terms of explanations for and solutions to health problems being based on rigid and historical notions of culture and cultural difference, where cultures reside in socioeconomic and power vacuums.

A potent contemporary example of racialisation is the medical discourse on consanguinity in explaining poorer birth outcome in the Pakistani origin population compared to the white population (Ahmad 1994). Whereas the data on infant mortality and congenital malformations—itself based on dubious categorisation and methods—presents a picture of inconsistency and confusion, this does not affect the magical belief that consanguinity is the direct cause of the high infant mortality and high rates of congenital malformations in the Pakistani population. The solution seems to rest, in this discourse, on changing marriage patterns and being more 'like us'—an approach which has a long history in ethnicity and health policy (see Ahmad 1993).

As anti-racism emphasised the role of institutions and ideology in the perpetuation of racism in society, combating racism, then, was not about preaching tolerance or changing attitudes but of changes in legal and institutional structures and practices. Anti-racism emphasised the shared experience of racism and discrimination of all racialised groups, leading to the adoption of 'black' as a symbol of political identity. As policy and practice, anti-racism became popular with many left-wing councils in the 1980s. The late 1980s witnessed a backlash against anti-racism, and politically-left councils generally, and criticisms from within the minority ethnic communities where many felt that the level at which anti-racism functioned undermined their cultural and religious values or heritage (Gilroy 1990; Modood 1988). Anti-racism, although once popular in social work, education and sections of social housing, never gained a firm foothold in health services. The predominant responses in health services remain around versions of ethnic sensitivity, often reduced to 'specialist provision', or interpreting services.

In terms of policy analysis the dichotomy of an over-structural (anti-racism) and an over-cultural approach (multiculturalism) is unhelpful. It is clear that structures, institutions and socio-material location of individuals and groups are important to their life chances and interaction with the state and its institutions. For the minority ethnic populations then, their generally poor housing, higher rates of unemployment and access to relatively poor quality of health care are important considerations (Central Statistical Office 1996). But equally, these populations are more than the sum total of racisms they confront. Cultural resources—religion, community institutions, families, links with kin abroad—are vital sources of strength and important to people's survival and success. To not acknowledge the importance of cultural resources in understanding and dealing with health and illness is, in many ways, to negate a vital aspect of human existence.

ETHNICITY AND HEALTH POLICY

Most early centrally driven interventions were aimed at promoting cultural change in minority ethnic communities with at best a marginal shift in health policy or practice. These interventions rested partly on the assumption that differences in health or use of services were located in differences in culture. Thus, as noted, rather than focus on major killers such as coronary heart disease, even as late as the 1980s, some major health care agencies like the Health Education Authority were instead focusing much attention on promoting birth control among minority ethnic communities. The often patronising and reductionist approach to early health policy on ethnicity has been criticised by numerous writers (e.g. Ahmad 1993; Bhopal & White 1993; Rocheron 1988).

More recently the purchaser–provider split in health services may have made it more difficult to pursue equal opportunities with vigour. For example, purchasers and providers within the same locality may have different conceptions of equal opportunities in employment or service delivery, or different commitment to these ideals. The ability of local minority communities to impact on purchasing may have been reduced through the loss of locally elected representatives on health authority and trust boards and the shifting of accountability of health agencies from the local level to the centre. Representation of minority ethnic groups as board members on health authorities and trusts remains limited (NAHAT/Kings Fund 1993). On the other hand, in theory at least, the needs assessment and contracting mechanisms do offer the potential for committed purchasers to influence developments at the provider level. However, beyond speculation, little is known about the potential for equal opportunity developments in the reformed National Health Service (NHS).

More positively, a number of recent developments offer some encouragement. The need for cultural sensitivity, and respect for religious values of all users is recognised in the NHS and Community Care Act, the Health of the Nation, The Patient's Charter, the Children Act 1989 and other policy documentation (cited in Department of Health 1989, 1991, 1992). The need to increase participation of minority ethnic members on health authority and NHS trust boards is acknowledged by the Department of Health as is the need to ensure equality of employment for minority ethnic nurses. Many of the centrally commissioned NHS research and development initiatives have encouraged applicants to consider in their submissions the needs of minority ethnic communities. And the Social Services Inspectorate (part of the Department of Health), has recently published a document on 'race' equality followed by publication of a review of literature on 'race' and social care (Butt & Mirza 1996; SSI 1995). Whether these developments effect any tangible change in the employment of minority ethnic staff or service provision remains to be seen. They must, however, be recognised as welcome leads from the centre.

Alongside these developments there has been continued interest in health policy and ethnicity by the Kings Fund, the Commission for Racial Equality (CRE) and policy as well as research interest by the Health Education Authority (HEA). The CRE has, in recent years, published guidelines and codes of practice on primary care services and other issues. The HEA's continuing survey of health and health needs of minority ethnic communities has provided valuable policy-oriented data on health and lifestyles; it is also developing work on coronary heart disease, haemoglobinopathies and other fields (HEA 1994a, b; HEA 1995). A number of databases, covering research and service contacts as well as published output, have been established (e.g. the Kings Fund *Share* project). The policy-maker or practitioner who wishes to take 'race' equality issues seriously is thus facilitated to do this both by policy directives and useful guidance and literature.

Alongside these official responses, community involvement in health and social care decision-making remains important. In the areas of haemoglobinopathies; mental health and increasingly, disability; community involvement and campaigning as well as development of a minority ethnic voluntary sector remain important. Although the minority ethnic voluntary sector remains underdeveloped and under-resourced its contribution to health and social care has been significant. The health oriented voluntary sector relies on different forms of funding both from local and national sources. Not insignificant in this respect has been the funding made available by the Department of Health (1996) and the NHS Ethnic Health Unit (1995). The latter, in particular, has attempted to have considerable involvement from the minority ethnic communities in identifying priorities for funding and many of the funded initiatives have been collaborative projects between statutory agencies and minority ethnic community organisations.

EPIDEMIOLOGY AND MINORITY ETHNIC HEALTH

Epidemiological literature predominates in the field of ethnicity and health. Reviews and critiques of this literature are available elsewhere (Ahmad 1993; Sheldon & Parker 1992; Smaje 1995). Here we focus on some selective but important elements. One important issue relates to the fascination in epidemiology with *relative* risk (i.e. higher rates of a condition in one group compared to another group, irrespective of the volume of morbidity or mortality). The emphasis on *relative* instead of *absolute* risk often leads to inappropriate priorities where effort may focus on the higher risk but low impact conditions as opposed to relatively lower risk conditions (e.g. cancers) which cause a far greater volume of morbidity and mortality. For example, tuberculosis has considerably higher prevalence among Britain's Asian communities compared to the general population but, as it is a relatively rare and treatable condition, total morbidity and mortality is relatively small. In contrast, cancers have a lower prevalence among minority ethnic groups compared to the general population. However, they account for far greater morbidity and mortality among the Asian communities than tuberculosis.

The tendency to concentrate on *relative* risk as opposed to *absolute* risk has served minority ethnic communities poorly. According to Bhopal and colleagues, the epidemiological literature on minority ethnic populations in the 1980s more accurately reflects the prejudices of the researchers rather than community needs or evidence-based service concerns (see Bhopal & White 1993). Bhopal and White refer to this inconsistency as the 'conflict between demand, need and provision'. This conflict encapsulates, first, the problems of health promoters from the ethnic majority controlling health promotion for ethnic minorities whom they understand poorly; secondly, paying insufficient regard both to epidemiological information and to the observation of ethnic minorities; and thirdly, a failure to involve, in a participative way, ethnic minority communities themselves.

The tendency in epidemiology to emphasise relative risk also has other drawbacks. It somehow gives the impression that research on minority ethnic communities is only legitimate if it compares the minority population (the experimental group) with the white population (the controls). At one level it espouses a simplistic logic that by having comparative data, the health service can be made aware of the differentials and act to reduce these differentials. Thus one can see the potential utility of evidence on social class differences in morbidity or mortality. But in relation to minority ethnic communities it gives rise to certain fallacies. First, it continues the historical tendency to regard the white community as the 'normal' against which the deviance of others must be measured and controlled (e.g. see Ahmad 1993; Said 1978). We believe that minority ethnic communities can and must be studied in their own right.

Secondly, it is important to distinguish between the risk factors which may explain a condition within a population and those which account for the differences between populations. For example, although smoking does not account for the increased prevalence of coronary heart disease among the Asian population compared with the European population, it remains an important risk factor for coronary heart disease within the Asian population (McKeigue & Chaturvedi 1996). This epidemiological bias in favour of studies focusing on relative risk raises questions both about the relevance of research knowledge to practice and the appropriateness and utility of policy interventions which follow.

EXPLAINING HEALTH INEQUALITIES

Although the evidence of inequalities in health status between Asian communities and the white population, and between and within Asian communities is clear, explanations remain contested. Four main explanations are forwarded. One (favoured) explanation locates inequalities in cultural differences: examples here include the 'consanguinity hypothesis' for explaining higher peri-natal mortality, stillbirth and congenital malformations among Pakistanis (Ahmad 1994) or dietary and other cultural practices for the higher rates of vitamin D deficiency in Asian children in the 1980s. Such explanations have, rightly, been criticised for their reductionist emphasis on one aspect of human existence and their failure to locate culture in its wider context of socioeconomic status, citizenship and access to services (see Donovan 1984; Ahmad 1993, 1996).

A second explanation has emphasised the racialised marginalisation of Asian communities—higher unemployment, inner-city residence, institutional racism—which hampers their life chances (see Ahmad 1993). The emphasis on cultural practices, as considered in this explanation, is regarded by many as no more than a decoy for racism. A third possible explanation rests on inequalities in health care provision. The existence of an inverse care law in health care is well recognised (Tudor Hart 1971) and governmental responses to this have included attempts at fairer distribution of funds to health regions to acknowledge this. In present-day Britain the inverse care law also has a racialised dimension; it is in the inner cities where most of the deprived minority groups reside and where health care remains at its poorest.

Finally, the categorisation of people into ethnicities or national groups itself hides more than it reveals. Ethnicity is difficult to define and represents only some aspects of personal identity (Ahmad & Sheldon 1993; Anthias & Yuval-Davis 1993). Previous definitions—routinely available data up to the early 1990s provided breakdown only by region or country of birth—as well as the current ethnic groupings, based on the 1991 Census categorisations, remain problematic. And the few studies which differentiate between the different populations within the same ethnic group (say Indians) by religion or language represent a picture of heterogeneous experience of health and health care—there are, for example, greater differences in birth outcome within the Indian population than between the Indian and other populations (see discussion in Ahmad 1994).

Ethnic inequalities in health and health care remain too marked not to be taken seriously. The relationship between ethnicity, socio-economic status and health care demonstrates that ethnicity does not determine destiny—the use of ethnicity as a primary category for grouping humanity is fraught with problems and its relationship to other aspects of human existence must be kept in mind.

ACCESS, QUALITY AND EQUITY

This section provides a rapid overview of some important themes in access to services: more detailed overviews are available in Ahmad (1993), Smaje (1995) and Ahmad and Atkin (1996); relevant survey data is presented in HEA (1994a) and Nazroo (1997). The evidence can be summarised under four inter-related headings: quality of care; access to services, including communication; use of services; and professional competence and attitudes.

QUALITY OF CARE

The operation of the inverse care law in health services is well recognised. Generally, better qualified practitioners and better equipped and resourced health services tend to be in the more affluent areas, areas with the least morbidity and mortality (Townsend & Davidson 1982; Tudor Hart 1971). Once we add access to private medical care for the affluent classes to this, the inequalities in quality of care become even more marked. Although recent data warn us against homogeneous treatment of all minority ethnic communities, for Pakistanis, Bangladeshis and African Caribbeans (and other minority groups) poverty, inner-city living, poor housing and unemployment remain trenchant realities (Central Statistical Office 1996). Inner-city areas are often the least well served in terms of quality of primary health care, relying on single-handed general practices with few facilities. In a rare study of quality of care to Asian and white maternity patients, Clarke and Clayton (1983) showed that general practitioners of Asian women were less likely to be on the obstetrics register and less likely to have postgraduate qualifications compared to general practitioners of white women. Quality of care was an independent risk factor: 'Asian and non-Asian mothers with general practitioners who were not on the obstetric list had more than twice the risk of a perinatal death.' Jain (1985) reported that a major reason for Asian women's relatively late booking into antenatal clinics was the late referral from their general practitioner. Literature on children's services remains limited. However, it is known that inner-city areas are less likely to have good management of asthma and require greater access for child accidents.

ACCESS

Access to health care is related to, among other factors, social class, gender and practitioner orientation (e.g. Cartwright & O'Brien 1976). Working-class users receive less positive consultations, including a shorter duration with the doctor, less information, less choice of treatment and a more directive consultation than middle-class patients. Similar findings were reported for women compared to men, and some researchers argued that, in terms of empathy and quality of communication, it was beneficial for women to have women doctors. Tuckett et al. (1985), however, argued for a more sophisticated model of doctor–patient communication in which they saw the patient acting as an 'expert', armed with their own lay knowledge and actively seeking an outcome which was consistent with their beliefs and experiences. Regrettably, the literature on doctor–patient communication and access has ignored issues of ethnicity.

Although one can postulate relevance of class, gender and doctor orientation for members of minority ethnic communities, the direct literature on minority ethnic patients, however, has concentrated on information, communication and doctor-choice. Numerous studies have shown minority patients to be less knowledgeable about available services (Ahmad & Walker 1997; Blakemore & Boneham 1994; Cameron et al. 1989; Darr et al. 1998; Firdous & Bhopal 1984).

While gender of practitioner may be important for appropriate health care to many women, it is reported to be a particular issue for Asian women (Theodore-Gandi & Shaikh 1988). Ahmad et al. (1989, 1991) argue that non-availability of female general practitioners who are fluent speakers of Asian languages may be compromising many Asian women's desire for same-sex consultations. Non-speakers of English face particular problems in terms of access—on the whole, the interpreter or linkworker schemes remain inadequate, with most users relying on kin, including young children for interpreting (e.g. Ahmad & Walker 1997). The ethical and practical problems of using qualified interpreters are discussed by Darr et al. (1998).

USE OF SERVICES

Evidence on differential use of both primary health and hospital services has accumulated over the last decade. Donaldson and Taylor's (1983) work based on hospital records showed areas of under- and over-utilisation, compared to the general population. Later work notes higher consultation rates for Pakistanis and Indian population compared to white population for people aged 16–64 years. For children, utilisation rates for Indian boys and girls and Pakistani girls were lower than for white children but higher for Pakistani boys (Balarajan et al. 1989). The recent HEA (1994a) survey shows an average one-month figure of 18 per cent consultations for the UK population compared to 36 per cent for Indian, 44 per cent for Pakistani and 45 per cent for the Bangladeshi population. The comparatively greater use of health care compared to the white population is also supported by other studies (Benzeval & Judge 1993; Johnson et al. 1983). Johnson et al. (1983) and the HEA (1994a) report very high registration rates with general practitioners for both white and Asian populations. However, none of these studies standardised for service need and thus the apparent greater use by some minority ethnic groups is difficult to interpret.

PRACTITIONER ATTITUDES

Practitioners exercise considerable power and discretion—their attitudes towards patients in terms of age, gender, ability or ethnicity do matter. For example, the medicalisation of disability and womanhood have been criticised by the disability movement and feminist critics (Morris 1991; Ussher 1991), and medicine's legitimisation of imperialism and racist marginalisation has also been noted (Littlewood & Lipsedge 1989). Ahmad and Husband (1993) note the distinction between formal and substantive citizenship; both are mediated by officials acting on behalf of the state where ideological, professional and personal prejudices can, and do, lead to discriminatory outcomes. Ideas about belonging and deservingness influence practitioners' judgement of individual and group rights to state welfare. This has also been noted in relation to access to medical services. Ahmad et al. (1991) and Wright (1983) have reported unfavourable attitudes held by general practitioners towards Asian patients: commonly held stereotypes included fussing over trivial complaints, inappropriate consultations, lack of care over own health and abuse of services. Ahmad (1993) and others have noted that medical professionals have favoured culture blaming explanations for a host of conditions and services: rickets, poorer birth outcome and tuberculosis have all been 'explained' with reference to deleterious cultural practices. Bowler (1993) has reported similarly unfavourable attitudes among midwives in relation to Asian maternity service users. Darr (1990) notes stereotypes employed by maternity services professionals in relation to thalassaemia; a finding also confirmed by Atkin et al. (1997).

Worryingly, combined with such negative attitudes is a degree of ignorance of certain conditions which are more commonly found among sections of minority ethnic communities. Many health professionals remain poorly informed on haemoglobinopathies (Anionwu 1993), a finding confirmed by widespread dissatisfaction with health professionals, especially consultants, among parents of children with sickle cell disorders or thalassaemia (Atkin et al. 1997).

CONCLUSION

The aim of this chapter has been to provide an overview of the health, health care and social context of minority ethnic people's lives in Britain. Demographically these populations remain diverse and this diversity is also reflected in their health status and access to services. Racism remains a reality of life for the many different racialised minorities. And as contemporary forms of racism employ the neutral language of culture, we must be cautious of discourses which locate ethnic differentials in health and health care in differences in cultural practices. As noted, available literature in health and social care remains skewed towards epidemiological and disease specific research. We have briefly reviewed the evidence on access, quality and equity; areas which show some improvements but still considerable inequalities. The improved recognition of minority ethnic health needs at the policy levels has happened at a time of weakened local democracy with an ambivalent relationship between local populations and health services: ambivalent in that while in principle purchasers should make the population needs the basis of commissioning, in reality the influence of local people on purchasing decisions seems to have diminished in the reformed NHS. The continued racialised marginalisation in most other walks of life (housing, employment, education, immigration) continues for the minority ethnic groups and is a continuing arbiter of health and illness and access to state welfare.

REFERENCES

Ahmad, W.I.U. (ed.) 1993 *'Race' and Health in Contemporary Britain* Open University Press, Buckingham

——1994 'Reflections on the consanguinity and birth outcome debate' *Journal of Public Health Medicine* vol. 16, no. 4, pp. 423–28

——1996 'The trouble with culture' in *Researching Cultural Difference in Health* eds D. Kelleher & S. Hillier, Routledge, London

Ahmad, W.I.U. & Atkin, K. 1996 *'Race' and Community Care* Open University Press, Buckingham

Ahmad, W.I.U., Baker, M.R. & Kernohan, E. 1991 'General practitioners' perceptions of Asian and non-Asian patients' *Family Practice*, vol. 8, no. 1, pp. 52–56

Ahmad, W.I.U. & Husband, C. 1993 'Religious identity, citizenship and welfare: The case of Muslims in Britain' *American Journal of Islamic Social Science* vol. 10, no. 2, pp. 217–33

Ahmad, W.I.U., Kernohan, E.E.M. & Baker, M.R. 1989 'Patients' choice of general practitioner: Influence of patients' fluency in English and the ethnicity and sex of the doctor' *Journal of Royal College of Practitioners* vol. 39, no. 321, pp. 153–55

Ahmad, W.I.U. & Sheldon, T. 1993 '"Race" and statistics' in *Social Research: Philosophy, Politics and Practice* ed. M. Hammersley, Sage, London

Ahmad, W.I.U. & Walker, R. 1997 'Health and social care needs of Asian older people' *Ageing and Society* no. 17, pp. 141–65

Anionwu, E. 1993 'Sickle cell and thalassaemia: Community experiences and official response' in *'Race' and Health in Contemporary Britain* ed. W.I.U. Ahmad, Open University Press, Buckingham

Anthias, F. & Yuval-Davis, N. 1993 *Racialized Boundaries* Routledge, London

Atkin, K., Ahmad, W.I.U. & Anionwu, E. 1997 *Evaluation of Services to Children with Sickle Cell Disorder or Thalassaemia Major* Ethnicity and Social Policy Research Unit, University of Bradford, Bradford

Balarajan, R., Yuen, P. & Raleigh, V. 1989 'Ethnic differences in general practitioner consultations' *British Medical Journal* no. 299, pp. 958–60

Benzeval, M. & Judge, K. 1993 *The Development of Population Based Need Indicators from Self-Reported Health Care Utilisation Data* Kings Fund, London

Bhopal, R. & White, M. 1993 'Health promotion for ethnic minorities: Past, present and future' in *'Race' and Health in Contemporary Britain* ed. W.I.U. Ahmad, Open University Press, Buckingham

Blakemore, K. & Boneham, M. 1994 *Age, Race and Ethnicity* Open University Press, Buckingham

Bowler, I. 1993. '"They're not the same as us?" Midwives' stereotypes of South Asian maternity patients' *Sociology of Health and Illness* vol. 15, no. 2, pp. 157–78

Butt, J. & Mirza, K. 1996 *Social Care and Black Communities* HMSO, London

Cameron, E., Badger, F., Evers, H. & Atkin, K. 1989 'Black old women, disability and health carers' in *Growing Old in the Twentieth Century* ed. M. Jeffreys, Routledge, London

Cartwright, A. & O'Brien, M. 1976 'Social class variations in health care and in the nature of general practitioner consultations' in *The Sociology of the National Health Service* ed. M. Stacey, University of Keele, Sociological Review Monograph 22

Centre for Contemporary Cultural Studies 1982 *The Empire Strikes Back: Race and Racism in 70's Britain* Hutchinson, London

Central Statistical Office 1996 *A Social Focus on Ethnic Minorities* HMSO, London

Clarke, M. & Clayton, D. 1983 'Quality of obstetric care provided for Asian immigrants in Leicestershire' *British Medical Journal* vol. 60, pp. 621–23

Darr, Aamra 1990 'The social implications of thalassaemia among Muslims of Pakistani origin in England' unpublished PhD thesis, University College, London

Darr, Aliya, Jones, L., Ahmad, W.I.U. & Nisar, G. 1998 *Ethnicity and Deafness: A National Overview* Policy Press, Bristol

Department of Health 1989 *Working for Patients* HMSO, London

——1991 *The Patient's Charter* HMSO, London

——1992 *The Health of the Nation: A Strategy for Health in England* HMSO, London

——1996 *Directory of Ethnic Minority Initiatives* Department of Health, London

Donaldson, L. & Taylor, J. 1983 'Patterns of Asian and non-Asian morbidity in hospitals' *British Medical Journal* no. 286, pp. 949–51

Donovan, J. 1984 *We Don't Buy Sickness, it Just Comes* Gower, Aldershot

Firdous, R. & Bhopal, R. 1984 'Reproductive health of Asian women: A comparative study with hospital and community perspectives' *Public Health* no. 103, pp. 307–15

Fraser, S. 1995 *The Bell Curve Wars: Race, Intelligence and the Future of America* Basic Books, New York

Gilroy, P. 1990 'The end of anti-racism' in *Race and Local Politics* eds W. Ball & J. Solomos, Macmillan, Basingstoke

Health Education Authority 1994a *Health and Lifestyles: Black and Ethnic Minority Groups in England* Health Education Authority, London

——1994b *Health-related Resources for Black and Minority Ethnic Groups* Health Education Authority, London

——1995 *Towards Better Health Service Provision for Black and Minority Ethnic Groups* Health Education Authority, London

Herrnstein, W. & Murray, C. 1994 *The Bell Curve* The Free Press, New York

Husband, C. 1994 *'Race' and Nation: The British Experience* Paradigm, Bentley, Western Australia

Jain, C. 1985 *Attitudes of Pregnant Asian Women to Antenatal Care* West Midlands Regional Health Authority, Birmingham

Johnson, M.R.D., Cross, M. & Cardew, S.A. 1983 'Inner city residents, ethnic minorities and primary health care' *Postgraduate Medical Journal* no. 159, pp. 664–67.

Littlewood, R. & Lipsedge, M. 1989 *Aliens and Alienists* Allen & Unwin, London

McKeigue, P. & Chaturvedi, N. 1996 'Epidemiology and control of cardiovascular disease in South Asians and Afro-Caribbeans' in *Ethnicity and Health: Reviews and Guidance for Purchasers in the Areas of Cardiovascular Disease, Mental Health and Haemoglobinopathies* eds W.I.U. Ahmad, T. Sheldon & O. Stuart, Centre for Reviews and Dissemination, University of York, York

Mercer, K. 1986 'Racism and transcultural psychiatry' in *The Power of Psychiatry* eds
P. Miller & N. Rose, Polity, Cambridge

Modood, T. 1988 '"Black", racial equality and Asian identity' *New Community* vol. 14,
no. 3, pp. 397–404

Morris, J. 1991 *Pride Against Prejudice: Transforming Attitudes to Disability* Women's Press,
London

Nazroo, J. 1997 *The Health of Britain's Ethnic Minorities: Findings from a National Survey*
Policy Studies Institute, London

NHS Ethnic Health Unit 1995 *Directory of Projects, 1994–95* NHS Ethnic Health Unit,
Leeds

NAHAT/Kings Fund 1993 *Equality Across the Board* Kings Fund, London

Rocheron, Y. 1988 'The Asian Mother and Baby Campaign: The construction of ethnic
minorities health needs' *Critical Social Policy* no. 22, pp. 4–23

Said, E. 1978 *Orientalism* Random House, New York

Sheldon, T. & Parker, H. 1992 'The use of "ethnicity" and "race" in health research:
A cautionary note' in *The Politics of 'Race' and Health* ed. W.I.U. Ahmad, Race
Relations Research Unit, Bradford University, Bradford

Smaje, C. 1995 *Health, 'Race' and Ethnicity: Making Sense of the Evidence* Kings Fund,
London

Social Services Inspectorate 1995 *'Race' and Community Care: An Inter-Agency Guide to
Good Practice* Social Services Inspectorate, London

Theodore-Gandi, B. & Shaikh, K. 1988 *Maternity Services Consumer Survey* Bradford
Health Authority, Bradford

Townsend, P. & Davidson, N. 1982 *Inequalities in Health: The Black Report* Penguin,
Harmondsworth

Tuckett, D., Boulton, M., Oslen, C. & Williams, A. 1985 *Meetings Between Experts: An
Approach to Sharing Ideas in Medical Consultations* Tavistock, London

Tudor Hart, J. 1971 'The inverse care law' *Lancet* no. 1, pp. 405–12

Ussher, J. 1991 *Women's Madness: Misogyny or Mental Illness?* Harvester Wheatsheaf,
Hemel Hempstead

Wright, C. 1983 'Language and communication problems in an Asian community' *Journal
of Royal College of General Practitioners* no. 33, pp. 101–04

8 Children's images of health

Gillian Bendelow & Pat Pridmore

In late modernity, the social and political concerns surrounding children's rights (e.g. the *Children Act* 1989 (UK) and the *United Nations Convention of the Rights of the Child* 1991), have been reflected within sociological debates around childhood, but also within debates about health and illness. The voices of children and young people have become an important focus within health research, especially with regard to health education and health promotion. Sociologists of childhood argue that, traditionally, much research has been *on* rather than *for* children, using adult categories, classifications and taxonomies into which children are expected to fit, and which regard them as incompetent, or at best as immature adults (see James & Prout 1990; Mayall 1996). Subsequently, there have been calls to develop 'child-centred' approaches which incorporate children's own ideas, beliefs and metaphors, and involve children in research in more ethical and humanistic ways (Kalnins et al. 1992; Mayall 1994). This chapter focuses on the use of the 'draw and write' technique, incorporating two studies which have used children's drawings in the UK and in South Africa. The recent upsurge of interest in the use of this method in health research reflects recognition of the need to develop innovative and participatory approaches which increase our understanding of children and how they see the world.

Using children's drawings as data has a long history within social science research encompassing psychology and psychoanalysis (see Pridmore & Bendelow 1995 for a detailed review of the use of children's drawings in research). However, as we have argued previously (Pridmore & Bendelow 1995), this research history is hardly 'child-centred' as drawings have not always been used to facilitate the so-called 'empowerment' of children; rather the opposite, to 'problematise' and diagnose abnormality and non-conformity. Therefore, the process of inverting this methodology to 'bottom-up' rather than 'top-down' collection of data needs to be undertaken with care and sensitivity if it is truly aiming to treat children as subjects rather than objects. The Brazilian educator Paulo Freire (1972) developed a method in which pictures were used not to transmit the educators' own messages to the learner but to reflect back to the learners the issues with which they themselves were concerned. The DELTA Training Programme (also known as the LEPSA technique) widely used by AMREF in Africa (Hope & Timmel 1984) draws on the philosophy and teaching of Freire. The information needed to identify the priority issues and concerns of the learners affords an opportunity for them to actively participate together with an animater/facilitator in conducting a survey and identifying priority issues and concerns. The animater then uses this information to develop relevant pictures (known as visual codes) which are presented back to the learners as triggers to stimulate discussion. Decoding the pictures to identify the issues expressed in the pictures through discussion raises the critical consciousness of the learners about the nature and root causes of their problems. Discussion then leads to a process of reflection and action (which Freire called praxis) to achieve positive change in their situation.

In similar ways, images have been widely used in health education and training to trigger discussion and seek solutions to health issues. Children's pictures, in conjunction with writing or dialogue, can be a powerful method of exploring the health beliefs of young children which inform health behaviours and influence health status (Barnett et al. 1994; Oakley et al. 1995; Pridmore & Bendelow 1995; Williams et al. 1989, 1989a, 1989b). The large-scale study by Williams et al. (1989a, 1989b) is the UK Health Education Authority's national study of primary school children. In this study 9854 children were asked to draw pictures and write explanatory labels around five key areas of health education—safety, relationships, eating, drugs and exercise/rest. The results provided the insight needed to develop more relevant health learning materials. Bendelow and Oakley (1993) and Bendelow et al. (1996) used the 'draw and write' technique to study children's beliefs of health, illness and cancer (see Case Study 1) and Occleston and King (1993) recently used the technique to evaluate school-based Child-to-Child programs.

Barnett et al. (1994) draw on experience from a number of studies ranging from small-scale local initiatives to a large-scale ongoing research program. The small studies report on the use of children's drawings to explore their health concerns and priorities in a sugar plantation in Zimbabwe, in a school in Liverpool, and in urban primary and secondary schools in Pakistan, Uganda and India. The large-scale research effort is aimed at establishing the current 'state of the art' concerning health education related to HIV/AIDS in Africa and Asia. The technique used in these studies involved children being asked to draw pictures of various health issues and then using these pictures as a basis for further dialogue with individuals or groups. This article makes a valuable contribution to promoting the potential of children's drawings and flags issues of concern around the responsible use of the technique and interpretation of the data collected. The second case study in this chapter used the 'draw and write' technique within Child-to-Child programs but with primary school children in Botswana (Pridmore 1993).

Although the technique is exploratory and is still in the process of being refined and developed, the two case studies provide an empirical demonstration of the high quality and sophisticated nature of the data collected in this manner.

CASE STUDY 1: HEALTH BELIEFS OF 9–10-YEAR-OLDS IN SOUTHEAST ENGLAND

The research described in this case study forms part of a larger study commissioned by the Women's Nationwide Cancer Control Campaign (Bendelow & Oakley 1993; Oakley et al. 1995) to explore levels of knowledge about cancer specifically and beliefs about health and illness generally, in children and young people.

Study sample

A sample of 100 children aged nine or ten in three primary schools in urban, rural and suburban areas of southeast England were interviewed. *School 1* is a small (approximately 100-student) mixed-sex primary school in rural Kent, well-resourced, with a range of parental occupations. *School 2* is a large (500-student) mixed-sex middle school in suburban Surrey in an extremely exclusive 'stockbroker' area. *School 3* is a primary school in the inner-London borough of Islington with a total of about 200 pupils, including approximately 30 per cent from ethnic minority backgrounds, and 10 per cent with special needs. Many of the children have materially deprived backgrounds.

On the first page of the schedule children were asked to give some basic demographic data. There are more boys (fifty-seven) than girls (forty-three) in the sample, and slightly more children from 'working-class' families. Social class was defined by the children's descriptions of what their parents do for a living, using parental occupation (as these were self-definitions it was sometimes problematic to tell from the children's descriptions what their parents do, for instance: 'He helps other schools with their problems and does fences'; or 'Thames water'!). The children were asked where they and their parents were born in order to try to yield some information about ethnicity. Most of the sample (86 per cent) come in the category of 'white British'. Although there is one child of Indian origin in School 1, and one child of Australian/Chinese parents in School 2, other ethnic minority categories are overwhelmingly found in School 3, in the inner-city area. Of the twenty-seven children who took part in the interviews from this school, four were Asian or Indian, three were Greek Cypriot and two were black British (from families originating in the Caribbean).

Children were also asked to describe who lived in their house or flat with them in order to establish types of household. Many of the children included pets and toys in their descriptions, for example: 'Mum, dad, two brothers, two cats, Superted and me'; 'Mum, tenant, hamster and me. Dad is dead'; 'Mum, sister, brother, sister, stepdad, two cats and me.'

Thirteen children in the sample lived in lone-parent households, all headed by females. The largest number of these (seven) were in School 1, with three each in Schools 2 and 3.

Method

A mix of group interviews and discussions was carried out in the three primary schools. Access was negotiated with the headteachers and relevant class teachers and letters requesting parental consent to the children's participation were sent home with the children. The children were also asked if they wished to take part in the project and there were no refusals.

In each of the three schools, the researcher was given free access to the whole class for a period of ninety minutes. The children were given pre-prepared sheets of paper which were blank apart from numbers indicating where to answer the questions asked by the researcher using the interview schedule. The schedule was an adaptation of the 'draw and write' technique devised by Williams, Wetton and

Moon (1989a, 1989b), including some questions specifically related to cancer. The children were guided through the schedule, and were able to ask questions if they were unable to understand the questions. When the schedule had been completed a group discussion was held, the purpose of which was to try to allay any anxieties that may have arisen from discussing 'sensitive' material with the children. For example, several children in School 3 were worried that having a nosebleed meant they had leukaemia; this arose from an episode of the television series *Neighbours* in which a character who was dying from the disease complained of constant nosebleeds. Reassurance was provided. Although the versatility of the data does enable statistical analysis, for the purposes of this chapter we will rely upon a simple qualitative analysis which identified themes and categories and broke them down by geographical location of the school (inner-city and suburban/rural) and gender.

Results

All the children wrote or drew at least two items in response to the requests to indicate factors responsible for health and ill health; most described between two and four, and some covered the whole page. On the whole, boys tended to draw more pictures per page than girls, but girls wrote more. Exercise and healthy eating were acknowledged by the children to be the most important factors in keeping healthy, whereas smoking and bad diet were cited most often as representing unhealthy behaviours. However, especially in terms of unhealthy behaviours, other items were mentioned which included both environmental as well as 'individualistic' factors. For example, inner-city children were more likely to mention violence and pollution.

What makes you healthy?: The major categories of response identified—diet/healthy food, fruit, vegetables, exercise, sport, hygiene, not smoking and sleep—broadly echo the Williams, Wetton and Moon study (1989a). The majority of responses centred on food and exercise. General indications of a healthy diet included fish, cheese, eggs, soup, cereals, 'not eating meat', milk, mineral water, milkshakes, vitamins and iron, and fruit is constantly mentioned so is listed separately, as is the case with vegetables. The category of hygiene includes cleaning teeth, washing and bathing.

What makes you unhealthy?: In similar fashion, on the next blank page, the children were asked to do the following: 'Please write or draw anything you think makes you unhealthy.' Again, the answers were organised into categories—smoking, diet, environment/pollution, violence, hygiene, alcohol, illness. Factors mentioned ranged from personal behaviour and lifestyles to more environmental issues. The category of *diet* includes the following responses: 'being fat', fatty meat, sugar, salt, pop/fizzy drinks, burgers/fast food, chips, crisps, fatty food, cakes, meat, chocolate, sugary food, red meat, 'too much food', 'unhealthy food', school dinners, beans, 'weetabix and lemon custard', 'fish salad', rape seed oil, dieting, no food, and anorexia. *Environment and pollution* includes 'smelly odours', smog, pollution, petrol, bad gases, car fumes, fumes, acid, factories, ozone layer, motorway, cars, running in road, microwaves, cutting down the rainforest, toxic waste, swimming in chlorine, bad water, dustbins, sun, heat, fire, lack of fresh air, computers, litter, and poison. *Violence* includes cuts, mugging, stabbing, knives, fighting, 'dangerous drunks', guns, nuclear arms, bombs, wars, and tanks. *Hygiene* includes 'dirty clothes', not washing, not brushing teeth, not cleaning teeth. *Illness* includes asthma, germs, and infection. Environmental and pollution factors were more frequently mentioned by children in the inner-city schools, and boys were more likely than girls to mention both violence and hygiene.

Beliefs about cancer: On another blank page, children were asked to: 'Please write or draw anything you know about cancer.' The written answers and drawings were again categorised into four main themes: (1) those connected with smoking, often showing fires in the body; (2) those showing bits of the body affected by cancer, often involving loss of hair; (3) drawings depicting cancer as cells; and (4) unpleasant faces, abstract demon-like figures.

Although nearly three-fifths of the children saw cancer as a fatal illness, only one-in-ten saw death as the inevitable consequence. Smoking featured in two-fifths of both the children's pictorial and written answers; more than three-quarters of their ideas about prevention were centred on the avoidance of smoking; and lung cancer was given as the most known cancer by a similar proportion. The perception about cancer next in importance was that of losing hair, which was mentioned by a third of the children, and vividly depicted in many drawings: this was obviously a source of anxiety across gender and schools.

Observations on Case Study 1

Although the method focuses on drawing, it still requires a certain degree of articulation, which may have been a problem for children whose first language was not English. However, all of the children in this sample were able to participate, although the quality of responses varied a great deal. There were two children in School 3 who were classed as having 'special needs' and were unable to read or write. However, they were still able to participate in the exercise by drawing pictures and through the assistance of the class helper who wrote down their responses.

The biggest problems encountered in this research were ethical ones: although we had gained consent from both parents and children, the classroom setting makes it very difficult for a child to refuse to take part. Some children asked whether the responses would be marked, or spellings checked, and were given reassurance that this was not the case, and that indeed they would not be seen by anyone other than the researcher. Also, it was not really possible to gauge the full extent of any anxieties raised by the research, especially with regard to cancer, but the group discussion afterwards was an attempt to address these. On the whole, the children expressed a strong desire for *accurate* knowledge, and the class teachers, who felt they knew the children well, thought they all benefited from the session.

CASE STUDY 2: HEALTH BELIEFS OF CHILDREN AGED 9–10 IN BOTSWANA

This case study presents the findings of an exercise carried out with primary school children in Botswana, to explore their beliefs about health and disease.[1]

The study sample

The sample comprised 111 primary school children aged nine or ten years. Of these children 100 were Batswana from schools near the capital city of Gaborone and eleven children were from an isolated settlement school for Bushmen children in Ghanzi District. Eighty-five of the Batswana children came from three similar rural schools within a 60-kilometre radius of Gaborone, where families subsisted on farming together with money earned by the men working in the mines in South Africa; whereas fifteen of the children were from an urban slum school in central Gaborone. The Bushmen children belong to a small marginalised ethnic group who are traditionally hunters and gatherers in the Central Kalahari Region of Botswana.

Method

The 'draw and write' exercise was used within an action research program which aimed to evaluate the effectiveness of children as health educators using the Child-to-Child approach (Pridmore 1993). All the children available in each school at the time of the school visit who were aged nine or ten years were involved in the exercise. However, in one particularly large rural Batswana school there was only time to involve the first fifty-three children who presented themselves in the classroom. In each school the draw and write exercise was conducted by the researcher during a visit which had previously been arranged to discuss some preliminary findings of the study program. Parents (and other community members), teachers and children had come for this meeting and it was therefore possible to obtain their consent for the draw and write exercise without giving prior notice. This avoided the possibility of children being rehearsed. At the time this exercise was carried out the researcher was well known as she had visited each school and worked with the children on many occasions during the course of the research program. She was therefore able to be present in the classroom to lead the exercise with the minimum of disruption.

Before starting the draw and write exercise the researcher trained one of the school teachers to help as a facilitator. During this training session it was agreed that only the Setswana words 'tshameka' (healthy), 'nwa' (unhealthy) and 'swa' (die) would be used. (The selection and use of these words was important as words influence thinking and response.)

Results

Each response consisted of a picture and a written comment. These were analysed together to identify major categories and sub-categories before individual responses were classified. The pictures were factual rather than symbolic and no attempt was made to use them projectively. There were no substantive differences in the data by gender or among the urban and rural Batswana schools and in most cases their responses have been reported together. There were important differences between the Batswana schools and the Bushmen school and their responses are recorded separately.

What makes you healthy?: The responses of the eleven Bushmen children fell into four categories—food, exercise, medicine and hygiene. By contrast, the responses of 100 Batswana children fell into only one—food. Five Bushmen children drew pictures of themselves involved in exercise whereas none of the Batswana children depicted exercise. Surprisingly, none of the children recorded sleeping, resting or keeping safe as causes of health.

What makes you unhealthy?: Seven out of the eleven Bushmen children drew pictures of unhealthy habits (drinking and smoking), and fighting and accidents were also frequently drawn. Only one child identified disease and one child drew herself 'being hungry'. In contrast, most (66 per cent) of Batswana children drew sugar and sweets, a few (10 per cent) drew children eating dirty food and water or not disposing of faeces in a hygienic manner. People taking traditional medicine, smoking and having worm infestations were also depicted, but rarely. Bushmen and Batswana children drew fewer pictures in response to this question than to the other two questions, which may reflect difficulty in understanding the notion of being unhealthy.

What do most people die from?: There was a greatly increased response rate for this question. Four categories were identified from Bushmen children—violence, accidents, wild animals and suicide. No diseases were recorded and this was puzzling because there was a high incidence of infectious childhood disease in the area. This may have been caused by children remembering the more violent causes of death more than the common-place or because disease was considered to be only one of many factors which ultimately resulted in death within their own understanding of the universe. The same four categories were identified in the pictures from Batswana children but there were also many pictures of diseases and sorcery (witches and spirits). Infectious diseases, (recorded by 90 per cent of Batswana girls but only 44 per cent of boys), included AIDS, tuberculosis, measles, mumps, polio, cholera, diarrhoea, scabies, diphtheria, chicken pox, malaria, leprosy and 'bacteria from water'. Non-infectious diseases recorded were heart trouble, eye trouble, 'aches and pains'. Suicide was recorded by twenty-one children (31 per cent of girls, 7 per cent of boys).

Observations on Case Study 2

This case study further illustrates the potential of the draw and write technique by describing how it was used in Botswana primary schools to explore beliefs about health, illness and death. Batswana children would clearly accept messages about healthy eating but might have more difficulty accepting other health messages such as the need for regular exercise, rest, relaxation, sleep, good personal hygiene and keeping themselves safe. Bushmen children would accept messages about exercise (playing, singing and dancing), bathing and eating enough food, but find it more difficult to accept messages about nutritious combinations of foods and keeping themselves safe. Children had particular difficulty with the concept of being unhealthy and did not appear to link being unhealthy with dying. The children found it particularly difficult to think of things they did (or could do) to make themselves unhealthy and the researcher observed that most Batswana children quickly drew pictures of sugar or sweets and then stopped. After a while some children continued drawing and filled up the page with drawings of other foodstuffs such as fruits, vegetables and staples even though they had drawn the same foodstuffs when asked to draw what made them healthy. These later drawings may not have been a true reflection of children's beliefs about being unhealthy but simply a desire to appear occupied and fill up the blank space. The study has shown that Batswana children perceived death to be caused both by diseases and by 'spirit people' and also suggested that there are discrepancies between the world view of Batswana and Bushmen children.

DISCUSSION

This chapter has provided an empirical demonstration of the high quality and sophisticated nature of the data which can be collected from young children using the exploratory draw and write technique.

Methodologically, there are considerable strengths around the potential for representation, versatility, replicability and universality. We hope to have demonstrated the value of using children's images as a means of interpreting the world in which they live and have emphasised that as a method, it allows for a more subjective and phenomenological input than many more traditional 'top down' approaches. In other words, the child's lived experience is able to be better represented than by the use of pre-determined and a priori adult categories. The method was especially valuable because the children enjoyed the process of drawing: it appeared to have encouraged them to relax, to concentrate their thoughts and to take time to reflect before expressing themselves. Most importantly, the methodology allowed children to express through drawing ideas for which they did not have words and then seek help to write about these ideas. Consequently, this methodology has the potential to enable all children to participate, including young children, children with special needs and those who cannot read or write or are unable to do so in the language of instruction.

It is significant that the school teachers and children involved in the two case studies appeared to have benefited from their involvement in the research. Some of the teachers said they had gained new insight into the children's perceptions of health; they were excited and surprised by the richness of the children's responses and considered draw and write to be a valuable method for their own classroom practice. The experience they gained in using this innovative 'bottom up' approach enabled them to become researchers and provided an effective catalyst for dialogue and critical reflection on current classroom practices.

Although the potential benefits of the draw and write technique are increasingly being recognised there are also limitations and concerns over its proper use which need to be addressed urgently if this technique is to be promoted widely for use with children. The power of this technique, deriving largely from the way in which the act of drawing can help to break down barriers, allows powerful emotions to be expressed; serious thought must be given to helping children come to terms with these emotions. Cases of special need must be followed up through further discussion or action. Issues of consent and confidentiality, interpretation and ownership of data are paramount.

There are also concerns over ownership and use of the drawings and writing. In both case studies the aims of the research were explained in simple terms to the children and it was stressed that participation was entirely voluntary. The question of confidentiality needs to be addressed. This is especially important where children are being asked to provide sensitive data, for example, relating to sexual practices or drug use which they may not want teachers to see. Researchers will need to think how confidentiality can be ensured while allowing the insight provided by the technique to inform action through feedback to the children, teachers and others. In Case Study 1, the aims of the research were explained in simple terms to the children and it was stressed that participation was entirely voluntary. Permission to keep their interview schedules and to use the drawings (anonymously) in any subsequent reports or publications was also asked of the children. In the Botswana exercise it was felt to be sufficient to gain the agreement of the children and stress that the exercise was not a test and that no marks were going to be given by teachers.

There are also concerns over interpretation and use of drawings as primary data. Most of the pictures collected in the case studies were realistic representations—for example, drawings of fruits or vegetables or people dancing—but in the UK study some of the depictions of cancer tended to be more abstract. This raises important concerns over their interpretation and where pictures are more symbolic it is argued that children need to interpret these drawings themselves and that their written or recorded comments must be used as the basis of analysis. Many experts are rightly sceptical about the validity of using children's drawings projectively (Thomas & Silk 1990) and the draw and write technique makes no claim to do this. Rather than being used in a diagnostic sense, this chapter contends that the use of children's drawing and writing is a simple way of exploring children's beliefs about health and of describing the society in which they live.

CONCLUSION

The draw and write technique is an innovative and participatory method of visualising health and as such it is a valuable research method. This chapter demonstrates that the technique can be used to explore the perceptions of young children about health and ill health and can be used in diverse cultural contexts to provide good quality data. The use of a 'bottom up' or child-centred approach enables children to take control and helps develop their capabilities. Although the draw and write technique is exploratory, and is in the process of being refined and developed, there is now a considerable body of research data to confirm that it is a powerful research method with considerable potential for curriculum development. It can be used to improve the relevance and effectiveness of educational interventions by helping to overcome the serious problems of design and delivery experienced by traditional health education programs which fail to address children's own experience and explanations for health and ill health. It can be used to tap into local health needs and concerns and adapt health messages to the local context. It allows for the study of difference and range, rather than seeing children as homogenous groups. However, the technique is still in the process of being developed and needs to be carefully and sensitively adapted for use in different contexts. Further consideration needs to be given to the constraints as well as the benefits of the technique if its potential for enabling all children to participate is to be realised.

NOTE

1   The study was conducted in Botswana, a large land-locked country in southern Africa where 85 per cent of primary-school age children now attend school but where over half of all households are living in poverty. The majority of the population are Bantu tribes but there is also a minority indigenous population of

Bushmen. The Bushmen are also known as Baswara but prefer to be called Bushmen to highlight their marginalised position.

REFERENCES

Barnett, E., Francis, V., de Koning, K. & Shaver, T. 1994 'Drawing and dialogue' unpublished document, The Learning Resources Group, Liverpool School of Tropical Medicine, Liverpool

Bendelow, G. & Oakley, A. 1993 *Young People and Cancer* Social Science Research Unit, Institute of Education, University of London, London

Bendelow, G., Oakley, A. & Williams, S.J. 1996 'It makes you bald: Children's beliefs about health and cancer prevention' *Health Education* vol. 96, no. 3, pp. 8–15

Freire, P. 1972 *Pedagogy of the Oppressed* Penguin, Harmondsworth, UK

Hope, A. & Timmel, S. 1984 *Training for Transformation Book 1* Mambo Press, Gweru, Zimbabwe

James, A. & Prout, A. 1990 *Contemporary Issues in the Sociological Study of Childhood* Falmer Press, London

Kalnins, I., McQueen, D., Backett, K., Curtice, L. & Currie, C. 1992 'Children, empowerment and health empowerment: Some new directions in research and practice' *Health Promotion International* no. 7, pp. 55–59

Mayall, B. (ed.) 1994 *Children's Childhoods: Observed and Experienced* Falmer, London
——1996 *Children, Health and the Social Order* Open University Press, Milton Keynes

Oakley, A., Bendelow, G., Barnes, J., Buchanan, M. & Nauseam Hasten, O. 1995 'Health and cancer prevention: Knowledge and beliefs of children and young people' *British Medical Journal* no. 310, pp. 1029–33

Occleston, S. & King, P. 1993 'Innovation in health promotion' *Community Participation Healthy Cities Newsletter* vol. 5, no. 2, June, Department of Public Health, Liverpool, UK

Pridmore, P. 1993 *Children as Health Educators Using the Child-to-Child Approach. Preliminary Report of a Field Study* Paper prepared for a UNICEF (Botswana) Consultation Meeting in Gaborone, July 1993, Institute of Education, University of London

Pridmore, P. & Bendelow, G. 1995 'Images of health: Exploring beliefs of children using the "draw and write" technique' *Health Education Journal* no. 54, pp. 473–88

Thomas, G.V. & Silk, A.M.J. 1990 *An Introduction to the Psychology of Children's Drawings* Harvester Wheatsheaf, Hemel Hempstead, UK

Williams, D., Wetton, N. & Moon, A. 1989a *A Picture of Health: What Do You Do That Makes You Healthy and Keeps You Healthy?* Health Education Authority, London
——1989b *A Way In: Five Key Areas of Health Education* Health Education Authority, London

9 Health and the discourse of weight control

Deirdre Davies

In general the issue of health and weight is assumed to have a straight-forward relationship. Most people in contemporary Western societies are aware, to a greater or lesser degree, that to be 'overweight' is 'unhealthy'. It could be argued that such an understanding lies at the level of commonsense knowledge, which is buttressed by the information and messages from public health authorities and through health promotions which emphasise that in order to be healthy, there is a need to be slim and weight controlled. The assumed links between health and weight are made explicit in the recommendation put forward by the Nutritional Taskforce of the Better Health Commission (cited in Santich 1995, p. 182) for a 25 per cent reduction in the prevalence of obesity by the year 2000, and in a newspaper headline stating 'Fat People Cost Us Millions', used to introduce an article about a health study on the cost of weight-related illnesses (*The West Australian* 1995, 6 April, p. 11). This chapter will explore these links by examining the concept of health and how it is articulated within the discourse of weight control.

The word discourse is used in the Foucauldian sense to refer to the cohesive and relational nature of knowledge, language and practices which surround—and indeed bring into being—concepts such as weight and overweight. Such a discourse makes some ways of knowing, seeing and speaking about weight allowable while leaving other ways of understanding and seeing marginalised and silenced. For example, it is difficult to see the generous proportions of the Japanese Sumo wrestler being viewed as athletic and strong within an Australian context, or that it was once thought that to be large and 'overweight', as measured against today's norms, was a sign of a strong constitution and good health. The discourse of weight control is best understood in terms of a governing discourse and as such is a strategy for social control. The discourse of weight control serves to regulate bodies—especially women's bodies—by a transformation of bodies considered 'overweight', and therefore out of control, undisciplined, deviant, and dangerously unhealthy. The transformation will, of course, involve weight loss leading to weight control, and begins with the recognition and incorporation of the self, by the self, into the category of 'overweight'.

The categorisation of bodies is achieved through the use of normalising height/weight tables (or Body Mass Index tables) and/or body size measurements such as the waist-to-hip ratio.[1] Leaving aside questions about how it is decided what constitutes 'overweight', and the validity of normalising standards such as height/weight tables, it must be recognised that there are real-life effects and social implications for people whose bodies are labelled as 'overweight'. A person perceived to be the bearer of 'excess' weight is considered to be the owner of a 'weight problem' because the categorisation of 'overweight' comes with an entire wealth of meanings about the 'overweight' body and about what it is to be an 'overweight' person. Such meanings have many sources, as the dominant knowledge and meanings which surround the concept of a 'weight problem' are generated through numerous experts and their specialist knowledges, such as medicine, epidemiology, psychology, nutrition, chemistry, and sport/fitness sciences.

It is therefore not surprising that the notion of a 'weight problem' has many facets and that the discourses surrounding body weight, in particular 'overweight', are quite varied and sometimes contradictory, while still retaining unifying themes due to the common knowledges upon which they are grounded. Thus, co-existent within the sphere of weight control there are dieting and exercise programs like 'Weight Watchers', 'Gloria Marshall', and 'Easyslim' based on food control (including calorie counting or portion control) and exercise regimes, alongside anti-diet programs such as *Fat is a Feminist Issue*,[2] 'Nectar' and 'Eat to Live', which work on the assumption that our bodies know best but we've forgotten how to listen to them. No matter how different, they remain joined in the assumption that there is a 'norm' in regard to 'fatness' and that there is a need to be weight controlled. Weight control literature in general, and programs like those already mentioned, regardless of the obvious differences, are embedded in common assumptions about weight, body size, beauty, sexuality, and health. As mentioned, it is the concept of health within the discourse of weight control which is the topic of this chapter. To explore how clearly the relationship between health and weight is seen within the discourse of weight control, and how is it articulated, the discussion will focus on the analysis of literature produced by the Heart Foundation of Australia, popular Australian weight control magazines, and Australian books on dieting advice. This will be followed by a brief discussion on the implication of these links in the lives of fifteen women interviewed who are considered 'overweight'. I argue that the governing discourse of weight control is not as totally dominating as might be supposed from a reading of the powerful and pervasive messages contained in weight control literature: that one must be slim in order to be healthy.

JOINING THE DOTS: THE LINKING OF
HEALTH AND WEIGHT

By interrogating the discourses surrounding weight control and concentrating on the issue of health within the discourse it becomes apparent the concerns over weight and health communicated to the general public lie within the language of epidemiology. In other words, much of the discourse surrounding weight control as it relates to health is indebted to research into the health of populations, and thus lies within the gamut of public health. The *Heart Facts 1992* report issued by the Heart Foundation of Australia in 1994 illustrates this point in the highlights, or report summary, with the statement: 'Far too many Australians remain at higher risk of heart and blood vessel disease through cigarette smoking, high blood pressure, high cholesterol, overweight and under exercise' (*Heart Facts 1992* 1994, p. 1). Such a statement only makes sense using the concepts of 'prevalence' and 'risk factors' constructed through epidemiological research. The next point made is that 'Overweight and obesity are becoming more common' (*Heart Facts 1992* 1994, p. 1). What is no more than a general observation nonetheless has a tone of condemnation, only understood in relation to the previous point on 'risk factors'. 'Overweight' and 'obesity' have become negatively implicated in health through association, via epidemiology. Excess weight is understood to be a causative factor in cardiovascular diseases through statistical correlations or associations with morbidity due to heart failure and heart-related conditions. This 'fact' is so accepted that the report's inclusion of weight under the section of 'Prevalence of Major Risk Factors' is left unexplained (as are the other risk factors mentioned) and merely involves a descriptive paragraph on the statistical instances of excess weight for the two sexes and different age groups. A second mention of weight is made in the discussion on lowering death rates through controlling 'risk' factors. But again it only describes the prevalence of 'overweight' in the studied population without any discussion on the link to death rates. The acceptance of weight as a causative factor can be seen in other publications by the Heart Foundation on *Living with Angina* (1993b), *High Blood Pressure—The Facts* (1994), and *Healthy Eating for the Heart* (1993a) with sections entitled respectively, 'Keep to a healthy weight', 'Control your weight' and 'Get that weight off' all given as strategies for controlling the above conditions.

The existence of debates questioning the very premise of so-called 'risk' factors is left silenced and disregarded within the Heart Foundation report and booklets. So taken for granted are terms like 'cholesterol' that it may be surprising to know it is a 'scientifically inaccurate' term which obviates distinctions and 'enables it to be given a range of roles in the body and in relationship to other risk factors that it does not have' (Hughes 1996, p. 2). With regard to the Heart Foundation literature, the links with mortality and risk factors become even more questionable in light of Hughes' observation that 50 per cent of deaths from coronary heart disease occur in the absence of any known 'risk' factors (Hughes 1996, p. 4). Experts also disagree on just how much 'excess' weight constitutes 'overweight'. How accurately does weight measure excess fat? Is the distribution of body weight (fat to be precise) more important as a health indicator than total body weight? (For discussions on these issues see Croft et al. 1995; Ernsberger & Haskew 1987; Garrow 1984; Pouliot et al. 1994.) In general, epidemiology fails to problematise research variables. Therefore, the search for statistical patterns in the population using such categories is accepted as a practical means by which to identify and explain the occurrence of disease and to decide which issues are to be considered health concerns within a population. These patterns are correlations which, via the language of epidemiology, are transmuted into causative factors as in the examples above. This is quite clearly the case in the Heart Foundation booklet, *Healthy Eating for the Heart*, where 'being overweight', along with eating too much fat and cholesterol, is given as a cause for high blood cholesterol (1993, p. 7). 'Overweight' is given the dubious position of an independent variable with high cholesterol a depende   nt variable, thereby establishing a statistically generated causative link between the two variables. Hence 'overweight' is labelled a cause of high cholesterol, while left unclarified is that it is just as possible that a diet high in fat/cholesterol may cause both high blood cholesterol and 'overweight'. 'Overweight' would then be seen as a dependent variable along with high cholesterol and cardiovascular disease. However, it should be kept in mind that to propose a relationship between any factors such as high blood pressure, high cholesterol, 'overweight', and cardiovascular disease is, in the first place, to accept the assumption that any of these variables or factors are linked at all. (For a full discussion on the problems of epidemiology see Petersen and Lupton 1996, ch. 2.)

Claims that 'excess' weight is causally related to ill health is not always dogmatically asserted. Sometimes arguments employ more speculative and tentative language, as seen, for example, in the phrases '*seem* to have a strong influence' (Heart Foundation of Australia 1994b, p. 9) or 'being overweight *tends* to raise blood cholesterol levels' [my emphasis] (Heart Foundation of Australia 1993, p. 13). Further, epidemiological research is contested within the discipline and larger scientific community through alternative readings of existing research data and the publication of dissenting research, for example Ernsberger and Haskew's *Rethinking Obesity: An Alternative View of its Health Implications* (1987), and the well known work of Ancel Keys (e.g. 1980, 1989). However, it is rare to find alternative reports in public health literature (e.g. Heart Foundation of Australia) or popular media. The 'facts' are presented as unequivocal and totally relevant to each individual. This is very clear in *The Diet Dilemma*, by Rosemary Stanton, a well known Australian author on nutrition, in which the statement 'Excess body fat is a health hazard' is supported by reference to a list of health problems including coronary heart disease, high blood pressure, some cancers, arthritis and gout (1991, p. 27). Stanton makes it clear that she is discussing 'excess body fat', not simply 'weight' but nevertheless writes about losing weight and 'overweight' in relation to health. The language used to discuss 'overweight' and its relation to each condition illustrates the absolute surety in which epidemiological data are presented to the general public, with statements like 'Medical researchers are now *agreed* that excess body fat is indeed a risk factor for heart disease' (1991, p. 30), and 'There is *no doubt* that excess body fat increases the risks of high blood pressure' [my emphasis] (1991, p. 31). Stanton is so sure about her position that she feels able to claim that 'Those who dispute this are often overweight themselves and look for some justification not to lose their excess fat' and that 'some have chosen to read only specific articles in medical journals' (1991, p. 27). As such she throws a blanket of surety over any contentious views while assuming a mantle of objectivity she denies to those with alternative views to her own. Those who would challenge current dictums are discredited by a bias supposedly borne of their own 'weight problem'. However, according to Santich, there is in fact a 'growing body of dissenters' (1995, p. 205) with influence and, importantly, credibility and 'a new era of dietary advice is on the horizon of the twenty-first century' (1995, p. 205). In her view, 'the bogeyman of overweight has had its day' (Santich 1995, p. 208).

As shown, there are moments within the discourse of weight control where the gross population statistics of the epidemiologist are apparent. Even if not always in strict numerical terms, the messages are at the very least couched in concepts such as 'risk' factors, prevalence, and cause, springing directly from statistical calculations of populations. However, it is often a more subtle percolation of knowledge that appears in magazines and popular media, by way of advice on lifestyle and the behavioural changes needed to attain a weight controlled body. The transition from the health of populations to individualised advice occurs because, even when health concerns are placed in a social/structural framework, the terms of reference remain the individual and individual bodies as perceived through a medical gaze. Within public health it is a medical model of the body, stemming from the scientific framework in which it is grounded, that is deployed in the same instance as concepts of population. The biomedical body is conceptualised as individualised but universally the same, 'natural', with a mind/body split, and often depicted in terms of a machine or system. It is based upon scientific knowledge which works upon the belief, and absolute confidence, that scientific endeavours have the ability to completely understand the body and illness. The locus of disease is understood to lie within the body and made obvious through the presence of signs and symptoms that require identification and interpretation to accurately name and control pathology. In so doing there is always a continual construction of what is to be considered 'normal' and 'healthy'. It follows that 'normal' body weight defined and constructed with the use of height/weight tables and understood as healthy body weight is at once reliant on the construction of the 'overweight' body, and indeed the 'underweight' body, as 'abnormal' and 'unhealthy'. Using a medical model, body features, characteristics and differences—in this case body size—come to be viewed as possible signs to be read for pathology and abnormality.

Integral to the medical model of the body and the identification of abnormality is the understanding that the body and its needs are quantifiable. It is the connection of the body to accurate measurement that forms the basis of a great deal of nutritional advice. Bryan Turner argues that modern dietary regimes are part of a wider strategy of 'rational calculation over the body' (1982, p. 267) and that iatro-mathematics, that is, the linking of nature to numbers with regards to the body, has made the body seem unquestioningly quantifiable. He further elaborates on the necessity of iatromathematics as a theoretical link for the existence of dietetics as we know it (Turner 1982, p. 259); to which one might add weight loss, fitness, exercise and general advice on well-being. The quantifiable and isolated body, or medical model of the body, persists throughout public health literature and information despite the analysis occurring at the level of populations, and claims to add the social and environmental dimensions to the identification of disease and causes of ill health (Petersen & Lupton 1996, p. 34). The result is what could be described as a bifocal gaze which enables public health to identify health concerns at the level of populations, through the science of epidemiology, at the same time as producing preventive measures directed at individuals, as seen in health promotion campaigns such as the 'Be Active Every Day—Heart Walks' campaign in which the newspaper advertisements published throughout 1996 began with '[d]id *you* take *your* heart for a walk today?' [my emphasis] (e.g. *The West Australian* 1995, 13 September).

With an approach to health focused on individuals comes the notion of personal responsibility built around the concept of rationality and the rational subject. The unacknowledged assumption is that if people are given the ability and knowledge they will make 'rational' choices about their own health care. Hence the focus for interventions revolves around questions of how to educate individuals, how to change socially condoned 'bad' habits/practices, and how to provide equitably the wherewithal for all sectors of society to partake of health-giving behaviour (e.g. see Hetzel & McMichael 1987). It follows that education is often a lynchpin for health promotion campaigns and a central feature within the discourse of weight control. Many weight control programs—such as 'Weight Watchers', 'Easyslim' and 'Gloria Marshall'—assume a pedagogical model. The emphasis on education can also be seen in diet and weight loss magazines with the format for information delivery generally following a recipe of question pages, health advisory sections and informative articles on a seemingly limitless range of topics. Such magazines are filled with inconsequential, seemingly unrelated information. One edition of *Weight Watchers* (June/July 1996) includes information on the healthful effects of laughter, the effect of smoking on wrinkles, food as preventive medicine, along with weight loss hints and diet plans. The information may sometimes seem spurious but is often backed up with statements and claims 'that recent research show . . .' or 'recent research has proven . . .'. It is at these times that the distant echo of epidemiology can most clearly be heard.

As already indicated, health understood as a societal issue through population statistics, or epidemiology, is at once constructed as an individual concern and responsibility. So along with health information in diet magazines, there is advice on personal behaviour through which the reader is continually reminded that it is the self who holds the responsibility. *Slimming* magazine well illustrates such overriding acceptance of personal responsibility in an article on metabolism and fat when it concludes that, despite our limited ability to change metabolism because of inheritance and hormones, we 'all have the power to get and keep our weight where it should be' and that although 'for some of us it's not easy . . . we can do it!' (*Slimming* 1996, April, p. 51). The reiteration of personal responsibility, and the need for personal control even in the light of individual genetic differences is pervasive, and appears in many guises throughout weight control literature. Stanton articulates it quite openly, in a discussion on the psychological reasons for losing weight, where it is acknowledged that discrimination against the 'overweight' is a problem and that 'We may be appalled by the societal problems of overweight people' (1991, p. 28). Stanton suggests we (that is, society) should try to eliminate the problem, but the final piece of advice is, 'The best way to avoid it may be to avoid being too fat' (1991, p. 28). In so doing Stanton places the onus for change squarely with the person labelled as 'overweight', for whom the only sensible decision is to lose weight. Once again the rational self emerges along with the notion of responsibility; one implicitly implying the other. A decision that fails to comply with the sensible suggestion of weight loss can only be understood as nonsensical; even irrational. It is inevitable that such a personal decision is also seen as a personal responsibility, and a failure to comply with health advice is seen as a dereliction of duty in the care of the self.

SPEAKING OUT OF TURN: 'I CAN BE
OVERWEIGHT AND HEALTHY'

I have been describing a 'victim blaming' paradigm which exists despite the best intentions of those who might claim otherwise. Excess weight (more specifically excess fat) is understood to be self-inflicted and a result of not managing one's body appropriately. Further, the 'overweight' body is understood to be a health 'risk' that is easily controlled by the self. The implication is that there is a lack of participation in one's own health care and that fault lies with the bearer of excess weight. In part, such a judgement is possible because the concept of health employed is one which understands it to be something to strive for and achieve, not just accept as fate or as a product of good genes. Within this framework, a body experienced by the self as being healthy, or at least not unwell, can still be defined as unhealthy by statistical measures and correlations with health problems of given populations.

Health is a term employed uncritically and without explanation throughout the terrain of weight control in the proliferation of literature and manuals on being 'overweight' and how to lose weight. However, it becomes clear on a closer reading that there is a particular concept of health being articulated within general health messages and the discourse of weight control in particular. Definitions of health are constructed around a concept of 'optimal' well-being and are no longer simply understood as an absence of disease. Health messages impel us to become the 'worried well' (Harris 1994), living and caring for 'sorts of "non-bodies" that experience "virtual illness" and "virtual health"' (Hughes 1994, p. 57) due to possibilities of illness and health 'risks' that position 'the body in a state of transitional ambivalence where bodies are both well and ill at the same time' (Hughes 1994, p. 57). The healthy body must be produced and worked towards because, even if there is an apparent absence of disease, health does not necessarily exist. That is not to say that all bodies are seen to be at the same degree of 'risk'. There are bodies that approximate, or align, more closely to images of optimal health—that is, the slender, clear skinned, fit, 'whole' body—and there are other bodies that do not, such as the 'overweight' body, the physically disabled body, the unclean body, and the 'leaking' body.

In such a social climate, it is difficult to conceive of a person considered 'overweight' finding it possible to speak about being in good health, as to be considered 'overweight' is to be part of a focal group in the governing discourse of weight control, and therefore a special target and concern for weight and health messages. Using interviews carried out with women categorised as 'overweight', I will briefly discuss how they were able to 'speak out of turn' about being in 'good health' as women of size. Thus far, I have concentrated on the ways health and weight are connected and on the powerfully prescriptive messages on the care of the self throughout weight control discourse. While not wishing to diminish the power of the governing discourse of weight control there is a need to acknowledge that the women I interviewed all spoke of being in good health, or of feeling well. This was possible because they applied very personal standards to their meanings of health, as epitomised by the following quotes. Alice, when asked if she had a healthy body replied, yes 'because I feel quite strong, I don't feel weak and enfeebled at all'. Alice describes her 'criteria' for health as

> really to be able to do things I want to do and to feel good. To be able to swim quite a way. I love swimming, I love being at the beach. To be able to walk a good distance . . . having a walk with friends . . . walking in a different country, doing a lot of walking . . . those things, that's what I consider good health.

Similarly, Shane describes good health as 'being able to walk up a flight of stairs without puffing, or [not] being all puffed out'. It became obvious that the women construct their sense of personal health predominantly around an absence of disease and illness, not around the understandings of health as a project that dominate the discourses of health and weight control.

The women all spoke from an individual experience of health and not as members of a health 'risk' category. Although the statistics of epidemiology would have their bodies configured as 'unhealthy', they have their own particular criteria by which they claim 'good health'. They speak from points of 'difference', in the face of health messages built upon 'experts' empiricist methodologies' (Harris 1994, p. 45) that would reduce their 'diversity to a question of measurement, to a matter of social norms' (Harris 1994, p. 45), and averages, which remove any 'particular content from the formal chain of thought and thus universalises behaviour, bodies and experience' (Harris 1994, p. 45). That all people unified through body size/weight will have a common or identical fate does not fit with what they know to be the lived experience of their lives, punctuated as lives are with the vagaries of chance, luck, contingencies and the unexpected. They live in the 'particular' and, although there may be some sense of anxiety about the management of uncertainty, or not meeting social demands of body size, there is also some confidence in difference. Such confidence is reinforced through experience and health stories about families and friends that sit in direct contradiction to dominant medical understandings about causes of disease and the maintenance of health.

The phrase 'lay epidemiology', coined by Davison et al. (1992) to describe the ways in which people construct their understandings of health and the incidence of ill health through the experiences of those around them (cited in Petersen & Lupton 1996, p. 51), provides the means by which to understand the importance of the contrary health stories told by the women interviewed. Beth, a woman aged in her mid-forties explained to me:

> . . . the number of people I know who are incredibly fit, dropped down dead at forty or forty five years old . . . One of my clients who is, what forty, he worked out. He did this, that and the other thing, put himself on a radical diet and lost a lot of weight. He had a massive stroke . . . he still comes in to see me and it's irreparable, oh dear, it is obviously a stroke . . . Another client, she used to work out two, three or four times a week, she had a stroke.

Kaz, a politically active woman, told a story from a news headline, about a young athlete who died of a heart attack

> . . . who looked a fit athlete in their twenties and collapsed . . . well excuse me, I don't think they were real healthy, you know what I mean. Twenty-year-old sports people are gonna drop dead (laugh) but I am sure that they had the best food intake, really good exercise and all that stuff that we perceive as good health. And well I am alive and they are not.

Kaz, although knowledgeable about 'health giving' practices, insists upon the inclusion of fate within her calculations on health and life and so states: 'that there are things that can go wrong, that you know it doesn't matter what you eat it's not gonna make a lot of difference.'

That is not to say that the women I spoke with take good health for granted or remain totally untouched by current directives to care for the self. Most find it is possible to ignore health messages to a point, but they inevitably find them more difficult to ignore when confronted by the rhetoric of foreboding deployed by health 'experts' in much of the information on weight and health. 'Overweight' is seen to have reached epidemic proportions and is named as the modern epidemic with constant references to the cost for 'the community'. There are forecasts that the 'overweight' individual is a time bomb waiting to go off, and according to Mr Shilton, a West Australian Heart Foundation spokesperson, 'the warning bells are sounding' (cited in The West Australian 1997, 3 May, p. 11). Terms such as '. . . premature death . . .' and '. . . a national problem . . .', pervasive within the Heart Foundation literature, are perhaps less obvious scare tactics but are no less dramatic. With such rhetorical devices it is hardly surprising that the concept of health as a project does not totally escape the women interviewed. For example, Shane has a clear concept of her program for good health which includes 'eating well, living a good reasonable lifestyle, no excesses, and perhaps being positive in your mind'. Alice reiterates this reflexive attitude to health as she states 'you should always be concerned about your health because I think it affects your mind too. You know I believe that you are connected to your body and you are a part of your body, and you know I think it makes you feel more positive if you are healthy.' It is apparent that ignorance and irresponsibility are not apt descriptions of these women's attitudes to health. All the women interviewed displayed a good general knowledge of health issues and a strong sense of responsibility in the care of the self. However, such care was not informed entirely upon medical and scientific knowledge, but rather, it was built upon a complex conglomeration of scientific and non-scientific knowledges and importantly through personal observations and experiences.

According to Petersen (1996) there is a potential for those seen to be in 'at risk' categories, who do not take up 'preventative action', to be seen as failing in their 'duties of citizenship' (1996, p. 56). It is clear there is a reality to this potential but it is equally evident that the women interviewed are able, in some ways, to avert implications that they are less than good citizens. By taking an individualised perception of health and size the women break what is seemingly a necessarily negative link between the two. Further, through a selective attention to directives on health care practices, such as less fat and more vegetables, they feel they fulfil current demands for individual responsibility and so remain, to a degree, guilt free about their body size. This point is crucial as the discourse of weight control constructs a sense of individual responsibility for 'the community' by reminders that one's 'overweight' body is a drain on the social body, and a burden to society resulting from an irresponsible lifestyle. Averting such messages proves to be even more complicated and yet strategic for women, who carry a double burden of responsibility. As mothers, women are caretakers of not just their own health but also that of their families and of future generations. The women interviewed, who are mothers, feel deeply the sense of responsibility they have for the health of their partners and children, both in the present and future. Delia, who knows herself to be particularly sensitive to comments due to her own size, when reflecting on her childhood, spoke about the string of diets her mother placed her on because of the pressure upon mothers to have the perfect child. She told me:

my mother-in-law often says to me about Mitchell's weight, or some-body else will say something to me about Mitchell's weight . . . they're doing to me what was done to my mother and people will always do that if a child is big, or what they class as a big size. Then people can't help themselves, they have to say something, because they think that you are sitting at home stuffing this child stupid and that's why it has a weight problem . . . they see it as something that has to be fixed because you see if a child has buck teeth they say why don't you take him to the orthodontist . . .

Several of the women are poignantly aware that because of their own size they are particularly concerned that their children not be 'over-weight' because it might reflect on them as bad mothers, and thus, by default, bad citizens.

CONCLUSION

The discourse of weight control is riven with health information and messages linking disease and ill health with body weight through the statistics of epidemiology. The credibility of this knowledge is rarely questioned publicly as science discourse is privileged in our decisions of truth and falsity (Harris 1994, p. 21). Harris argues that what becomes disqualified is our own low ranking, local and self-knowledge (1994, p. 21), or as Harding refers to it: 'knowledge based in experience' (1987, p. 184). Although accepting that there is a general disregard for 'local' knowledge within expert discourses this chapter would suggest that the women interviewed give credence to their own personal knowledge and experiences. This is especially so when those experiences put into stark relief the inconclusiveness of expert knowledge at the level of individuals. The women interviewed do speak about being in good health but they also remain alert to issues of health woven through the governing discourse of weight control.

NOTES

1 The waist-to-hip ratio (WHR) represents the numerical difference between the waist and hip circumferences, for example when the waist measures 80 centimetres and the hips measure 85 centimetres, the waist-to-hip ratio would be 80/85 = 0.94. Results of greater than 0.95 for men and 0.80 for women are understood to indicate possible health risks. Debates ensue over the most accurate WHR cut-off points for defining high-risk categories.

2   Susie Orbach's book *Fat is a Feminist Issue: The Anti-Diet Guide to Permanent
    Weight Loss* (1978) is generally understood to be resistant to weight loss and
    dieting. However, I would argue that underlying her thesis is the demand that
    women should lose weight and that 'excess' weight is abnormal and a sign of
    pathology.

REFERENCES

Croft, J. et al. 1995 'Waist-to-hip ratio in a biracial population: Measurement, implica-
    tions, and cautions for using guidelines to define high risk for cardiovascular disease'
    Journal of the American Dietetic Association vol. 95, no. 1, pp. 60–64
Davison, C., Frankel, S. & Davey Smith, G. 1992 'The limits of lifestyle: Re-assessing
    "fatalism" in the popular culture of illness prevention' *Social Science & Medicine*
    vol. 34, no. 6, pp. 675–85
De Swann, A. 1990 *The Management of Normality: Critical Essays in Health and Welfare*
    Routledge, London
Ernsberger, P. & Haskew, P. 1987 'Rethinking obesity: An alternative view of its health
    implications' *The Journal of Obesity and Weight Regulation*, special edition, vol. 6,
    no. 2, Summer, Human Sciences Press Inc., New York
Garrow, J. S. 1984 *Treat Obesity Seriously: A Clinical Manual* Churchill Livingstone,
    Edinburgh
Harding, S. (ed.) 1987 'Feminism and methodology' in *Social Science Issues* Open
    University Press, Milton Keynes
Harris, P. 1994 *Expert Knowledge and Everyday Life* unpublished PhD thesis, Murdoch
    University, Perth, Australia
Heart Foundation of Australia 1993 *Healthy Eating for the Heart: A Guide to Lowering
    your Cholesterol* National Heart Foundation of Australia, Canberra
——1993 *Living with Angina* National Heart Foundation of Australia, Canberra
——1994 *Heart Facts 1992* National Heart Foundation of Australia, Canberra
——1994 *High Blood Pressure—The Facts* National Heart Foundation of Australia,
    Canberra
Hetzel, B. & McMichael, T. 1987 *The L S Factor: Lifestyle and Health* Penguin Books,
    Ringwood
Hughes, M. 1994 'The risks of lifestyle and the diseases of civilisation' in *Annual Review
    of Health Social Sciences: Embodiment* eds B.S. Turner et al., vol. 4, pp. 57–78
——1996 'Screening for cholesterol: Reducing the risk of coronary artery disease or
    increasing the opportunities for regulation of lifestyle?' Paper presented to Health
    Plenary: The Politics and Sociology of Screening, at The Australian Sociology
    Association Annual Conference, University of Tasmania, 5 December 1996
Keys, A. 1980 *Seven Countries: A Multivariate Analysis of Death and Coronary Heart
    Disease* Harvard University Press, Cambridge, MA
——1989 'Longevity of man: Relative weight and fatness in middle age' *Annual Medicine*
    vol. 21, pp. 163–68
Orbach, S. 1978 *Fat is a Feminist Issue: An Anti-Diet Guide to Permanent Weight Loss*
    Paddington Press, New York
Petersen, A. 1996 'Risk and the regulated self: The discourse of health promotion as
    politics of uncertainty' *Australian and New Zealand Journal of Sociology* vol. 32,
    no. 1, March, pp. 44–57

Petersen, A. & Lupton, D. 1996 *The New Public Health: Health and Self in the Age of Risk* Sage, London

Pouliot, M. et al. 1994 'Waist circumference and abdominal sagittal diameter: Best simple anthropometric indexes of abdominal visceral adipose tissue accumulation and related cardiovascular risk in men and women' *The American Journal of Cardiology* vol. 73, no. 1, March, pp. 460–67

Santich, B. 1995 *What The Doctors Ordered: 150 Years of Dietary Advice in Australia* Hyland House, Melbourne

Slimming Australia 1996 *Slimming* Mason Stewart Publishing, Sydney, April

Stanton, R. 1991 *The Diet Dilemma* Allen & Unwin, Sydney

The West Australian 1995 'Did you take your heart for a walk today?' advertisement for the Be Active Everyday health promotion campaign supported by Healthways and Australian Heart Foundation, Wednesday 13 September

——1995 'Fat people cost us millions' headline, Thursday 6 April, p. 11

Turner, B. 1982 'The government of the body: Medical regimens and the rationalisation of diet' *The British Journal of Sociology* vol. 33, no. 2, pp. 254–69

Weight Watchers 1996 *Weight Watchers* magazine, June/July, Weight Watchers, Sydney

10 Containing the body

Wendy Seymour

L eaky bodies worry us. We are anxious about bodily fluids. We
spend a good deal of our lives monitoring and regulating the foods
and liquids we consume and the bodily wastes which result from this
ingestion. The preoccupation transcends age, gender, class and racial
affiliation: we all keep watch on our bodies. We engage in routine
and largely taken for granted bodily surveillance as we monitor the
passage of substances in and out of the body and engage in activities
designed to prevent the untoward leakage of bodily fluids. While the
management of these tasks is seen as a private, personal issue, continence is assumed to be part of the responsibility of adult citizenship.
Bodily continence concerns us throughout our lives. We live in fear
that our bodies will let us down.

Occasional attacks of diarrhoea or vomiting unsettle us: fear of
contamination by the products of other people's bodies provokes
national anxiety, as well as personal concern. The current underutilisa-
tion of vaccination programs may reflect fears of introducing
'impurities' into the body: anxieties concerning bodily contamination
reflect prevailing ideas at different historical times (Turner 1996,
p. 98). The management of infant incontinence is often the subject
of parental worry and discussion. Regular menstruation will be a part
of most women's lives for forty years, and few women are sanguine at
the prospect of the menopause. Ageing of the body brings new
challenges to bodily continence for both men and women. These issues
are inevitable aspects of our lives.

In addition to these routine matters, many people experience
specific conditions that intensify the anxieties and exacerbate the
management problems associated with a leaky body. Conditions which

break down the neurological control of muscular sphincters, inflammation which disrupts the systematic functioning of bladder and bowel, or injuries which impair organ integrity put new demands on the already vulnerable body. Inflammatory bowel disease, nephritis, prostatic disease, and bladder and bowel dysfunction associated with spinal cord injuries are some of the more common conditions that challenge bodily continence. The HIV/AIDS crisis has exacerbated our fears of contamination and boundary trespass (Butler 1990, p. 132). While the mundane management of bodily continence involves us all, people with conditions such as these must live with the anarchy, disorder and unpredictability of their bodies. No longer taken for granted, bodily management takes on heightened importance in their lives. The smells and leakages associated with disrupted excremental processes revoke maturity in adult bodies. The rigorous monitoring of bodily ingestion challenges the freedom of choice presumed by adult men and women: stigma, shame and embarrassment are evoked by evidence of failure to contain the body.

Why does the issue of continence preoccupy us? Why do we devote such energy to containing the body? All of us have bodies which will leak and spill from time to time, but the anxieties related to incontinence seem greater than the experience of individual discomfort. Does continence have implications beyond the personal distress associated with a leaking body? Do our anxieties related to the permeability of the body and its boundaries reflect wider social concerns? Can the embodied self survive in a leaky container?

This chapter will examine the issue of bodily continence from a number of perspectives. While the primary focus is on bodies which are phenomenally experienced—lived individual bodies/selves—these bodies are explored in relation to the social body, the body used as a schema for thinking and conceptualising about society and culture. Battles for control and subversion are continually waged in this context. Although the body is the site of enormous political and social control, the body is also a powerful site for contestation and transformation.

CONTINENCE

The chapter will draw on data from an empirical study of twenty-four people with varying degrees of bodily paralysis resulting from a range of serious conditions, material which is developed more fully in a recently released publication (Seymour 1998). Most of the informants have sustained damage to their spinal cord. The loss of muscle power associated with these conditions is usually obvious but few people realise that deep and superficial sensation, vasomotor control, bladder and bowel control and sexual function may also be lost. Since spinal cord damage is permanent, rehabilitation is directed towards utilising the remaining intact functions and developing strategies for maintaining essential bodily functions. Care of the bladder and the bowel must become obsessional, since neglect of these vital parts of the body can have extremely serious clinical consequences (Jones & Davidson 1988, p. 109). While the loss of bowel and bladder control associated with these conditions provides dramatic examples of faecal and urinary incontinence, the broader issue of bodily continence involves a range of fluids and substances which engage with the body in a variety of ways.

The informants graphically describe the experience of living in a leaking body. Anthony says, 'You can't control when you urinate, nor do you know when you are using your bowels. It is very scary, and very threatening. The need to protect yourself means that you do not open up to people.' Joy claims that 'You lose all your modesty—you know, shitting and urinating in front of people and stuff like that. It really hurts your pride.' Ken says

> One of the most demeaning and belittling things is not having control over your bowels. It creates enormous feelings of powerlessness. I was having accidents daily, more than daily. Every time I did anything physical, my bowels would move, not much sometimes, but enough to create a helluva mess and a smell.

Frances describes her early experiences as 'excruciating'. 'I was mortified every time it happened. I hated the fact that people had to come to change the sheets. It was just awful. I can remember that I was smelly, I was just vile, the gas that was coming from me was just terrible.' Bridget, too, is unequivocal that the loss of bladder and bowel function was the worst aspect of her disability, 'I had to wear these big nappies at first. With the suppositories you flood all over the toilet. It was a real hassle.' Although Mark's injury was many years ago he still remembers 'the mess, you know, shitting myself, having accidents, and that went on for quite a number of years after I left the unit'.

Unlike babies in the animal kingdom, the human baby is born with an 'unfinished' body (Gehlen 1988, p. 4). The newborn baby cannot fend for itself but must depend on others to attend to its nourishment, shelter and the management of sleep and bodily excretions. Gradually infants learn to control aspects of their bodies, and attend to their own needs. The child's internal bodily processes are regulated as well as the child's behaviour, appearance and view of the world. Civilisation is, thus, an ongoing process of body taming. Human bodies have to be trained, manipulated, cajoled, coaxed, organised and disciplined in order to fit into society (Elias 1978). Civilised life depends on the successful presenting, monitoring and interpreting of bodies; culture is a product of the complex interweaving of the body and society. The body is neither a product of biology nor a product of society. The body is 'simultaneously, conjointly and concurrently socially and organically founded' (Turner 1992, p. 7). Although society plays a critical role in the constitution of the body, it is the body which may present society with its potentiality and with its most formidable resistance.

SOCIALISATION

Toilet training is a potent vehicle for introducing a child to the concept of shame (Lawler 1991, p. 137). Civilising the bladder and bowel to conform to social rules about the timing and placement of bodily wastes involves a systematic process of encouraging the baby to take on the parent's attitudes, and through the parent, the values of the wider social group to which the parent belongs, in relation to these activities (Turner 1987, p. 85). This process is achieved through orthodox behaviour modification strategies where children are rewarded for behaving in a way that conforms to their parents' values, and punished when they do not.

The concept of modesty—the acknowledgement of the need to privatise the 'private parts' of the body (Elias 1978, pp. 31–32)—has developed alongside the processes designed to civilise the body. The sequestering of particular parts and functions of the body that are 'best not talked about' makes people vulnerable to embarrassment and shame (Elias 1978, p. 190).

A well-socialised adult understands the need to protect the sensibilities of others from untoward sights, sounds and smells that may emanate from the body. Public health messages are based on similar imperatives (Petersen & Lupton 1996). A responsible citizen must work on their own body in order to defend it against moral, bacteriological and physical invasion. At the same time the citizen must assume responsibility for ensuring that these bodily regimens are sufficiently rigorous to protect others from contamination. In the contemporary era a citizen is expected to assume onerous responsibilities for monitoring, discipling and controlling their body. But how much control does an individual have over their body in a context of disease, damage and rapidly escalating global risk? (Beck 1992; Petersen & Lupton 1996). Disease and illness have long been imbued with moral implications (Turner 1996, p. 97). Contemporary public health is still a moral enterprise (Petersen & Lupton 1996): the 'new' public health remains embedded within a discourse which underlines the responsibilities and duties that individuals should assume in relation to their bodies in return for the privilege of citizenship. Health economics are played out in a multitude of sites, but within the context of modern hospital management, the insurance industry and the new public health we are witnessing an increasingly direct linkage between individual behaviours and disease or trauma. While victim blaming is by no means a new invention, the recent emergence of the concept of the 'entrepreneurial self'—the self who is expected to live life in a prudent and calculating way, well informed and mindful of the risks to the body—is clearly a product of the retreat from the welfare state and reliance on markets to regulate the economy (Petersen & Lupton 1996, p. xiii).

In this context people who have sustained damage to their bodies through trauma or accidents involving alcohol or drug usage, travelling at high speeds or risk-taking behaviours such as diving into shallow water or hang-gliding are particularly susceptible to implications of irresponsibility. They may feel a heightened sense of obligation to manage their anarchic body in a manner which will cause as little further distress to others as possible. Successful body management, especially in the area of bodily continence, will provide evidence of a renewed sense of responsibility and commitment to core social values.

Continence then, can be seen as the conquest of the body by society, a victory which is reinforced by the context of privacy, modesty, propriety and shame within which the bodily activities take place. The victory, however, is always tentative. Our anxieties about continence reflect our perpetual fear that the body may defy its years of careful socialisation and training and reassert its pre-civilised nature. The unregulated permeability of bodily fluids represents a serious source of danger and pollution (Butler 1990, p. 132). Conditions or practices which refocus attention to particular areas of the body, or redefine the expectations of activities previously taken for granted are distressing because they threaten to disrupt the stability of the body and question our status as properly civilised, responsible citizens.

Formal bladder and bowel retraining in rehabilitation units aims to condition the bladder and the bowel to empty at convenient times and in convenient places, a process not unlike the toilet training procedures of childhood. A young child learns to be ashamed as part of the social process of toilet training. While the sense of 'feeling like a baby' sums up the experiences of most of the informants, these people have well established attitudes towards bodily continence. Their sense of shame is fully developed. To attempt to reconcile such feelings about oneself with the inexorable reality of incontinence in the face of other people's revulsion to bodily products is a constant attack on the embodied self.

Although Mary claims that 'bladder problems are endless' she continues, more forcefully, to say:

but I don't think that there is a word bad enough to describe the problems associated with the bowel. Bladder training is a euphemism. It doesn't train your bladder at all, it just means that you beat your bladder to it. As far as my bowels are concerned, I go once a day. Something may or may not happen, and it's a revolting process. I've been down the suppository track. I have ended up having to do it with a gloved hand, what's called 'manual removal'. In my case it's a very messy occupation, and it prevents me going away to stay overnight. What on earth would I do if I found myself with a toilet that is unsuitable, and I made an awful mess that I'd have to clean up?

Rosemary has an ileostomy bag for urinary elimination; faecal material, though, must be manually removed from her bowel. Her mother has done this for her all her life, but as Rosemary says, 'Now I am getting older I should try to do this for myself'. Alister claims that he was not distressed by the rigorous, formal program of bladder and bowel management that is central to spinal injury rehabilitation. He was able to see the catheterisation and suppositories as 'practical measures which just had to be done. Well you have no choice. You either do it or you don't cope.' Jenny is less phlegmatic. 'With the lack of bladder control, you were constantly having to have your sheets changed—every few hours, day and night. I found all of that a real intrusion. There were lots and lots of jokes, "Oh you're wet again", and "Didn't your mother toilet train you?", or whatever.' Alister's attitude towards this aspect of rehabilitation is rare; most of the men and women perceive the practices and implications arising from this loss as a destructive incursion into their embodied selves, and a recurring attack on their bodily integrity and self-esteem throughout their lives.

The perineum may be a relatively small area of the body, but it contains a concentration of bodily openings. Danger is focused in this area because of the pathway these orifices offer between the body and the outside world. Semen, vaginal secretions, faeces, urine and blood pass from the body: bacteriological, physical and moral invaders may enter the body through these external portals. If the body provides a schema for society as Mary Douglas suggests (1966), it is not hard to see how this part of the body is invested with inordinate importance. Sex and excretion are thus highly dangerous activities. Our ideas of cleanliness and purity are closely aligned with these activities.

It is in this small, but highly defended part of the body where society may be most threatened. In no other part of the body is the tension so tightly drawn. While few able-bodied men and women are unaware of the volatile nature of the perineal area, most people develop a range of strategies to divert themselves and the attentions of others from this dangerous territory. The lifelong preoccupation with bodily eliminations and relentless concentration of energy and attention to the genital area are the issues to which people with body paralyses must attend. Yet this context of leaking fluids and permeable boundaries may also be a site of contestation and new possibilities.

For a considerable time, however, most of the informants expressed profound distress at what they termed the 'abnormality' of their situation. As George says, 'the worst impact of bowel and bladder loss is the abnormality of it all'. For several years he didn't go anywhere 'because it was just too hard'. He now manages all the aspects of bowel and bladder function himself. Joy, too, feels this loss most profoundly. 'I miss the feeling of wanting to go to the toilet, you know, you miss things like that, the feeling of a full bladder or just going to the toilet. I dream about it all the time. In my dreams it's so real, it feels like it's real.' Because some of the sensory nerves were spared in Anthony's spinal injury, the retraining program was more likely to be successful. He speaks of 'the great joy and excitement I had when I started to be able to go to the toilet and use my bowels again—the sensation and the feeling!' The elation at achieving what seem such mundane goals after two years of effort highlights the dramatic impact of this aspect of bodily damage.

Eating and drinking are major preoccupations of our lives. While biomedicine sees these activities as fundamental to the survival of the human organism and as risk factors in some diseases, recent developments in the sociology of food and consumption (Crotty 1995; Falk 1994; Lupton, 1996a; Mennell et al. 1992; Turner 1992, ch. 6) have expanded such restrictive notions. When we eat and drink we engage in a complex range of personal and social acts which may have little overt connection with survival or disease prevention. Clearly the rationalisation of eating practices and the growth of dietary sciences epitomise Foucault's connection between the body, knowledge and power (Turner 1992, p. 192), yet food and drink are also associated with appetites, desires, comforts, satisfactions, sexualities and other bodily pleasures which have far less rational connotations.

Rehabilitation of the leaky body involves strict adherence to a range of bodily regimens. Desires and appetites for food and drink must be modified in order to discipline the body and regulate its fluids. The body is subdued by means of painstaking experimentation and monitoring of bodily processes. It is only by constant surveillance of the body and monitoring of its fluids that the chaotic body can be restored to a semblance of order, a fragile truce.

Pam describes the extensive program of bodily surveillance in which she engaged before she developed some strategies for control. She says, 'I went through a process of measuring what I drank. I used to sit on the portable commode by the hour just finding out how long it took to come through and then measure it.' Pam claims that it took about six months after she returned home from the rehabilitation unit to develop some confidence in her bladder, although she still has accidents. Many years later she still monitors her intake very carefully, but social functions, sickness and even climatic variations can threaten this uneasy equilibrium.

Not surprisingly, this process encourages the men and women in the study to reconceptualise their bodies in terms of a well-integrated, but simple, hydraulic system of pipes, plumbing, substances and fluids (Turner 1992, p. 184). Inputs are carefully manipulated to ensure satisfactory outputs. Constant attention must be given to the timing and nature of the food and drink taken into their bodies in order to minimise the possibility of inopportune leakage. The body is seen as a machine that requires continual surveillance for optimal perfor-mance, and in order to operate in a manner which will not offend others. Dietary management, careful living and regular habits serve to produce a well-contained body which will not threaten society by its anarchic activities. Anxieties associated with the uncontrolled leakage of bodily fluids are reassured by evidence of strict observation of bodily regimens associated with the government of the body (Turner 1992, p. 192). Clearly these bodies have come to epitomise the notion of the mechanical body which lies at the heart of biomedicine.

Although many of the informants have been successful in devising ways to manage their wayward bladders and bowels to fit their own lifestyles, most live with a heightened sense of the risks involved in failing to balance the tensions between bodily input and output. The necessity to continually monitor these activities compromises the spontaneity and freedom of choice we associate with eating and drinking. While such practices will result in a degree of predictability for many people, this regulation threatens to subordinate the body. Rigorous self-surveillance, discipline and deference to regimens of diet and timetables of bodily evacuation must surely challenge the embodied self. But just as appetite and sexuality are major threats to the aestheticism which underpins religious vocation (Turner 1992, p. 178), so too are appetites and sexualities key areas for subversion of the regulated body. While dietary regimes may subdue the body, the desire and appetite for food may subvert this regulation.

Adulthood is characterised by a well-managed, continent body. Evidence of the ability to control the body correlates with the capacity to control and manage public affairs. This association is not diminished by occasional lapses, such as adult men vomiting after a drinking binge. Evidence of 'boyish' behaviour may in fact highlight the skills that men more usually employ to control their anarchic bodies, and demonstrates the likelihood that they will be similarly successful in administering the chaos associated with corporate life.

Women's bodies are typically portrayed as leaky and unreliable. Mysterious blood issuing from the hyster or uterus, with a regularity linked to the moon's cycle (Rowland 1988, p. 30)—small wonder that women have been seen as dangerous, hysterical lunatics. The 'uncleanness' of menstrual blood has been hedged with taboos, rituals and exclusory practices by different societies throughout the ages (Douglas 1966). Even pornography, which seems to stop at nothing, excludes displays of menstruating women (Lawler 1991, p. 106). The regularity and predictability of menstrual periods have done nothing to ameliorate their danger. Even today, despite the exposure associated with the newly discovered commercial advantages of menstrual accoutrements, menstruation is still a subject shrouded in mystery. Public exposure can be a double-edged sword. Recognition of pre-menstrual syndrome, for instance, has only provided more 'scientific' evidence for women's recurring 'irrationality' and hence legitimated their continual exclusion from positions of responsibility and power (Martin 1987, ch. 7; Ripper 1994; Rowland 1988, pp. 34–35).

In late modernity corporate and government management is concerned with containing boundaries and controlling leakiness in efficiency, costs and information. Regular surveillance, accountability and monitoring provide evidence of rational management and identify areas which require further containment, restructuring, 'downsizing' and control. If women's bodies epitomise leakiness and lack of containment and leaking bodily fluids are associated with 'leaky' reasoning, women's presence in organisations and governments in times of economic crisis is simply too difficult to manage. It is not hard to discern notions of menstruation as 'failed production' (Martin 1987, p. 45) or the revisiting of old associations of irrationality and menstruation underlying some attempts to explain women's underrepresentation in higher management structures at the end of the century (Lupton 1996b, p. 93).

The 'breakdown' of older women's bodies greatly intensifies the forebodings associated with women's bodies in general. While we may be reassured that the dangers related to pregnancy, childbirth and menstruation are past, hot flushes, night sweating, irritability, mood swings, unpredictable vaginal bleeding and urinary incontinence exacerbate the spectre of an unregulated, anarchic and chaotic body. A variation of the 'entrepreneurial self' (Petersen & Lupton 1996) is evoked to dismiss women who complain of symptoms by suggesting that these events could have been prevented by more careful management (Greer 1991, ch. 5). The possibilities of pleasurable, nonreproductive sex merely add to the dangers associated with the bodies of older women.

If babies' bodies leak and women menstruate for nearly forty years, if people with bodily paralysis and other medical conditions lose control of their bladder and bowels and ageing bodies simply cannot be contained, we must concede that there are indeed very few people who can feel confident in the continence of their bodies. Is it only the bodies of men who have passed childhood but not yet reached old age that we should trust?

Unlike women's sexuality which has long been portrayed as dangerous to men (Petersen & Lupton 1996, p. 78), men's heterosexual participation has largely escaped public anxiety. Gay men's bodies, however, have been subject to intense scrutiny (Petersen & Lupton 1996, p. 85). Moral panic is engendered by the perception of AIDS as the 'gay disease' and the person with AIDS as the 'polluting person' (Butler 1990, p. 132). That these diseases are transmitted through the exchange of bodily fluids reinforces the threat that permeable body boundaries present to the social order. Any kind of unregulated permeability constitutes a site of danger and pollution. In terms of the heterosexual construction of gendered exchange, homosexuality *is* boundary trespass (Butler 1990, p. 132).

CONCLUSION

Taming the body is a remarkably efficient process. The rational management of the potentially unruly body is seen to benefit others, as well as contributing to society more generally. Operating within a moral framework of shame, modesty and propriety, and encouraged by the rewards which accrue to virtuous, responsible citizens in a civilised society, it is small wonder that bodily containment preoccupies us.

The late twentieth century world is replete with risk and danger. While our bodies have always worried us, recent years have brought increasing fears about our bodies and a deepening sense of foreboding that we shall be unable to protect our bodies against the 'invading antigens of hypermodern culture' (Kroker & Kroker 1988, p. 16). While faith in science and medicine have sustained us until now, the realisation that we are entering a new stage of global risk fills us with profound apprehension.

The intense concern associated with bodily fluids accompanying the AIDS epidemic focuses attention directly on the body. Biological fundamentalism—the generation of a panic-based 'temperance movement' to maintain the cleanliness and safety of bodily fluids (Kroker & Kroker 1988, p. 11)—seems our best defence against invasion of the body by the diseases of modern civilisation, but these measures will never alleviate our fear that it will be our own body which will betray us (Lupton 1994, p. 64).

While we fear that science and medicine can no longer protect our bodies from disease, leaky bodies have far more fundamental implications: leaky bodies endanger society. Our ideas of crisis and social disorder are articulated through theories of bodily disorder and disease (Douglas 1966, 1973). Is it the leaky, unreliable, troublesome body which threatens to overwhelm society? Women's bodies, old bodies and sick bodies may defy containment: these bodies may leak and spill. Heterosexuality is situated within the safe parameters of conventional gender relations, reproduction and family life, but the boundaries of the homosexual body are ill-defined and dangerous. Leaky bodies threaten to destabilise society and its categories. Bodies lacking self-containment constitute 'a disorder which threatens all order' (Grosz 1994, p. 203).

While the body is subject to moral regulation and control, the body is also the site of struggles and competing discourses which may challenge the rational management of the body. Embodiment involves the active participation of the body; it engages the body and the mind. Pleasures, appetites and desires may subvert years of careful socialisation.

The body is the arena for a vast array of persuasive forces which may threaten rational control and challenge ideas of what bodies are and what they should do. In the process of exploring new possibilities for pleasure, bodies may also challenge society: new political and social possibilities may be revealed. A well-regulated body may comfort us: our preoccupation with boundaries and containment is not surprising. Yet the context of leaking fluids, permeable boundaries and seeping orifices may also be a site of innovative and creative opportunities.

REFERENCES

Beck, U. 1992 *Risk Society: Towards a New Modernity* Sage, London
Butler, J. 1990 *Gender Trouble: Feminism and the Subversion of Identity* Routledge, London
Crotty, P. 1995 *Good Nutrition? Fact and Fashion in Dietary Advice* Allen & Unwin, Sydney
Douglas, M. 1966 *Purity and Danger: An Analysis of the Concepts of Pollution and Taboo* Routledge & Kegan Paul, UK
——1973 *Natural Symbols: Explorations in Cosmology* Penguin Books, Harmondsworth
Elias, N. 1978 *The Civilizing Process: Vol. 1: The History of Manners* Urizen Books, New York
Falk, P. 1994 *The Consuming Body* Sage, London
Gehlen, A. 1988 *Man. His Nature and Place in the World* trans. C. McMillan & K. Pillemer, Columbia University Press, New York
Greer, G. 1991 *The Change: Women, Ageing and the Menopause* Hamish Hamilton Ltd, London
Grosz, E. 1994 *Volatile Bodies: Towards a Corporeal Feminism* Allen & Unwin, Sydney
Jones, G. & Davidson, J. 1988 'How spinal cord paralysis affects body image' in *Altered Body Image—The Nurse's Role* ed. M. Salter, John Wiley & Sons Ltd, Guildford
Kroker, A. & Kroker M. (eds) 1988 *Body Invaders: Sexuality and the Postmodern Condition* Macmillan, Hampshire
Lawler, J. 1991 *Behind the Screens: Nursing, Somology, and the Problem of the Body* Churchill Livingstone, Melbourne
Lupton, D. 1994 *Medicine as Culture. Illness, Disease and the Body in Western Societies* Sage, London
——1996a *Food, the Body and the Self*, Sage, London
——1996b 'Constructing the menopausal body: The discourses on Hormonal Replacement Therapy' *Body & Society* vol. 2, no. 1, pp. 91–97
Martin, E. 1987 *The Woman in the Body: A Cultural Analysis of Reproduction* Open University Press, Milton Keynes
Mennell, S., Murcott, A. & van Otterloo, A. 1992 *The Sociology of Food: Eating, Diet and Culture* Sage, London
Petersen, A. & Lupton, D. 1996 *The New Public Health: Health and Self in the Age of Risk* Allen & Unwin, Sydney
Ripper, M. 1994 'The engendering of hormonal difference' in *Just Health: Inequality in Illness, Care and Prevention* eds. C. Waddell & A. Petersen, Churchill Livingstone, Melbourne

Rowland, R. 1988 *Woman Herself: A Transdisciplinary Perspective on Women's Identity* Oxford University Press, Melbourne

Seymour, W. 1998 *Remaking the Body: Rehabilitation and Change* Allen & Unwin, Sydney

Turner, B. 1987 *Medical Power and Social Knowledge* Sage, London

——1992 *Regulating Bodies: Essays in Medical Sociology* Routledge, London

——1996 *The Body & Society: Explorations in Social Theory* 2nd edn, Sage, London

11   A good enough death?

Beverley McNamara

Dying is not often discussed in the context of health, and indeed each could be viewed as the antithesis of the other. However, 'health' and 'dying' are not discrete states, and the degree of relativity between the two varies for philosophical as well as practical reasons. A good death which implies a degree of quality and dignity in the dying process is more closely aligned to the concept of health than a 'good enough' death or even a 'bad' death. Also, the ageing population in advanced industialised societies[1] has meant that the gradual decline of health to a state of ill health and further to a state of dying may be a protracted stage of a person's life. Much of what happens to a person during this time of failing health and approaching death will be determined by the pathology of their disease as well as their physical strength and personal resolve. Yet individual characteristics cannot fully explain the circumstances of each person's journey towards death. Cultural responses to dying and death as well as broader social structures frame the experience of each individual.

There are two distinct things that happen to the terminally ill person: the death of the body and the 'passing' of the person (Cassell 1975, p. 45). Dying, therefore, is not simply a biological fact, but a social process; and death, not a moment in time, but a social phenomenon. The meanings of both dying and death are not invariant (Gavin 1995, p. 75); they are constructed differently over time and in different cultural contexts (Aries 1974; Metcalfe & Huntington 1991). For terminally ill people, therefore, it is not just their health or ill health that matters, but the manner in which dying and death is understood when and where their life ends. In this chapter I will explore some of the issues that arise in the time before death, when

terminally ill people, together with their families and health professional carers, negotiate the circumstances of dying. While most of the
discussion is relevant to all terminally ill people, I will illustrate
theoretical perspectives with examples drawn from my ethnographic
fieldwork in Australian hospices and palliative care services. Most
people who use these services suffer from cancer, though palliative
care is now becoming increasingly more available to people with other
non-malignant diseases.

The terminally ill person's experience, particularly their quality
of life, will be influenced largely by their ability to participate in
decisions that are made about them in the last days of their life. These
decisions might relate to life-prolonging medical treatments, to issues
of pain control and the degree to which the dying person is conscious,
or even to the place and the time of death. Decision-making at the
end of life seems particularly important in the current climate of
patient 'empowerment' and individual responsibility. Individualism,
however, often becomes more a rhetorical construct than an observ-
able and effectual reality when dying people, exhausted by illness and
grief, negotiate with varying degrees of ability and support, the circumstances of their own deaths. How then can we understand death
to be good; or are most deaths simply 'good enough'? I propose five
inter-related factors which inform the manner in which people die in
advanced industrialised societies. These are: (1) cultural constructions
of individualism; (2) the terminally ill person's altered conceptions of
self and their capacity for autonomous decision-making; (3) social
location and structural constraints; (4) biomedical culture; and (5)
local moral culture. These five factors influence the extent to which
each person's dying and ultimate death can be understood as 'good'
or 'good enough'.

DEATH: 'GOOD' OR 'GOOD ENOUGH' IN HOSPICE?

The Good Death is an idealised concept, particularly in the context
of a hospice and palliative care setting, where terminally ill people
who have stopped curative treatments are cared for in a supportive
environment. Good death, which literally means euthanasia (Veatch
1976), has here been reconstructed to mean a process where the
terminally ill person, their family, and the health professional team
share a mutual acceptance of the terminally ill person's approaching
death and engage in shared decision-making. Above all, this manner
of dying is said to be dignified and peaceful. Many factors impinge

upon the realisation of this ideal which I have detailed elsewhere (McNamara et al. 1994, 1995) but for the purposes of the discussion in this chapter it is important to note that Good Deaths can only happen if the dying person, the family and the health professionals all agree with what is happening in the time before death. It is also significant that when people are dying from cancer and other chronic illnesses they require substantial medical and nursing care. The stage upon which these dramas unfold therefore, is most significantly that of medicine.

While the area of hospice and palliative care has traditionally been viewed as relatively marginal to mainstream medicine, it still tends to be part of the vast cultural system of biomedicine. The hospice–palliative model of care, based upon the broader social movement of hospice evident in North America and Britain, arose in response to the inappropriate, technological and clinical approach to dying people that was evident in the 1960s and 1970s. There has been a large degree of integration of the palliative care model into the mainstream of medical care, but this model still continues to serve as a symbolic critique of how dying people are managed in other terminal care settings. Yet paradoxically, hospice and palliative care is dependent on the structural and ritual foundations of medicine and the national health care system. Such tension forms a backdrop for the ideological framework of hospice and palliative care which focuses on the needs and wishes of the individual patient and their close social circle.

Many health professionals who work within the area of hospice and palliative care have often expressed reservations about the ideal of a Good Death, considering either open discussion concerning death or shared decision-making to be problematic. An alternative way of looking at the interaction that takes place in the time before death is to propose the idea of a death that is 'good enough'. A 'good enough' death has been described by two prominent palliative care practitioners as a death 'as close as possible to the circumstances the person would have chosen' (Campbell 1990, p. 2) and 'a death with integrity, consistent with the life that person has led' (Komesaroff et al. 1995, p. 597). Both of these interpretations are consistent with the recent theoretical position that authority over dying should be invested in the individual. Closer examination of these seemingly humanistic and person-centred definitions, however, reveals that the focus on the individual can be empowering on one hand, yet on the other hand, it can act as a means to shift the locus of responsibility. A 'good enough' death does not happen through the individual conception of self in relation to what the dying person was or what they wanted, but to what they see themselves as being now and what they are able to decide upon now. Furthermore, the death is 'good enough' because it is close enough to individual wishes. The question arises: what factors constrain individual wishes? In order to understand the implications of a 'good enough' death it is necessary to trace the social and historical contexts of individualism in relation to medical care.

THE INDIVIDUAL'S AUTHORITY OVER DYING

The concern with the authority of the individual over dying can be traced broadly to two trends: first, a societal preoccupation with individuality; and secondly, a growing dissatisfaction among the lay and professional communities with both the power and limitations of medicine. With regards to the first of these trends, Kellehear (1996, pp. 88–89) has noted that present attitudes towards death are 'forged from the material and social conditions of the baby-boomer generation'. He suggests that focusing on the individual has become a moral and ethical imperative. Moller (1990) contributes to this discussion by arguing that the technological development of modern society, with its associated bureaucratic rationality, has created an ideology of individualism.

Both Bauman (1992) and Elias (1985) have argued that the self-care policy of survival (individual concerns with health and fitness of the body) construes death as an individual event. Furthermore, they have commented on the increasing secularisation and privatisation of contemporary society. The group of people who gather around the bed of the dying person generally do not have a shared system of belief, be it religion, magic or science, to temper what Elias (1985) has called the loneliness of dying. The degree to which death has become taboo (Gorer 1965; Aries 1981) or sequestrated from public view (Mellor & Shilling 1993) within society is a contentious issue (Kellehear 1984; Walters 1991). However, there seems to be an agreement within the literature that the privatisation and subjectification of the experience of death 'results in the increased presence of considerations of death for individuals' (Mellor 1993, p. 12).

The second trend which has led to the re-examination of the authority of the individual over dying points to a critique which comes from both within and without the profession of medicine. Social scientists have been prominent in the discussion surrounding the use of technology as a means of unnecessarily prolonging life, delaying death or even engaging in a conquest of death (Parsons et al. 1972; Illich 1976; Lock 1996). It has been suggested that the medical model makes it difficult, if not impossible, to decide that any given person shall be allowed to die (Muller & Koenig 1988). Responding to these criticisms, Kelner and Bourgeault (1993) have suggested that health professionals must concede their professional autonomy and enter into a partnership with patients in end of life decision-making. In Chapter 18 of this volume, Kellehear traces the recent public expectation of control over dying to the rise of the New Public Health which has fostered empowering social forces for the individual.

This message of empowerment and the dissatisfaction of community members with the medicalisation of death, most evident in the social movement of hospice in North America and Britain, but also in popular media presentations, has influenced many members of the medical profession to varying degrees. North American surgeon Nuland, whose book *How We Die: Reflections on Life's Final Chapter* (1994) has gained a large popular readership in the English-speaking world, while critical of medical technology, cautions that inevitably the rescue credo of high technology medicine overrides personal choice. In the Australian context the message of community dissatisfaction with end of life treatments appears to have reached some medical practitioners:

> Many health professionals believe that more people can have better deaths, that enough is known to make dying more tolerable for many of us, and that too many of today's problems rest with the attitudes of providers as much as with anything else. (Baume 1993, p. 792)

A recent survey made clear that end of life treatment is 'significantly determined by an array of individual characteristics of the doctor and not solely by the nature of the medical problem'. However, it was also noted that, of the doctors surveyed, most believed that they adhere to patient and family wishes when they are known, providing the patient has not requested euthanasia (Waddell et al. 1996, p. 540).

The focus on the individual and that person's ability to be part of the discussions surrounding their dying has become a feature of the modern hospice–palliative model of care within Australia. Hunt, a doctor and pioneer in hospice and palliative care in South Australia writes the following:

> The principle of autonomy was neglected in terminal care before the development of hospice and palliative care—most patients were ill-informed of their situation, and they were submissive to medical paternalism. The palliative mode emphasised the importance of sensitively informing patients about their state of health and the treatment

options available to them, and stressed the importance of patients being involved in decisions about their quality of life. The shift to the palliative mode, therefore, moved the power base in the relationship between health carers and patients, from professional domination to increased patient autonomy. (1994, p. 131)

Whether the principle of autonomy in terminal care can be traced solely to the development of hospice and palliative care is debatable given the social and historical contexts of both individuality in dying and death and the growing consumer dissatisfaction with all medical care. However, suffice to say this social movement both grew out of and further fuelled the impetus for patient autonomy in terminal care, which has now begun to reach beyond the bounds of hospice and palliative care. Nevertheless, it seems that in the discussion regarding patient autonomy there is an oversight which relates to the way in which 'individual' or 'self' is taken as a priori and not seen as relevant to the way decisions are made. Yet in the course of daily practice terminally ill people, their loved ones and health professionals are consistently confronted with conflicting understandings of individuality, self, personhood, autonomy, and so on.

DYING IN ADVANCED INDUSTRIALISED SOCIETIES

So far in this chapter I have argued that the ability to participate in decision-making at the end of life has become a feature of 'modern' dying. Furthermore, participation and empowerment have become principal criteria in determining whether a person has a 'good' or 'good enough' death. As the Good Death is an idealised concept which is often unrealised, a 'good enough' death appears to be a far more workable definition with which to link participation in end of life decision-making. The following five inter-related factors inform the manner in which people die in advanced industrialised societies. They illustrate the degree to which cultural and individual responses, as well as broader social structures, frame the experience of each terminally ill person.

Social constructions of individualism

Just as dying and death are understood to mean different things at different times and places, the concept of individual or self is historically and socially constructed. When the two concepts of 'dying' and 'individual' are linked we are confronted with multiple interpretations of what it might mean for a person to die. 'Westernised' interpretations of individuality can vary from a death with defiance model of rebellion depicted in Dylan Thomas' poem 'Do not go gentle into that good night' (Ramsay 1975, p. 82), to the individual supremely in control of their own deathbed (Aries 1974). Foucault has added further dimensions to interpretations of the self by arguing that 'discourses', understood to be a collection of related statements or events, profoundly affect the possibilities for individual expression (Petersen 1994, p. 6). Following Foucault, we can see how discourses which promote individualism in dying may encourage the terminally ill person to make available their own subjectivity for management and control. Their grief, for example, while entirely individual, may be managed with the aid of professional support. The communal death rituals of earlier times and more traditional cultures, are consequently replaced by a privatised and professional relationship which tinges emotional subjectivity with pathology.

Individualism can be construed to be both liberating and obstructive. In the hospice–palliative care model an individual who is thought to have a Good Death interacts with others and is aware and accepting of approaching death, whereas the individual whose death is 'good enough' does it their own way but must consequently take responsibility for their own actions. Individual expression in this latter context is thought to be negative and a barrier to therapeutic intervention. This can be illustrated by the terminally ill person who refuses to discuss their approaching death and also by the dying person who may not comply with medication routines in terminal illness. Focusing on the individual, therefore, serves to provide specific treatments and support suited to the needs of each person, but it also clouds the issue of responsibility for action and inaction.

Notions of individuality also vary from culture to culture. For many Asian cultures, in particular, the individual may not be understood outside of social connectedness to others. The Confucian Chinese concept of personhood—jen—does not end at the boundaries of the skin but extends into the family and the intimate social circle (Kirmayer 1988, p. 78). Similarly in Japan, ningen—the term for person—means 'human between-ness' and defies Western individualistic notions of self (Kimura 1991, p. 235). As Kleinman (1988, p. 11) reminds us, many members of emerging industrialised societies, as well as members of multicultural societies, may view the body as 'an open system linking social relations to the self, a vital balance between inter-related elements in a holistic cosmos'. These conceptualisations fall outside of the Cartesian mind–body split so prevalent in Western notions of the individual (Gordon 1988). It seems little wonder then, that the disjunction between Western understandings of individualism and those of many other cultural groups can complicate cross-cultural interactions in health care settings. For example, truth telling in relation to dying is not a universally held ethic. It is not unusual in a hospice and palliative care setting to find that an Italian, Greek or Chinese family will refuse to allow their dying loved one to be burdened with the knowledge about their future. Conceptualisations of self and responsibility are, in this context, vastly different from the Westernised Christian medico-centric beliefs shared by most health professionals.

Altered conceptions of self

Social construction theories of the individual or self offer explanations of how groups of people share broad understandings of what person-hood means. However, these theories do not tell us a great deal about how the terminally ill person thinks and feels throughout the experi-ence of disabling chronic illness and existential crisis. Kelly and Field (1996, pp. 250–51) suggest that bringing the body into analytical focus helps us to see the interplay between self and identity and to 'manage sociologically the relation between biological and social facts'. With this kind of conceptual framework we can see that self need not be situated 'within' the body, but 'with' the body. A significantly changed body will therefore be a significantly changed self, yet that person's sense of identity and their ability to cope with terminal illness will also continue to be linked to past experiences or 'life themes' (Zlatin 1995). The important point here is that the terminally ill person will function and think differently from the way they did when they were a healthy individual. Each person will have a unique set of circum-stances which will alter their own conceptions of self and their own ability to make autonomous decisions.

Many palliative care professionals cite weakness and fatigue as one of the most disabling symptoms of terminal illness because there is little that can be done to alleviate this state of powerlessness. This manifestation of terminal illness is just one of the many symptoms which will influence the dying person's conception of themselves. Nausea, vomiting, breathlessness, constipation, diarrhoea, oedema (swelling), smell from infections and wounds, confusion and pain are also associated variously with disease and with intervention proc-edures. Knowledge of approaching death, whether this is implicit or explicit, and its associated anticipatory grief, further complicates self-knowledge and the capacity to act to change circumstances. It seems little wonder that the meanings of a Good Death can be vastly different for terminally ill people than for health professionals. While health professionals draw increasingly on notions of self-control and self-efficacy in their conceptualisations of 'good' and 'good enough' deaths, many terminally ill people question why dying takes so long, and as a recent study has suggested, characterise a good death as 'dying in one's sleep', 'dying quietly', 'with dignity', 'being pain free' and 'dying suddenly' (Payne et al. 1996). Nevertheless, if this is what many people want, terms like 'quietly', 'dignity' and 'suddenly' should not go unquestioned. The meanings of dignity, for example, are multiple: some people believe euthanasia is a dignified death while others believe it is unlawful killing. And what does dying 'suddenly' mean? Does the use of this word mean people would rather not have control over the circumstances of their death? Further still, the degree to which a person can be empowered or even the extent to which their wishes can be met needs to be understood in the context of social structure.

Social location and structural constraints

Any meaningful analysis of individual autonomy in decisions surrounding terminal illness and death needs to focus upon the individual's unique experience. Yet this micro-perspective needs to be understood within a structural framework which includes an understanding of each person's location within society as well as a knowledge of the macro-organisational contexts of the social world. Each individual negotiates their own illness and dying trajectories with varying degrees of ability and support due to their own place in society. The degree to which a terminally ill person has control, or is able to actively engage in decision-making has been linked to age (Rinaldi & Kearl 1990) and to patient residence and the degree to which staff set limits upon their own involvement with patients and families (Mesler 1995). Further-more, elements which determine the terminally ill person's social location such as gender, ethnicity, social class and educational back-ground and the kinds of social supports they receive must be understood in the light of entrenched social inequalities. The termi-nally ill person's access to power should also be seen in contrast to that of the health professionals who care for them. For example, a doctor who is dying of cancer can very easily negotiate their own medical management with the aid of colleagues, but an Aboriginal person is unlikely to benefit from very basic forms of support other than those provided by their own disadvantaged communities.

The inequalities of care for people suffering from terminal illnesses are institutionalised, but there is also an alarming element of chance which may affect the quality of their lives before death. We can see that a person suffering from cancer, on first consulting a doctor, begins a series of consultations, investigations and interventions, through which they will come into contact with various people who may obstruct or facilitate decisions regarding dying and death. The health professions are by no means a homogenous group. Their beliefs and actions vary greatly, particularly in this time of public and professional discussion of end of life decisions. Terminal care within Australia varies greatly: from high technology intensive care facilities to sup-portive hospice and palliative care services; some people die at home, but more die in nursing homes or hospitals; most people die in urban locations, while country communities suffer relative disadvantage. The degree to which a terminally ill person engages in decisions about their dying and death will therefore be mediated by their access to power and to the place and time of their death. If resources are channelled into facilities which support the needs and wishes of individuals and their families, rather than providing the latest in high technology curative treatments, people will be better able to maintain some degree of authority in the last days of their lives.

Biomedical culture, individualism and death

There have been significant changes in health professionals' responses to dying people in recent years, yet it would be premature to propose that the authority of the individual has supplanted the biomedical culture and social organisation of medicine. Medicine continues to frame the experience of individuals throughout their illness and dying trajectories. This powerful presence seems a little ironic given that medicine, with all of its technological mastery, has not wrought much change in lowering the incidence or raising the cure rates of chronic illnesses like cancer (Costain Schou 1993, p. 239). While artificial respirators and organ transplants have introduced an ambiguity about the definition and time of death, people do continue to die. However, many health professionals believe that medicine has not reached its potential for easing the burdens of dying people. Implicit in this view is the fundamental belief that if medicine cannot control death, then at the very least it should control the circumstances of death.

Even within the practice of hospice and palliative care, which proposes that death is a 'natural' part of life to be accepted when it comes, there is a very prominent view that the symptoms of dying should be treated at all cost. Some palliative care practitioners worry whether total alleviation of pain should be a goal of terminal care, yet many also are caught up with the imperative to treat and to act with whatever treatments may be current. This view may seem quite understandable when confronted with the physical devastation of diseases like terminal cancer. However, medical and cultural views of suffering overlap to obscure answers for those who seek a 'correct path' to care for dying people, particularly when that path aims to include the individual and their family in the decision-making process.

Western culture is permeated with the view that pain is growth, yet it is also very influenced by the medico-scientific approach to pain (Bendelow & Williams 1995). Most palliative care practitioners articulate a distinction between suffering and pain, but fail to conceptualise suffering in the same manner that they have contained pain within a neat neuro-physiological explanatory framework. They are far more willing than many of their colleagues in other disciplines to cross the boundary between the rationally and objectively measured sensation of pain and the lived embodied experience of pain. Yet pain that can be measured is considered a priority because this gives the impression that pain can be controlled. Additionally, measured pain serves to act as a potentially achievable audit of credibility for the health professional who must be seen to be doing their job in order to guarantee that the job will continue.

Illich (1976, p. 271) notes that in traditional cultures, '. . . pain was recognised as an inevitable part of the subjective reality of one's own body'. Such pain was made tolerable by integrating it into a meaningful setting. An original intention of the modern hospice movement, as articulated by its founder Dame Cecily Saunders (Saunders & Bains 1983, pp. 65–66), was to create an environment which was supportive to the search for meaning through pain and in the most adverse circumstances. This most fundamental philosophy is often overshadowed by the medico-scientific dimension of pain which focuses on the 'sensation' of pain rather than the meaning and experience of pain. In Australian hospice and palliative care the rhetoric of individualism must be questioned: does the control of pain by experts supersede the provision of a meaningful setting whereby the individual may learn to tolerate the sensation of pain if that is their wish? What may seem like a romanticised view here is, rather, a fundamental problem for both the terminally ill person and their professional carers. Many dying people fear pain, but also feel

dissatisfied with the debilitating side effects of pain controlling medications such as morphine. The health professional may likely be faced
with a dilemma: how can the terminally ill person articulate their
needs and desires if their cognitive function is altered by medications,
yet how can they focus on autonomous decision-making if they are
incapacitated by pain? More sophisticated medications are offered as
a solution, yet a cautionary note needs to be sounded about the
reliance upon technology's capacity to provide answers to suffering.
Overuse of medical technology will not only anaesthetise dying people
to pain, it may also anaesthetise individuals to the act of dying.

The local moral world

Kleinman (1992, pp. 128–29) suggests that in order to describe and
interpret interpersonal and intersubjective illness experience, ethnog-
raphers should set about conceptualising *local worlds* of illness and
care. Within the local world, actions have cultural, political, economic, institutional, and social relational sources and consequences.
However, local worlds need be understood as moral worlds where
people recreate local patterns of '*what is most at stake* for us' in our
living and dying. Following Kleinman we can see that 'what is most
at stake' in the context of terminal illness may be different for
individuals, yet no matter how contested or fragmented the local world
is, there is a shape or coherence which makes them recognisable as a
particular form of living and dying. The integrity of the terminally ill
person and their capacity to assume some kind of authority over dying
needs to be set within the local world. Some of the larger scale
political, socioeconomic and cultural forces that impinge upon the
local world of the terminally ill person have been outlined. Further
moral dimensions complicate the process of deciding how dying will
be managed.

The religious and cultural beliefs of the dying person, the person's
family and the health professionals who care for them often influence
the manner in which a terminally ill person dies. Furthermore, the
philosophy and organisational culture of services for terminally ill
people may constrain the degree to which the individual can make
autonomous decisions. This needs to be set into a social context where
the management of dying and death is highly contested. So while the
Northern Territory in Australia passed legislation allowing euthanasia
(July 1996), it was subsequently overturned in the Senate (March
1997). Furthermore, hospice and palliative care services have made a
public stand against legalised euthanasia and presented a report which

informed the Senate decision. Terminal sedation is a common practice in hospice and palliative care services, either at the request of the dying person, or at the discretion of the health professionals when the dying person is incapacitated. However, this assistance to die is not considered euthanasia as health professionals believe their intention is to alleviate the distressing symptoms of the dying person and not to deliberately end their life. If we ask the question 'what is at stake?' it becomes clear that the moral and ethical principles of a group determine the boundaries of individual authority over dying.

CONCLUSION

The preceding discussion has illustrated many of the concerns that face dying people, their families and their health professional carers. While the micro-context of each terminally ill person's experience of suffering and their ability to be involved in decision-making at the end of life is unique, it must also be situated within historical, social and cultural contexts. These contexts inform our understanding of what it means to die, as well as influencing the degree to which we may be able to participate in the circumstances of our deaths. Individual characteristics cannot fully explain the circumstances of each person's experience of dying. So rather than proposing that the terminally ill person might have a 'good' or 'good enough' death based upon their capacity for interpersonal interaction and autonomous decision-making, an alternative way of looking at the dying and death may be to consider it 'good enough' relative to social as well as individual factors.

Many of the factors that influence the individual's experience of dying are social: the social location of the individual and their access to power; cultural understandings of dying, death and individuality; the political and economic organisation of medicine and health care; and the moral dimensions of shared decision-making. Yet the actual experience of terminal illness is also embodied and personal. A person who experiences terminal illness and approaching death will be changed by the experience. The experience is not a series of isolated events, but a process of deterioration, interrupted by unpredictable changes and re-evaluations. If each person's death is considered as unique relative to the kinds of considerations that have been outlined in this chapter we will be better able to acknowledge individual agency, structural constraint, culture and change.

While a growing body of literature in the sociology of dying, death and bereavement has contributed to our understanding of death in advanced industrialised society, further socially-oriented research is needed to elaborate the social and the embodied experience of dying. This is particularly important in view of the fact that most deaths in advanced industrial societies occur as the result of long-term disease conditions where it is likely that people will be aware of their approaching death. This chapter goes some way towards conceptualising issues that are of concern to all those who value individual empowerment in end of life decision-making.

NOTE

1   The terminology used to describe the kinds of societies Australians, New Zealanders, British and North Americans live in is often disputed in social science discourse. The term 'Western' is thought to convey a geographical meaning which is inappropriate in the context of changing and globalising forces. Yet a term is needed to describe the influence of certain kinds of philosophical thought that have contributed to contemporary knowledge. In this latter case I have used the term 'Western'. Elsewhere I have employed the terms 'advanced' and 'emerging' industrialised countries, both of which may be multicultural to varying degrees.

REFERENCES

Aries, P. 1974 *Western Attitudes to Death* Johns Hopkins University Press, Baltimore, MA
——1981 *The Hour of Our Death* Allen Lane, London
Bauman, Z. 1992 *Mortality, Immortality and Other Life Strategies* Polity Press, Cambridge
Baume, P. 1993 'Living and dying: A paradox in medical progress' *The Medical Journal of Australia* vol. 159, pp. 792–94
Bendelow, G. & Williams, S. 1995 'Transcending the dualisms: Towards a sociology of pain' *Sociology of Health and Illness* vol. 17, no. 2, pp. 139–65
Campbell, A. 1990 'An ethic for hospice', paper presented at The Australian Hospice and Palliative Care Conference, Adelaide, 22 November
Cassell, E. 1975 'Dying in a technological society' in *Death Inside Out: The Hastings Centre Report* eds P. Steinfels & R. Veatch, Harper & Row, New York
Costain Schou, K. 1993 'Awareness contexts and the construction of dying in the cancer treatment setting: "Micro" and "macro" levels in narrative analysis' in *The Sociology of Death: Theory, Culture, Practice* ed. D. Clark, Blackwell, Oxford
Elias, N. 1985 *The Loneliness of Dying* Blackwell, Oxford
Gavin, W. 1995 *Cuttin' the Body Loose: Historical, Biological, and Personal Approaches to Death and Dying* Temple University Press, Philadelphia
Gordon, D. 1988 'Tenacious assumptions in Western medicine' in *Biomedicine Examined* eds M. Lock & D. Gordon, Kluwer Academic Publishers, Dordrecht
Gorer, G. 1965 *Death, Grief and Mourning in Contemporary Britain* Cresset, London
Hunt, R. 1994 'Palliative care—the rhetoric–reality gap' in *Willing to Listen Wanting to Die* ed. H. Kuhse, Penguin Books, Ringwood

Illich, I. 1976 *Limits to Medicine. Medical Nemesis: The Expropriation of Health*, Marion Boyars, London

Kellehear, A. 1984 'Are we a "death-denying" society? A sociological review' *Social Science and Medicine* vol. 18, no. 9, pp. 713–23

——1996 *Experiences Near Death: Beyond Medicine and Religion* Oxford University Press, Oxford

Kelner, M. & Bourgeault, I. 1993 'Patient control over dying: Responses of health care professionals' *Social Science and Medicine* vol. 36, no. 6, pp. 757–65

Kelly, M. & Field, D. 1996 'Medical sociology, chronic illness and the body' *Sociology of Health and Illness* vol. 18, no. 2, pp. 241–57

Kimura, R. 1991 'Fiduciary relationships and the medical profession: A Japanese point of view' in *Ethics, Trust, and the Professions: Philosophical and Cultural Aspects* eds E. Pellegrino, R. Veatch & J. Langan, Georgetown University Press, Washington

Kirmayer, L. 1988 'Mind and body as metaphors: Hidden values in biomedicine' in *Biomedicine Examined* eds M. Lock & D. Gordon, Kluwer Academic Publishers, Netherlands

Kleinman, A. 1988 *The Illness Narratives: Suffering, Healing and the Human Condition* Basic Books, New York

——1992 'Local worlds of suffering: An interpersonal focus for ethnographies of illness experience' *Qualitative Health Research* vol. 2, no. 2, pp. 127–34

Komesaroff, P., Norelle Lickiss, J., Parker, M. & Ashby, M. 1995 'The euthanasia controversy: Decision making in extreme cases' *The Medical Journal of Australia* vol. 162, pp. 594–97

Lock, M. 1996 'Death in technological time: Locating the end of meaningful life' *Medical Anthropology Quarterly* vol. 10, no. 4, pp. 575–600

McNamara, B., Waddell, C. & Colvin, M. 1994 'The institutionalisation of the Good Death' *Social Science and Medicine* vol. 39, no. 11, pp. 1501–08

——1995 'Threats to the Good Death: The cultural context of stress and coping among hospice nurses' *Sociology of Health and Illness* vol. 17, no. 2, pp. 222–44

Mellor, P. 1993 'Death in high modernity: The contemporary presence and absence of death' in *The Sociology of Death: Theory, Culture, Practice* ed. D. Clark, Blackwell, Oxford

Mellor, P. & Shilling, C. 1993 'Modernity, self-identity and the sequestration of death' *Sociology* vol. 27, no. 3, pp. 411–31

Mesler, M. 1995 'The philosophy and practice of patient control in hospice: The dynamics of autonomy versus paternalism' *Omega* vol. 30, no. 3, pp. 173–89

Metcalf, P. & Huntington, R. 1991 *Celebrations of Death: The Anthropology of Mortuary Ritual* 2nd edn, Cambridge University Press, Cambridge

Moller, D. 1990 *On Death Without Dignity: The Human Impact of Technological Dying* Baywood Publishing, New York

Muller, J. & Koenig, B. 1988 'On the boundary of life and death: The definition of dying by medical residents' in *Biomedicine Examined* eds M. Lock & D. Gordon, Kluwer Academic Publishers, Netherlands

Nuland, S. 1994 *How We Die: Reflections on Life's Final Chapter* Chatto & Windus, London

Parsons, T., Fox, R. & Lidz, V. 1972 'The "gift of life" and its reciprocation' *Social Research* vol. 39, pp. 367–415

Payne, S., Langley-Evans, A. & Hillier, R. 1996 'Perceptions of a "good" death: A comparative study of the views of hospice staff and patients' *Palliative Medicine* vol. 10, pp. 307–12

Petersen, A. 1994 In A Critical Condition: Health and Power Relations in Australia Allen & Unwin, Sydney

Ramsay, P. 1975 'The indignity of death with dignity' in Death Inside Out: The Hastings Centre Report eds P. Steinfels & R. Veatch, Harper & Row, New York

Rinaldi, A. & Kearl, M. 1990 'The hospice farewell: Ideological perspectives of its professional practitioners' Omega vol. 21, no. 4, pp. 283–300

Saunders, C. & Baines, M. 1983 Living With Dying: The Management of Terminal Disease Oxford University Press, Oxford

Veatch, R. 1976 Death, Dying and the Biological Revolution Yale University Press, Connecticut

Waddell, C., Clarnette, R., Smith, M., Oldham, L. & Kellehear, A. 1996 'Treatment decision-making at the end of life: A survey of Australian doctors' attitudes towards patients' wishes and euthanasia' The Medical Journal of Australia vol. 165, pp. 540–44

Walters, T. 1991 'Modern death: Taboo or not taboo?' Sociology vol. 25, no. 2, pp. 293–310

Zlatin, D. 1995 'Life themes: A method to understand terminal illness' Omega vol. 31, no. 3, pp. 189–206

PART 3

Care matters

What constitutes care? More specifically, what constitutes just and equitable care? What exactly is meant by patient 'participation' in medical treatment and health care? How do the media shape our perceptions of health care? How much trust do we, and should we, invest in those who are charged with caring for our health? These are some of the questions addressed by the chapters in this Part.

The word 'care' has strong evaluative connotations. It includes cure—a focus on the episodic, the biological, and clinical procedures. But it also includes the continuous, the contextual, and the whole person (the 'holistic' perspective). When we speak of 'caring for' someone, it is likely to evoke images of selfless devotion to others, attending to their physical, psychological and/or emotional needs. Professional nursing work is widely seen as the archetype of caring work, involving a great deal of emotional and physical labour on behalf of people who are dependent in some way on others. It is work that involves constant, close personal contact with those who are, in most cases, strangers. The intimacy involved in attending to their bodies—washing, dressing wounds, dispensing medicines, and so on—as well as their emotions (their fears, doubts, and psychological discomfort), calls for an extraordinary degree of skill, patience, empathy, and dedication. Caring work is also likely to evoke images of femininity, since, regardless of milieu, it is undertaken mainly by women.

Caring need not involve these connotations, however. There is no necessary connection between femininity and care, for example, and caring need not involve the emotional content found in nursing and parental roles. In some contexts, caring implies little more than surveillance and 'treatment' of the physical body (commonly the case with medical care), or no involvement of a 'care-giver' other than the self ('self-care'). Furthermore, one needs to recognise that any care practice inevitably involves some degree of power and influence over, and objectification of, those who are 'cared for'. Thus, even in nursing, which involves so much empathy and 'giving', the nurse retains overall control of the form of interactions with the patient and does not generally make the reciprocal disclosures that would be expected of a more equal relationship (May 1992). Sociologists, ever attentive to history, culture and social context, have examined how our images of care come into being and are sustained, and how the content of caring work is shaped by the particular settings in which it is practised. Any 'just sociology of health' worth its name will be concerned with the meanings and contexts of 'care' and 'caring', and with exploring the changing nature of health care practices. So it is with the chapters that follow.

The first four chapters focus specifically on medical care: cultural images of medicine and health care, trust in medical authority, uncertainty in medical decision-making, and the structure of general practice. They reflect a number of more general themes and perspectives in contemporary sociology, including the analysis of discourse and representational practices, the concept of trust, and analyses of professional knowledge, professional power, and professional practice, and of their interconnections. In Chapter 12, Deborah Lupton examines popular media portrayals of medicine and health care, focusing on television drama and news reporting. Given the dominance of the media in our lives, as a source of information and visual imagery, it is important that its discourses on 'the body', health, illness, the patient, health care and health professionals be opened to detailed and critical sociological scrutiny. In this chapter, Lupton is concerned with the ways in which the media establish and maintain particular 'ways of seeing' 'the body', medicine and health care, focusing on dominant discourses, and on the use of linguistic and visual devices. As she argues, media present diverse representations of modern medicine, as 'saviour, the font of hope, and as the site of malpractice, despair, greed and human error', both reflecting and contributing to uncertainty, and the consequent need for information to provide security. However, there has been no overall challenge to the status of doctors as arbiters of truth on 'the body' and its illnesses. Despite increasing cynicism about, and criticism of, doctors, patients continue to invest a great deal of faith in scientific medicine and doctors' expertise. In Lupton's view, the representation of medicine and medical practice in the media conform to broader emphases on the autonomy of the self, as a responsible agent and manager of risk.

Although expert knowledge may be losing its certainty, individuals are still compelled to trust abstract systems and knowledges, and to continually weigh up risks and benefits. Medical stories, she argues, provide a way of working through the complexities of modern life, involving both the desire for control and recognition of the reality of uncertainty.

In Chapter 13, Ann Daniel explores in detail the role of trust in medical authority. In her view, trust is 'an integral dimension of social life', providing the basis for cooperation. As a rational feeling, it helps us cope with uncertainties, difficulties and dangers, and arises from recognition of our dependence on others. Thus, we all invest a great deal of trust in other categories of persons and in social arrangements, which take on particular symbolic significance in our lives—'the father', 'the teacher', 'the doctor' etc. However, as symbols, they are susceptible to being overturned. Trust can quickly turn to mistrust, leading to a redefinition of social relations, involving withdrawal and resentment by both parties to the interaction. This applies to inter-action between doctors and patients no less than to other kinds of interactions. As Daniel argues, as people concerned with the avail-ability and quality of medical care, we place great trust in the medical profession and in individual practitioners. But only up to a point! Daniel examines the significance of trust in professional systems, and its relevance to expert–client interactions. She also discusses the relevance of reputation and of discipline (in the Foucauldian sense) to trust in medical authority. As she concludes, trust in both the medical profession and in medical practitioners is always tempered by a measure of distrust, the effect of which is to limit the authority of medicine to its clinical domain.

In Chapter 14, Gillian Hatt discusses the failure of the medical discipline to acknowledge uncertainty and the implications of this for clinical decision-making and health care policy. As part of its efforts to maintain the trust of the public, outlined above, the medical profession, with support from health care policy-makers, have down-played the appearance of doubt in clinical decision-making. As Hatt explains, medical educators have trained students to believe that uncertainty is a manifestation of ignorance, weakness or failure; a view that is upheld by patients who have been led to believe in the objectivity and precision of medical science. Hatt examines sociolog-ical analyses of uncertainty in medicine, and the particular contribution of social constructionism to the analysis of clinical un-certainty. She then uses the example of the measurement of a patient's blood pressure to emphasise the uncertainty surrounding clinical decision-making in the case of what appears to be an unproblematic, 'scientific', procedure. The socioeconomic implications of the failure of medicine to avoid dealing with the issue of uncertainty, Hatt argues, need to be more fully explored. The view that medicine is precise and certain, reinforces the view of health care policy-makers that medical practice can be organised in a more rational, cost-effective way, because it is supposedly easier to differentiate between 'effective' and 'ineffective' diagnostic and therapeutic decisions. However, this often leads to a reduction in time allocated to the exchange of information between clinician and patient, leading to greater distrust and uncertainty in the ability of the medical profession to provide health care equitably.

In Chapter 15, Valerie Clifford reports on a study of a new kind of general practice—the Aurora Health Centre—established by four women doctors in New Zealand. Work environments, and general practice in particular, are seen as male-dominated public domains, and as separate from the domestic, private sphere, occupied mainly by women. In medical practice, this generates inequalities in working conditions, in doctor–patient relationships and patient choice in health care. The four women doctors who are the focus of this study have attempted to achieve some balance in, and control over, their work environment, while delivering 'good quality medical care'. That is, they have sought to achieve a 'patient-centred' and a 'doctor-centred' practice. The chapter discusses the relationship between the doctors' work and other aspects of their lives, and their ideals and how these are reflected in the practice setting and in patient care. The study is based upon extensive fieldwork, involving observations of the practice, reading of various documentation, individual interviews and group discussions with the doctors, and a survey of patients. At the time of the study, the practice was deemed to be successful by some criteria, for example, it had survived its first three years of operation and had a full patient list. However, there remained some unresolved problems and tensions. These are discussed in detail in the chapter, and some suggestions are offered for furthering the ideals of the Centre.

The final three chapters in this Part examine care in the context of an increasingly deregulated health care system and the emergence of new personal roles and responsibilities associated with the so-called new public health. Increasingly, individuals are being called upon to play a greater role in their own health and medical care: to care for themselves to prevent illness and promote 'well-being' and, when sick, to play a more active role in their own healing. In line with this latter tendency, we have seen the development of a new language of patient 'participation' or patient 'empowerment'. But what do these terms mean in practice, and what are the implications for those who are subject to these new strategies of care? Can one achieve social justice objectives in a deregulated health care system? These chapters go some way towards answering these specific questions, while contributing more generally to our understanding of the impacts of changing social contexts on the meanings and content of care.

In Chapter 16, Julie Mulvany reviews sociological arguments and evidence relating to psychiatry and 'mental illness', and considers the contributions that sociologists can make to informing the policy of 'de-institutionalisation'. Sociologists have offered diverse contributions to our understanding of mental health, as Mulvany explains, through, for instance, investigations into social responses to people suffering from a psychiatric disorder and the analysis of the social factors that influence the cause and incidence of 'mental health problems'. By expanding our approach to the study and conceptualisation of the area commonly referred to as 'mental illness' (or 'psychiatric disability', the term preferred by Mulvany), sociologists contribute to challenging dominant medical definitions and approaches. The move towards community based care in recent years has revealed shortcomings in the medical model, in particular its neglect of the effects of poverty, social security policy and inadequate housing on those diagnosed as seriously mentally ill. Mulvany critically examines the discourse of 'community care' as it operates in Australia, highlighting in particular the tendency to over-look the social circumstances and experiences of people suffering from serious psychiatric disability when living in the community. To this end, she examines research regarding the housing circumstances of such people, which she believes 'alerts us to the dangers of assuming that de-institutionalisation will be successful if the needs of the psychiatrically disabled continue to be conceptualised in narrow clinical terms'. Through the application of their conceptual, analytical and research skills, sociologists, she believes, can make an important contribution to the assessment of the post-de-institutionalisation process.

In Chapter 17, Saras Henderson examines nurses' and patients' perceptions of participation and its influence on patient involvement in their own care. Because, as noted above, professional nursing work always contains some element of control, the move towards a more patient-oriented approach to care would seem to be an essential element in the creation of a more just health care system. However, although practising nurses are in favour of patient participation, and studies indicate that patients experience positive outcomes, as

Henderson indicates, there is some evidence to suggest that there is an incongruity between nurse attitudes and behaviour. In a context of financial constraints and the pressure for early patient discharge, the demand for participation will not go away, and so nurses, who are most involved with patients, need to take a leading role in the promotion of the concept. It is important to know whether patients can effectively care for themselves once at home. In Henderson's view, it is only through active involvement while in hospital that patients will be prepared for self-care when discharged. As a first step in understanding how patient participation is initiated and maintained while patients are in hospital, an interview study was conducted with a sample of nurses and patients in order to gain insight into the meaning of participation for both. The chapter discusses the findings, drawing on nurses' and patients' own comments, and identifies some major conceptions of participation shared by both parties. There is a mismatch between the ideal of patient participation and reality of practice, argues Henderson, which calls into question the nursing profession's philosophy of holistic care and patient involvement. She offers some likely explanations as to why it might be difficult to bridge the theory/practice gap.

Finally, in Chapter 18 Allan Kellehear explores the recent emergence of the idea of the active involvement of a person in the process of their own dying. Kellehear traces the history of dying from the Middle Ages to the present in order to present a broad context for his discussion of the contemporary Western emphasis on individual control over dying. He is concerned with the impact of a new health discourse—and more specifically the New Public Health—on our understanding of dying, and on debates about 'euthanasia'. In Australia, the recent euthanasia debate has reflected a shift away from the idea that doctors should always endeavour to prolong life to the notion that doctors could assist people to take their own life in certain circumstances. Such a shift is only possible, Kellehear argues, when 'health' and 'dying' cease being seen as opposites and begin to converge. The idea of the passive patient approach to health care has been predominant for most of the period since the eighteenth century when health and health care began to be medicalised. However, dissatisfaction with this idea has grown since the 1960s, gaining momentum with the emergence of 'healthism' philosophy in the 1970s and 1980s, and the New Public Health, with its focus on personal and community 'empowerment'. With the New Public Health, the individual began to be seen as an active agent in their own health outcomes who is entitled to assistance from those who are able to provide it. (On this point, see also Bev McNamara's Chapter 11.) Nevertheless, as recent events have shown, the idea of euthanasia remains contentious. On 26 March 1997, the Australian Senate passed a Bill to override the Northern Territory Euthanasia Bill, and the merits and dangers of euthanasia continue to be debated by politicians, members of the clergy, and the general public. In his chapter, Kellehear discusses a number of implications of the new philosophy of dying, especially in light of religious and humanistic concerns about the protection and sanctity of the individual.

REFERENCE

May, C. 1992 'Nursing work, nurses' knowledge, and the subjectification of the patient' *Sociology of Health and Illness* vol. 14, no. 4, pp. 473–87

12 Medicine and health care in popular media

Deborah Lupton

The medical profession and the practice of medicine have provided the stuff of gripping television, radio and film drama and newsworthy events for decades. It is estimated that at least fifty-five drama and comedy series centring on doctors were aired on the three major American television networks from the start of commercial television in the late 1940s to the late 1980s (Turow 1989, p. xviii). Recent years have witnessed an emergence of a spate of new medical dramas, including the American *ER* and *Chicago Hope* and the Australian *Medivac*, as well as the 'docu-dramas' portraying real-life situations of patient care such as *RPA*, based on the activities in Royal Prince Alfred Hospital in Sydney. So too, studies of news coverage of medical and public health stories have shown that these topics receive a high level of prominence overall. One recent content analysis of Australian metropolitan newspapers published in 1993 showed that science and medicine was one of nine major topical areas identified, comprising 7 per cent of all news stories, with medical stories accounting for most of the reports in this category (Henningham 1996). Another study found that medical and public health issues regularly made the front page of a major Australian metropolitan newspaper, appearing in this prominent spot in over one-third of editions published over the year-long study period (1993–94) (Lupton 1995a). Health and medical stories are also dominant in Australian television news and current affairs programs (Chapman & Lupton 1994).

Research would certainly suggest that the lay public has a strong interest in health and medical issues in the media. Series such as *ER* and *RPA* regularly appear among the top programs in lists of television ratings in Australia. A survey of over 4000 British and American adults found that of six different issue areas reported in the news media, by far the highest level of self-reported interest was that for new medical discoveries. The respondents were also more likely to say they would read newspaper stories with headlines concerning medical issues compared with other topical areas (Durant et al. 1989). Australian research has also found that the popular media are used by members of the lay public as an important source of information about health and medical issues (Kassulke et al. 1993).

In this chapter, I discuss the ways that the popular media portray health and medical issues. This has been a central research interest of mine for some time, and I draw in this chapter on a range of studies I have conducted, focusing in particular on television drama and news reporting. My interest in the popular media, regardless of the genre, is in identifying the dominant discourses on the body, health, illness, the patient, health care and health professionals in these texts, or the ways in which language and visual imagery convey certain meanings about these phenomena. The notion of discourse sees language and imagery as having a constitutive role in producing social relations and notions of reality. From this perspective, language and imagery are viewed as a form of social practice, a mode of action as well as a mode of representation (Fairclough 1992, p. 63). More specifically, in relation to the concerns of the sociology of health and medicine, my assumption is that such language and imagery serve to shape and constitute our embodiment, our understandings and experiences of and practices around health and illness, our interactions with doctors and other health care workers. I am also interested in the cultural and historical contingency of discourses and meanings around the body, health, illness and medicine; that is, their changing and often contradictory nature.

A focus on power is an integral feature of analyses of discourse, for a discourse is often used in the interests of maintaining or reproducing power relations (Fairclough 1992; Parker 1992). Dominant discourses generally support the status quo rather than challenge it, reproducing and legitimising the power of dominant social groups and institutions. In media representations of health and medicine, particular social groups, institutions and bodies of knowledge are routinely positioned as elite, as commanding authority and as objects of personal and institutional deference. As will be detailed below, for example, medical practitioners are generally depicted as the most powerful group of health workers in the popular media, with their practices, knowledge base and professional associations receiving far more attention and given far more credence than those of other health workers, particularly practitioners of alternative medicine. Various narratives and discourses associated with the body, disease and health care are used in the media to support this positioning.

When media workers such as journalists, editors, photographers, camera operators, writers, actors and directors produce their accounts of health and medicine, they do so as members of a particular social world or culture. They draw upon pre-established discourses and meanings, and in doing so, reproduce them (Tulloch & Lupton 1997). Thus, for example, when in the early 1980s AIDS was first portrayed in the media, a number of pre-established discourses and meanings were invoked to 'make sense' of this new disease. In Australian press reports of AIDS, the discourses and meanings drawn upon included comparing AIDS to the plague, drawing a binary opposition between 'innocent' and 'guilty' people with HIV/AIDS based on understandings about the extent to which they engaged in practices believed to be deviant, and employing military metaphors to describe the 'fight' or 'war' against AIDS (Lupton 1994). In Australian television drama and mainstream documentaries, the notion of the gay man or injecting drug user with HIV/AIDS as stigmatised outsider, or the figure of the passive, 'innocent' female victim of HIV, were commonly employed (Tulloch & Lupton 1997, ch. 4).

Discourses, however, as noted above are not static, and are subject to change over time. As Fairclough notes, 'power struggle occurs both in and over discourse' (1992, p. 56), and this struggle is an important feature of social change. Discourses compete with each other for attention, and sometimes new, subjugated or radical discourses gain prominence over more established or politically conservative discourses. In the case of health care, for example, the discourse of consumerism has emerged over the past two or three decades, which has challenged the power of doctors to make decisions about patient care. The popular media have sometimes taken up this discourse of consumerism in representing the medical encounter and medical politics, particularly in news reporting.

DRAMATIC PORTRAYALS

Fox (1993, pp. 154–55) summarises the major patterns of representing medicine and doctors in television and cinematic drama. He identifies seven key discourses in this representation. They are as follows:

1   The doctor as paragon or hero figure, usually portrayed as male and white, and as motivated by altruism, with a strong faith in rationalism, scientific medicine and medical technology.

2   The doctor as human figure, again predominantly male and white but depicted as interested in the lives of his patients.

3   Doctors/medicine as emotional broker, depicting doctors as dealing not only with patients' physical problems but also successfully counselling them on their emotional or personal problems.

4   Health care as alienation, or the notion that doctors may themselves suffer from personal or health problems, find the practice of medicine difficult, or engage in nefarious practices.

5   Health care as bureaucratic or inefficient: portrayals which suggest that scientific medicine is not quite as successful or humane as more positive representations would suggest.

6   Health and the human condition: a cynical or 'postmodern' representation of medicine and health care, in which patients and health care workers alike are portrayed as alienated within the medical system, with scientific medicine offering little hope or solace for either group.

7   Health and medicine as comedy.

What is interesting about these discourses is that they all currently co-exist in popular representations of medicine and health. In previous times, however, some have been more dominant than others. In his historical overview of American television medical dramas, Turow (1989) notes that during the 1960s, while issues such as medical incompetence and malpractice did come up occasionally on these shows, they tended to be dealt with as rarities. Doctors' overall professionalism, idealism and dedication tended to be privileged. Thus, if a doctor was shown making a mistake and being sued for malpractice, it was dealt with in the context of the narrative as an excusable outcome of the uncertainties of medicine and the occasional need for heroic and sometimes risky measures to combat disease (Turow 1989, p. 73). Turow argues that this type of representation lasted well into the 1960s but began to change into the 1970s, during which time doctors were represented as more 'human', experiencing difficulties in their private lives and sometimes even shown as making professional mistakes. Karpf (1988) and Bury and Gabe (1994) make similar observations of changes over time in the portrayal of doctors and medical practice in British television.

In the 1990s, there is a trend evident in popular media in the representation of uncertainty and risk in relation to medicine and public health. The discourses of 'health care as alienation' and 'health care as bureaucratic and inefficient' are far more dominant compared with the pre-1970s medical dramas discussed by Turow. For example, one of the two major American television medical dramas currently screened in Australia, *Chicago Hope*, constantly raises ethical issues around surgical procedures and debates the financial issues of high technology medicine. In the first two seasons of the series (shown in Australia in 1995), the hospital's resident lawyer was one of the main characters, portrayed as constantly seeking to find ways of dealing with patients' threats to sue for medical negligence or appealing to the courts to approve highly unusual surgical procedures. The other American medical drama, the rather more adrenalin-filled *ER* (set in another Chicago hospital's emergency medicine department), highlights the doctor characters' personal foibles and problems, and depicts the occasional medical disaster, including the death or near-death of patients because of doctors' or nurses' mistakes.

Despite this trend, however, very positive portrayals of doctors and medical practice remain in such dramas. Both *ER* and *Chicago Hope* also depict medical practitioners and other health care workers as highly dedicated to their jobs, to the point that their personal lives are often compromised and their own happiness is denied. They are also shown as efficient in their work, constantly saving patients from death through their dedication and medical expertise, with mistakes depicted as rare events rather than usual. Both dramas have a glossy visual style, featuring largely attractive doctors, nurses and patients.

Contemporary Australian and British medical dramas have tended to have more of an ironic edge compared with these American dramas. The British series *Cardiac Arrest*, for example, which began screening in Australia in 1996, is a cross between satire, drama and black comedy. *Cardiac Arrest* falls squarely into Fox's sixth discursive category, in which medicine is portrayed as offering little hope to either patient or health care workers. It is a clear and bitter critique of the hospital system under the funding and administrative problems of the British National Health Service. For example, one of the episodes in the first series shown in Australia included the character of a young idealistic doctor, just out of medical school, who was forced to work three nights and three days solid because the hospital administrators wanted to save money. The doctor was shown as desperately tired and reaching the end of his tether, not caring what he was doing by the end.

The hospital administrators and surgeons in *Cardiac Arrest* are depicted as nasty, uncaring types, with the junior doctors and nursing staff portrayed as long-suffering and overworked, near desperation point most of the time or else engaged in high jinks and tasteless practical jokes to relieve the pressure. The style of the series is more gritty and less glossy compared with the American series. The patients in the series are far less glamorous and are often depicted as suffering in conditions of disarray, their needs neglected by the overworked or cavalier staff. Rarely are they shown as miraculously getting better through the interventions of the doctors and nurses. Heroicism, the 'doctor as paragon' discourse, rarely makes an appearance in this series. The doctor characters are portrayed as dishevelled, highly dissatisfied in their work, grey with fatigue, sexually obsessed and bickering among themselves. (See Bury & Gabe (1994) for similar comments on another British medical drama, *Casualty*.)

In my study of the 1994 season of the now defunct Australian medical drama *GP*, which ran for eight years on the ABC, I noted that a strong aspect was a juxtaposition of social issues with medical issues evident in this series and the blurring of the boundaries between the two (Lupton 1995b). Rather than illness and disease being predominantly depicted in the modernist tradition as entities capable of being isolated from the rest of the patient's body and their social context, there was a continual focus in the episodes examined on the social location of the patient (albeit confined within the temporal limits of a fifty-minute episode and the conventions of the television drama series genre). Unlike many other medical dramas, the plots of *GP* often did not end with the patient being cured or the problem being solved. The doctor characters, although shown as dedicated and interested in their patients, were also portrayed as having occasional lapses of judgement, and being criticised by their patients, who were often portrayed as militant rather than as passive and grateful recipients of the doctors' care.

GP, therefore, was not nearly as bleak as *Cardiac Arrest*, but was less supportive of the discourse of heroic medicine than *ER* and *Chicago Hope*. Unlike the latter two series, where the use of high technology equipment and medico-scientific jargon is a large part of creating the atmosphere of the surgery and the emergency room, *GP* devoted more attention to human relations, drawing on the 'doctor as emotional broker' discourse more frequently. This may partly have been a function of the specific focus of *GP*, which, as the name suggests, concerned the activities of a group of general practitioners (GPs) working in a suburban Sydney clinic and dealing with the day-to-day problems of their patients. As is the case in real life, GPs see far more routine and banal problems than do medical specialists or surgeons. There is less opportunity for them to be depicted as heroic, saving patients' lives on the operating table using high medical technology.

Another factor, however, potentially shaping differences in
representation between series such as the Australian *GP* and the
British *Cardiac Arrest* and contemporary American medical dramas, is
the differences in the cultures and politics of medicine in Australia
and Britain compared with the United States. Both Australia and
Britain have state-funded systems of medical care, whereas health care
in the United States is privatised. This provides a different context
within which to portray the practice of medicine. Further, American
medicine tends to be far more aggressive and scientifically oriented
than British medicine, with a greater emphasis on tests, surgical
procedures and immediate action (Stein 1985; Payer 1989). Australian
medical culture probably falls somewhere between the American and
British approaches.

NEWS PORTRAYALS

In news reporting, as in dramatic portrayals, there are a number of
different and sometimes conflicting discourses on medicine and health
care circulating. These conform to the seven major discourses identified by Fox described above. There is somewhat of a difference in
emphasis in news reports of medicine and health compared with
dramatic portrayals, however, because they are different genres. Television or cinematic drama is produced with the major intention of
engaging audience members' emotional responses, drawing them in
with a strong narrative that has some sort of ending, or closure. There
is no assumption, necessarily, that dramatic portrayals need to be
realistic in representing social groups, institutions or events, because
it is accepted that drama is fiction. While the producers of many
medical dramas strive for accurate portrayals of the medical treatment
they are depicting in a quest to create authenticity, often employing
doctors as consultants to advise on such details, realism is not the
central purpose of this genre.

News reporting, in contrast, bears the values of realism and 'truth'.
Indeed, the legitimacy of news reports is founded on their claim to
'tell the truth' about news events. The producers of news reports seek
to engage their audiences by presenting stories about subjects that are
considered to be important, to be new, to affect the audience member
in some way, to be unusual and to have local, national or global
significance. This is particularly the case of 'hard' news, which tends
to be composed of reports of accidents, conflicts, crimes, an-
nouncements, discoveries or other recent events deemed to be

newsworthy (Bell 1991, p. 14). Newsworthiness is based on such features as negativity, proximity, novelty and relevance, the extent to which elite social groups are involved and the degree to which the issue can be personalised (pp. 157–58).

In the case of news reports of health and medicine, events or issues which involve a new medical discovery or treatment, unusual medical research findings or those which contradict previous advice and conflict between elite groups tend to be most often reported. Hence, the discourses of 'doctor as paragon/medicine as font of hope', 'health care as alienation' and 'health care as bureaucratic or inefficient' tend to receive prominence. The first discourse supports the notion that medicine is making continual progress by reporting new advances in treatment or covering stories about the successes and dedication of individual doctors. The second discourse feeds on the confounding of this first discourse, often sensationalising cases where doctors have been found guilty of medical negligence or assault or mistreatment of their patients, and the third raises issues of political relevance and often features conflict between doctors' associations and government. All these discourses have personal relevance for members of the audience, the vast majority of whom seek help for illness from doctors on a regular basis and are therefore likely to have an interest in both the successes and the failures of medicine and its practitioners.

A study I conducted with a colleague examined one week of prime-time news and current affairs programs on Australian television in March 1993 (Chapman & Lupton 1994, ch. 3). We found that the health and medical stories centred on the narrative themes of 'the bizarre', 'moral tales and falls from grace', 'medical miracles' and 'low-tech prevention'. The first category, 'the bizarre', included stories that focused on visual portrayals of ill, wasted or unusual bodies, such as those of body builders using steroids, Siamese twins undergoing a separation operation and people in developing countries dying in a famine. 'Moral tales and falls from grace' included stories on medical negligence: in these cases, the 'fall from grace' involved doctors whose heroic status was compromised by their mistakes. In contrast, stories conforming to the 'medical miracles' narrative theme built on the 'doctor as paragon' discourse by including news of medical discoveries and new technologies promising to alleviate human suffering. The 'low-tech prevention' theme diverged from the previous theme by including stories about non-medical or preventive health solutions to ill health, such as the importance of including vegetables in one's diet to prevent heart disease. This last theme was not as common as the 'medical miracles' theme, which we concluded was due in part to the demands of television for arresting visual material:

> Viewers cannot 'see' a healthy diet working to protect against heart disease in the same way as they can witness heart surgery being performed by the high priests of medicine, clustered around an operating table with the very organ pulsing in their bloodied hands. (Chapman & Lupton 1994, p. 92)

In another analysis I conducted of over 5000 articles on medical practitioners and medical practice published in major Australian newspapers and news magazines between January 1994 and March 1995, it was found that the most frequently appearing topic was 'Medical malpractice and medical negligence/mistakes' (included in 9 per cent of the articles). The topic 'Legal action against doctors by patients' was also included in a relatively high percentage (5 per cent) and ranked as the equal fourth most frequent topic. Stories about 'bad' doctors included those who had murdered their wives, had contributed to serious illness or death of a patient and failed to prescribe appropriate treatment for a patient or missed signs of a serious disease (particularly newsworthy when such cases involved infants and children or young, attractive women). There were also a number of stories about doctors who were charged with sexually harassing or assaulting their patients, and those charged with defrauding the state by claiming for consultations with patients they had not actually seen or for surgical procedures they had not carried out. However, these types of reports were not very dominant overall: stories about sexual abuse comprised only 1 per cent of the total of reports in the study, while those about Medicare fraud accounted for less than 1 per cent.

While the frequencies of topics tells us something about which issues are considered most newsworthy by members of the press, and which individuals, groups and events are more likely to have a presence in news coverage, there is much more to the meaning of news accounts. Unusual or conflictual items may not appear as frequently as other topics, but the tenor of reporting may have the effect of making such stories more memorable and interesting to readers. The language used in headlines, in particular, is important in framing the meaning of news events and social groups and in attracting readers' attention to the news story. The recurrence in newspaper headlines about doctors of such phrases as 'Doctors contributed to the death of injured toddler', 'Dead man's family felt "let down" by doctors', 'Doctors accused of sexplay with patients', 'Boy blames doctor for brain damage', 'Doctors admit aiding death', 'Cheating doctors made to pay up', 'Patient accuses doctor of sexual assault', 'Doctor banned for sex attack', 'Dying mother sues two doctors', 'Doctor "bashed" patient', 'Doctors leave patients to die', and 'Doctors "fail to listen to patients"' bespeak the existence of strong emotions around the issue of the medical profession's conduct and expertise.

As these headlines suggest, negative news stories often contain lurid combinations of the word 'doctor/s' (or, less frequently, synonyms such as 'surgeon/s' or 'GP/s') with other words linking them to murder, death, sexual assault and misconduct, negligence and greed. The study also found, however, that medical science was also commonly portrayed as successful and providing hope, particularly for very ill infants and children, people with cancer and women suffering infertility problems. Stories on economic and budget issues related to health care (which accounted for 5 per cent of the total) typically depicted members of the medical profession as attempting to fight against difficult working conditions so as to do their best by their patients. Articles were often illustrated with photographs of doctors protectively cradling infants or young children, demonstrating their caring side, or intent in operating theatres, working on a difficult surgical procedure.

News stories also still tended to use doctors as figures of authority and knowledge, routinely employing such phrases as 'Doctors say . . .' or 'Doctors warn . . .'. Doctors were dominantly represented, therefore, as holding cultural and social authority (Elston 1991, p. 61), in terms of possessing the power to act as the major news sources and actors in news stories on medical matters. Compared with other interested parties, such as patients, consumer groups, nurses, allied health professionals and alternative medical practitioners, doctors receive far more prominence as the voices of authority on matters medical (see also Lupton (1995a), for similar findings). This is particularly the case if they are male rather than female (Lupton 1995a). Conservative medical associations, such as the Australian Medical Association, and the doctors who lead them receive far more prominence than do left-leaning, more marginalised professional associations such as the Doctors' Reform Society.

Docu-dramas or 'fly on the wall' programs (also called 'reality television') such as RPA, the Australian series mentioned earlier, are interesting in that they combine features of current affairs or documentary reporting with elements of drama. RPA, which began screening on Channel Nine in 1995, is based on the activities of real doctors and other health care workers with real patients in a real hospital. They are followed and filmed by camera crews, with footage later edited. As such, RPA conforms to the 'realism' and 'factual' demands of news or documentary reporting. It differs from the news genre, however, in constructing a narrative that is more similar to a dramatic serial or a soap opera than a documentary. Audiences of programs like *RPA* are encouraged to identify with the plight of the patients they see portrayed and to be interested in their progress. The series introduces individual patients and their doctors and other health care workers and then follows their fate over a number of episodes, like characters in drama series. Most news reports and documentaries, in contrast, are 'one-off' productions.

RPA is also far less 'hard-edged' than most news reporting, focusing on 'human interest' and tugs on the heartstrings instead. The emotions of patients and their relatives as they deal with serious illness and major surgery is a central feature of the program. The doctors and other health care professionals in the hospital are never shown in an unfavourable light, but rather as constantly caring and efficient in their work. Numerous scenes in each half-hour episode show patients telling their doctors how grateful they are for their expert assistance, and there is very little emphasis in the series on operations that go wrong, or on patients who fail to get better or who die. The inevitable disasters and tragedies that occur in all hospitals, and which are portrayed even in the glossier medical dramas such as *ER* and *Chicago Hope*, are not included in this series. The overall effect, indeed, is that of a public relations exercise for the hospital featured in *RPA*.

CONCLUSION

As shown in this chapter, popular media portrayals of medicine and health care oscillate between depicting modern medicine as saviour, the font of hope, and as the site of malpractice, despair, greed and human error. Depending on the particular genre of media, various discourses are taken up more often than others. Most media portrayals rarely present either a totally positive or wholly negative representation of medicine and those who practise it (although exceptions are *RPA* and *Cardiac Arrest*, which tend to portray a very rosy and a very bleak view of medicine, respectively). The tenor of media representations is important, because they both serve to reproduce major currents in the broader society and to contribute to 'ways of seeing'. In their portrayal of health and medicine, whether in news accounts, documentaries, drama or government-sponsored health promotion advertisements, the media are reflecting and reproducing the high level of uncertainty, accompanied by the consequent need for information and detail to provide security, that is part of the late modern era. They contribute significantly to a heightened awareness of risk, danger and uncertainty by covering such issues as the potential side effects of medical treatment or the tendency of some doctors to sexually assault their patients or make mistakes about medical treatment.

Some writers have suggested that the contradictory discourses circulating on medicine and health care in the popular media provide a space for alternative discourses to be generated, for the power of scientific medicine to be challenged (e.g. Fox 1993, pp. 156–67). As I have shown, it is certainly the case that doctors, in particular, are subject to often contradictory portrayals in the popular media, portrayed as both heroes and sinners. Nonetheless, they remain firmly positioned as the dominant authorities on medical issues. The very blackest and most cynical of discourses, that representing medicine as offering little hope for either patients or doctors, appears rarely in the popular media. There is little suggestion from the research here discussed that any other group is significantly challenging the cultural and institutional power of members of the medical profession or of scientific medicine as the most appropriate way to treat illness and disease. Nor is it necessarily the case that members of the lay public want to mount such as a challenge. Research eliciting the views of patients continues to show that while some may be more cynical about doctors and more willing to be critical of them than in previous eras, patients in general continue to invest their faith and trust in scientific medicine and doctors' expertise (e.g. Lupton 1996, 1997).

The pattern of representation of medicine and medical practice in the popular media conforms to broader changes in people's understandings of the self and their relationship with expert knowledges. More so than in the past, individuals are seen as autonomous actors, disembedded from traditional ties with others, their problems their own concern. It is seen as their responsibility to deal with risks, to seek out knowledge about them and deal with them individually by engaging in self-regulation (Beck 1992; Giddens 1994). Choice has become obligatory in everyday life, which has become governed by decisions, often based on the claims of expert knowledge rather than on tradition (Giddens 1994, p. 76). Trust in abstract systems and knowledges, such as those of medicine and medical practice, remains a necessary part of life. Yet expert knowledges themselves are no longer certain and are subject to dispute between experts, and the media often report these disputes. Because of the divided and contestable nature of expertise, trust cannot be fully invested in expert knowledges and abstract systems. As a result, lay people are placed in a situation of continually weighing up risks and benefits, wanting more and more information about how to prevent illness and disease but often finding that such information does not serve to solve their dilemma or provide ontological security.

Medical stories attract audiences because they strike at the fundamental concerns and uncertainties of late modern life, a time when we like to think that our lives (and our deaths) are under our control but know at heart that unanticipated disaster may always strike, confounding our best-laid plans. As Tulloch and Lupton have put it, 'The media provide a "window on risk", a means of working through the complexities of human relationships and of demonstrating the ills to which human bodies may become prey' (1997, p. 216). Stories which show doctors performing dramatic life-saving operations, extolling the wonders of scientific medicine, or those which reveal doctors' foibles and personal failings, or which show the occasions when medicine can 'go wrong', hold equal potential to attract audiences' attention. The prevalence of medical and health stories in the news and the high ratings afforded medical dramas and docu-dramas is evidence of this.

REFERENCES

Beck, U. 1992 *Risk Society: Towards a New Modernity* Sage, London
Bell, A. 1991 *The Language of the News Media* Blackwell, Oxford
Bury, M. & Gabe, J. 1994 'Television and medicine: Medical dominance or trial by media?' in *Challenging Medicine* eds J. Gabe, D. Kelleher & G. Williams, Routledge, London
Chapman, S. & Lupton, D. 1994 *The Fight for Public Health: Principles and Practice of Media Advocacy* British Medical Journal Publishing, London
Durant, J., Evans, G. & Thomas, G. 1989 'The public understanding of science' *Nature* vol. 340, pp. 11–14
Elston, M.A. 1991 'The politics of professional power: Medicine in a changing health service' in *The Sociology of the Health Service* eds J. Gabe, M. Calnan & M. Bury, Routledge, London
Fairclough, N. 1992 *Discourse and Social Change* Polity Press, Cambridge
Fox, N. 1993 *Postmodernism, Sociology and Health* Open University Press, Buckingham
Giddens, A. 1994 'Living in a post-traditional society' in *Reflexive Modernization: Politics, Tradition and Aesthetics in the Modern Social Order* eds U. Beck, A. Giddens & S. Lash, Polity, Cambridge
Henningham, J. 1996 'The shape of daily news: A content analysis of Australia's metropolitan newspapers' *Media International Australia* vol. 79, pp. 22–34
Karpf, A. 1988 *Doctoring the Media: The Reporting of Health and Medicine* Routledge, London

Kassulke, D., Stenner-Day, K., Coory, M. & Ring, I. 1993 'Information-seeking behaviour and sources of health information: Associations between risk factor status in an analysis of three Queensland electorates' *Australian Journal of Public Health* vol. 17, pp. 51–57

Lupton, D. 1994 *Moral Threats and Dangerous Desires: AIDS in the News Media* Taylor & Francis, London

——1995a 'Medicine and health on the *Sydney Morning Herald*'s front page' *Australian Journal of Public Health* vol. 19, pp. 501–08

——1995b 'GP: a postmodern medical drama?' *Australian Journal of Communication* vol. 22, pp. 108–20

——1996 '"Your life in their hands": Trust in the medical encounter' in *Health and the Sociology of Emotion* Sociology of Health & Illness Monograph Series, eds J. Gabe & V. James, Blackwell, Oxford

——1997 'Consumerism, reflexivity and the medical encounter' *Social Science & Medicine* vol. 45, no. 3, pp. 373–81

Parker, I. 1992 *Discourse Dynamics: Critical Analysis for Social and Individual Psychology* Routledge, London

Payer, L. 1989 *Medicine and Culture: Notions of Health and Sickness in Britain, the US, France and West Germany* Victor Gollancz, London

Stein, H. 1985 *American Medicine as Culture* Westview, Colorado

Tulloch, J. & Lupton, D. 1997 *Television, AIDS and Risk: A Cultural Studies Approach to Health Communication* Allen & Unwin, Sydney

Turow, J. 1989 *Playing Doctor: Television, Storytelling, and Medical Power* Oxford University Press, New York

13 Trust and medical authority

Ann Daniel

In this chapter I will examine medical authority as a matter of power conceded by the communities in which the medical profession practises its art. The line I am taking is that we, as people concerned about the availability and quality of medical care, are prepared to trust that profession and individual practitioners—up to a point. Without that concession of trust a practitioner cannot practise and without a generalised trust a profession loses its authority. That trust is not absolute. It is conditioned by a multiplicity of beliefs, values, needs and perceptions at a personal level as well as by the guarantees of competence and care which a profession wrests from the state.

This approach takes a different path from the usual one where medical dominance can be seen as the outcome of the power-plays of a masterful and resourceful consortium which won a monopoly of its market for services from all other potential contenders and negotiated aggressively with the powers that be, usually the state, to legislatively authorise its monopoly. Yes, such accounts are true. But, like all attempts to find the truth, it is only part of the truth. This chapter is simply another part of the whole truth which I suggest we can never totally discover or understand. In following this proposed line of inquiry we should grasp a number of concepts. In particular such an approach draws on notions of trust, discipline, reputation and, of course, profession, specifically the medical profession. Like all concepts that are crucial to a sociological analysis these terms stand for contested ideas. Nonetheless, arguments over definitions should not blur their usefulness. Debates about definition can be met by saying what we mean by the sociological constructs we use. They can then be used to throw light on such questions as how medical dominance emerged and how it may be threatened. So, the ideas of trust, discipline, profession and reputation are examined in what follows. They are significant in the creation and maintenance of medical dominance and the promotion of medical authority.

Many years ago medicine secured from the state a licensed monopoly to practise its art for the purpose of curing disease and alleviating suffering and disability. By 'the state' I mean the various agencies of governance, created by law, which order any society (one of the most readable papers describing the Australian state was written by Michael Pusey in 1988). The state has played a pivotal part in the establishment of monopolies of professional service provision. The actual time when the medical profession achieved that licensed monopoly varies from country to country. You might read about the battles to gain medical sovereignty in the United States in Paul Starr's social history (1983) or of the strategies used by Australian doctors in Evan Willis' classic analysis of medical dominance (1983). Early in this century medicine had assumed dominance of the health field in North America, most countries of Europe and Australia. And throughout this century the medical profession has maintained its primary authority, although there have been significant attempts by other interests to restrict or subvert medical power. In this chapter I am not retracing those histories, nor am I detailing the way the medical profession continues in its uneasy autonomy–dependence relationship with governments. The stresses and strains of that partnership with reference to a major industrial conflict in the 1980s have been examined in earlier writing (Daniel 1990). Here I take as given the medical profession's historical achievement of dominance in health matters and focus on how it is sustained and how it is threatened.

This chapter reflects on matters of trust and the way this feeling mediates the relation between practitioner and patient and between profession and society. It examines the links between trust and authority in practitioner–patient encounters and investigates what sustains that trust and what erodes it. I will argue that trust concedes professional authority. And in making that connection I will indicate the conditions for trust which apply in health settings. My initial point is a simple one. If I do not trust the physician I will withdraw my permission for their treatment.

Let us look more closely at this notion of trust.

MUNDANE TRUST

Trust is implicit in the practices of everyday life and so is readily taken for granted. Trust is the beginning of cooperation. Other motivations will do the same—fear or self-interest can deliver collaboration with another, but these require a heavy apparatus of scrutiny, supervision and sanctions for both sides, or one side, to get what is wanted. The prisoner who does not trust the gaoler acts out of fear of being found out and punished. The worker who does not trust the competence of the boss may comply without complaint in the hopes of promotion or, at least, keeping the job. Foucault's story of Panopticon, where an all-seeing presence is set at the centre of an institution, exemplifies a powerful way to instil docile conformity without any recourse to trust (Foucault 1984a). Ann Game's analysis of her interviews with a boss and 'his' secretary tells of a relationship where cooperation rested on self-interest and trust did not come into it (Game 1991). A relationship imbued with trust is different. Trust is a feeling that facilitates cooperation in a most economic fashion.

Trust, as an integral dimension of social life, has been flagged by so many sociologists (e.g. Coleman 1990; Durkheim 1957; Giddens 1990; Luhmann 1979; Parsons 1967; Simmel 1950). 'Trust in the broadest sense of confidence in one's expectations is a basic fact of social life' (Luhmann 1979, p. 4). Without some measure of trust we would not leave our house, or venture on the road. Everyday life is only possible under conditions of trust. Without it the terrors of paranoia disable us. Trust is learned from infancy as the effective way of coping with the threat of uncertainty and complexity. The learning continues through life experience and engagement in everyday discourses.

As part of this generalising, simplifying process the persons or social arrangements to be trusted become *symbol complexes*, beyond our ken and our manipulation, but to be invoked to work or intervene for us. As symbols these systems, individual or social, signify specific powers but are at the same time susceptible to overturning. The ultimate in such constellations of ideas of trustworthiness are often colloquially termed 'motherhood statements'—a set of comforting concepts which are not to be questioned. Every event in matters of trust is sensitive and significant; that which is trusted is invested with a simplified image, becomes a symbol in a field of trust, which the symbolic controls. In this process there is no requirement for, no possibility of, detailed explanation. It is sufficient that it is 'the father' or 'the teacher' or 'the doctor' who is trusted. Trust is heightened by the perception of symbols which reassure—the comfort of hands, the wall lined with books, the white coat, the procedures of testing. Trust simplifies so that the fearful unknown can be visualised, can be knowable and, hence, controllable.

Trust, however necessary, is not a stupid or vacuous response to a need for confidence in reciprocal understandings and expectations. It is a rational and considered feeling. I think about trust when I drive on a highway; there I expect that every driver will keep to the correct side of the road, but I am cautious lest an oncoming driver does not or cannot respect those expectations. Moreover, the scope of trust is defined and relative to persons or systems. Trust arises in relationship, an emotion discovered through experience, but distrust may equally be found—'Familiarity is the precondition for trust as well as distrust' (Luhmann 1979, p. 19). Trust is usually tempered by the possibility of distrust. Such distrust erupts when the threshold of trust is over-reached and this presumption prompts an adverse reaction. Typically the person distrusted at first responds with forbearance, then shifts to caution and eventually resentment. Distrust tends to endorse and reinforce itself in the course of social interaction and the distrusted person can take that attitude as an exemption from the moral obligations initially accepted. Distrust, which easily slips into mistrust, becomes a self-fulfilling prophecy. Then, where distrust or, worse, mistrust permeates social relations, danger threatens more fearfully and the risks loom larger. (To be sick is alarming; to distrust nurse or doctor escalates into terror. But, think too about the nurse's reaction to my regarding their every approach, or each injection, with horror.) Either trust or distrust can establish the mind-set which interprets events and reinforces itself—and so redefines the relationship between people. The absence of trust is a problem which can prevent the other's attempts to provide a service. We focus in this chapter on the systems of professional medicine and the requirement for trust as the condition for its work. Where distrust prevails a system's controls are directed to restoration of trust. Self-regulation can obviate distrust by patently punishing any individual practitioner's self-exemption from moral obligations. This has become a crucial disciplinary function for professional associations.

TRUST IN PROFESSIONAL SYSTEMS

This talk of trust in a system or an individual introduces an obvious distinction emphasised by several sociologists. Who or what is trusted; system or individual? In Durkheimian terms the system, the collective, generates trust, is trustworthy. The individual merely stands for the system; the individual's significance is exemplary and symbolic. Trust assumed by a system potentiates its capacity to comprehend and deal with complexity and to gain time and achieve distant effects. Giddens explains this further by pointing to two categories of trust: that accorded an individual, as in a loving relationship, and that conceded to a system, as in reliance on professional expertise. He gives neither primacy. For Durkheim, of course, the social precedes the individual. The system, such as a profession, generates the milieu in which trust in individuals also may flourish. Trust, a condition of sociality, allows time for problems to be resolved. In a situation of risk and uncertainty trust reduces social complexity by going beyond available but inadequate information and generalising expectations of behaviour to provide guaranteed security. System trust subsumes the demand for increasing expert knowledge and vests control over individual practitioners in the system itself.

Decisions about trust bear strongly on the professional–client relationship. The complexity with which the expert deals is typically baffling and alarming in the risks it poses. Trust reduces the client's apprehension of external complexity and uncertainty by substituting an inner confidence in the simplification and control held out by the expert. For example, the lawyer's interview with the client seizes the salient issues from the client's catalogue of fears and anxieties and ties these into a pertinent legal framework. The lawyer takes charge and reworks the issues so that they may be resolved as best as can be for the client. Another commonplace example would be the decision to entrust a construction project to a builder, and engineer, or an architect. While the client keeps a watchful eye on progress the complexities of design and technical detail are left to the experts. It becomes their problem.

Because trust is demanded where there is a sense of ignorance or inability, the knowledge/expertise distance between professional and client necessitates trust in large measure. This holding is diminished when patent inconsistencies in expert knowledges appear; then a pragmatic acceptance of abstract systems becomes questionable. For instance, the debates around the practices of midwives and obstetricians attendant at childbirth can whittle away the trust which birthing women allow to either expert system. Although arguments among health service providers from any disciplines may advance science in the long run, they can readily disrupt the trust people place in those health professionals.

This brings us to the explicit relevance of trust to client-professional relationships. I have mentioned at several points Niklas Luhmann's brilliant analysis of trust. In a more accessible way the American sociologist, Bernard Barber, has examined trust and the way it works in major institutions including the professions (Barber 1983, pp. 131–62). His book shares much of Luhmann's perspective. It is, however, an easier read. Trust, he explains, comes with setting expectations of others. These expectations are definitive in a professional encounter and constitute the community's conferral of the identity and status of profession. As clients we bring trust into the relationship. That concession of trust is a manifestation of the status we, as a community, allow to that profession and the confidence which we, as individuals, concede to a specific practitioner. The client–professional encounter can continue only under conditions of trust in the person and the system. This is not to say that there are no elements of distrust. There often are. Indeed, trust can be readily upset by insignificant as well as obviously important things. The client's reliance is prompted by their problems, difficulties and anxieties. It is emotionally tense, albeit rationally determined; and issues not relevant to the matter in hand may become disturbing enough to undermine trust. Trust is a way of simplifying and going on despite the insecurity of inadequate knowledge in risky circumstances; the 'leap of faith' implicit in trust may be rational, but, in the instability of a dangerous situation, small, seemingly irrelevant things can upset it. If the practitioner's demeanour or dress or speech breaches the bounds of conventionality we can become alarmed and mistrustful of their competence or care.

Barber worries about the diminishment of public trust in significant institutions, especially in science and the professions. First, the very high profile of science and technology makes us anxious. Such powerful knowledge is potentially dangerous. Can the scientists and the practitioners of science be trusted to be good? Secondly, trust is challenged by the growing demand for personal autonomy—egalitarianism and resistance to collectivisation—which resists the authority of knowledge, of science. Thirdly, trust is diminished by the prevalence of education. The spread of knowledge and competence promotes the public's scepticism. Faith in the 'magic' of professions may be dissipated in the context of a better-educated public sensitive to notions of individual autonomy and egalitarianism and nervous about the depredations of science. This reading of the shifts in public regard for professions, especially for medical science, anticipates critical issues which tell against trust.

Trust in a profession is a special case of the trust implicit in everyday activity. But, why, given the risks involved, do we put a measure of trust in a profession, or, at least, in a practitioner? It can only be because of expectations of what that consultation and subsequent cooperation can do for us. Trust is a matter of expectations based on experience and the experience of others. Those experiences are implicit in reputation. We trust those dear to us because we know them, we have learned through experience that they are trustworthy. Yes, that can be a risky business but we persist, because we want to trust particular persons. When it comes to the more impersonal institution of a profession and of the people practising that profession we depend, perhaps, on some personal experience, and, to a larger extent, on public reputation. Reputation is a matter of credit, distinction, good fame: reputation is the recognition of the quality of what people hold themselves out to be. It is a consciousness of and respect for status, for an honourable position.

THE RELEVANCE OF REPUTATION

The medical profession, a powerful exemplar of profession, zealously guards its reputation as the *sine qua non*, the necessary condition, for its practice. It is not just that doctors, like everyone else, value their reputation. Without a strong reputation for high competence, special knowledge and concern for our welfare, doctors cannot practise. We would not otherwise trust them and so would not allow them to lay hands on us. Those who do not believe in the reputation so valued by the medical profession do not put themselves into the hands of the doctors. But those who mistrust medicine to that extent are in the minority. Trust, which is prerequisite for any client–practitioner relationship, is needed in very large measure where the practitioner treats the body or the mind of the person. That is why doctors make much of the 'sacred doctor–patient' relationship! This is claimed to be the particular nature of the profession and especially of the medical profession.

So what do people and the professionals themselves believe is capable of producing such a reputation that they permit all the analyses and interventions commonplace in medical treatment? We entrust our secrets to the doctor and accept, most times, their interpretation, their diagnosis. We allow them to explore our bodies, to prescribe drugs for our condition, to order regimes of health, to cut and enter and excise our organs. Such trust relies on reputation for knowledge and skill of a very high order. Quite simply we submit to the diagnosis and treatment because we believe that the medical practitioner knows and is skilled in the disciplines of medicine. Discipline in its multiple meanings applies readily to the practice of a profession and generates, to a large extent, its reputation.

DISCIPLINE

The term discipline postulates the field of knowledge itself, the inculcation of knowledge, mental and moral training, identification and definition of standards, surveillance, and sanctions imposed when standards are transgressed. This concept links knowledge and power, a connection forged for those making ready for and then living a professional career. Foucault (1984a, 1984b) wrote of discipline as a form of surveillance, exercise and examination subjecting the individual to the power of the norm, to standardisation. But the power exerted in discipline is not merely negative; it is enabling. This specific technology of power, that is, discipline, produces reality; it makes real the ideal of mastery over a field, or over oneself. Discipline, which has positive as well as negative effects, is a power that may be taken over as well as submitted to (Foucault 1984a, pp. 188–205). Professionals in training must engage with and submit to discipline in order to make it their own. Professions have taken over discipline to command knowledge and expertise. But there is no reprieve from its exercise. Discipline recurs endlessly and, like the skill of the gymnast, is lost when not practised. In everyday language the term 'professional' conjures up notions of excellence, of constant practice producing knowledgeable skill and expertise.

Foucault argues that professional authority has sprung from the power of the disciplines grown and cultivated by disciplinary practices. Educational institutions, among others, employ such practices in the training, exercising and examining of students. Teaching and learning in universities are undertaken in such ways. An exemplar of disciplinary practice is medical science where is found the ascent of power tied to scientific knowledge and the disciplinary normalisation of the learned college (see Foucault's essay on 'the birth of the asylum', 1984c, pp. 162–66 and, for a larger exposition, *The Birth of the Clinic* 1973). The systematic construction and ordering of empirical knowledge about disease and disability is a huge and continuing medical project. Medical science and the status it attained became major sources of medical power.

To this authority of powerful knowledge was added the legitimated power or authority explicit in the state's legislative action. The state ruled that only the certified holders of that knowledge may practise medicine. The presence of these twin sources of power in one profession is not envisaged in Foucault's analyses. He claimed that the disciplines supplant law as a source of power. He sees one form of power waxing as the other wanes. A persuasive and detailed criticism of this thesis can be found in Hunt and Wickham's excellent work, *Foucault and the Law* (1994, pp. 20–24, 46–71). They argued that the charismatic authority of discipline and the legal authority of the state can operate together. In the interest of examining the discipline of medicine the collaboration between profession and state to deliver a monopoly of medical practice should not be ignored. That legislated authority is crucial for medical dominance (Johnson 1972, 1982). But, at this juncture we are intent on discovering what is the professional monopoly that medicine asserts and the state has approved. Discipline is paramount in those claims.

Discipline in the sense of both knowledge and practice is central to what professions hold out as their authority. They build their reputation on the stability of such claims. The discipline of medicine begins with examination for entry to the professional faculty. There, education and training readily take on connotations of the sacred. Education can be seen as a form of ritual, most notably in universities where elite education forges a bond among the acolytes in a sacred realm (Collins 1990). The aspiring professionals participate so intensively that they come to identify themselves with the subject of the curriculum, that scheme which fits together bits of knowledge, connects up the bits of experience and invests the whole with meaning. Curriculum is remarkably significant to teachers' sense of self and in medicine is carefully patrolled by the most learned teachers *cum* practitioners, the professors of medicine whose surveillance ensures the integrity and conformity of the discipline. The students perceive the significance of all this, make it their own and are thus imbued with a sense of being special, apart, in following an elite calling.

The disciplinary practices, enforced in university and maintained by learned society and college, are ostensibly directed to the expansion of knowledge and refinement of techniques. But they quite materially and unequivocally secure the knowledge base as citadel and exclude unschooled contenders for professional status. Only those who have been selected, have submitted to the discipline of the medical school and have succeeded through examination, are permitted to become practising interns (Becker et al. 1961; Collins 1979; Murphy 1988). Through these procedures the authority of medicine is sustained, its reputation for expertise and integrity is justified, and so the grounds of trust are exposed and trust itself is vindicated. Professional training ensures that discipline has been taken into the individual's soul. Self-discipline then impels a person to obey the code, to perform at best independently of surveillance.

This interrogation of the effects of discipline should not depreciate the significance of a profession's striving for autonomy and authority. Medicine has secured its authority by a variety of strategies that monopolise knowledge and expertise and, in collaboration with the state, exclude the amateur whose knowledge is not certified, whose practices have not been disciplined in the regulatory, approved manner (Daniel 1990, pp. 49–65). The process of training, however, anticipates professional authority and inculcates values about intellectual excellence, good teamwork, self-discipline and endurance of lengthy periods of study and practice. (Regrettably this process often engenders arrogance towards workers presumed to be subordinate to the new doctor's authority. The elapse of time can effect a cure for this condition.) Discipline continues through hard work and long hours and, most esteemed of all, the development of intellectual acumen in dealing with each patient's 'case'. These processes are highly valued in the collegiate whose experienced practitioners are unmoved by the neophytes' complaints of arduous or oppressive conditions. 'We were trained that way and so must you be.' Doctors in training and in practice are expected to be dedicated to their vocation and to show total commitment to the disciplines of work. Professional reputation celebrates a tradition of arduous and difficult training and acclaims continuing application and devotion to the discipline. The ideal is the engendering and sustaining of excellence.

Medical authority, which is founded on the disciplines of clinical knowledge, instilled in the university and replenished by constant practice, is the authority of expertise. It is reinforced by legislative definition and exclusiveness. Writing of medical dominance in the US Paul Starr tells of the dual sources of that profession's power. Its social authority is a domination by virtue of legislation and regulation. Its cultural authority is initiated by medicine's claims to scientific knowledge and technical expertise and only secured by community acceptance of these claims. Cultural authority is embedded in values and meanings held to be valid, important and trustworthy and is conceded because the community believes that it needs the services medicine holds out. The faithfulness of cultural authority to community ideals, values and meanings supports relations of trust between patient and doctor (Starr 1983, pp. 3–17). Clinical knowledge and skill are required, but more is needed. Doctors must be of good repute if they are to be trusted with authority in their sphere, in the knowledge of health and illness. Now there is the rub. Ethical behaviour is a further issue in the shifts between trust and mistrust.

A discipline is a body of knowledge. But discipline is more than that. It is practice subject to examination which produces expertise. It is the force, the energy and focusing of energy which creates the expert, the professional. In thinking of discipline it is useful to recall sporting narratives where the 'professional' athlete, swimmer, footballer, or whoever, masters their sport by dint of knowing, practising, concentrating over many years. This is a significant feature of the training of the professional practitioner. The public face of such disciplined mastery is awesome capability. And there lies a problem. Knowledge and its correlate power come into play in practice, when their application may be very dangerous. Doctors are involved in the life of individuals and communities. The doctor can be found at the centre of a disaster area as well as in the mundane setting of the consulting room where they deal with lesser worries. In the course of doing their work doctors become the recipients of intimate secrets. Being privy to intimate secrets puts professionals in a superior position as well as one of trust. The practitioner's sense of responsibility in keeping secrets while using that information to help is a matter of concern to the patient. So, the public presentation, the reputation of profession must go beyond the image of knowledge, expertise and practised excellence.

Science, including medical science, is dangerous. The evil doctor is a fearful stock figure of horror movies. The drunken or the careless doctor is almost as disturbing. Perhaps more than any other profession medicine must convince its public of both the excellence of its practice and the moral integrity of its practitioners. The powerful must be good, or, at least, seen to be good. Alvin Gouldner points to this human predilection for imputing goodness to power as a general condition for trust and for sociality; this is 'a dissonance-reducing strategy of avoidance of the reality of power' (1971, p. 488). Patients require reassurance if they are to accept and comply with professional judgement. This trust is built on the profession's reputation for responsibility and care as well as its presumed high level of knowledge and skill. Discipline can govern practice and instil habits of ethical responsibility and so condition professional standing and reputation. If people are confident about the claims about high standards and firm regulation, trust is possible despite the anxieties, or terrors, of illness, disability or death. The alternative, the failure of trust, is a grim prospect for any profession. Medical practice, in particular, is not possible when trust fails.

There are other threats to medical authority. Some come from the state itself with its interest-driven bureaucracies. These are charged with managing the populations under their control and monitoring the services which the state oversees. For a discussion of this historical development turn to Foucault's analysis of 'pastoral power' (Foucault 1973), or Perrow's persuasive essay on 'a society of organizations' (1991); and for specific health and medicine-related examples see Daniel (1994). The medical profession sees these incursions as attacks by government. This old vulnerability is the negative side of medicine's interdependent partnership with governments. Recently the profession has become alert to an attack on its autonomy mounted from the marketplace. Large public companies are exploiting the profitable possibilities of health insurance and hospital services. In these marketplace manoeuvres an independent medical profession poses a problem for cost control. The profession faces a pincer movement from the public (government) sector and from private enterprise. This twin assault may subjugate the profession even in its domain of clinical practice. Paul Starr tells of this two-pronged development already apparent in the US in the late 1970s (1983, pp. 420–49). The Australian profession has been somewhat protected in recent decades by extensive public funding of medical and hospital care, but this bulwark is diminishing and its professional association, The Australian Medical Association, is taking a determined stand against health insurance and hospital corporation plans for cooption of medicine.

These forces threaten medical authority from outside the profession, but there are also fault lines opening within professional ranks. One is the emergence of a profound critique of professions from within the academic profession as well as the social sciences. In his highly significant last book Alvin Gouldner (1979) claimed that intellectuals, particularly professionals, were now realising their command of scientific discourses, on which so much in contemporary society depends. The 'intellectuals' were assuming the role of a new elite. Gouldner dwelt on the power of knowledge as cultural capital within a general theory of capital and hence the potential of knowledge to produce a new class of intellectuals. He indicated two forms: the rational discourse of practical mastery and the critical discourse which questions the paradigm of scientific knowledge and expertly trained practice. Rational discourse becomes the official form of professional knowledge—characteristically useful knowledge with practical application. But, there has also developed a critical discourse which questions the main paradigm of objective scientific knowledge and expertly trained practice. This vocal and critical minority may call everything into question, even rational thought and inquiry. Martin and Szelenyi

(1987) developed this distinction further and pointed to the 'practical mastery' of engineers, chemists and a range of skilled people. They differentiated this command of knowledge from 'symbolic mastery' which is applied in analysis of the ways of thinking, abstraction and the construction of knowledge. The difference between practical knowledge with its empirical certainties (it works—mostly) and the critical analyses of all forms of knowledge practised by some intellectuals who may be found in leading clinical and 'natural' science research units as well as in the humanities and some social sciences. Discipline in a profession drives towards both forms of mastery. The aim is to be knowledgeable, skilful and critical so that knowledge is productive of further knowledge. (Foucault mounted such a critique of specifically medical knowledge in *The Birth of the Clinic*.)

University education, which is integral to professional training, emphasises abstract, esoteric knowledge, as well as critical analysis and evaluation of the organisation of knowledge. At the same time professional training through the clinical years promotes the skilful application of that knowledge (cf. Freidson 1994, pp. 176–78). This division troubles professions which perceive a major threat to reputation coming from the self-critique. There in the universities, which reproduce the professions, lies the potential for deep distrust (Collins 1990; see also Abbott 1988, pp. 52–58; Burrage, Jarausch & Siegrist 1990; Derber et al. 1990). But, there is a dislocation between the profession's base in the university and its practical application to the human condition. Academic knowledge legitimates professional work by identifying it with the abstraction and status of science; yet, while it is remarkably inventive, academic knowledge is not practical. The 'science' of medicine is organised into logically consistent, abstract classifications; when put to work it must be assembled differently to mesh with the contingencies of clinical case and context.

The critical analysis of knowledge which is alive and well in many university departments is itself a firm discipline restraining the excesses of faith in medical miracles. Recall the discussion of trust early in this chapter. Trust is a rational feeling which helps us deal with uncertainties, difficulties and dangers. It arises from the recognition that we cannot do everything for ourselves; that we need other people and expect them to act well towards us. In knowing where to direct these trusting expectations we draw on our own and other people's experience. This is a reliance on reputation which becomes crucial in getting help to deal with troubling conditions and alarming situations. It is central to negotiations of trust between patients and doctors.

CONCLUSION

A feeling of trust facilitates reliance on a profession in the person of the practitioner. That feeling, in turn, is prompted by regard for the ethical knowledge and power held in the profession; its reputation for capability and care. Professions operate in fields of danger where the person—whose life, possessions or well-being are at risk—entrusts the outcome to the practitioner's command of a realm of knowledge and expertise. The renown of the profession, and the professional, is calculated to inspire trust. Discipline and celebration of discipline create the reputation on which the client relies. It should not surprise that the dependence of the patient, stressed by illness, disability, or disease, gives rise to medical dominance. But the relation is more complex than that. It is a relationship based on trust tempered by a measure of distrust. The imminence of distrust underlines the rationality of reason. We are never quite sure of the capability and care of others. We trust the profession and medical practitioners—up to a point. This limits the authority of medicine to its clinical domain. There, despite multiple threats, it remains sovereign. But thus far and no further.

REFERENCES

Abbott, A. 1988 *The System of Professions: An Essay on the Division of Expert Labor* University of Chicago Press, Chicago

Barber, B. 1983 *The Logic and Limits of Trust* Longman, London

Becker, H.S., Geer, B., Hughes, E.C. & Strauss, A. 1961 *Boys in White: Student Culture in Medical School* University of Chicago Press, Chicago

Burrage, M., Jarausch, K. & Siegrist, H. 1990 'An actor-based framework for the study of professions' in *Professions in Theory and History: Rethinking the Study of the Professions* eds M. Burrage & R. Torsendahl, Sage, London

Coleman, J.S. 1990 *Foundations of Social Theory* Belknap Press of Harvard University Press, Cambridge MA

Collins, R. 1979 *The Credential Society* Academic Press, New York

——1990 'Market closure and the conflict theory of the professions' in *Professions in Theory and History: Rethinking the Study of the Professions* eds M. Burrage & R. Torsendahl, Sage, London

Daniel, A. 1990 *Medicine and the State: Private Autonomy and Public Accountability* Allen & Unwin, Sydney

——1994 'Medicine, state and people: A failure of trust?' in *Just Health: Inequality in Illness, Care and Prevention* eds C. Waddell & A. Petersen, Churchill Livingstone, Melbourne

Derber, C., Schwartz, W.A. & Magrass, Y. 1990 *Power in the Highest Degree: Professionals and the Rise of a New Mandarin Order* Oxford University Press, New York

Durkheim, E. 1957 *Professional Ethics and Civic Morals* trans. A.C. Brookfield, Routledge & Kegan Paul, London

Foucault, M. 1973 *The Birth of the Clinic: An Archaeology of Medical Perception* Tavistock Publications, London

—— 1984a 'The means of correct training' in *The Foucault Reader* ed. P. Rabinow, Penguin Books, Harmondsworth

——1984b 'Panopticism' in *The Foucault Reader* ed. P. Rabinow, Penguin, Harmondsworth

——1984c 'The birth of the asylum' in *The Foucault Reader* ed. P. Rabinow, Penguin, Harmondsworth

——1988 *Politics, Philosophy, Culture: Interviews and Other Writings* Routledge, New York

Freidson, E. 1994 *Professionalism Reborn: Theory, Policy and Prophecy* Polity Press, Cambridge

Game, A. 1991 *Undoing the Social: Towards a Deconstructive Sociology* Open University Press, Milton Keynes

Giddens, A. 1990 *The Consequences of Modernity* Polity Press, Cambridge

Gouldner, A.W. 1971 *The Coming Crisis of Western Sociology* Heinemann, London

——1979 *The Future of Intellectuals and the Rise of the New Class* Macmillan, London

Hunt, A. & Wickham, G. 1994 *Foucault and Law: Towards a Sociology of Law as Governance* Pluto Press, London

Johnson, T. 1972 *Professions and Power* Macmillan, London

——1982 'The state and the professions: Peculiarities of the British' in *Social Class and the Division of Labour: Essays in Honour of Ilya Neustradt* eds A. Giddens & G. Mackenzie, Cambridge University Press, London

Luhmann, N. 1979 *Trust and Power* John Wiley, London

Martin, Bill & Szelenyi, I. 1987 'Beyond cultural capital' in *Intellectuals, Universities and the State in Western Modern Societies* eds R. Eyerman, L.G. Svensson & T. Soderqvist, University of California Press, Berkeley

Murphy, R. 1988 *Social Closure: The Theory of Monopolization and Exclusion* Clarendon Press, Oxford

Parsons, T. 1967 *Sociological Theory and Modern Society* Free Press, New York

Perrow, C. 1991 'A society of organizations' *Theory E Society* no. 20, pp. 725–62

Pusey, M. 1988 'State and policy' in *A Sociology of Australian Society* eds J.S. Western & J. Najman, Macmillan, Melbourne

Simmel, G. 1950 *The Sociology of Georg Simmel* Collier-Macmillan, London

Starr, P. 1983 *The Social Transformation of American Medicine* Basic Books, New York

Willis, E. 1983 *Medical Dominance: The Division of Labour in Australian Health Care* Allen & Unwin, Sydney

14 Uncertainty in medical decision-making

Gillian Hatt

Harry Collins (1985, pp. vii) suggests that knowledge can be likened to a 'ship in a bottle of truth', because 'once it is in the bottle of truth it looks as though it must always have been there and will never get out again'. In this chapter I will prise out medical knowledge from its 'bottle of truth', in order to address some of our common assumptions about the nature of clinical practice. As I argue, the issue of uncertainty is rarely acknowledged by the medical profession, and by the 'population at large', who are subsequently encouraged to have unrealistic expectations about the anticipated outcomes of clinical decision-making. I will suggest that because the medical discipline tends not to acknowledge uncertainty, health care policy legislators believe that clinical practice can be organised in more rational and cost-effective ways, leading to an efficient, equitable and quality health service (Lupton & Najman 1995) founded on the principles of scientific rationalism (Hicks 1995).

Turner (1995) argues that it is not clear whether medical institutions and health behaviour can be understood in terms of economic models of efficiency. In both free market and welfare systems of health care, which have undergone processes of economic rationalisation, many commentators have argued that differences in health status among different social classes have remained relatively constant. Drawing on data from the 1980 UK Black Report on infant mortality rates, Townsend and Davidson (1982, cited in Turner 1995) argue that although the infant mortality rate of the lowest classes had declined, the gap between the upper and lower classes had increased. This suggests that although one outcome of restructuring health care organisation might be greater efficiency (based on the assumption that clinical practice is a 'certain' and 'scientific' practice), a corresponding shift towards a more egalitarian system of health care may not be attained.

Contemporary social theories emphasise that we are living in an age of increasing uncertainty. For example, postmodernism has drawn our attention to the instability of knowledge, particularly the uncritical confidence we have had in science. Bauman (1992) indicates that in a postmodern age there is no authoritative standpoint from which to know the world. Thus, it appears that the status of expert knowledge is becoming increasingly contestable (Carter 1995, p. 146). This is particularly obvious in the case of medical knowledge, where it is evident that medicine is no longer seen as a concrete body of 'scientific objectivity'. Many commentators, both within and outside the medical profession suggest that the power of the medical profession is seen to rest as much on uncertainty as on technical expertise (McKee & Clarke 1995). Logan and Scott (1996, p. 598) for example, conclude that clinicians cannot afford to avoid uncertainty or pass it off as an 'inherent aspect of the art of medicine' because certainty is delusion, and 'only uncertainty is definite'. Reinforcing this view, Hunter suggests that:

> Medicine then, is a science-using, judgement based practice committed to the knowledge and care of human illness and characterised by its varied and ingenious defences against uncertainty. Because disease is culturally defined and not simply 'out there' in nature and because human beings are ultimately unknowable, medicine's knowledge is fundamentally, ineradicably uncertain. (Hunter 1991, p. 47)

Mechanic (1996) suggests that all social institutions, including medicine, have fallen from the public trust. Although we may point to wider social trends to explain this phenomenon, Mechanic indicates that changes in medicine have exacerbated this problem: in particular, the way in which medicine has come to be seen as a corporate marketplace, where primary emphasis is placed on profit maximisation. Alongside these developments, Beck (1992) indicates that 'health risks' have become a 'systematic way of dealing with the hazards and insecurities induced and introduced by modernisation itself' (cited in Scott & Freeman 1995, p. 151). Such socially constructed and regulated 'risks' have become a major issue for lay people and experts, journalists and governments (Gabe 1995, p. 1). It is apparent then, that an emphasis on uncertainty is a significant feature of contemporary health care (and life in general) for both patients and clinicians.

Although clinical uncertainty has been identified as a major factor common to the key controversies being debated with regard to health care policy determination (Logan & Scott 1996, p. 595), both the medical profession and health care policy-makers downplay the appearance of doubt in clinical decision-making (McKee & Clarke 1995). 'Traditional' medical education has instilled in its students the belief that uncertainty is a manifestation of ignorance, weakness or failure, and this view is often held by patients who have been led to believe in the objectivity and precision of clinical decision-making. The socioeconomic implications of this avoidance of dealing with the issue of uncertainty by the medical profession clearly need to be investigated. Ironically, the dominant view of the medical profession which constructs clinical decision-making as a precise, certain and scientific practice reinforces the view of health care policy legislators that medical practice can be organised in more rational, systematic and cost-effective ways. An effect of this is that health care economists are likely to respond that in order for a health care system to function more cost-efficiently, ineffective care must be swept away through the competitive purchasing of health care services. The subsequent economic pressures which may evolve as a result of this frequently lead to a reduction in time available for the direct exchange of information between clinician and patient, and are likely to produce greater uncertainty and imprecision.

The language of militarism which has had a pervasive influence on both the practice and financing of medicine in most Western health care systems appears dysfunctional in the new language of the health care economy (Annas 1995). In the language of the market, health care providers market products to consumers, who purchase them on the basis of price and efficiency, and the goal of medicine becomes a healthy bottom line instead of a healthy population (Annas 1995). Logan and Scott (1996) indicate that the recognition of the uncertainties contained within medical practice may arise from a response to greater demands for accountability and cost-effectiveness: 'The simplistic analyses used by health-care purchasers coupled with theories of management, and practice dictates of economic so-called science, together serve to mask the complexities of health care and the uncertainties inherent in human behaviour' (Logan & Scott 1996, p. 595).

A discussion of uncertainty within the context of clinical practice is also important because it is the thread connecting litigation, threats to job security, challenges to professional status, the role of doctors within new market organisations, and curriculum development in clinical schools (Logan & Scott 1996). Guidance in developing techniques to handle issues raised by uncertainty do not feature prominently in most medical schools curricula, and the incorporation of social science and medical ethics courses in undergraduate teaching has had little impact. The underlying assumption continues to be that clinical discourse is purely conceptual, propositional and algorithmic, operating in a realm free of bodily constraints and governed by its own logical rules (Johnson 1987, p. xx).

SOCIOLOGICAL ANALYSES OF UNCERTAINTY IN MEDICINE

The majority of sociological studies of uncertainty (Armstrong 1980; Atkinson 1984; Fox 1957) in clinical practice have tended to focus on the way in which uncertainty is dealt with in terms of medical curricula. In this chapter, my overriding concern is the recognition of uncertainty within processes of clinical decision-making. Like Harvey (1996) I perceive both 'certainty' and 'uncertainty' to have significant socially constructed elements to them. This infers that both certainty and uncertainty can be achieved through the deployment of particular strategies involving specific bodies of knowledge (such as scientific knowledge) and artefacts (such as clinical procedures and technological devices), which are associated with mechanisms of professional power and social relations.

Harvey (1996) distinguishes between 'achieved certainty' and 'achieved uncertainty'. Because certainty is bound up with control over knowledge, the ability of clinicians to determine the extent of uncertainty in a particular clinical situation enables them to gain control over the situation. This analysis indicates that in certain circumstances 'achieved certainty' will be emphasised. This refers to the process whereby specific methods and techniques are drawn upon to create the illusion of certainty. One example might be the use of technology in Intensive Care Units where it might appear to the patient's relatives that any uncertainty is being technologically controlled (Harvey 1996, p. 86). In opposition to this, Harvey suggests that 'achieved uncertainty' is established when perceptions of risk are exaggerated so that everyone is seen to be vulnerable and in need of medical surveillance. An example of this would be the way in which obstetrics frequently constructs all women as being 'at risk', with women who favour home deliveries considered to be at 'high risk'.

This perspective suggests that 'uncertainty' may be seen to be a strategy which is socially negotiable and dynamic. Like certainty, uncertainty may be considered to be what clinicians define as uncertainty, and this is a social practice which must be accomplished through a number of strategies.

At a more general level, attempts are made to eradicate uncertainty at all stages of the clinical consultation. For example, frequently the doctor's 'write-up' of the clinical consultation in the patient's clinical record is a reconstruction of an actual event, in which uncertainty is effectively written-out of the account. Similarities can be drawn here between the reconstruction of accounts of scientific practice. Gooding (1990), for example, has compared the structure of Michael Faraday's scientific discoveries as they were framed at the laboratory bench with the structure subsequently attributed to it in a published report of the discovery. Making a narrative imposes temporal structure on a process so as to enable logical structure to be read into it. The uncertainty which the physician may have encountered either attempting to make a diagnosis or deciding about treatment is often not expressed; neither is the tacit knowledge that the physician may have developed.

On the basis of a series of participant-observation studies and interviews which I conducted in a series of clinics in Melbourne, it was possible to establish a number of ways in which uncertainty was apparent in clinical practice. The first was in cases where 'formal' medical knowledge (the type learned in medical school) cannot be routinely or reliably applied. This often refers to statistical definitions of normality and abnormality, or 'standardised' procedures for diagnosis and treatment. The clinician may be unsure about the 'degree of fit' between this 'formal knowledge' and the symptoms presented by the patient which confound the situation. This is because textbook idealisations give prototypical cases and every individual case varies in detail. The doctor thus becomes the detective, working on incomplete, uncertain and context-specific knowledge. Such information is often 'tailored' according to their previous clinical experience of certain cases.

Turner (1995) indicates that within the context of statistical theory, a distinction is made between rejecting a hypothesis which is true (type 1 errors) or accepting one which is false (type 2 errors). This is frequently the same problem which is presented to the medical practitioners when they are faced with making a clinical diagnosis. Based on probability they must decide whether illness is present or not. Turner indicates that clinicians are much more likely to accept the hypothesis that there is an illness rather than rejecting such a proposition. As Scheff (1963, cited in Turner 1995) suggests, in a context of permanent uncertainty, doctors are more likely to over-prescribe than under-prescribe. This is because it is considered better to intervene using treatment which may not be life-threatening, than not to intervene and risk the patient dying. However, this process is not always recognised by those involved. Frequently, medical practitioners criticise their colleagues for 'over-diagnosing' and ordering unnecessary tests and procedures. A clinician, writing in the 'clinical problem solving' section of a major medical journal, comments on the decisions made by a fellow colleague:

> As a practitioner of the art of medicine, I am struck by how technology was used and abused in this case. The clinical diagnosis was apparently not acceptable to the patient and the practitioner, so numerous tests were performed essentially to prove negative results. (Aptekar 1995, p. 539)

Another clinician, commenting on the same 'clinical problem solving' case study, stated that it illustrates why the cost of medicine is so high because 'thousands of dollars were spent on unnecessary tests and procedures' (Coleman 1995, p. 539). Likewise, another commentator felt that the cost of attaining absolute diagnostic certainty in every instance was not just the economic cost to society, but also the cost to the patient in terms of time, anxiety and life-threatening complications—'the most invasive approach is often not the most appropriate' (Thibault 1995, p. 539).

When clinicians make a diagnosis they must synthesise a series of clinical 'facts' and 'data' drawn from a variety of sources about an individual patient. They must then address how the individual disease attributes identified in the clinical study of a patient relate to the types of disease classification which are detailed in medical textbooks (Blois 1986, p. 225; Eddy 1988, p. 54). Fogel (1980) indicates that often physicians depend more on their 'sense' of the situation than on general medical knowledge. Emphasis is put on aspects of non-verbal communication, such as tone of voice, facial expression, gestures, whether subjectively the doctor thinks the patient 'looks sick', and so forth. The doctor becomes the detective, working on incomplete, uncertain and context-specific knowledge. A general practitioner whom I interviewed commented on this process: 'I mean, while there are textbooks written, GPs often tailor or interpret that information to suit the individual that is in front of them' (general practitioner, Melbourne, 1993).

This indicates that clinicians often compensate for this uncertainty by drawing on 'commonsense' understandings of the situation. Therefore, rather than applying 'generalised rules' to explain the clinical phenomena under observation, this suggests that the clinician must frequently renegotiate these 'rules'. Shotter (1993, p. 93) suggests that the rule-following model is inadequate because 'people do not just follow rules they also create them as well (as well as challenge, change and correct them, and in applying them, check out with others whether they have applied them correctly)'.

Berg (1992) makes a similar point when he suggests that the biomedical model may not be the frame of reference which structures clinical consultation, as medical practice does not always adhere to universal rules. Berg introduces the concept of 'routines' to express how the decisions which clinicians frequently make are all routinely performed and embody the 'safety of the norm'. Medical practitioners develop their own routines in the process of practising medicine. This type of action is justified because the individual clinician is doing what everyone else is doing. Berg's contribution to the literature is of importance because it leads to a critical questioning of the extent to which the assumed 'rule basis' of clinical knowledge is able to structure localised decision-making.

In addition to situations where 'formal' medical knowledge cannot be routinely or reliably applied, the second type of uncertainty which it is possible to define refers to cases where there is an acknowledged lack of clinical knowledge. An example would be situations in which test results are missing, or need to be performed, and their absence prevents the clinician from making a 'certain' diagnosis.

To construct a diagnosis the physician needs a lot of different types of information in order to build up a sufficient clinical picture. This leads to a degree of uncertainty about how to combine all the observational data ranging from laboratory test results (some of which may be missing or awaiting analysis), to ethical issues and vague clinical impressions (Blois 1986). Fogel (1980) indicates that often clinicians depend more on their 'sense' of the situation than on general medical knowledge. Data are elicited from the patient in order to evaluate the complaint—reliance is put on non-verbal communication, tone of voice, facial expression, gestures, whether they 'look sick', and so forth. Fogel (1980) indicates that 'experience teaches doctors to allow for effects such as the nature of the human relation between doctor and patient on the patient's presentation—patients confide in some people and not others; they minimise or exaggerate symptoms, depending on whom they are addressing' (Fogel 1980, p. 1307).

The third type of uncertainty is the situation where the novice or learner (a medical student for example) is still coming to terms with the entirety of medical knowledge. Renee Fox (1957) pioneered much of the early work in sociology of medicine studies which sought to address the significance of uncertainty in clinical education. This work, set within a functionalist framework, sought to account for how the medical novice (or trainee) becomes equipped with the necessary knowledge, values and attitudes to enable them to be regarded as a competent member of the medical profession (Atkinson 1984). Fox emphasised that 'training for uncertainty' was a necessary part of the process of professional socialisation, which led to the accumulation of professional norms and values. Therefore, although uncertainty may be identified as problematic to clinical decision-making, Fox stressed that it was important to realise that uncertainty was a significant component of medical knowledge and practice.

Armstrong (1980) indicates another view of uncertainty which is bound up with the way in which medical education is situated within a scientific paradigm which promotes a 'certain' and concrete world of 'facts'. For example, recent sociological interpretations of uncertainty in clinical practice (Armstrong 1980; Atkinson 1984) have emphasised that medical students are 'just as likely to treat knowledge as a series of more or less discrete "facts", "topics" and so on, to be learned or not, to be forgotten and revised and so on'. Atkinson (1984) suggests that in many contexts some notions of 'uncertainty' are promoted in clinical education, which projects the view that practitioners must learn to rely, at times, on their own personal experience. This view, Atkinson believes, does not create a state of uncertainty for the medical practitioner involved but leads to the assumption that drawing on personal experience may be warranted for creating conditions of 'certainty'.

The fourth type of uncertainty refers to situations in which clinical phenomena are presented to the clinician for which standard knowledge or representations do not yet exist. The clinician attempts to make sense of what appears to be a 'novel phenomenon', they cannot explain their uncertainty due to a lack of clinical knowledge or expertise.

THE SOCIAL CONSTRUCTION OF NORMALITY
AND ABNORMALITY

One theoretical perspective which may be adopted to explain the phenomenon of clinical uncertainty is *social constructionism*. The social constructionist perspective emerged during the 1960s, within the context of an increasingly critical sociology of health, illness and medicine. Berger and Luckmann stated in the *Social Construction of Reality* (1967) that what we take to be 'facts' are the result of social interactions between people and their interpretation of these. This infers that when we talk about 'reality' and 'knowledge' we draw attention to the way in which these are socially constructed, and mediated through social relations. Lupton (1994, p. 11) suggests that the social constructionist approach does not necessarily call into question the reality of disease or illness states or bodily experiences, but 'emphasizes that these states and experiences are known and interpreted via social activity and therefore should be examined using cultural and social analysis'. Social constructionists draw attention to the way in which concepts of disease are not necessarily universal, ahistorical or unrelated to the society in which they emerge, but are rather context specific. Descriptions of wide variations in the forms of intervention which clinicians take when treating illness, and the rates at which these are done, has challenged the idea of there being a universalised body of medical knowledge (*Lancet* 1995, p. 1449).

This suggests that concepts of 'health' and 'illness' may have different definitions in different historical periods and cultural contexts, and such a view challenges the assumption that medical knowledge is a coherent and universal body of knowledge. For example, Turner (1995, p. 202) indicates that there are major differences in the classificatory and diagnostic frameworks between societies. He indicates that this is particularly evident in cases of acute mental illness. A patient of any age who is admitted to a mental health hospital in the UK is ten times more likely to be diagnosed as manic depressive than an individual exhibiting the same symptoms in the US. Likewise, Atkinson (1978) has suggested that differences in suicide rates may often be an effect of different classificatory procedures which are used to determine the cause of an individual's death.

Evidently, this lack of 'standardisation' causes problems for the medical practitioner. The uncertainty and doubt which arises from this may be a result of the socially negotiated distinction between what is labelled as 'normal' or 'abnormal', and the difficulty of applying 'universal truths' to the context of individual patients (Hatt 1992). Such determinations of 'pathological' and 'healthy' physiology are concepts of value embedded with political, economic and technological imperatives.

THE EXAMPLE OF 'BLOOD PRESSURE'

One example of a procedure and a concept which is frequently taken to be unproblematic by many people (and thus not a cause of uncertainty) is the measurement of a patient's blood pressure. If we look at this more closely we see that this isn't necessarily the case. There are wide variations in both the definition of 'normal', 'high' and 'low' blood pressures and the treatment of 'abnormal' blood pressure levels in different cultural contexts within what we might call 'Western medicine'. Historically, the measurement of blood pressure has been considered to be a 'scientific procedure' which yields accurate 'hard' data. For example, Maurice Craig published an article in *Lancet* in 1900 suggesting that because of the uncertainties that psychiatrists faced when making a diagnosis, it would be more reliable to make such diagnostic decisions on the basis of blood pressure and pulse readings. As a rule of thumb, Craig indicated that in melancholia the blood pressure tended to be high, while in cases of mania, the pressure tended to be low.

One of the fundamental problems associated with introducing blood pressure measurement into clinical practice at the beginning of this century was the difficulty associated with ascertaining what levels of blood pressure should be determined 'normal' from 'abnormal'. An archival analysis of the medical literature illustrates that accompanying the development of blood pressure measuring devices in the late nineteenth century there was an ongoing controversy regarding the most effective instrument for measuring blood pressure, the definition of 'normal' blood pressure levels, and the significance of measuring blood pressure in various clinical states. The desire to measure physiological parameters in order to ascertain 'normal' distributions in the population was a major preoccupation of late nineteenth-century and early twentieth-century clinical practice. The body became a normalised, mechanised entity which needs to be systematically explained with scientific precision.

'Expert' authorities such as the World Health Organization (WHO) have attempted to set some degree of standardisation in definitions of 'normal' blood pressure (allowing obviously for variables such as gender, age, and so forth). However, this knowledge is frequently contested in the process of clinical decision-making, when the doctor must re-evaluate such standards in order to see whether they are applicable to the context of a particular patient. In many respects, as well as diagnosing patients, clinicians must also perform a 'diagnosis' on the knowledge which they have acquired during clinical training. This re-interpretation of knowledge is reflected in processes of clinical decision-making where the relevance of such knowledge may be re-evaluated. For example, the clinician may ask: 'This patient's blood pressure is high, but what should I regard as "normal" for this patient?'

The manner in which knowledge is socially constructed is well borne out in a recent controversy in the medical (and popular) literature—the diagnosis and treatment of low blood pressure. During the early 1990s several British medical practitioners published articles which took issue with the German medical profession's treatment of low blood pressure. Historically, within the context of British medical practice (and also Australian medical practice) low blood pressure (or hypotension, as it is clinically known) has been regarded to be a 'good thing' or a 'non-existent clinical syndrome'. British medical practitioners have felt that the treatment of low blood pressure as a primary condition (in an otherwise healthy patient) is unwarranted. This position is in stark contrast to the approach to treating low blood pressure in Germany. Within German medical practice, low blood pressure is frequently treated due to the undesirable psychological and physiological side effects which it is thought to produce, such as giddiness, headaches, anxiety and tiredness. A recent study concluded that:

> The dangers of high blood pressure are well recognised but the clinical importance of low blood pressure is controversial. Several recent studies reported an increased prevalence of fatigue, crying, or psychological dysfunction associated with low blood pressure.[1] Although a hypotensive syndrome manifested by subjective symptoms has been accepted in Europe, it has been dismissed in the United Kingdom and United States.[2] (Barrett-Connor & Palinkas 1994, p. 308)

In response to this debate, several British psychiatrists were prompted to publish some 'new' findings, which contradicted both of the above positions. This research challenged both the view that low blood pressure was a 'good' thing (as British medical practitioners had suggested), and the German view that low blood pressure *causes* a number of undesirable effects. Some of the conclusions of this new research were that low blood pressure could be viewed, in some cases, as an *effect* of some underlying psychological morbidity, such as depression. What is more, it was suggested that this phenomenon was more common among women. This reinforced the views of the 'type of patient' who was most likely to be 'afflicted' with hypotension, which had been presented in earlier studies. For example, Robbins (1982, p. 28) stated that 'subjects receiving the hypotensive label from practitioners were typically women with less education and income'. Robbins also advocated a link between low blood pressure and 'low mood', with women considered to be at 'greater risk' of developing this phenomenon.

By referring to the medical literature from the late nineteenth century onwards (when blood pressure measuring devices became popular) we see the hypotensive sufferer being constructed in a number of different ways. Within the context of psychiatric practice at the beginning of this century, links were drawn between those institutionalised as 'maniacs' who frequently displayed lower blood pressures than those considered to be 'normal'. During the First World War soldiers were often monitored physiologically, and research illustrated that low blood pressure was common among neurasthenic or shell-shocked soldiers in the upper ranks, whereas soldiers in the lower ranks suffering from the trauma of war were more likely to be diagnosed with hysteria (which historically has been regarded as a 'feminine' diagnosis, and thus it was considered that this signalled a personal crisis in masculinity). A medical practitioner whom I interviewed commented on the 'gendering' of low blood pressure in this way:

> This just happens to be a cultural symptoms package that is more common in women than men. In the First World War as I mentioned to you, the whole question of neurasthenia and neurasthenic disorders were found in men. Sixty-thousand English soldiers were made invalids with it. This was a man's disease earlier in the century. (Hospital Consultant, Melbourne, 1993)

What does this case study tell us about the social construction of medical knowledge and the notion of uncertainty? First, it is obvious that 'Western medicine' is not a homogeneous body of medical knowledge. Low blood pressure is explained in a variety of ways in different cultural and historical contexts, resulting in a multiciplicity of views, and evoking varying degrees of uncertainty. A Hospital Consultant whom I interviewed summed this up:

> You've got to say something, and you've got to say something you can do something about. In England you say it's the nerves and give some valium. In Germany you say it's your BP and give some ergot. It just reflects our medical incompetence. I don't mean incompetence in a negligent sense, but our medical ignorance is such that despite the very sophisticated nature of modern medicine there are a lot of gaps in our knowledge and this is a very elegant example of what happens in a controversial area that's not nailed, and of course there'll be conflicting opinions . . . And it'll be cultural. It'll not only be doctors. It'll be a cultural thing how they handle this gap in scientific knowledge. (Hospital Consultant, Melbourne, 1993)

It is also evident from the low blood pressure case study that within different historical and cultural contexts we see the hypotensive individual being constructed in a number of different ways. Alongside attempts to determine the clinical significance of low blood pressure was the construction of a type of patient most likely to be regarded as 'hypotensive', and the subsequent emergence of various bodily identities associated with this diagnosis. Examples of these are the 'neurasthenic' (Chamberlain 1929; Cowing 1912; Wessely 1990) in the early part of this century, and more recently the 'neurotic female patient' (Robbins 1982; Shapiro 1982), an identity which continues to persist in a number of guises—depressed, hypotensive, neurotic or 'eating disordered'. These models and metaphors inform not only how bodies are represented, but also construct how these individuals live within their bodies. This means that we come to regard our embodied ethos as socially constituted. We are 'made sense of' by the physiological parameters which we display in clinical tests, our physical appearance, and the subsequent diagnosis which is made, which renders us into a classification of a certain type of 'body'.

UNCERTAINTY AND THE FINANCING OF HEALTH CARE

The issue of uncertainty has become acute in a context of financial constraints. Rationing is a feature of all Western health care systems by virtue of the fact that the demand for medical care exceeds the resources which societies are willing to commit to health care (Fuchs 1984; Gross 1994; Heginbotham 1992). Salmon (1995) states that current mortality and morbidity patterns represent phenomenal inequality in the distribution of health. He indicates that death and disease rates are not only influenced by environmental and personal attributes, but also the nature of the health care system, 'the kinds of products and services offered, who becomes the "target market", and on what terms the products and services are sold' (Salmon 1995, p. 13). The 'corporatisation' of health care organisation in the US, which is dominated by the profit motive, would be an obvious example here.

Gross (1994) draws a distinction between 'implicit' and 'explicit' rationing of health care provision. 'Implicit' refers to the type of rationing which has been evident in Britain since the National Health Service (NHS) was established in 1948. Global constraints are imposed which limit the resources that are generally available. Under this system it is assumed that the clinical judgement of doctors will ensure rational use of resources, therefore giving clinicians 'clinical autonomy' (Gross 1994, p. 30).

In a system of explicit health care rationing, policies limit the access of particular groups of the population to particular medical services. This model is particularly dominant in the US health care system, where the fee-for-service system discourages many people from seeking health care. External controls are placed on length of hospital stays, tests and procedures, physicians' fees and the use of drugs (Gross 1994, p. 17).

Palmer and Short (1994, p. 6) indicate that the Australian health care system is 'the product of a diverse range of economic, social, technological, legal, constitutional and political factors, some of which are unique to Australia'. Historically, it is possible to see the influence of both the US and the British health care systems in the provision of health care in Australia.

Logan and Scott (1996, p. 595) state that although the uncertainties inherent in medical practice have been ignored or obscured, their implications are exposed through changes in health service organisation, in particular processes of economic rationalisation, which promote greater demands for accountability and cost-effectiveness. Ironically, they argue that uncertainty and precision may be increased as a result of economic pressures leading to a reduction in the time available for the direct exchange of information between clinicians and patients. The basis for such rationalisation, Logan and Scott (1996) suggest, is often founded on gross misunderstandings about the nature of science and scientific method which contribute to misconceptions about the accuracy of clinical prediction.

Several commentators have emphasised the way in which medical care is different from the types of commodities that people generally buy on the market. Changing structures of health care provision have encouraged patients to be distrustful of health care providers. In the health care marketplace the patient is seen to be a 'consumer' who must choose wisely from a range of 'health care commodities' that are available. Palmer and Short (1994, p. 42) detail some of the problems associated with explaining the workings of the health care system by reference to a simple demand and supply model which many economists and politicians use. This is principally because such a model does not take into consideration the uniqueness of health care in comparison to other 'commodities'.

Turner (1995, p. 201) also indicates that 'it is not clear that medical institutions or health behaviour can be understood appropriately in terms of economic models of efficiency'. He refers to work by Daniels (1985) which states that the underlying problem in the organisation of health care is the apparent contradiction between efficiency and equality. This infers that it is impossible to develop a radically egalitarian system of health care which runs as a cost-effective service (Turner 1987, p. 200). Other commentators (Arrow 1963, cited in Turner 1987) emphasise the problem of applying utility models from economic theory to the systems of medical care in mixed economies. This is because buying medical services is dissimilar to purchasing other goods on the market. The consumer (the patient) is often unsure of their needs, and must place their trust in their service provider (the doctor). Due to the patient's uncertainty, it is left to the physician to judge the effectiveness of the service (the treatment) offered, in contrast to other goods which they might purchase in the 'market place'.

CONCLUSION

In this chapter I have addressed the way 'uncertainty' is frequently not acknowledged by the medical profession as a significant factor that is evident in clinical decision-making. I have argued that disregarding uncertainty in this way in an attempt to construct situations of 'certainty' has socioeconomic implications. By characterising the clinical decision-making process as a 'certain' activity, based on rational principles that can be employed in a number of contexts, this frequently supports the view that health care systems can become increasingly more effective and cost-efficient, because it is easy to differentiate between 'effective' and 'ineffective' diagnostic and therapeutic decisions. Many commentators are doubtful that this is attainable. They draw attention to the uniqueness of health care, aside from other 'commodities' on the market, and indicate that clinical uncertainty and the 'messiness' of 'doing medicine' complicate these matters significantly. As McKee and Clarke (1995, p. 104) suggest, 'the issue is the validity of applying models based on rational decisions and perfect information to complex adaptive systems'. Ironically, the unwillingness to tackle the issue of uncertainty is frequently due to professional desires to construct medical practice in a 'scientific paradigm' which is devoid of such supposedly 'subjective' elements. However, this may be seen to legitimate processes of economic rationalisation, and create greater uncertainty and distrust in the ability of the medical profession to provide health care equitably, reducing access for socioeconomically disadvantaged groups.

238   CARE MATTERS

NOTES

1   See Bengtsson et al. (1987), Pilgrim et al. (1992) and Wessely et al. (1990).
2   See Robbins et al. (1982) and Pemberton (1989).

REFERENCES

Annas, G.J. 1995 'Reframing the debate on health care reform by replacing our metaphors' New England Journal of Medicine vol. 332, no. 14, pp. 744–47
Aptekar, D.W. 1995 'Clinical problem solving: The appropriate degree of diagnostic uncertainty—response' New England Journal of Medicine vol. 332, no. 8, p. 539
Armstrong, D. 1980 'Health care and the structure of medical education' in Medical Education and Primary Health Care ed. N. Noack, Croom Helm, London
Arrow, K.J. 1963 'Uncertainty and the welfare economics of medical care' The American Economic Review vol. 53, no. 5, pp. 941–73
Atkinson, P. 1984 'Training for certainty' Social Science and Medicine vol. 19, no. 9, pp. 949–56
Barrett-Connor, E. & Palinkas, L.A. 1994 'Low blood pressure and depression in older men: A population based study' British Medical Journal vol. 208, pp. 446–49
Bauman, Z. 1992 Intimations of Postmodernity Routledge, New York
Beck, U. 1992 Risk Society: Towards a New Modernity Sage, London
Bengtsson, C. et al. 1987 'Prevalence of subjectively experienced symptoms in a population sample of women with specific reference to women with arterial hypotension' Scandinavian Journal of Primary Health Care pp. 155–62
Berg, M. 1992 'The construction of medical disposals: Medical sociology and medical problem solving in clinical practice' Sociology of Health and Illness vol. 14, no. 2, pp. 151–81
Berger, P. L. & Luckmann, T. 1967 The Social Construction of Reality Allen Lane, London
Blois, M.S. 1986 'Diagnosis versus diagnostic programs' Medinfo 86 Elsevier Science Publishers, North Holland, pp. 225–27
Carter, S. 1995 'Boundaries of danger and uncertainty: An analysis of the technological culture of risk assessment' in Medicine, Health and Risk: Sociological Approaches ed. J. Gabe Blackwell, Oxford, pp. 133–51
Chamberlain, F.N. 1929 'The treatment of low blood pressure' Lancet vol. 1, p. 889
Coleman, L.R. 1995 'Clinical problem solving: The appropriate degree of diagnostic uncertainty—response' New England Journal of Medicine vol. 332, no. 8, p. 539
Collins, H.M. 1985 Changing Order Sage, London
Cowing, W.H. 1912 Blood Pressure Technique Simplified Taylor Instrument Companies, Rochester NY
Daniels, N. 1985 Just Health Care Cambridge University Press, Cambridge
Eddy, D.M. 1984 'Variations in physician practice: The role of uncertainty' Health Affairs vol. 3, pp. 74–89
Fogel, B.S. 1980 'Reply to Blois: Clinical judgement and computers' New England Journal of Medicine vol. 303, no. 22, p. 1307
Fox, R. 1957 'Training for uncertainty' in The Student-Physician eds R.K. Merton & P.L. Kendall, Harvard University Press, Cambridge
Fuchs, V. R. 1984 'The "rationing" of medical care' New England Journal of Medicine vol. 311, pp. 1572–73
Gabe, J. 1995 Medicine, Health and Risk: Sociological Approaches Blackwell, Oxford

Gooding, D.C. 1990 *Experiment and the Making of Meaning* Kluwer, Dordrecht, Netherlands

Gross, E.B. 1994 'Health care rationing: Its effects on cardiologists in the United States and Britain' *Sociology of Health and Illness* vol. 16, no. 1, pp. 17–37

Harvey, J. 1996 'Achieving the indeterminate: Accomplishing degrees of certainty in life and death situations' *Sociological Review* vol. 44, no. 1, pp. 78–98

Hatt, G.L. 1992 'What is low blood pressure' *Lancet* vol. 338, p. 1049

Heginbotham, C. 1992 'Rationing' *British Medical Journal* vol. 304, pp. 496–99

Hicks, N. 1995 'Economism, managerialism and health care' *Annual Review of Health Social Sciences* pp. 36–60

Hunter, K.M 1991 *Doctors' Stories: The Narrative Structure of Medical Knowledge* Princeton University Press, New Jersey

Johnson, M. 1987 *The Body in the Mind: The Bodily Basis of Meaning, Imagination and Reason* Chicago University Press, Chicago

Lancet 1995 'Leap of faith over the data trap' vol. 345, pp. 1449–50

Logan, R.L. & Scott, P.L. 1996 'Uncertainty in clinical practice: Implications for quality and costs of health care' *Lancet* vol. 347, pp. 595–98

Lupton, D. 1994 *Medicine as Culture* Sage, London

Lupton, G.M. & Najman, J.M. 1995 *Sociology of Health and Illness* 2nd edn Macmillan, Melbourne

McKee, M. & Clarke, A. 1995 'Guidelines, enthusiasms, uncertainty, and the limits to purchasing' *British Medical Journal* vol. 310, pp. 101–04

Mechanic, D. 1996 'Changing medical organisation and the erosion of trust' *Milbank Quarterly* vol. 74, no. 2, pp. 171–89

Palmer, G. & Short, S. 1994 *Health Care and Public Policy: An Australian Analysis* Macmillan, Melbourne

Pemberton, J. 1989 'Does constitutional hypotension exist?' *British Medical Journal* vol. 298, pp. 660–62

Pilgrim, J.A. et al. 1992 'Low blood pressure, low mood?' *British Medical Journal* vol. 304, pp. 75–78

Robbins, J.M. et al. 1982 'Treatment for a non-disease: The case of low blood pressure' *Social Science and Medicine* vol. 16, pp. 27–33

Salmon, J.W. 1995 'A perspective on the corporate transformation of health care' *International Journal of Health Services* vol. 25, no. 1, pp. 11–42

Scheff, T.J. 1963 'Decision rules, types of error and their consequences' *Behavioural Science* vol. 8, pp. 97–107

Scott, S. & Freeman, R. 1995 'Prevention as a problem of modernity: The example of HIV and AIDS' in *Medicine, Health and Risk: Sociological Approaches* ed. J. Gabe, Blackwell, Oxford, pp. 151–71

Shapiro, M. 1982 'Low blood pressure: An extinct diagnosis' *Canadian Medical Association Journal* vol. 126, pp. 887–88

Shotter, J. 1993 *Cultural Politics of Everyday Life: Social Constructionism, Rhetoric and Knowing of the Third Kind* Open University Press, Buckingham

Thibault, G.E. 1995 'Clinical problem solving: The appropriate degree of diagnostic uncertainty' *New England Journal of Medicine* vol. 332, no. 8, p. 539

Townsend, P. & Davidson, N. 1982 *Inequalities in Health: The Black Report* Penguin, London

Turner, B.S. 1987 *Medical Power and Social Knowledge* Sage, London

——1995 *Medical Power and Social Knowledge* 2nd edn, Sage, London

Wessely, S. et al. 1990 'Symptoms of low blood pressure: A population study' *British Medical Journal* vol. 301, pp. 362–65

15 Looking after patients and doctors

Valerie A. Clifford

Traditionally the work environment has been seen as the public space inhabited by men while women occupy the domestic private space. Men were seen to be focused on their careers while women concentrated on raising the family. As women have begun to compete with men demanding careers in the public arena, they have taken with them a different orientation to employment, seeing their home lives as being as important as their work lives (White et al. 1992). Marshall (1984) illustrated how women have the same motivations to work as men but practical difficulties explain why they do not translate this into action. Women accept the impossibility of separating their private lives from their paid work lives as they still carry the main responsibility for the maintenance of family life (Dobson 1994; O'Regan 1992; Pringle & Collins 1996).

Work environments generally are not 'family friendly' (Liddicoat 1996) and to achieve the flexibility they need in their lives women, over the past two decades, have been leaving large organisations, more often than men, to set up their own businesses. This allows them to arrange their own work environments and work practices. These businesses have succeeded more often than those established by men (Auster 1988; Davidson & Cooper 1992; van Auken et al. 1994; Welsh 1988). While first generation women entrepreneurs were seen to be forced through economic pressure to set up their own businesses, the second generation entrepreneurs have been seen to be acting to fulfil their needs for achievement, independence and control rather than financial rewards (Gregg 1985; Lee-Gosselin & Grise 1990; Neider 1987; Olsson 1992). Women are seeing a small, stable business and balance between their professional and personal lives as important, and the need for challenge as greater than the need for promotion (Lee-Gosselin & Grise 1990; White et al. 1992).

In primary health care women doctors are mostly employed sessionally in male-run general practices. In this position they are unable to control their hours of work or the way they practise medicine. Lorber's (1993) study found that, to be in control of how they practised medicine, women doctors needed to be working in their own practices. In this study four women doctors argue that inequalities in their work environments crucially affect their own lives, doctor–patient relationships and patient access to choice in health care.

This chapter describes a study of a new general practice established by four women doctors at the end of 1991 during its fourth year of operation. The women doctors set up their own practice in an attempt to achieve some balance in their lives and to give them control over their work environment, while delivering good quality medical care. The doctors wanted to achieve both a patient-centred and a doctor-centred practice. The study explores the relationship of their work to the rest of their lives, their ideals and how these are reflected in the organisation of their practice and in patient care.

METHOD

In order to gain insight into how these doctors seek to achieve their goals I undertook fieldwork in the clinical setting in which they worked: the Aurora Health Centre. First, I had to negotiate attachment to the team. After approaching the doctors, a series of meetings were held between the Aurora staff, with and without my presence. My proposal was accepted in the spirit that it would be part of the doctors' and staff's self-reflection on their professional practice and that the doctors and staff had a right not to cooperate at any stage if they chose and that no material would be published without their permission. At each stage my involvement with the practice was at the team's invitation. Their willingness to involve me in all aspects of the practice demonstrated their commitment to the ideals on which the practice was established.

During my year's attachment to the Centre I observed the practice in progress by spending time in the waiting room, the reception area and the office. I read documentation about the practice including past minutes, business plans, newspaper reports and articles written by the doctors. I conducted individual interviews with the doctors, all staff members and an external facilitator who has worked with the group since its inception. These interviews were taped and transcribed and their scripts returned to the interviewees. Further interviews were held where staff wished to amend or elaborate on their scripts. I also held group discussions with the doctors. I attended the weekly practice meetings, educational evenings, conflict resolution meetings and social events. I also ran a patient survey through questionnaires given out at reception and interviews arranged by the receptionists.

All the material, plus my own fieldnotes were entered on the Nud*ist computer program and subjected to a content theme analysis. Papers resulting from the analysis were circulated among the doctors and staff and time was allocated at practice meetings and doctors' meetings to discuss and negotiate the content. This has resulted in two joint conference presentations with the doctors, as well as other papers (Clifford 1996; Clifford & Cocks 1996; McIlroy & Clifford 1996). The analysis also resulted in the team holding further meetings to review and institute new organisational processes and to draw up a five-year strategic plan.

THE IDEALS

The practice was established in 1991 by four women general practitioners and one receptionist. They set up a new practice rather than buying an established one so that they were not bound by the existing expectations of colleagues and patients. By 1995 it had thirteen staff plus an attached physiotherapy unit. After four years of existence the practice was deemed to be a business 'success' in that it had survived its first three years and had a full patient list and patient satisfaction was high (Clifford & Cocks 1996). However, for the doctors there were unresolved tensions.

The ideals of the practice echo those found in other feminist organisations: (1) to give equal value to their work lives and their home lives; (2) to have control over their work environment and work practices; and (3) to give good quality patient care (Davidson & Cooper 1992; Hawken 1996; Nathan 1996; Olsson 1992; O'Regan 1992; Still 1996; Weeks 1994; White et al. 1992).

(1) To give equal value to work life and home life

The four doctors all worked part-time, offering the equivalent service of two full-time doctors. The doctors arranged their hours to suit their personal schedules, for example, starting at 9.15 a.m. so that a child could be taken to school, swapping sessions to help each other out and covering for each other's holiday periods. As in Marshall's (1984) study of women managers, when at the Centre the doctors were fully committed to their patients but they did not want to be 24-hour-a-day doctors: *'our families and our interests outside medicine are equally important to us.'* The doctors saw their private lives as *'valid and valuable'* and talked about putting boundaries around their work and making the workplace flexible to allow a life alongside work.

(2) To have control over work environment and work practices

The doctors sought to avoid the management styles they had encountered in the practices in which they had previously worked. Leadership styles range over a continuum from management being competitive, rational, objective, analytic and strategic with formal, hierarchical power structures. At the other end of the continuum, management is seen to be collaborative, intuitive, subjective, egalitarian and concerned with a quality product and to view power as shared within groups (Applebaum & Shapiro 1993; Hawken 1996; Olsson 1992). Stereotypically, male managers are seen to operate in the former fashion and women in the latter. The structures and processes established in an organisation reflect the dominant management style. Weeks' (1994) study of Women's Health Centres showed women developing a group-centred model of leadership while Craddock and Reed (1993) illustrated the problems women met trying to transform an existing hierarchically structured health clinic to one based on an holistic model of health, where staff offering different types of help to clients were equally valued by the professionals themselves.

The doctors wanted to work in a nurturing environment; one which involved caring for each other and being aware of each other's needs (and that of all the staff at the Centre). The doctors wanted to work as a team of people, respecting each other's skills, working cooperatively and on an equal basis. Similar values were held in the Women's Health Centres studied by Weeks (1994). Trust and honesty were the words often used to describe the environment. The staff affirmed that the atmosphere at the Centre was very supportive, caring and accommodating to the requirements of their personal lives. The doctors were conscious of looking after their own health and well-being as well as that of their patients.

The work practices at the Centre were organised cooperatively, all the staff being considered to be on an equal footing and each respected and valued for the contribution they made to the whole project. The doctors took responsibility for different administrative aspects of the practice such as the wages and employment contracts and the building, while the non-clinical staff took responsibility for their area of work, for example, reception, nursing. The partners have had to learn to trust each other to get on with their delegated responsibilities and not to interfere if they feel things could have been done a different way.

> Yes you have to rely on other people, and sometimes you have to say well 'I wouldn't have done it that way', but can I live with it, and if the answer is yes I can live with it, you shut up even if you would have done it a different way. (Doctor)

All staff are invited to the weekly practice meetings, which are the hub of communication in the practice. With mostly part-time staff, good communication is essential and the doctors are aware of the important strategic roles the full-time nurse and full-time receptionist play in communication channels. The agenda for the meetings is accumulated over the week, in the minutes book, to which all staff have access. The agenda is frequently too long for the one hour allowed for the meeting. The meeting serves the function of bringing the staff together socially and keeping everyone in touch with the numerous issues involved in running a business and a health service. It allows many decisions to be made at short notice. O'Regan (1992) discussed the need for weekly meetings to keep communication channels open and to stop comments being passed unconstructively behind the filing cabinet. The practice has also variously held monthly business/financial meetings for the doctors and regular clinical peer review meetings for the doctors and nurses. Social gatherings were also held periodically.

Early on the doctors drew up a business plan and a set of ground rules. The ground rules, effectively, became part of the job description for each position at the Centre. The ground rules include such things as honesty, confidentiality and caring.

Decision-making is on a consensus basis, which was described by the staff as a process by which everyone was involved in discussion and felt that they had had their views heard and even if they did not agree with the final decision, that they could live with it (a process described by Stanford et al. (1995) as participative leadership). If issues cannot be resolved at the weekly meeting further time is allocated.

Workshops have been held intermittently with an outside facilitator. The first one, before the practice opened, focused on team building and the contribution each person could bring to the practice.

Subsequently they have been used to resolve emotionally charged issues. These meetings have had the effect of dissipating emotional tensions that have built up over the year as people have got progressively more tired and new issues have had to be confronted. Two of the doctors also meet regularly with individual supervisors outside the practice as they feel it necessary to talk through the emotional demands of the Centre with a detached third party.

> Right. The first level is probably anybody who has got an issue, we try and sort it out directly with the others involved I suppose. If those people felt it should be discussed at the meeting, we go to the meeting, and then if the issues still weren't resolved then we'd probably organise a separate time to actually look at that issue specifically. If that wasn't sufficient then what we have done on several occasions in the past is that we've actually invited an independent person to come in and help us resolve issues. And that has been really effective . . . When the four of us were first setting up the business she looked into how we might work together and drew out some very interesting characteristics about each of us that we didn't know about each other . . . get people working in a much more cooperative sort of way. (Doctor)

(3) To give good quality patient care

The doctors in the study saw the management philosophy of the practice as reflected in patient care; hierarchical work structures and relationships lead to inequalities in doctor–patient relationships, lack of consultation and lack of involvement in decision-making. In New Zealand the government financing of general practice—through subsidies of patient visits—has meant that maximisation of income is achieved by seeing as many patients as possible per day. This has led to an average appointment time of eight minutes and a reluctance by doctors to make home visits. It also has repercussions on the type of medicine practised and the relationship between doctor and patient; general practitioners, at times, being perceived as skilled technicians focusing on the bio- or biopsycho-aspects of medicine (Campbell & Howie 1992; Risdale et al. 1989; Roland 1989; Wilson 1989).

For their patients the Aurora doctors wanted to provide quality medical care at an affordable price. Quality care, for them, included patients having a chance to explain what they wanted to say and being listened to, having access to the most appropriate care for them whether medical, counselling or information. The doctors wanted to create a caring, comfortable environment for patients and to offer an holistic approach to their health care. They wanted to have less hierarchical relationships with their patients and to fully involve the patients in decisions about their treatment. One of the main practical implications of this philosophy has been allowing initial consultations of thirty minutes to take a full medical history and standard appointments being fifteen minutes long.

THEORY INTO PRACTICE

Conducting the study over the period of a year allowed observation of the way the structures and processes established worked in practice and the extent to which they reflected the desired ideals.

An essential part of the day-to-day running of the Centre, and the communication system, was the weekly meeting. The ground rules made a commitment to practice meetings having equal importance to clinical work, to punctuality and investing time to resolve issues. All the staff attested to the importance of the weekly meetings in the running of the practice and for staying in touch with each other. In reality the weekly meetings were placed at the end of a busy week when people were tired and demands on their time had built up. No-one in the practice was in the habit of taking a 'lunch hour' so this was not an automatically available time slot. The meetings turned out to be very fluid affairs with attendance and punctuality waxing and waning, overfull agendas that could not be done justice to in an hour, patient appointments ran late, food had to be fetched and consumed and the staff be back on deck at the end of the hour. There were no regular items on the agenda, for example, a practice manager's report or nurse's report. So, despite requests for some of these they eventuated only peripatetically. Part-time staff who attended infrequently found it difficult to claim space for their issues. The pressure on the Friday meeting had led to them being more task-oriented and less a time for social contact.

To expect a one hour meeting (which is frequently less) to fulfil the function of meal break, socialising and business is perhaps too idealistic and was subsequently reconstituted. The lack of time and energy for further meetings meant that staff were becoming out of touch with each other's opinions and feelings. The doctors met only irregularly and the clinical meetings had stopped. Investing time in the future development of the practice proved difficult during the year of the study. A strategic planning exercise was not followed through for a whole year and plans that demanded more commitment of time, especially evenings and weekends, were not being addressed. As one staff member commented:

> *I think it's really great that we have our weekly meetings . . . we all know we have got to be on time, we all know we need to all listen, but what happens sometimes is that we get so busy that I'll sometimes find they don't, I might not mention the things that help everyone hold everything together, we just run out of time, it's not like I feel we fail, it's just because we need to just keep looking at those things, just keep tightening up those things we've all said are important.* (Staff member)

The problem of communication between a predominantly part-time staff brings up the question of the emotional level at which the Centre operates. On one level the doctors have to maintain their relationship which was described by the facilitator as a marriage of

> *. . . four really strong people who really want to make sure that communication systems are good and I think it is like any marriage, I think they are just constantly working on it . . . every now and again they have a bit of a blow out, like we all do in any of our relationships and that they need to go back and have a really good look at the basics again.* (Facilitator)

On another level the partners are trying to maintain relationships of equality, honesty and trust throughout the Centre. These ideals require knowing each other really well and this arises from spending quality time together, which becomes increasingly difficult as more people are involved.

The philosophy of equality for all was eagerly embraced by all the staff when the practice was small, but began to be queried as the practice grew larger. All of the staff were enthusiastic about working at the Centre but three of the part-time staff did not think in terms of equality of staff. They did not know that they could attend the weekly meetings, have their say on issues or put items on the agenda. They saw themselves as employees with bosses, although benign bosses.

The issue of equality was thrown into relief in 1995 by the appointment of a part-time practice manager. At the beginning of the year one of the doctors expressed apprehension about the post affecting the power balance in the practice and this became an issue as responsibilities for jobs shifted or did not shift as expected and processes became disrupted. James and Saville Smith (1992, p. 40) describe 'processes shaping the exercise of power'. As discussions took place about lines of responsibility basic philosophies began to be questioned.

I wonder how real it was to start with, when we weren't busy. Now we can be consensual but the doctors are the partners and they are the ones who have the most to gain out of this practice, 'cos it is theirs. A consensual/communist philosophy maintains that everyone gets the same amount out of the business. I don't . . . I have just become more aware that the doctors are the financial partners and my commitment doesn't have to be on the same level and I have come round to thinking that it shouldn't be . . . the doctors have to take on board now the responsibilities of employers. (Staff)

Staff began to re-define decision-making in the practice and see the four partners as being equal in having the financial responsibility for the business but themselves as paid employees. They began to question the weight given to their opinions and to withdraw from decision-making. However, this situation was not sustained as the staff realised that all the decisions would affect their working environment and relationships and it was in their interests to be involved with them.

As awareness of the employer–employee relationship grew views differed as to the advisability of trying to run a business and hold all employees as friends.

I think that it is really difficult to establish a relationship with staff that is almost on an equal footing without causing practical problems in dealing with issues that arise. And my feeling has been in the last few weeks that that has reached a stage at times where decision-making has almost become impossible for the partners because of concern about staff-response, staff feelings about being involved or not in the decision-making . . . the practical side is, those people are always going to receive salary. The partners are not always going to receive a profit and so some decisions are their responsibility and theirs to be made . . . if you are going to try and have that sort of relationship there still needs to be a boundary and maybe the way of dealing with that is to make it more firm, that there is actually an agreed thing that beyond this point these are our responsibilities as the employer. (Doctor)

The doctors' responses to these developments have been ambivalent; on the one hand, withdrawing into doctor-only meetings, to decide how they feel about things and what they want out of the situation and, on the other, putting extra time and effort into involving staff. It has also led to the re-defining of jobs and responsibilities and the restructuring of reporting procedures.

I think there is a feeling of loss of control with what's happening and a desire to keep some control over it. And the way that they have gone about it . . . is to set up committees . . . with the subcommittees reporting back to the Friday meetings and that may well work fine . . . but it may end up meaning that they immerse themselves in a level of detail that just wastes their time. (Staff)

. . . how much do we delegate and how much we retain control . . . delicate balance. (Doctor)

The questioning of equality in the practice reflects on the ideal of consensus decision-making. This is now seen as a very time-consuming process and relies on the complete honesty of the participants. Time is one thing that we have seen to be at a premium at the Centre and honesty requires a high degree of emotional involvement.

. . . but I have some sense that some of the things we have had conflict over have got papered over and may well re-emerge. I don't think that's because we're particularly bad at it or whatever, I sort of think that is human nature. And I think conflict resolution, you may come out with an answer but it's seldom to everybody's satisfaction and I think we've put a lot of emotional effort and energy into quite a lot of our conflict resolution and our work in general . . . I think it has potential to bond and also the potential to split us asunder. I doubt that all male practices do much of it and if they do I suspect they do it in quite a different way. (Doctor)

We do try hard to be consensual, but I actually found that I had never worked in an environment where we try to do that so hard and it is actually incredibly difficult to do. (Staff)

The facilitated meetings at the Centre have been held annually and seem to be a time for re-evaluation and team building. The staff find the meetings very draining because of the high level of emotional contact that they demand. Some of the staff feel that these meetings should be regular scheduled events, once or twice a year and others feel that they are not necessary, that the Centre does not need to function on this emotional level.

But it seems quite a good idea to get together about once a year. Winter seems a better time, because I think people are more likely to be having difficulties in winter, if you're not feeling well, or the weather's foul or you're overtired. Things seem to be a little more down and I think it's important people make contact emotionally from time to time. I would quite like us to actually have a time, at least once a year where we actually talk about how we're all feeling about things. (Doctor)

This level of emotional involvement is very demanding. As staff leave and are replaced by fresh faces, and as new positions open up and change people's jobs, relationships need constant attention and adjustment. The way the Centre approaches team building and maintenance may need to be addressed. Structures need to be in place to ensure the cohesion of the team and that working processes are overt (Traquair 1993; Walker 1993).

I suppose I don't know how to (tell them). It is the whole start. It is easy to start sounding bitchy about it and then things come right and it is okay so I get cowardly and think 'oh what the hell' . . . (Staff)

The main thing that has changed as we have got bigger is that we don't meet so often as we are busier and women resist it. (Doctor)

The original team worked together to build the practice, discussing and exploring their philosophies and suitable organisational structures, making an open declaration of, and commitment to, those ideals. As new members join the team their acceptance of the philosophy of the Centre may not be grounded in practical experience of those ideals. The Centre may need to address the induction of new staff to the philosophy and practice of the Centre and in terms of getting to know the person and the person getting to know the team. They may also need to consider whether it is necessary to sustain the present level of emotional involvement for the practice to function on its philosophical base. Focusing on systems and procedures may remove some of the interpersonal tensions, allowing criticisms to be directed to the processes rather than to personalities.

The doctors at Aurora have provided the quality medical care they envisioned. The patient survey showed high levels of satisfaction, particularly in the relational and holistic health areas deemed important by the doctors. The patients frequently commented that everyone at the Centre was addressed by their first name and not just the patients, which is common practice elsewhere. The patients emphasised the time available for them to explain their problems, the doctors gathering a variety of knowledge about their conditions, sharing it with them and discussing several different treatment possibilities. They were encouraged to consider these and to be fully involved in the treatment decision.

However, as the doctors become more focused on the financial side of the business and discuss ways of increasing income, some of their medical practices come into question. As general practitioners in New Zealand receive government subsidies according to the number of patients they see each day, allowing patients fifteen minutes rather than eight minutes for appointments immediately halves their potential income. This and other practices that potentially reduce income are recognised by the doctors but at present are seen as 'non-negotiable' in terms of their vision of patient care (Clifford 1996). However, even within their desired medical practices there are efficiency gains that could be made that would increase income and could be addressed by the doctors, such as ensuring that they see ten patients per session (their target break-even number) and doctors and nurses charging for all the visits as per schedule.

CONCLUSION

The three goals of the doctors at the Aurora Health Centre are intricately intertwined, achievement in one area affecting success in another. The women set up a new practice so that they could introduce an alternative model of general practice in terms of organisation and patient care. The doctors portray Olsson's (1992) second generation women entrepreneurs who were seen to establish their own businesses in order to satisfy their needs for independence and control rather than being primarily motivated by financial rewards. The doctors had recognised that, initially, setting up the business would be time consuming but had aimed towards lightening their work load, and increasing their remuneration, by the end of the first three years. At the time of the study this goal had not been achieved and now that the initial challenge and satisfaction of establishing the business has subsided the financial basis of the practice is more figurative with a focus on the pay levels of locums and the remuneration levels in other (male) general practices. The doctors have found that to achieve their first ideal, of giving equal value to their home and work lives, they must be able to afford to work less hours in order to be able to contain their work time. Earning more per session would allow them to buy in more staff to spread the workload. Part of the role of the practice manager has been to relieve some of the administrative burden from the doctors, but this still does not give them the hours and flexibility that was their goal. They have found running the practice to be more expensive than anticipated: the advice they received, that 55 per cent of the business income would go on overheads, has turned out to be true. They have also found that the paper work involved with patient care requires them to spend extra sessions at work, outside of their surgery hours, and these are not income-generating hours.

The delimiting of work time is also problematic in relation to the style of management and environment chosen by the women. Consensus decision-making and establishing a nurturing environment are all very time intensive and require input out of 'office hours'. There is, therefore, a conundrum between the structures and processes chosen and the desire to contain work involvement.

Collaborative work requires constant attention to team building and team maintenance to keep the commitment and involvement alive (Opie 1996; Weeks 1994). At the Centre the weekly meetings and social events are an important part of the relational and business processes. Some of this work went on serendipitously with the use of the external facilitator and appeared to have been vital in establishing the team and the team's continued coherence. However, there are no in-built review mechanisms or induction processes for new staff in which they could make a commitment to the team, and where the role they would play in the whole was made explicit and their contribution to the team clarified. As staff change and teams enlarge this is an important process.

Regular reviews are necessary in a participatory model of management, such as this, to ensure that the mechanisms in place are adequate to sustain the process. The case study illustrates a subtle, and unintended, shift from a participative model of management, involving joint decision-making, to a consultative model, where staff are consulted and then the managers make the decision (Stanford et al. 1995). As situations are continually in a state of flux, vigilance is needed to recognise when processes are being subverted and for participants to consider whether this is a change that they want or not. The comments of some of the Aurora staff indicated an inability to use existing structures effectively to deal with the concerns that arose and that a change of model may be acceptable if it were overt and agreed. The annual facilitated meetings, although not constituted as such, may have provided a forum for periodic reflection on practice and may need to be recognised as such and formally instituted.

The egalitarian philosophy espoused on the establishment of the Centre needs to be reconsidered. There is a fundamental difference in the position of the doctors and the staff relating to the financial ownership of the business and, therefore, ultimately in terms of responsibility for the practice. The power in the hands of owner-managers is well described in Riordan and Riordan's (1993) study of small family businesses where some decisions made in the interest of the family were not necessarily in the interests of the business. The Aurora doctors could make decisions that suit their lifestyle choices rather than ones that are in the best interest of the practice. There may also be occasions when democratic leadership styles and decision-making may or may not be appropriate and where a variety of styles needs to be available to the group with a mechanism for deciding when the various processes will be used. Marshall's (1995) women managers described changing their leadership styles to suit the situation.

The doctors see the ethos of the organisation as directly reflected in the doctor–patient relationship. The practice of the principles of egalitarianism and collaboration in patient care are also time consuming, and in the business arena 'time is money'. Under present government funding arrangements the more time general practitioners spend with their patients the less money they make. To sustain the ideals of Aurora to run a doctor-centred and a patient-centred practice requires the doctors to constantly confront their ideals and reaffirm or renegotiate them. They provide a successful alternative model of patient care which may be demanded by an increasingly information literate and consumer rights-oriented population. The study highlights the financial and management implications of this style of medical care.

> If we go out of business, we do nobody a favour. I actually think we can't have all that we wanted, like we wanted to have a low cost service to patients, one of quality service to patients, want to give patients time, equally wanted to have time for ourselves and we wanted a reasonable remuneration from that. And I don't think you can have all of those things. (Doctor)

ACKNOWLEDGEMENT

I would like to thank all the staff at the Aurora Health Centre for trusting me with this project and for their time, cooperation and friendship as it has developed.

REFERENCES

Applebaum, S. & Shapiro, B. 1993 'Why can't men lead like women?' *Leadership and Organisation Journal* vol. 14, no. 7, pp. 28–34

Auster, E. 1988 'Behind closed doors: Sex bias at professional and managerial levels' *Employee Responsibilities and Rights Journal* vol. 1, no. 2, pp. 129–44

Campbell, J.L. & Howie, J.G.R. 1992 'Changes resulting from increasing appointment length, practical and theoretical issues' *British Journal of General Practice* vol. 42, no. 360, pp. 276–78

Clifford, V.A. 1996 'Women's ways of working: A study of a feminist general practice' in *Proceedings of Women and Leadership: Power and Practice International Conference* eds S. Olsson & N. Stirtin, Massey University, Palmerston North, pp. 123–36

Clifford, V.A. & Cocks, T. 1996 'Is there room for caring in the world of business', paper presented at *Sixth Western Pacific Regional Conference of the International Medical Women's Association,* Auckland

Craddock, C. & Reed, M. 1993 'Structure and struggle in implementing a social model of a well women clinic in Glasgow' *Social Science and Medicine* vol. 36, no. 1, pp. 67–76

Davidson, M.J. & Cooper, C.L. 1992 *Shattering the Glass Ceiling. The Woman Manager* Paul Chapman Publishing Ltd, London

Dobson, S. 1994 'Women and psychiatry—Struggles, strivings and social justice' Public Lecture Series in *Women in Leadership Programme 1993* ed. P. Carrols, Edith Cowan University, Perth

Gregg 1985 'Women entrepreneurs: The "second generation"' *Across the Board* January, pp. 10–15

Hawken, D. 1996 'Feminist management practice in the social services' in *Proceedings of Women and Leadership: Power and Practice International Conference* eds S. Olsson & N. Stirtin, Massey University, Palmerston North, pp. 205–20

James, B. & Saville-Smith, K. 1992 'Feminist perspectives on complex organisation' in *The Gender Factor: Women in New Zealand Organisations* ed. S. Olsson, Dunmore Press, Palmerston North

Lee-Gosselin, H. & Grise, J. 1990 'Are women owner-managers challenging our definitions of entrepreneurship? An in-depth survey' *Journal of Business Ethics* vol. 9, no. 2, pp. 423–33

Liddicoat, L. 1996 'The impact of the family friendly workplace on management and employees' in *Women and Leadership: Power and Practice International Conference* eds S. Olsson & N. Stirtin, Massey University, Palmerston North

Lorber, J. 1993 'Why women physicians will never be true equals in the American medical profession' in *Gender, Work and Medicine: Women and the Medical Division of Labour* eds E. Riska & K. Weger, Sage, London, pp. 62–76

McIlroy, J. & Clifford, V.A. 1996 'Safeguarding the health and well-being of the medical family: The Aurora Experiment four years on', paper presented at *Sixth Western Pacific Regional Conference of the Medical Women's International Association,* Auckland

Marshall, J. 1984 *Women Managers: Travellers in a Male World* John Wiley & Sons, Chichester

——1995 *Women Managers, Moving On* Routledge, London

Nathan, J. 1996 'The role of the leader in the establishment of the New Zealand Ministry of Women's Affairs' in *Proceedings of Women and Leadership Power and Practice International Conference* eds S. Olsson & N. Stirtin, Massey University, Palmerston North, pp. 331–48

Neider, L. 1987 'Preliminary investigation of female entrepreneurs in Florida' *Journal of Small Business Management* vol. 25, no. 3, pp. 22–29

Olsson, S. (ed.) 1992 *The Gender Factor: Women in New Zealand Organisations* Dunmore Press, Palmerston North

Opie, A. 1996 'Potential or problems: Collaboration in research teams' *New Zealand Sociology* vol. 11, no. 1, pp. 38–65

O'Regan, M. 1992 'Daring or deluded? A case study in feminist management: M. O'Regan in interview with Mary Varnham 1992' in *Feminist Voices. Women's Studies Text for Aotearoa/New Zealand* ed. R. Du Plessis, Oxford University Press, Oxford, pp. 197–208

Pringle, J. & Collins, S. 1996 'Pakeha women run organisations' *Proceedings of Women and Leadership: Power and Practice International Conference* eds S. Olsson & N. Stirtin, Massey University, Palmerston North

Riordan, D.A. & Riordan, M.P. 1993 'Field theory: An alternative to systems theories in understanding the small family business' *Journal of Small Business Management* vol. 31, no. 2, pp. 66–78

Risdale, L., Carruthers, M., Morris, R. & Risdale, J. 1989 'Study of the effect of time availability on the consultation' *Journal of the Royal College of General Practice* vol. 39, no. 329, pp. 488–91

Roland, M. 1989 'The efficient use of time in general practice' *Journal of the Royal College of General Practice* vol. 39, no. 329, pp. 485–86

Stanford, J.H., Oates, B.R. & Flores, D. 1995 'Women's leadership styles: A heuristic analysis' *Women in Management Review* vol. 10, no. 2, pp. 9–16

Still, L. 1996 'Women as leaders: The cultural dilemma' in *Proceedings of Women and Leadership: Power and Practice International Conference* eds S. Olsson & N. Stirtin, Massey University, Palmerston North, pp. 63–76

Traquair, N. 1993 'The primary head' in *Women in Educational Management* ed. J. Ozga, Open University Press, Buckingham

van Auken, H.E., Rittenburg, T.L., Doran, B.M. & Hsieh, S.F. 1994 'An empirical analysis of advertising by women entrepreneurs' *Journal of Small Business Management* vol. 32, no. 3, pp. 10–28

Walker, C. 1993 'Black women in educational management' in *Women in Educational Management* ed. J. Ozga, Open University Press, Buckingham

Weeks, W. 1994 *Women Working Together: Lessons from Feminist Women's Service* Longman Cheshire, Melbourne

Welsh, M. 1988 *The Corporate Enigma: Women Business Owners in New Zealand*, GP Books, New Zealand

White, B., Cox, C. & Cooper, C. 1992 *Women's Career Development: A Study of High Fliers* Blackwell, Oxford

Wilson, A. 1989 'Extending appointment lengths—The effects in one practice' *Journal of the Royal College of General Practice* vol. 39, no. 318, pp. 24–25

16 Psychiatric disability and community based care

Julie Mulvany

It has been estimated that 20 per cent of the Australian population will be affected by mental health problems and mental disorders at some time in their lives (National Health and Medical Research Council 1992). At any one time 3–4 per cent of the population suffer from severe mental disorders (Australian Health Ministers 1992, p. 7). The costs to the community in terms of lost productivity and treatment expenses are high (National Health and Medical Research Council 1992).

People with a history of mental illness face discrimination and stigmatisation (Campbell & Heginbotham 1991). They are more likely to experience poverty and neglect than those suffering from most forms of physical illness (Warner 1985). In 1990 concern for the plight of those suffering from psychiatric disabilities culminated in a national inquiry into human rights and mental illness. The report concluded that:

> It is clear from the evidence presented in this report that the cost of mental illness in terms of human lives and suffering is enormous. In addition to the pain suffered by consumers, these costs include disruption to family life, and sometimes unbearable pressures on other family members who feel powerless to assist the person who is ill. (Human Rights and Equal Opportunity Commission 1993, p. 15)

A number of recent national and state government inquiries and reports have drawn attention to the disadvantage experienced by people suffering from a psychiatric disability. The abuse suffered by people while living in both public and private psychiatric institutions (such as Chelmsford, Townsville, and Ballarat) has been documented. A Royal Commission, for example, was held into the Chelmsford

Hospital in Sydney where twenty-four people died in the 1960s and 1970s as a result of 'deep sleep' therapy (Bromberger & Fife-Yeomans 1991). People suffering from psychiatric disabilities have been neglected by the health and welfare systems. They have been given low priority in general government programs relating to education, employment and income support. Community based social and 'generic' disability programs and services have disregarded their needs (National Health Strategy 1993).

WHAT IS MENTAL ILLNESS?

The dominance of the medical profession in the definition of illness ensures that the most accepted conceptualisations of illness follow medical ideas about illness and its causes (Busfield 1986). These schema focus on the biological nature of disease and conceptualise illness as 'discrete, distinctive entities, differentiated from one another in terms of their causes, symptom patterns, course and outcome' (Busfield 1986, p. 36). In a biomedical model of health, illness is regarded as a physiological problem related to changes in bodily functioning. Thus physical symptoms of illness can be identified and treated by medical intervention, using technologies such as drugs and surgery. The focus of intervention is the individual patient and members of the medical profession are seen as being most appropriate to deal with the problem.

Psychiatry, as a branch of medicine, draws heavily on this model in its conceptualisation of mental disorders. Psychiatrists identify and differentiate between different types of mental disorders largely in terms of clusters of symptoms. Although we commonly speak of 'mental illness' as if it is one particular disorder there are a number of generally accepted classification systems of serious psychiatric disorders such as the *Diagnostic and Statistical Manual of Mental Disorders* *(DSM–4)*, developed by the American Psychiatric Association.

The major categories of serious disorders include schizophrenia, the most commonly diagnosed psychotic condition. A second major group of disorders is the affective psychoses, involving mood disorders such as manic-depression and major depression. A third category of disorders is anxiety disorders that include obsessive-compulsive disorders and phobias. Finally, there is a category of organic mental disorders such as Alzheimer's disease and Korsakoff's psychosis. Most psychiatrists make a distinction between mental disorder and intellectual disability or mental retardation.

SOCIOLOGY AND THE STUDY OF MENTAL HEALTH

Sociologists have made a major contribution to our understandings of mental illness and psychiatry. Their work can be divided into two main areas of interest. A major body of work focuses on the ways in which mental illness is socially constructed. An analysis is made of the social organisation of psychiatry, including an analysis of the development of particular categorisations of mental disorder and the application of psychiatric diagnoses by psychiatrists. In addition, community understandings and perceptions of mental illness are examined.

Sociologists interested in analysing medical conceptualisations of mental illness have identified a number of problems associated with these conceptualisations. They dispute the claimed 'scientific' status of the psychiatric study of mental disorders. For example, the inability to identify objective indicators, such as physical manifestations of disease in the body (Pilgrim & Rogers 1993) and the lack of agreement between psychiatrists regarding the diagnosis and treatment of different mental disorders is criticised (Brown 1987). Labelling theorists claim that the psychiatrist's interpretation of the significance of the potential patient's behaviour is crucial (see Scheff 1966; Schur 1971). Their research suggests that the application of diagnostic categories is influenced by factors such as the gender, race and class background of both the client and the psychiatrist rather than being determined by the identification of an objective sign of 'illness' (see Loring & Powell 1988). The value neutrality of the classification of particular psychiatric disorders is challenged. Writers point to the way behaviours viewed as deviant or immoral—such as homosexuality, hyperactivity in schoolchildren and political dissidence in the Soviet Union—have been conceptualised as illness (Conrad 1975; Szatz 1961).

A further concern of sociologists working in this area is the consequences that flow—in terms of the social response to people suffering from a psychiatric disorder—from the way mental disorder is conceptualised by the medical profession. Sociologists argue that the narrowness of the psychiatric focus excludes an examination of the social context within which illness occurs and leads to social policy interventions that rarely target broader socioeconomic issues. A sociological approach assumes that biological factors do not directly determine a population's health but are 'mediated through a society's social organisation' (Davis & George 1993, p. 31). Most sociologists do not deny that mental disorders exist or that biophysical factors may play a role in the aetiology of particular kinds of mental illness.[1] The sociologist is concerned, though, to examine how social factors such as interpersonal relationships, cultural practices, patterns of social organisation and wealth distribution influence both the incidence of mental disorders and the way people suffering from these disorders are treated in our society.

The second major area of interest for sociologists concerned with mental health issues is a focus on mental illness as a social product (Busfield 1989). The contribution social experiences and social structural factors make to the development of symptoms of mental illness and distress is studied. Research has examined the way social factors influence the cause and the incidence of mental health problems and exacerbate existing mental health problems. Sociological studies of psychiatric institutions (Goffman 1961; Strauss et al. 1964), for example, have made a major contribution to understandings of the effects of institutional care on inpatients. Goffman wrote about the effects of stigma on people suffering from a psychiatric disability and the negative effects of labelling by medical personnel on a patient's self-concept and identity during their incarceration in a psychiatric institution. This work was instrumental in leading to a reassessment of the treatment of the mentally ill in large psychiatric institutions.

An outstanding example of the way one's location within the social structure can influence health states is the relationship between poor health and low socioeconomic status. The relationship between socioeconomic status, whether measured by occupation, income, education, or geographical location, is consistent. Men and women of all ages from low socioeconomic status brackets have higher death rates and report higher levels of illness than those in higher status brackets (Commonwealth Department of Human Services and Health 1994).

A number of sociological studies have identified a relationship between mental illness and socioeconomic background. One of the first sociological studies of the relationship between class and mental disorder was conducted by Hollingshead and Redlich (1958) in America. They divided their sample into five classes and found that people diagnosed as mentally ill were more likely to be located in the lowest socioeconomic group. Epidemiological studies conducted in Europe, the US and the UK indicate a relationship between low socioeconomic status and the incidence of major mental disorders (Dohrenwend & Dohrenwend 1969; Faris & Dunham 1939; Kessler et al. 1994; Srole et al. 1962).

Despite the body of research showing a relationship between social class and mental illness there is little consensus on its significance in terms of causality. Some argue that location at the lower end of the socioeconomic scale exposes one to social conditions that precipitate or exacerbate symptoms of a psychiatric disorder. There is a growing body of epidemiological research, for example, that identifies a relationship between mental illness and stressful social circumstances and life experiences (Busfield 1989). A number of writers agree that stresses associated with location in lower socioeconomic classes lead to the development of particular kinds of mental illness. A recent study, for example, examined the effects of the rural economic crisis during the 1980s in America on the mental health of a representative sample of Nebraskans (Ortega et al. 1994). An impairment scale was used to measure depression, anxiety and psychosocial dysfunction. A relationship was found between levels of psychological distress, particularly depression and the downturn of the rural economy. The results also suggest that social factors such as the degree of integration of the community and the availability of social supports may explain the differential reaction of farmers to the crisis.

A number of studies have shown that children from poor social backgrounds experience more mental health problems than children from higher socioeconomic backgrounds (McLeod & Shanahan 1996). McLeod and Shanahan (1996) found that the early experience of poverty affected depression in later years of life. Warner (1985), on the basis of a wide ranging analysis of research into schizophrenia, argues that material conditions 'mold the course and outcome of the illness and influence, along with other factors, its prevalence' [original emphasis] (Warner 1985, p. 2). A central thesis of his book Recovery from Schizophrenia is that a positive relationship exists between prognosis for schizophrenia and employment options.

An alternative explanation of the correlation between low socioeconomic background and the incidence of serious psychiatric disorders is what has become known as the drift thesis. This thesis contends that people suffering from a psychiatric disability become concentrated at the lower end of the social strata as a result of their illness. Many people suffering from serious psychiatric disabilities are likely to be impoverished (Community Mental Health Policy and Planning Group 1989; Hage 1990; Naufal 1992). They have reduced employment prospects and are likely to be recipients of the disability pension (National Health Strategy 1993, p. 51). The social security benefits they receive do little to compensate them for the extra costs they encounter due to their disability (Naufal 1992; Sach & Associates 1991).

There is little doubt that the relationship between poverty and mental illness is significant. The nature of this relationship must be further explored by sociologists. We need to know what aspects of an impoverished lifestyle contribute to the development of particular mental disorders and/or exacerbate their symptoms. To what extent is there a likelihood that people suffering from serious psychiatric disabilities will drift into poverty because of a range of cultural, economic and political factors?

In the light of the increasing interest in health promotion and disease prevention the identification of risk factors associated with mental illnesses is crucial. Link and Phelan argue that research should analyse the social conditions that 'put people at risk of risks' (Link & Phelan 1995, p. 80). This involves moving beyond a focus on 'individual-level risk factors' to an analysis of the relationship between social conditions and health and illness (Link & Phelan 1995, p. 81). They are concerned that there has been an increase in research into the relationship between stress and psychiatric disabilities in the last few decades but a decline in research on the relationship between psychiatric disorders and socioeconomic status.

A number of writers utilise the concept of disability to assist them in their analysis of the social context of health and illness. The World Health Organization (WHO) makes a distinction between impairment, disability and handicap (WHO 1980, reprinted 1989). Impairment refers to bodily dysfunction resulting from injury or disease, such as organic brain damage or the loss of a limb. The term disability is used to describe the lack of function resulting from the impairment, for example, a loss of memory or the inability to walk. The WHO uses the term handicap to refer to the disadvantage experienced because of negative social reaction to impairment, for example, discrimination.

The WHO distinctions have been criticised (see Oliver 1990; McDermott & Carter 1995). Oliver argues that this terminology leads to a focus on the abnormality of particular individuals. Attention is directed towards treating a pathological condition instead of examining the wider social context within which the individual is living. Oliver, referring to physical disabilities, prefers to define disability as 'the disadvantage or restriction of activity caused by a contemporary social organisation which takes no or little account of people who have physical impairments and thus excludes them from the mainstream of social activities' (Oliver 1990, p. 11). As Fulcher (1989, p. 27) points out, 'a medical discourse links impairment and disability'. By conceptualising disability as the problem of an individual this discourse depoliticises the circumstances of the disabled. Oliver's conceptualisation of disability demands an identification of the social, political and economic conditions that restrict the life opportunities of someone suffering from an impairment.

A focus on disability inevitably exposes the impact of social conditions. Disability is seen as a condition resulting from social constraints, rather than as a sign of illness, requiring medical treatment. For the remainder of this chapter the term psychiatric disability will be used when referring to people who have been diagnosed as suffering from a serious mental disorder.

The sociological work discussed above suggests ways of expanding our approach to the study and conceptualisation of the area commonly referred to as 'mental illness'. The importance of examining the contribution social factors make to health states—including their role in the construction of disability—has been emphasised. In addition, sociologists are concerned with the social consequences of particular conceptualisations of mental disorder for the way people suffering from a psychiatric disability are treated.

DEINSTITUTIONALISATION AND COMMUNITY BASED CARE

The most significant change in the area of mental health policy has been the treatment of people suffering from a psychiatric disability within the community rather than in psychiatric institutions. The number of psychiatric hospital beds in Australia declined from 281 beds per 100 000 people in the early 1960s to forty beds per 100 000 people in the 1990s (National Health Strategy 1993). Despite assumptions that the movement to community based treatment in Australia for people with a serious psychiatric disorder is beneficial, a comprehensive assessment of de-institutionalisation has not been undertaken.[2] Anecdotal evidence suggests that many people suffering from serious psychiatric illness remain socially isolated and impoverished. In 1994 the National Inquiry into Human Rights and Mental Illness was reconvened in Victoria. The Inquiry concluded that despite the development of a range of potentially progressive policies there were major inadequacies associated with their implementation. Overall spending on mental health in Victoria had declined, mental health services were fragmented and uncoordinated and the mental health system 'is not meeting the demands placed on its services' (Human Rights and Equal Opportunity Commission 1995, p. 94).

We can identify within mental health policy a discourse about the importance of community based care. Policy responses, however, appear to be based on simplistic understandings of concepts of community care. In many instances what is meant is the delivery of health services within the community rather than in hospitals.[3] They fail to target social structural factors that affect an individual's experience of illness. For example, in an attempt to integrate the services provided by hospital and community mental health centres, most states in Australia are developing area based mental health services. The range of programs offered by these services includes 'assessment, crisis intervention teams, domiciliary services, and rehabilitation and living skills programs' (National Health Strategy 1993, p. 22). Many people suffering from serious psychiatric disabilities, however, also require a range of disability and social support services including employment and training, accommodation support, respite care, recreation and independent living and training. Many mainstream services are reluctant to include people with serious psychiatric disabilities in their programs and members of the mental health sector still see the provision of community services as chiefly their responsibility (National Health Strategy 1993).

The sociological critique of medical conceptualisations of mental illness directs us to conduct detailed examinations of the social circumstances and experiences of people suffering from serious psychiatric disability when living in the community (Cook & Wright 1995). In the final section of this chapter we will examine, therefore, research regarding the housing circumstances of people suffering from serious psychiatric disorders. This research alerts us to the dangers of assuming that de-institutionalisation will be successful if the needs of the psychiatrically disabled continue to be conceptualised in narrow clinical terms.

HOUSING PROBLEMS FOR THE PSYCHIATRICALLY DISABLED

A fundamental requirement for life in the community is satisfactory housing. Yet the housing circumstances of many people suffering from a serious psychiatric illness are deplorable. Research in the UK, the US and Australia has identified a range of housing problems faced by people suffering from a psychiatric disability. Financial constraints are the most obvious. The lack of low-cost housing options is well documented in the literature (see the National Housing Strategy 1992).

A second problem relates to inappropriate options and limited choice within the housing market (Burt 1991; Carling 1990). There is a chronic shortage of suitable housing for the psychiatrically disabled in countries such as Australia, England and America (Dear & Wolch 1987; Lamb & Lamb 1990). A recent study found that in Victoria, people with disabilities were 'vastly over-represented in low quality accommodation' (Naufal 1992, p. 7). The majority of people suffering from a psychiatric disability in Australia appear to be concentrated in one of a limited number of housing types. These include Special Accommodation Houses (SAHs), hostels, community residential units, rooming houses, cheap hotels, congregate housing and crisis accommodation. It could be suggested that a de facto policy of segregation and stigmatisation exists because of the extensive use of boarding and rooming houses by people suffering from a psychiatric disability.

A third problem is a lack of supportive housing services available for people with serious psychiatric disability. Traditionally, community based services have focused on medical treatment and social psychological rehabilitation. Housing and support needs have been neglected. Finally, the rights of the psychiatrically disabled are often disregarded in the housing sector. Hostels, Community Residential Units and SAHs are not covered by tenancy legislation and hence residents have little protection against eviction or invasion of privacy. Stresses related to dealing with tenancy issues had resulted in some respondents being re-hospitalised (Codsi 1993).

In a study conducted in Melbourne on the housing needs of people suffering from a serious psychiatric disability (Mulvany 1997) respondents cited a range of practical obstacles that hindered them from obtaining accommodation. These included a scarcity of information concerning housing options and advice about how to secure accommodation. They lacked access to transport to inspect appropriate accommodation. Many experienced problems meeting accommodation setup costs, such as payment of bonds and forward rental payments. They lacked money to buy basic items of furniture.

Many of the respondents in this study reported difficulties in asserting their rights and expressed feelings of vulnerability to exploitation and discriminatory practices in the housing market. Respondents who tried to find accommodation in the private sector reported being discriminated against because they were in receipt of a pension. One-third of respondents said they believed they had been denied housing because of their psychiatric illness. For people who are often struggling to cope with the symptoms of serious psychiatric illness, as well as the side effects of medication, these problems may become insurmountable.

A number of studies suggest that there are many mentally ill people among the homeless (Bachrach 1984; Hage 1990). Herrman

(1990) in a study of the homeless in inner-Melbourne found that 12 per cent of the 382 interviewed suffered from a mood disorder and 18 per cent from a psychotic disorder. Many live permanently in crisis accommodation centres where their social support needs are unlikely to be met (Hage 1990). An 'incipient homeless population' has also been identified. These are mentally ill people living in temporary accommodation:

> in the homes of their friends and relatives; in places they can not afford to hold onto; in dwellings from which they are in danger of being evicted; and in spaces that are not adequate dwellings, such as caravans, cars, garages, sheds, and even boxes. (Kearns et al. 1991, p. 1)

HOUSING EXPERIENCES AND MENTAL HEALTH

Poor housing conditions can have a negative impact on the mental health of residents. In a study of the housing needs of people suffering from psychiatric disability in Melbourne, the majority of respondents reported that their housing affected their mental health (Mulvany 1997). Factors they saw as negatively affecting their health included harassment, excessive noise, lack of privacy, overcrowding, conflict with neighbours and insecurity of tenure. Housing that facilitated their access to support and community facilities was valued. The ability to exert greater control over the nature and form of one's housing environment was associated, by respondents, with a more positive sense of identity and independence. Stress caused by unsatisfactory housing is particularly difficult for many psychiatrically disabled people who are faced with a range of other stresses, such as low income, lack of social networks and chronic psychiatric symptoms.

A study by Appleby and Desai (1987, p. 515) found that high residential mobility was related to an increased number of hospital admissions, 'isolation, disruptive family situations, and homelessness'. They cite research by Caton and Goldstein (1984) which 'found that highly stressful living conditions were related to mobility and rehospitalization' (Appleby & Desai 1987, p. 516). Stable housing arrangements seem to be associated with longer stays in the community (Taylor et al. 1989). Conversely, length of stay in hospital may be increased solely because of the inability to find suitable housing within the community for the patient (Carling 1990; Hage 1990). The provision of a stable housing environment for the newly discharged patient is important if community support systems are to be re-established (Appleby & Desai 1987) and maintained (Korr 1988).

Housing must be seen as constituting much more than the provision of physical shelter. It plays a pivotal role in facilitating or constraining access by people suffering from psychiatric disability to a range of community activities and supports. Factors associated with housing location, such as proximity to transport and friends, are of major importance if consumers are to be able to access community facilities and services, engage in work and recreational activities and be able to visit friends and relations. The location and form of housing can facilitate or retard social isolation and the development of confidence and self-respect.

HOUSING AND SUPPORT

Research from America and Australia identifies the crucial role accommodation support services can play in facilitating stable housing for many people suffering from serious psychiatric disabilities. Accommodation support programs provide client-identified support services at the client's chosen accommodation. This research illustrates the growing recognition that the social context of housing is crucial: 'housing which does not have support is like support to people who have no housing—it won't work' (Robson 1995, p. 88). An evaluation of a small housing support program in Melbourne identified improvements in the quality of life of many of the participants since their involvement in the program and argues that rates of hospitalisation can be reduced by the provision of supported accommodation (Robson 1995). The Macaulay Community Support Association in Melbourne provides social support to public housing tenants suffering from psychiatric disabilities.

> Data for Macaulay has shown hospital readmission has been reduced by up to 80% and a similar reduction for days spent in hospital was achieved for the 30 people who had been in the service for more than three months in 1990. (Naufal 1992, p. 33)

A New Zealand study of housing and health needs of people suffering from serious psychiatric disabilities points to the way in which aspects of housing such as noise, lack of privacy, overcrowding and lack of security can increase levels of psychological stress (Smith et al. 1994). A conclusion of this research, though, is that 'the presence of social support seems to have a generally beneficial influence on psychological distress (and, presumably, vice versa), regardless of the level of exposure to housing stressors' (Smith et al. 1994,

p. 256). Policy intervention, the authors argue, should be directed towards ways of building up the friendship networks of people suffering from serious psychiatric disability.

> This can be done in a number of ways: creating links to organisations that can provide information about jobs, housing or educational pursuits; making connections with helpful people and healthy places; and searching out interesting activities and recreational outlets. (Smith et al. 1994, p. 258)

Respondents in a Melbourne housing study (Mulvany 1997) were asked what support services they found useful. The types of supports identified by respondents can be divided into the categories of medical, financial, emotional and practical 'daily living' assistance.

The area of support mentioned most frequently related to the provision of 'practical assistance'. Respondents wanted information about such things as the availability of housing options, public transport in the area, how to obtain employment and how to access pensions. Some required assistance in organising their choice of housing, obtaining furniture and household appliances, organising home repairs and finding friendly people with whom to share housing. Others required assistance with daily living activities such as shopping, banking, washing, cooking, housework and budgeting. Forms of advocacy were also mentioned, such as having access to a legal advocate to assist with bonds and rules and regulations regarding living in rented accommodation. The provision of transport to such things as appointments and shopping was cited.

Many respondents wanted to be involved in the range of activities available to all community members such as recreational and entertainment facilities. They wanted access to excursions, trips, cheap holidays, films and games. They spoke of the need for day centres where recreational activities would be available. They emphasised the importance of these activities as a means of overcoming boredom, giving them something to look forward to, helping them utilise their time and as a way of meeting people.

Inappropriate housing exacerbates symptoms of illness. Appropriate housing is fundamental to the integration of people with psychiatric disabilities in the community. Socioeconomic factors and discriminatory practices prevent many people suffering from psychiatric disabilities from maintaining secure and permanent housing. Many of the problems individuals face on a daily basis and the supports they require are non-clinical. The importance of the provision of practical 'daily living' support for many people living in the community with serious psychiatric disabilities should not be underestimated.

CONCLUSION

In this chapter I have reviewed some of the work of sociologists interested in the study of psychiatry and mental illness. I have examined sociological work which explores the negative relationship between low socioeconomic status and health states. In my discussion of housing I have identified ways in which impoverished and stressful social circumstances can exacerbate symptoms of illness and create social situations in which dealing with psychiatric disorder becomes very difficult. As Cook and Wright (1995, p. 97) suggest, for many people suffering from serious psychiatric disability 'their lifestyles are as disabling as their mental illnesses' (see Segal & VanderVoort 1993). An understanding is required of the complex relationship between medical symptoms and socioeconomic factors. Symptoms do not occur in a vacuum and can be exacerbated by social factors and circumstances. Unsuitable living conditions can produce annoyance, frustration, anger, depression, despondency and lack of hope and motivation. These responses can exacerbate or be mistaken for illness symptoms. The ability to identify the relative influence of social as well as medical factors should provoke more appropriate intervention decisions.

I have also reviewed work of sociologists concerned that ideas about appropriate treatment continue to be conceptualised in narrow medical terms. Such a conceptualisation of mental disorder deflects attention from the effects of poverty, social security policy and diminishing housing markets on the lives of people diagnosed as seriously mentally ill.

It appears that problems with the implementation of the policy of de-institutionalisation are in part related to a failure to acknowledge and understand the social context of illness. The process of de-institutionalisation was essentially a passive process, either by the release of patients from institutions or the reduction in the number of hospital admissions. The active component, the provision of community care and support, has yet to be demonstrated. Detailed research is required that explores exactly how social, cultural, economic, political, and medical factors impinge on the lives of the psychiatrically disabled. The challenge for sociologists is to bring to bear their conceptual, analytical and research skills to constructively assess and inform the post-de-institutionalisation policy process.

NOTES

1   A number of writers, often referred to as the anti-psychiatrists, challenged the very notion of mental illness. Szasz (1961) believed that the symptoms associated with a diagnosis of mental illness were related to 'problems in living'. Scheff (1966) argued that most of the symptoms associated by psychiatrists with mental disorders developed because of the way the diagnosed patient was treated by community members and health professionals.

2   Research conducted in the United States and England identifies major problems associated with de-institutionalisation in these countries (see, e.g. Bean & Mounser 1993; Benson 1994).

3   The National Mental Health Policy, for example, states that one means of reducing the stigma and discrimination faced by people with mental disorders is 'by changing the approach to service delivery from institutionalised to community care' (Australian Health Ministers 1992, p. 12).

REFERENCES

Appleby, L. & Desai, M.D. 1987 'Residential instability: A perspective on system imbalance' *American Journal of Orthopsychiatry* vol. 57, no. 4, pp. 515–24

Australian Health Ministers 1992 *National Mental Health Policy* AGPS, Canberra

Bachrach, L. 1984 'The homeless mentally ill and mental health services: An analytical review of the literature' in *Report prepared for the Alcohol, Drug Abuse and Mental Health Administration* US Department of Health and Human Services, Washington DC, April

Bean, P. & Mounser, P. 1993 *Discharged from Mental Hospitals* Macmillan, London

Benson, P. 1994 'Deinstitutionalization and family caretaking of the seriously mentally ill: The policy context' *International Journal of Law and Psychiatry* vol. 17, no. 2, pp. 119–38

Bromberger, B. & Fife-Yeomans, J. 1991 *Deep Sleep* Simon & Schuster, Sydney

Brown, P. 1987 'Diagnostic conflict and contradiction in psychiatry' *Journal of Health and Social Behaviour* no. 28, pp. 37–50

Burt, H. 1991 *Creating A Place* Ecumenical Housing Unit, Melbourne

Busfield, J. 1986 *Managing Madness: Changing Ideas and Practice* Hutchinson, London

——1989 'Sexism and psychiatry' *Sociology* vol. 23, no. 3, pp. 343–64

Campbell, T. & Heginbotham, C. 1991 *Mental Illness, Prejudice, Discrimination and the Law* Dartmouth, Aldershot

Carling, P.J. 1990 'Major mental illness, housing, and supports: The promise of community integration' *American Psychologist* vol. 45, no. 8, pp. 969–75

Codsi, J. 1993 *Missing The Mark: A Report on the Tenancy Problems and Needs of People with Disabilities in Victoria* Shelter Victoria, Melbourne

Commonwealth Department of Human Services and Health, 1994 *Better Health Outcomes for Australians* AGPS, Canberra

Community Mental Health Policy and Planning Group 1989 *Mental Health Services into the 21st Century: A Time For Planned Change* Pre Budget Submission to the Minister For Health, Melbourne

Conrad, P. 1975 'The discovery of hyperkinesis: Notes on the medicalization of deviant behavior' *Social Problems* vol. 23, no. 1, pp. 12–21

Cook, J.A. & Wright, E.R. 1995 'Medical sociology and the study of severe mental illness: Reflections on past accomplishments and directions for further research' *Journal of Health and Social Behaviour* (extra issue) pp. 95–114

Davis, A. & George, J. 1993 *States of Health* 2nd edn, HarperEducational, Sydney

Dear, M. & Wolch, J. 1987 *Landscapes of Despair: Deinstitutionalisation to Homelessness* Princeton University Press, Princeton, NJ

Dohrenwend, B.P. & Dohrenwend, B.S. 1969 *Social Status and Psychological Disorder: A Causal Inquiry* Wiley, New York

Faris, R. & Dunham, H. 1939 *Mental Illness in Urban Areas* University of Chicago Press, Chicago

Fulcher, G. 1989 *Disabling Policies* Falmer, Sussex

Goffman, E. 1961 *Asylums* Penguin, Harmondsworth

Hage, M. 1990 *People with Mental Disorder and Homeless* Council to Homeless Persons, Melbourne

Herrman, H. 1990 *Homelessness and Severe Mental Disorders* National Health and Medical Research Council, Commonwealth of Australia, Canberra

Hollingshead, A. & Redlich, F. 1958 *Social Class and Mental Illness* Wiley, New York

Human Rights and Equal Opportunity Commission 1993 *Human Rights and Mental Illness, Report of the National Inquiry into the Human Rights of People with Mental Illness* AGPS, Canberra

——1995 *Human Rights and Mental Illness, Report of the Reconvened Inquiry Into the Human Rights of People With Mental Illness (Victoria)* AGPS, Canberra

Kearns, R., Smith, C. & Abbott, M. 1991 'Dwellers on the threshold: Housing poverty and mental health in urban New Zealand' Paper presented to the Biennial Congress of the World Federation for Mental Health, Mexico City, August 18–23

Kessler, R., McGonagle, K., Zhao, S., Nelson, C., Hughes, M., Eshleman, S., Wittchen, H. & Kendler, K. 1994 'Lifetime and 12-month prevalence of DSM–111-R psychiatric disorders in the United States: Results from the National Comorbidity Survey' *Archives of General Psychiatry* no. 51, pp. 8–19

Korr, W.S. 1988 'Outpatient commitment: Additional concerns' *American Psychologist* September, pp. 748–49

Lamb, H. & Lamb, D. 1990 'Factors contributing to homelessness among the chronically and severely mentally ill' *Hospital and Community Psychiatry* no. 41, pp. 301–14

Link, B.G. & Phelan, J. 1995 'Social conditions as fundamental causes of disease' *Journal of Health and Social Behaviour* extra issue, pp. 80–94

Loring, M. & Powell, B. 1988 'Gender, race and DSM–111: A study of the objectivity of psychiatric behaviour' *Journal of Health and Social Behaviour* vol. 29, no. 1, pp. 1–22

McDermott, F. & Carter, J. (eds) 1995 'Mental disorders: Prevention and human services research' *Commonwealth Department of Human Services and Health, Issues for Research, No. 4* AGPS, Canberra

McLeod, J.D. & Shanahan, M.J. 1996 'Trajectories of poverty and children's mental health' *Journal of Health and Social Behaviour* vol. 37, September, pp. 207–20

Mulvany, J. 1997 *Housing Needs of the Mentally Ill* Swinburne Centre for Urban and Social Research, Melbourne

National Health and Medical Research Council 1992 *Prevention in the Mental Health Field* AGPS, Canberra

National Health Strategy 1993 *Help Where Help is Needed* Issues Paper No. 5, National Health Strategy, Canberra

National Housing Strategy 1992 *Housing Choice: Reducing the Barriers* Issues Paper no. 6, AGPS, Canberra

Naufal, R. 1992 *Double Disadvantage: Housing for People with a Disability in Victoria* Victorian Council of Social Service and the Office of the Public Advocate, Melbourne

Oliver, M. 1990 *The Politics of Disablement* Macmillan, London

Ortega, S.T., Johnson, D.R., Beeson, P.G. & Craft, B.J. 1994 'The farm crisis and mental health: A longitudinal study of the 1980s' *Rural Sociology* vol. 59, no. 1, pp. 598–619

Pilgrim, D. & Rogers, A. 1993 *A Sociology of Mental Health & Illness* Open University Press, Buckingham

Robson, B. 1995 *Can I Call This Home? An Evaluation of the Victorian Housing and Support Program for People with Psychiatric Disabilities* VICSERV, Melbourne

Sach & Associates 1991 *The Housing Needs of People with Disabilities* Discussion Paper, National Housing Strategy, AGPS, Canberra

Scheff, T.J. 1966 *Being Mentally Ill* Weidenfeld & Nicolson, London

Schur, E. 1971 *Labelling Deviant Behaviour* Harper & Row, New York

Segal, S. & VanderVoort, D. 1993 'Daily hassles of persons with severe mental illness' *Hospital and Community Psychiatry* no. 44, pp. 276–78

Smith, C., Smith, C., Kearns, R. & Abbott, M. 1994 'Housing stressors and social support among the seriously mentally ill' *Housing Studies* vol. 9, no. 2, pp. 245–61

Strauss, A., Schatzman, L., Burcher, R., Ehrlich, D. & Sabshin, M. 1964 *Psychiatric Ideologies and Institutions* Free Press, Glencoe, ILL

Strole, L., Langner, T., Michael, S., Opler, M. & Rennie, T. 1962 *Mental Health in the Metropolis: The Midtown Manhattan Study* McGraw-Hill, New York

Szasz, T.S. 1961 *The Myth of Mental Illness* Hoeber-Harper, New York

Taylor, S.M., Elliott, S. & Kearns, R. 1989 'The housing experience of chronically mentally disabled clients in Hamilton, Ontario' *Canadian Geographer* vol. 3, no. 2, pp. 146–55

Warner, R. 1985 *Recovery from Schizophrenia* Routledge & Kegan Paul, London

World Health Organization 1980 (reprinted 1989) *International Classification of Impairments, Disabilities and Handicaps* WHO, Geneva

17 Nurses and the ideal of patient participation

Saras Henderson

This chapter presents research into nurses' and patients' perceived understanding of the meaning of participation and its influence on patient involvement in their own care. Patient participation has become the catchphrase in health care in recent times. Brearley (1990, p. 4) defined participation as 'being allowed to become involved in a decision-making process or in the delivery and evaluation of a service, or even simply being consulted on an issue of care'. Health consumer groups are now questioning the dependent role of patients within the Parsons' theory of sick role emphasising that there should be autonomy and self-determination from the patient's perspective (cited in Kim et al. 1993). Waddell and Petersen (1994, p. 137) have also emphasised that patients should be empowered through being allowed to participate in their care. The bases for this thinking are attributed to ethical, legal and social reasons (Sutherland et al. 1989). There is pressure from professional nursing bodies and consumer lobby groups for nurses to change from a paternalistic philosophy of care to one in which there is patient autonomy and empowerment. The issue of informed consent has been revisited since nurses continue to work within the premise that there is implied consent when the patient is admitted into hospital. There is an emphasis on patients, as health consumers, having access to information and participating in care (Biley 1992; Brearley 1990). These concerns are congruent with society's current concept of social justice and equality.

Practising nurses are of the opinion that patients should participate in the planning, implementation and evaluation of care in keeping with nursing's philosophy to provide holistic care (Waterworth & Luker 1990). Studies have demonstrated that when patients participate, they experience positive outcomes. These include greater satisfaction with care, a sense of control, decreased vulnerability and stress of hospitalisation, and being effectively prepared for discharge (Brearley 1990; Giloth 1990). Despite these positive outcomes, there is literature to indicate that there is incongruence between nurses' proparticipatory attitudes and the reality of what is actually practised by nurses. Brearley (1990) claimed that patient participation is a demand that will not go away and nurses, being most involved with patients, need to take the lead in promoting this.

Financial constraints within the health care system in Australia have resulted in reduced beds available for hospitalisation. Thus, several hospitals have opted for the early discharge program (*Health Observer* 1994). Wolf et al. (1994) therefore argue that patient participation is a necessity if nurses are to assist patients to care for themselves effectively once discharged. The Diagnosis Related Group (DRG) system of funding for hospitals in Australia also reinforces the participation ideal. Under this system, monies are paid prospectively to hospitals for patient outcomes rather than retrospectively for services rendered. Hence, hospitals aim to discharge patients as quickly as possible in order to benefit under the DRG system. This is acceptable if patients do not suffer any adverse effects such as complications from being sent home too early. It is all very well discharging patients early but can they care for themselves effectively once home? It is suggested that it is only through the active involvement of the patient while in hospital that they can be prepared effectively for discharge.

An insight into the understanding of the meaning of participation held by nurses and patients can be the first step in exploring and describing how patient participation is initiated and maintained while patients are in hospital. Ashworth et al. (1992) suggested that in any given social world, the assumptions and understanding of the actors must be congruent if there is to be consensual behaviour.

METHODOLOGY

This chapter is based on research involving qualitative research methodology. A purposive sample of thirty-three nurses and thirty-two patients was obtained from four hospitals in Western Australia. The purposive sampling technique requires selecting informants who are knowledgeable about the topic and who are willing to share experiential information about the phenomenon being studied (Morse 1989). The nurses and patients were interviewed using unstructured open-ended questions.

The criterion for including patients was that they had to have had at least three days in hospital, be able to speak English, and be mentally and physically capable. Patients in medical and surgical wards at Perth metropolitan hospitals were selected. The study is limited by the fact that only English-speaking informants were selected. It was decided to exclude non-English-speaking informants because of the difficulties involved with the use of interpreters. Eighteen patients were female and fourteen were male. The mean age was fifty-nine years. The number of hospitalisations varied, with some patients being first time admissions while others had been in hospital several times. The sample was composed of patients of mainly European background, although it did contain non-Europeans.

A sample of nurses who worked at the patients' bedside and who were employed at Level One and Level Two (as per the West Australian Nursing Career Structure) were interviewed. This sample was drawn from the same medical and surgical wards from which the sample of patients was drawn. Level One nurses comprised a combination of newly graduated nurses and nurses with several years of practice. These nurses worked under the supervision of Level Two nurses. Level Two nurses had expertise in their area of practice and had proven skills in communication, leadership and management. Twenty-six nurses were female and seven were male. The mean age of the nurses was thirty-five years, and two-thirds had university degrees. The ethnicity of the nurses was varied.

Permission to conduct the research was obtained from the Ethics Committees of the hospitals. Written consent was obtained from the informants for interviews and to audiotape the interviews. Informants were assured of confidentiality and anonymity. The interviews were approximately sixty minutes in duration. They were audiotaped and transcribed verbatim. The initial interview questions were broadly focused to encourage informants to speak freely about their perceptions of the meaning of participation. The later interview questions allowed the researcher to explore issues brought out by the informants. Five nurses and seven patients were re-interviewed to further clarify responses ascertained from the first interview.

The transcribed interviews were coded and major categories were developed. The categories from each of the taped interviews were then compared with categories developed from other transcribed interviews for common links. Credibility of the findings was established by having other researchers independently analyse slices of data and then compare coded categories and interpretations. Informants were contacted after analysis to verify the researcher's findings.

As the sample size was small and the research was qualitative, the reader should appreciate that the findings should only be placed within the context in which the study was conducted and are not necessarily generalisable. An Australian study by Irurita (1994) showed that patients perceived being consulted by nurses as a tenet of quality care. Furthermore, she found that patients wanted to participate in their care but perceived that this was not occurring. The findings of this research have the potential to provide answers to the question of why patients are not actively participating in their care. Exploring the meaning of participation from the nurses' and patients' perspective, therefore, seemed an appropriate start.

FINDINGS

In summary, the findings indicated that there was a lack of consensus in the conceptual understanding of the meaning of patient participation among nurses and patients and between nurses and patients. The conceptual understanding included the aspect where informants internalised the components of what participation encompassed, that is, whether patients should be involved in decision-making about all aspects of their care or only in some aspects of their care. Analysis of data showed that nurses and patients tended to have three different conceptualisations of the meaning of participation. These were: complete input from patients; partial input from patients; and minimal input from patients. These differing conceptualisations resulted in styles of participation which fell on a continuum, ranging from 'inclusive participation', to 'partial participation' to 'exclusive participation'. The nurses' and patients' understanding influenced the expectation and enactment of both parties regarding the degree to which patients actually participated and the extent to which nurses encouraged participation. In the following section, the conceptions and styles of participation will be discussed. Strategies used by nurses and patients in relation to each style will be described. Excerpts from narrative texts will be used to emphasise nurses' and patients' perspectives.

INCLUSIVE PARTICIPATION

In this style of participation, both nurses and patients conceptually understand that participation means involvement of patients in all areas of care. Both parties are of the view that patients should have input into meeting their own *hygiene needs*, be consulted on the type of *pain control*, and be part of the *decision-making* process regarding treatments. The informants perceive that nursing care is a cooperative process. They believe that there should be equal input from both parties, provided patients are well enough to participate and are fully informed. An example of nurses' comments in support of the above statement include:

> *Participation involves patient input from admission to discharge as long as well enough . . . to be involved in activities of daily living and decision-making . . . it means having a voice to speak out re care; evaluating what's been done and refusing treatment if not happy without ramifications from the health professional!* (Nurse)

> *Participating, to me, is patients being involved in their own hygiene care if able; know about their medication and even self medicate. If they* [meaning patient] *do not want a particular type of surgery for example, laparoscopic versus open surgery, then they should be able to choose . . . it's up to us, nurses, to provide the patient with the relevant information and be an advocate for them so that they can participate in all aspects.* (Nurse)

Patient comments demonstrate that they perceive participation to include all aspects of care, for example:

> *I think I can judge for myself the kind of nursing care that I need . . . I ask for information because I have got to know what is going on with me . . . this is so that I can work with them* [meaning nurses] *to meet our goals . . . I don't look for control in the hospital, I look for cooperation in the things that they are aiming for in helping me get better and move me along the recovery trail.* (Patient)

> *As a patient, I am willing to accept that they* [meaning nurses] *have their expertise but I have mine and we are equal in that way . . . I think there has to be mutual cooperation between doctors and nurses and patients . . . there should be none of these one-upmanship . . . They need to consult me because I know my body better than anyone, it's not like working with a machine!* (Patient)

From the above comments it can be inferred that both nurses and patients perceive that care should be mutually driven, thus embracing the concept of social equality. Nurses seem to appreciate that patients need to be well enough and have the necessary information in order to participate. Therefore, they perceive that they should volunteer information to patients without being asked and encourage patients to share information with them, for example:

> It is a two-way street between the nurse and patient . . . they [meaning patients] are not to lie there passively and be administered to . . . we need to provide them with information . . . we need feedback from them about how they are going . . . I always tell my patients that they have rights and encourage them to ask questions so that they are informed . . . (Nurse)

The above comment by a nurse highlights the point that some nurses want patients to move away from the passive role and be involved in their own care. Similarly, patients with this view expect to be informed and consulted so that they can participate in all aspects of care. This is suggested by Salvage (1990, p. 44) whose survey indicated that patients wanted to be given sufficient information so that they could make rational choices in their care. Some patients in this study stated:

> I think, they [i.e. nurses and doctors] should give you as much information as they can about your stay so you are not under plain dark authority . . . I mean a lot of patients have not been in hospital before and they don't know what to expect . . . I think patients should know what they are in for, what is going to happen, so that they can have a say in what is being done. (Patient)

When there is inclusive participation, patients are able to be involved and are encouraged by nurses to fully participate in all aspects of their care. This includes having an input into their activities of daily living, deciding on pain management and making decisions about their treatment regimes. In inclusive participation, both nurses and patients engaged in behaviour termed in the data as 'partnering'. There was mutual information sharing, and the nurse and patient transacted and negotiated with each other to maximise patient participation in all aspects of care. For example:

> I tried not to take too many pain killers . . . I might take them in the morning and at night before bedtime . . . the nurse was pretty good about it . . . she let me decide when I wanted them and I felt she was okay about it . . . sometimes, in the shower, the nurse wanted to assist me but I told her 'look, I can manage myself so you can leave me' and the nurse left me alone . . . we got on really well. (Patient)

Often with this style of participation, the nurse acted as the patient's advocate, especially where medical decisions were involved

such as whether the patient should have chemotherapy or radio-
therapy, as demonstrated by this comment:

> Well, I encourage self-determination and I encourage patients to seek
> other opinions . . . they have the right to make their own decisions
> and if they don't accept a particular treatment that has been recom-
> mended by the doctor . . . then I support them absolutely one hundred
> per cent if they decide 'no'. (Nurse)

This comment supports the Ashworth et al. (1992, p. 1430) contention that nurses, being part of society, should accept the ethos of
individual freedom and responsibility and therefore encourage patients to
have input into their care. Data analysis indicated that for partnering to
occur, nurses need to be the patient's advocate, that is, to speak up or
act on behalf of the patient. Nurses need to be prepared to undertake
complex and sometimes controversial roles in order to act in the best
interest of patients. This sometimes involves negotiating with doctors.
Sines (1994) argues that this stance may be difficult for some nurses. To
'be the guardian of patients' rights and be a champion of social justice
in providing care', nurses often face opposition from doctors. This is
because doctors believe that it is their responsibility to discuss medical
treatment issues with patients and not the nurses (Sines 1994, p. 899).

However, if the patient is too sick to participate, the nurse still
consciously thinks about the patient's input and, where appropriate,
consults with the relatives of the patient. The nurse also guided and
directed the patient until such time as the patient was able.

> If the patients are sick, keeping them comfortable is uppermost in my mind
> but I still act as their advocate. For example if the doctor gets really 'gung
> ho' and invasive in his treatment, I will try and take him aside and explain
> that perhaps he should consult with the rellies [relatives]. (Nurse)

It was evident from the analysis that the *ideal* of inclusive participation was occurring at the research sites. With this style of
participation, patients believe that they are fully able to participate
as appropriate and state that they feel in control and less vulnerable
about their hospital experience. The translation of the ideal into
behaviour, however was only infrequently noted at the research sites.

PARTIAL PARTICIPATION

Both nurses and patients with this style of participation conceptualise
participation as patients having input into meeting their *hygiene needs*

and making decisions about *pain control* if able. However, both parties perceive that patients should not and cannot make decisions about their *treatment plans*. Nurses believe that they should be helping patients and taking control as patients are in hospital to get better. The reason for this thinking by nurses seems to be related to the perception that patients lack medical knowledge, such as:

> *I mean with very basic things like when they want their shower . . . just those basic things* [they should have control]. *I don't really see they have control in much else . . . often, things are not fully explained to patients about their treatments so they are not in control of the knowledge of what is happening . . . they don't have the whole story.* (Nurse)

> *Some nurses are driven by the belief that doctors and nurses know best . . . so we encourage patients to do as instructed by us . . . patients should cooperate and comply to what sort of advice we give them because they* [patients] *don't have the expert knowledge to decide!* (Nurse)

Patients share the same view as nurses in this conceptualisation of participation. Patients are of the opinion that nurses 'know best' and that they should cooperate with nurses in whatever they asked them to do, giving nurses control. Patients perceive that nurses and doctors are the experts and 'gatekeepers' of information. This view is not uncommon, as Tuckett et al. (1987) found that patients often saw themselves as having a 'competence gap' and therefore expected to take advice on trust and not question what they are told. As such, patients with this conceptualisation believe that it is up to the experts to provide them with the necessary information if they perceive that patients need information. For example:

> *Certainly they* [nurses and doctors] *should, in my opinion, give you the information as needed . . . they are trained to know better. I am a farmer and not a doctor or nurse . . . if they don't know more, they shouldn't be here!* (Patient)

> *I think you need to cooperate with everything that goes on because you don't know exactly why some things are being done . . . I only know that if you don't have the knowledge, you can't really provide any input . . . so you cooperate . . . surely they wouldn't be doing anything unless necessary, they know what needs to be done.* (Patient)

Accordingly, with this style of participation, the concept of patient participation seems to take a back seat in the conscious minds of patients and nurses. Nurses and patients therefore engage in behaviour suggested by the data as one of 'guidance' from nurses and 'cooperation' from patients. The patients receive procedural information from nurses without asking. Nurses, however, only give treatment information to patients when they request that information from them. There is no mutual information sharing. In partial participation, nurses encourage patients to take control of meeting their hygiene needs as appropriate. As with pain management, nurses sometimes offer patients alternatives and get the doctor to write up alternative medication. However, nurses with this conceptualisation of participation do not advocate for patients to help them to make decisions about treatments. Nurses use such behaviour as coaching, prompting, directing and gentle persuasion to guide patients and to gain their cooperation, as shown in these nurse comments:

> In the shower, I stand back and sort of encourage them. I would say like 'how about washing your legs' or whatever . . . just a bit of verbal prompting and it does work. I will for example, direct them to pop the cream on or their Ted stockings . . . you know I just encourage them [patients] to go for a walk with prompting them and they do cooperate. (Nurse)

> I would give them the option like if they would like to get out of bed and go for a walk but I would say it in such a way without letting them [patients] say 'no'. I can't let them lie back in bed for the next 56 hours or whatever . . . I try to coax them to move for their own good. (Nurse)

The patients' behaviour with this conceptualisation of participation is one of cooperating with nurses and taking the passive role. Interestingly, patients feel comfortable about cooperating with the nurses because of the knowledge gap as indicated earlier. This is supported by Harrison and Cameron-Traub (1994, p. 153) whose study showed that patients often saw their role as one of cooperation with nurses; that is, not wanting to impede nursing care by being uncooperative. These authors also found that patients perceived that the doctor was in charge and that nurses were there to follow doctors' orders with little decision-making powers.

> You can take control to a certain extent like what you want to do for the day or if you want the pain killer stopped but treatments don't fall within that parameter . . . I suppose you have got to stay within what they say, to get better, so you cooperate with them. I cooperate with them because I am here to be looked after and the doctors are here to

*set the program and the sister [meaning nurse] is here to follow suit
. . . so what is there but to cooperate.* (Patient)

*The nurses are in control . . . after all they are your anchor and you
are dependent on them especially if you are a bed patient, you cannot
get up and un-hitch yourself . . . therefore, you pretty well go along
with them . . . after all they are professional people and looking after
you.* (Patient)

Partial participation by nurses and patients was evident frequently
in the data. Both nurses and patients seemed to accept the notion of
'nurse knows best' and enacted their behaviour accordingly. McCormack (1993, p. 341) has questioned whether the professionalisation
of nurses has allowed them to fall into the rhetoric of thinking and
believing that they do know what is best for patients, thereby ignoring
the real needs of patients. In this present research, while patients were
satisfied with their hospital care, they expressed concern that they
sometimes were not fully sure of what to do or expect about their care
once discharged. In retrospect, patients felt that they should have been
given more control over their care in hospital so that they could care
for themselves more effectively at home.

*When I went home I got my wound wet and it got a bit red and inflamed
. . . when I went back into hospital, the nurse said I should have kept it
dry. You see, in hospital, the nurses always covered it and I didn't need
to do anything . . . They took care of everything . . . I think we should
be involved so we know what to do once home.* (Patient)

EXCLUSIVE PARTICIPATION

In this style of participation, nurses and patients perceive that participation encompasses patients listening to nurses and doing as they are
told with regards to meeting their own hygiene needs, pain control
and treatment plans. Analysis indicates that exclusive participation
occurs in hospitals to some extent but not as frequently as partial
participation. The notion that there is implied consent when patients
are admitted to hospital seems to foster the perception that nurses are
clearly in charge and patients are there to follow orders. Patients
believe that they should conform and 'toe the line' so that they get the
necessary care to recover. Patients with this conceptualisation of
participation state that they do not wish to be labelled as 'difficult';
and thus do as they are told. Both nurses and patients are of the view

that nursing care is nurse-driven with patients taking a submissive role, as indicated by these statements:

I acknowledge patients have rights but I don't believe in giving in to what they want . . . they often don't know what is best for them so we have to take charge . . . we would hope that they [patients] have a positive outlook and conform. (Nurse)

In some ways, I expect them [patients] to be subservient . . . and yes, it is a role of dependency and maybe that's what I, as a nurse, feel patients should feel . . . maybe I am creating an expectation from patients that they conform to my views. (Nurse)

Patients with this conceptualisation believe they need to toe the line; that is, do exactly as asked by nurses without question. It also includes totally complying with nurses' orders without consideration for their own feelings, as highlighted by these patient comments:

I think the nurses have got the upper hand . . . you are there because something's gone wrong and it's got to be rectified and they know what they are doing . . . they [nurses] are the ones that . . . well, they have got the upper hand, haven't they . . . the patients are really floundering in the dark. (Patient)

I think if you toe the line, the girls [nurses] will definitely look after you . . . if you don't toe the line, the girls get their backs up . . . you should do what you are told as you are dependent on them . . . therefore, you pretty well got to go along with them . . . I think you have to as you have no option. (Patient)

It may be suggested that the above nurse and patient comments reflect nurses' views that they are in control and patients' perceptions of vulnerability while in hospital. This was also demonstrated in a study by Waterworth and Luker (1990) that showed that patients appeared to value being able to trust nursing staff and 'toe the line' rather than to participate in their own care. The patients in the above study were so preoccupied with 'staying out of trouble' that they took on a submissive role. Some patients with this conceptualisation perceive the nurse to be clearly in charge. Both nurses and patients equate the nurse–patient interaction with the teacher–pupil interaction, as seen in the following comments:

I suppose we expect them to follow instructions from nursing and medical staff . . . in some ways to be subservient, I suppose, probably to make our job easier. (Nurse)

Basically they [patients] are unwell and they are here to be looked after . . . I suppose ideally, we expect them to accept whatever treatment they are offered. You see they are not in a position to make decisions because they don't have the knowledge. (Nurse)

I think, just try and be a good patient, try and abide by the hospital rules and what the nurses want you to do, not to be difficult . . . I suppose to listen to their advice. (Patient)

I feel the nurse is like a teacher in the classroom. The nurse is in charge of the ward and has the right to use her professional judgement. (Patient)

In exclusive participation, contextual factors such as time and length of patient hospital stay seem to have little effect on the degree to which patients participate. The nurses are mainly engaged in doing technical tasks. Asking patients to participate in their hygiene needs does not appear to be a conscious decision on the part of nurses. It just happens to be the lowest form of participation which fits into the repertoire of nurses' work routine. Similarly, patients also do not consciously think of initiating participation. They were primarily concerned about helping nurses and being 'good patients'. Hence, they believe that they should carry out hygiene needs as able. There is evidence in the data that the concept of participation is not important to nurses and patients with this conceptualisation of participation.

The drive on the nurses part seems to be how to get through the technical tasks and get the work done within the shift rather than planning care based on the decision to involve patients in all aspects of care, that is, meeting hygiene needs, making decisions about treatment regimes, and pain management. If nurses encourage patients to perform their own hygiene needs, it appears to be a consequence of their routine work and nothing more. Patients, on the other hand, want to get better as quickly as possible and all they are concerned about is listening to nurses' instructions and complying.

The strategy used in this conceptualisation is nurses overshadowing the patient and the patient 'toeing the line'. This situation occurs because the concept of patient participation is not consciously thought of and enacted. This is evident in the sense that nurses and patients who subscribe to this conceptualisation have to think hard to tell the researcher what patient participation means. Thus, patients only participate in meeting their hygiene needs by default and sometimes inappropriately. Patients are just told what the nurses are going to do to them, leaving them uninformed about what is really happening to them. As the patients' stance is such that they do not think it their place to ask questions, these patients are not in a position to make informed decisions.

CONCLUSION

In this chapter the conceptual understanding of patient participation by nurses and patients and its influence on participation was presented. Conceptions of participation were identified and described. It is interesting to note that partial participation seems to be the most common style enacted with exclusive participation occurring to a lesser extent. Inclusive participation—the ideal—was enacted least of all.

Empowering patients and allowing and encouraging patients to take an active role in their care has been espoused as a desired outcome by the nursing profession (Pyne 1994). The findings of this research, however, indicate that there is a discrepancy in what has been espoused and what is actually enacted in the practice setting. More specifically, this research highlights that there is considerable lack of consensus in the conceptual understanding of what participation means to nurses and patients. This had led to varying degrees of patient participation and a lack of consistency in nurses' promotion of the ideal. Partial participation seems to be occurring frequently in the practice setting. Even though nurses and patients are not too concerned about this occurrence, the nursing profession needs to take a closer look at why partial participation is occurring because it is not the ideal. The issue of power imbalance between nurses and patients especially with the style of exclusive participation is disconcerting. As patients do not want to be labelled as 'difficult' and miss out on care, they simply comply with nurses' instructions or 'toe the line'. This is of concern because it is not in keeping with society's value in empowering patients and enhancing social equality. This situation also calls into question the nursing profession's philosophy of holistic care and patient involvement. The scope of this research did not extend beyond exploring the views of patients with European and English-speaking backgrounds. This limitation needs to be redressed in future research by using more non-European and non-English-speaking patients.

Salvage's (1990) explanation may be worth addressing at this point. She explains that even though nursing has embraced the view of patient-centred care, it is still driven by routine and task-oriented care. Salvage further explains that there is literature to show that nurses continue to perceive 'real nursing' as doing practical tasks. This had resulted in nursing practice being mechanistic in nature with low priority placed on interacting with patients and actively promoting involvement. It is suggested that nursing re-visit its practice paradigm and move away from task-oriented care to one in which the patient plays a pivotal role. The other area that needs to be examined is nursing education. If the concept of holistic care which involves patient participation is taught to students at universities, why then are nurses not able to successfully promote this in clinical practice? Perhaps nursing curricula are only concerned with outcome measures in learning. The process of how to actually involve patients may need to be taught to nursing students. Certainly this issue should be investigated. Future research is therefore required to fully explore the issue of patient participation.

REFERENCES

Ashworth, P.D., Longmate, M.A. & Morrison, P. 1992 'Patient participation: Its meaning and significance in the context of caring' *Journal of Advanced Nursing* no. 17, pp. 1430–39

Biley, F.C. 1992 'Some determinants that effect patient participation in decision making about nursing care' *Journal of Advanced Nursing* no. 17, pp. 414–21

Brearley, S. 1990 'Patient participation: The literature' Royal College of Nursing Research Series, Scutari Press, England

Giloth, B.E. 1990 'Promoting patient involvement: Educational, organisational, and environmental strategies' *Patient Education and Counselling* no. 15, pp. 29–38

Harrison, L. & Cameron-Traub, E. 1994 'Patients' perspectives on nursing in hospital' in *Just Health: Inequality in Illness, Care and Prevention* eds C. Waddell & A.R. Petersen, Churchill Livingstone, Melbourne

Health Observer 1994 'Silver chain promote early discharge' May, p. 18

Irurita, V. 1994 'From person to patient: Nursing care from the patient's perspective' Nursing Research Unit, Curtin University of Technology, Bentley

Kim, H.S., Holter, I.M., Inayoshi, M., Shimaguchi, S., Ryder, R.S., Kawaguchi, Y., Hori, R., Takezaki, K., Leino-Kilpi, H. & Munkki-Utunen, M. 1993 'Comparison of patients' and nurses' attitudes in Finland, Japan, Norway and the USA' *International Journal of Nursing Studies* no. 30, pp. 387–401

McCormack, B. 1993 'How to promote quality of care and preserve patient autonomy' *British Journal of Nursing* vol. 2, no. 6, pp. 338–41

Morse, J.M. 1989 *Qualitative Nursing Research: A Contemporary Dialogue* Aspen, Gaithersburg, MD

Pyne, R. 1994 'Empowerment through use of the code of professional conduct' *British Journal of Nursing* vol. 3, no. 12, pp. 631–34

Salvage, J. 1990 'The theory and practice of the new nursing' *Nursing Times* vol. 86, no. 4, pp. 42–45

Sines, D. 1994 'The arrogance of power: A reflection on contemporary mental health nursing practice' *Journal of Advanced Nursing* no. 20, pp. 894–903

Sutherland, H.J., Llewellyn-Thomas, H.A., Lockwood, G.A., Tritchler, D.L. & Till, J.E.

1989 'Cancer patients: Their desire for information and participation in treatment decisions' *Journal of the Royal Society of Medicine* no. 82, pp. 260–63

Tuckett, D., Boulton, M., Olson, C. & Williams, A. 1987 *An Approach to Sharing Ideas in Medical Consultation Meetings Between Experts* Tavistock, London

Waddell, C. & Petersen, A.R. 1994 *Just Health: Inequality in Illness, Care and Prevention* Churchill Livingstone, Melbourne

Waterworth, S. & Luker, K.A. 1990 'Reluctant collaborators: Do patients want to be involved in decisions concerning care?' *Journal of Advanced Nursing* no. 15, pp. 971–76

Wolfe, G.A., Boland, S. & Aukerman, M. 1994 'A transformational model for the practice of professional nursing' *Journal of Nursing Administration* vol. 24, no. 4, pp. 51–65

18 Health and the dying person

Allan Kellehear

At 9.30 a.m. on 2 January 1997, a 52-year-old person by the name of Mrs Janet Mills became the second person to take advantage of the Northern Territories Euthanasia Bill. She had a rare form of skin cancer and her doctor assisted in her suicide. Mrs Mills' last reported words were 'peace at last'. But for those of us left behind in the wake of her death it was not peace but rather a war of words which remained.

To understand what particular influences led Mrs Mills to look to her doctor—a person committed to health care—to help her take her life, we need to look at the contemporary connections between our evolving ideas of health and the experience of dying. When we think about health, dying is the last thing on our minds, except perhaps the thought that being as healthy as possible may help us avoid it. And when we think about dying we often think of the absence of health or rather, the deterioration of health associated with dying. So on first thoughts, and for many people, the ideas of health and dying are opposite ones.

The aim of this chapter, however, is to demonstrate that the recent euthanasia controversy is a natural and logical outcome of an increasingly popular view that health and dying should not be opposites—they should instead be synonymous. Just how this particular association of ideas has come to enjoy a certain ascendency can only be understood by examining how both 'health' and 'dying' have gradually come to converge in the minds of increasing numbers of people this century.

In our examination, the first part of the chapter will take the reader through a quick review of the social history of dying. The second part of the chapter will compare that history with the parallel history of our experience and ideas about health. Finally, the last section of the chapter will examine the emergence of the New Public Health Movement and its increasing impact on the way we view all health matters and, by extension, matters to do with dying.

A SOCIAL HISTORY OF DYING

The name that immediately comes to mind when discussing the history of dying is Phillipe Aries, the famous French historian of social ideas. Aries wrote several books and papers (1974, 1981) outlining what he saw as the retrograde cultural changes to death being experienced during his time. In the mid-twentieth century dying was considered an embarrassing and stigmatised activity.

From around the Middle Ages to the beginning of the nineteenth century dying was an event controlled by the dying person. Through much personal experience of seeing other people die and also because of a more personally observant relationship to one's own body most people 'knew' when they were gravely ill or mortally wounded. Awareness of dying did not need a doctor's opinion. People relied on their own observations into this process.

Once becoming aware that they were to die soon, the dying would prepare for their death by organising those attending into tasks. Sometimes clerics would be sent for. At other times, when clerics did not perform the 'last rites' for non-clerics, those who attended the dying would be asked to pray or sing for the soul of the dying person. Later, in the late eighteenth and early nineteenth centuries, the last words of the dying became important to those around the deathbed. Words about the nature of life and the mercy of God or advice about the family and its needs were particularly valued.

Increasingly, as European people moved into the nineteenth century with some wealth, words of wisdom and advice were combined with instructions on what to do with personal property and fortune. When it became apparent that the wishes of the dying were not always respected by families, particularly wealthy families, the legal will took on a certain obvious importance. In most of these cases, the essential observation made by Aries was the centrality of the dying person to these events, the unequivocal authority and control that dying persons exercised by directing those around them.

Gradually, over the course of a hundred years or so, that authority waned, and then succumbed to the encroachment of professionalism in law, medicine, the funeral industry, but also changes within the family itself. The rise of the urban, wage-earning family in late nineteenth–early twentieth century Europe meant that community ties and networks decreased. Instead, small, private families with fewer relatives but more money bought in services formerly provided by themselves or their community.

Doctors' advice was sought. Funeral professionals performed functions that elderly women formerly performed in the old villages. Wills were drawn up because the sentimentality of family relations meant that those surrounding the dying saw their task primarily in terms of comforting words rather than dutiful actions. Complementing these changes to the private lives of families were other changes in the sphere of public institutions.

Medicine increased its knowledge and expertise about the body, no longer requiring elaborate stories from the patient to make a diagnosis. A study of bodily emissions and other symptoms led to a greater understanding of the hidden ways of the body. A doctor could suspect greater problems and poorer prospects than the patient could detect naively and by their own wits. An understanding of infection led to a growing concern for isolating patients. And public hospitals, formerly places with higher mortality rates than the general community, now became places where both patients and doctors shared the one aim—cure.

Aries documented these numerous social and cultural changes carefully, interweaving his accounts with those of fellow historians of the family, economy, and of epidemiology and public health. He has been criticised by, among others, the British historian David Cannadine (1981) for over-emphasising the Catholic experience of dying; for over-selecting from bourgeoise experiences of dying and assuming this to be the experience of the wider population, particularly the proletariat and working classes. He has also been criticised for sentimentalising, even romanticising, the image of dying in the Middle Ages.

But these criticisms notwithstanding, Aries was reacting to his contemporary situation. This was the situation and circumstances of dying in the mid-twentieth century, a time when dying had come to be seen as medical failure. Hospitals isolated the dying from other patients. Doctors felt that the knowledge of dying would so shatter a person's hopes and mental stability that they no longer felt obliged to make the patient aware of their impending death. Compared to an earlier time, however imperfect, of relative autonomy and control, the dying in Aries' time were disempowered people who were often left to die alone, and ignorant of their fate until hours from it.

Aries, however, was not alone in looking for reasons for this shameful situation and in the 1970s social and behavioural scientists wrote extensive critiques and theories about the social and clinical reasons behind the situation (Brim 1975; Feifel 1977; Garfield 1978). Geoffrey Gorer, an English anthropologist, felt so strongly about it he entitled his most famous work on this subject, *The Pornography of Death* (1976). In his view, death had become the great taboo after sex itself. Talk of death was so feared, it so revolted or embarrassed people of the day, that such talk and the images associated with it could be seen as 'pornography'.

The 1960s were the low ebb in discussions and arrangements surrounding death. At the end of that decade the psychiatrist Kubler-Ross published *On Death & Dying* (1969) and insisted in that work that we start listening to the dying person again. Across the Atlantic, the pioneering English nurse Cicely Saunders made similar arguments when attempting to set up a special place for the care of the dying—a hospice (Saunders & Baines 1983).

The aim of hospice and palliative care is to provide a series of medical and nursing interventions designed around the idea of part restoring control to the dying person. Priority among these interventions was symptom control—particularly control over incontinence, breathing difficulties, and pain. The clinical interventions were designed to help restore a certain level of health. Permitting the dying person an improvement of quality of life, these interventions enhanced levels of physical mobility and comfort.

A further priority was to permit a certain level of social functioning and comfort normally enjoyed at home. In this way, visiting hours were made more flexible, private decorations and belongings from home were encouraged and this included visits from pets. The desire to maintain minimum levels of familiar social context was a major departure from the traditionally restrictive controls and routines of the hospital.

Robert Kastenbaum, a psychologist and the editor of the longest-running academic journal of death studies in the US (*Omega*), expressed some of the earliest reservations about this pursuit of what he called 'healthy dying'. Kastenbaum (1979) argued that the expectations that some people have for this last phase of life might be more than many would expect during the normal course of life. An obsession with prolongation of life through aggressive interventions such as radical surgery and chemotherapy may now have been enjoined by an equally concerted attempt to 'improve' quality of life at the end of it.

Both Kastenbaum, and more recently Kearl (1989), have argued that the booming literature on near-death experiences has further increased people's expectations, both patients and clinical staff, of not only a dying with minimum fuss and discomfort but a positively pleasurable death. The euphoric descriptions of out-of-body experiences and reunions with deceased friends and relatives so often associated with the near-death experience adds to the desire of many to go out in good and spectacular style let alone with simple dignity.

This increasing attention to the importance of 'quality of life' has not, however, been a simple reaction to some remembrance of a period of poor quality of life for the dying in the 1960s. Nor are the aims of the current palliative care and hospice services responding to some nostalgic notion of bourgeoise autonomy remembered by the French historians such as Aries. The centrality of the concern for 'quality of life' is only *shaped* by those forces, not *created* by them; the pursuit of quality of life has been an evolving one in the health area in general.

A HISTORY OF HEALTH CARE

The fact that dying people controlled their deathbed exits during the Middle Ages should surprise few when one remembers the absolute autonomy they enjoyed during any ordinary period of illness. Before the advent of modern understandings of anatomy or physiology doctors relied on a different method to ascertain a clinical problem (Jewson 1976).

The doctors, like most people during this period, assumed that the body was like the physical world itself—it contained ill winds, cold and hot cauldrons of fluid, wet and dry influences, and periods of harmony and balance such as that enjoyed by the stars against a night sky. The patient was the key to the state of this 'weather' system within the body because only the patient could report on these internal and changing states. The doctor's role was to gently help piece this story together from their patient's experience.

The doctor's task was then to put the many feelings and thoughts about the body that the patient held about their current experience into a coherent story with which the patient could identify. When this task was complete, a 'diagnosis' was achieved and a treatment designed. In this way, the patient's experience was at the very centre of the production of medical knowledge. At this time then, it was the patient who was the most powerful and controlling person during illnesses including the final one—dying. Jewson (1976) called this the period of 'bedside medicine'.

As the public hospital system opened up across Europe in the eighteenth century, and as these filled with the poor, doctors were able to engage in unprecedented experiment (Waddington 1973). Advances in surgery and the increased access to and study of autopsy gave eighteenth-century doctors a new understanding of basic anatomy and physiology. Slowly a clinical system of signs and symptoms emerged which permitted doctors to formulate a diagnosis with minimal assistance from the patient. The advent of this 'hospital medicine' meant that the patient's experience declined in importance. The body of the patient, conscious or otherwise, could now be 'read' by physical examination, and treatment instigated.

Later still, in the late nineteenth and early twentieth centuries, laboratory medicine enabled samples of a patient's body to reveal more through examination of blood, urine or tissues. During this period—a period which enjoyed its greatest influence up to the 1960s—the role of the good patient had turned full circle from its Middle Age counterpart. The age of interventionist medicine was at its height during this time.

No longer a participant, the 'good patient' was the compliant one, a passive person who took their doctor's advice. When there was nothing more to do, from a doctor's point of view, there was nothing more for anyone to do. In the case of dying people, this usually translated in professional terms to 'failure', and in social terms, to rejection and segregation of the dying. In those days, health was an inheritance, and if you lost it, the doctor's pills and surgery were your main chances of having it restored. If the doctor could not help you, there was little you could do either but perhaps wait for the end, whenever that end came.

Around the 1960s, as I observed earlier, there was substantial dissatisfaction with the idea of the passive dying person but this was part of a general, more widely felt dissatisfaction with the passive patient approach to health care. New studies from Public Health and Community Medicine began to show that substantial health gains could be achieved by thinking, not in terms of heroic interventions, but rather prevention.

The limitations of surgical and pharmacological interventions were being debated and slowly recognised. If lung cancer could not be cured perhaps we could avoid the things which seemed to cause it, for example tobacco. If the replacement of damaged hearts was so costly and the domain of a privileged few, perhaps we could take steps to prevent the necessity for their replacement in the first place. If high fat diets, too much salt, or a sedentary lifestyle were shown to be key factors in causing heart disease perhaps we could avoid them. The key to the success of implementing this insight was the ability to get people to actively cooperate. This collective desire on the part of the medical profession and governments interested in containing health costs was the birth of the New Public Health movement.

Both professional advice and government monies began to pour into prevention messages—*you* can do something for your health, live better, live longer, experience greater quality of life. Health promotion became a central weapon in the war against morbidity and mortality. Occupational health and safety became issues in workplaces and courts all over the country. People began to jog, cycle, and 'work out' at the local gym. Others not only avoided 'fat' or 'salt', they became vegetarian. Stress became an enemy, with some people attending relaxation classes and others joining meditation, Tai Chi, or yoga groups.

Not long after Jewson wrote his famous article documenting the ascent of hospital and laboratory medicine, Crawford (1980) was documenting the 1970s obsession with health. Not only were people actively encouraged to believe that they could exercise control over their health through dietary and other lifestyle changes under their direct control, those who declined to be similarly engaged were the subject of moral disapproval.

A new moral imperative emerged that saw, among other attitudes, fat people defined as 'over' weight and smokers as anti-social. Asking for your fish to be beer-battered attracted stares of disbelief from one's dining companions. Crawford coined the term 'healthism' for this attitude and these experiences. These changes to the way health was understood and experienced by many people heralded the entry of an interesting and important political value for all stakeholders in the health system and it was this: although *control over the production of medical knowledge* remained with the professionals, from now on *control over outcomes* was to be increasingly viewed as the patient's responsibility.

This recent shift to link professional expertise to a new collaborative promotion of patient autonomy and control arose from the adoption of insights from health education, behavioural sciences and adult learning theories of the 1970s and 80s (O'Connor & Parker 1995). Around the mid-1980s this 'individual responsibility' model began to be overtaken by a revisionism moving into the next and latest phase of the New Public Health.

Critics were arguing that the individual responsibility approach did not go far enough and carried with it the disadvantage of 'blaming' the victim for their disease. The individual was not the only influence responsible for health and illness and to expect the individual to carry sole responsibility for outcomes was to deny these other influences. The health system at large—governments and their policies on roads, health, housing, employment or workplace safety—all these and more played a role in health maintenance and promotion.

The *Ottawa Charter* from the World Health Organization (1986) embodied this recent view. Health promotion was about developing personal skills; enabling, mediating and advocacy; strengthening community action and creating supportive environments; and finally, re-orienting health services to help enhance these other 'empowering' social forces for the individual. From now on, *not only should individuals expect control over their health outcomes they should also expect help from those who are able to provide the relevant assistance*. We are now ready to re-examine the events in the Northern Territory.

SOME SOCIOLOGICAL OBSERVATIONS

The famous sociologist, C. Wright Mills (1959), argued that one of the central tasks of sociology was to describe what kinds of men and women are ascendant in a society. In this way he urged us to understand that social types of people are a product of the prevailing ideas of the times. Just as the active sick and dying person of the Middle Ages gave way to the ascendancy of a more passive type, so too the passive dying person is gradually being replaced by, or assuming position alongside of, a new kind of active and controlling dying person.

In this way, Janet Mills was not some highly eccentric person with idiosyncratic ideas about death, dying and medical practice. Janet Mills was a rather public example of a growing number of people who endorse and support the view that she should be able to control the outcomes of what some people call 'the final illness'. Janet Mills represented a new type of dying person, and a fine individual example of attitudes and actions which, in principle, are perfectly aligned with the values of the New Public Health. Why, then, all the controversy?

First, the current connection between health and dying is poorly recognised by many observers. This is because we are emerging from an immediately preceding period where these ideas have been seen as opposites. Even the New Public Health is a philosophy frequently identified and confined to issues of illness prevention and health maintenance. In this rather ironic way, the current public health discourse reflects old assumptions about death and dying—that those experiences exist somehow outside of discussions about 'health matters'. This sometimes means that many health workers do not view the euthanasia controversy in public health terms yet.

Often these public health workers are delighted that so many of the population take the public health messages so seriously. But some of these same professionals are dismayed when they see some of these people take those messages and principles so much to heart that they attempt to use them even on their deathbeds. The new expectation of collaboration—at the deathbed—is a source of ambivalence and confusion, even surprise for them.

Secondly, for most people in the secular world, dying is no longer a religious issue. Without religious frameworks in which to interpret the meaning of final pain, loss, and questions about one's future, or apparent lack of it, other frameworks will be employed to do that private, psychological work. To view dying as primarily the 'final illness' is to acknowledge that the dominant framework now, for many people, is a health care one.

The New Public Health ideas indicate that one can expect to take a certain amount of responsibility for one's health outcomes and, since death is the one certain outcome, the only real question for a dying person is *how* is one to die? For dying people, the answer to that question is firmly linked to issues about their remaining time and the quality of that time. Both of these issues are tied to one's relationship with the prevailing health services, in particular, doctors. The question of the meaning of 'quality of life' is the subject of much dispute. Is it intervention for care or does it also involve help with ending life?

In this way, do people who are dying expect, as Kastenbaum asserts, more than they would expect during a normal course of life? Do they, moreover, train their sights on a positively, pleasurable death?

The answer to the first question must be emphatically in the negative because, as we have seen, people commonly expect what they are reasonably led to expect. At the moment, the health promotion messages to which people are daily subjected point to health values which are now considered to be realistic and reasonable—self-determining and self-maintaining, but at the same time collaborative and participatory.

When seriously ill, the current health promotion messages talk of 'policies which support health' and 'strengthening community action'. Ill people can expect traditional interventions and treatments but they can also expect assistance in maintaining control over the outcomes they have fought so hard to achieve during a life of health maintenance. In the present era of public health they do not expect 'more', they expect what they are currently led to expect in today's health promotion messages. And they are led to believe that these are not unreasonable.

Does the publicity surrounding near-death experience lead people to see dying as attractive? This is doubtful. Preceding most near-death experiences are rather detailed descriptions of personal suffering. Indeed, all the bestselling biographical works in this genre emphasise the fact that the near-death experience comes at the end of a period of deep or prolonged physical and psychological crisis (Kellehear 1996). The near-death experience might change some people's view of death, but it will seldom alter their view of dying.

There are two further observations to make about the recent social changes at the centre of current concerns over euthanasia. We should first remember that these changes, and the conflict which arises from them, are not completed changes but rather features of a *period in transition*. Some health workers and their patients are keen to bring the principles of the New Public Health to bear on the experience of dying and to help themselves control that element of outcome important to them both—the how and when of dying.

Other people resist the connection between contemporary ideas of public health and how these apply in the context of dying, preferring instead to see the issues in the old terms of medical control and resistance to death and patient acceptance. Death chooses its own timing, and not the patient or doctor (Kelner & Bourgeault 1993; McNamara, Waddell & Colvin 1994).

Just as critically, we should also recall that not everyone has embraced even the older wave of 'healthism' emergent in the 1980s. The professional and white collar groups in society seemed to have embraced these new health ideologies much more than the unskilled and semi-skilled working classes. Being proactive in health matters, holding a critical questioning and discursive relationship with one's doctor, has been largely the province of those whose occupational status and means have approached those of the medical practitioner. More traditional, passive roles persist in other sections of the community.

The second characteristic of this period of transition concerns the relationship between religion and health. The issues underlying the euthanasia controversy are also not clearly and cleanly in the province of health care—for health workers or for those dying. Notwithstanding my earlier remarks about health issues becoming the dominant way of interpreting the problems of dying, many people remain ambivalent and in transition over matters to do with religion. This is regularly illustrated around *all* matters to do with the deliberate taking of human life—abortion, the death penalty for criminals, euthanasia or suicide. How does one balance a religious or humanist concern for the protection and sanctity of life with an emerging health system that advocates *individual responsibility* and teams that idea with the equally fertile one of *advocacy and assistance from the health services?* Are we to say: Health promotion for the healthy only? Are we to continue to say to dying people that the principles that govern our understanding of health and illness do not apply to you—one rule for you, and a different one for the rest of us?

These questions have answers that differ as widely as the different groups who clamour to answer them. The one sociological observation to remember when hearing those answers is that the current wave of interest in physician assisted suicide is largely a function of a worldwide health promotion movement. In the cost-cutting environment of the late twentieth–early twenty-first centuries, the health promotion ideas of the New Public Health will influence the act of dying in substantially greater ways in the future.

Those who would attribute the current push towards assisted suicide to some small but vocal sectional interest in society clearly fail to see the giant which stands behind it—the New Public Health. Any debate about the morality of assisted suicide, then, cannot and should not be separated from a wider debate about the moral and social worth of the New Public Health. We are now finally in a position to see that the real surprise that Janet Mills left literally in her wake was how much her 'good death' resembled our increasingly popular notions of 'good health'.

CONCLUSION

Health Promotion ideas within the New Public Health, of course, are not the only social influences responsible for our current interest in euthanasia, although these ideas are central to explaining a particular type of euthanasia—the physician assisted form. (For an introduction to other types of euthanasia see Mason and McCall Smith (1994, p. 315). More broadly, as Howarth and Jeffreys (1996) argue, the ageing and gentrification of Western populations and the decline of religious authority have also played important roles in promoting wider interest in this subject.

Further to those observations we should also add the rise of the legal-individual rights discourse in health care and the changing relationship between doctor and patient. There has been a shift— readily illustrated in the changing language of the area from 'professional service' to that of 'providers' and 'consumers'. This has correspondingly changed the content and style of mutual expectations and exchanges in this relationship.

Nevertheless, emphasising the role of modern health promoting ideas, such as those now associated with public health, underlines two important lessons for anyone with an eye for social change. First, although much of the current debate about euthanasia draws its vocabulary from old institutional sources such as religion or law, it is health, and especially our current ideas about health, which provide the very source and substance for our expectations. Health now drives our understanding of dying.

Finally, the parallel history of health and dying tells us that above all these are political histories and not merely social ones. If the sixteenth century depicted the dying person as the powerful and controlling figure around the deathbed, and the twentieth century saw this power transfer to the doctor, the twenty-first century seems to be moving towards a *participatory* model. The current conflicts over roles and responsibilities surrounding death and dying reflect the shifting movements of power elsewhere in the health care system. In this way, the debates about how we die will reflect, once again, our ongoing debates about how we wish to live.

REFERENCES

Aries, P. 1974 *Western Attitudes Toward Death* Johns Hopkins University Press, London
——1981 *The Hour of Our Death* Allen Lane, London
Brim, O.G. (ed.) 1975 *The Dying Patient* Russell Sage, New York
Cannadine, D. 1981 'War and death, grief and mourning in modern Britain' in *Mirrors of Mortality: Studies in the Social History of Death* ed. J. Whaley, Europa, London, pp. 187–242
Crawford, R. 1980 'Healthism and the medicalisation of everyday life' *International Journal of Health Services* vol. 10, no. 3, pp. 365–89
Feifel, H. (ed.) 1977 *New Meanings of Death* McGraw-Hill, New York
Garfield, C.A. (ed.) 1978 *Psychosocial Care of the Dying* McGraw-Hill, New York
Gorer, G. 1976 'The pornography of death' in *Death: Current Perspectives* ed. E.S. Schneidman, Mayfield, Palo Alto, CA, pp. 71–96
Howarth, G. & Jeffreys, M. 1996 'Euthanasia: Sociological perspectives' *British Medical Journal* vol. 52, no. 2, pp. 376–85

Jewson, N.D. 1976 'The disappearance of the sick man from medical cosmology 1770–1870' *Sociology* vol. 10, no. 2, pp. 225–44

Kastenbaum, R. 1979 '"Healthy dying": A paradoxical quest continues' *Journal of Social Issues* vol. 35, no. 1, pp. 185–206

Kearl, M.C. 1989 *Endings: A Sociology of Death and Dying* Oxford University Press, New York

Kellehear, A. 1996 *Experiences Near Death: Beyond Medicine and Religion* Oxford University Press, New York

Kelner, M.J. & Bourgeault, I.L. 1993 'Patient control over dying: Responses of health care professionals' *Social Science and Medicine* vol. 36, p. 757

Kubler-Ross, E. 1969 *On Death and Dying* Macmillan, New York

Mason, J.K. & McCall Smith, R.A. 1994 *Law and Medical Ethics* 4th edn Butterworths, London

McNamara, B., Waddell, C. & Colvin, M. 1994 'The institutionalisation of the good death' *Social Science and Medicine* vol. 39, pp. 1501–08

Mills, C.W. 1959 *The Sociological Imagination* Oxford University Press, New York

O'Connor, M.L. & Parker, E. 1995 *Health Promotion: Principles and Practice in the Australian Context* Allen & Unwin, Sydney

Saunders, C. & Baines, M. 1983 *Living with Dying: The Management of Terminal Disease* Oxford University Press, Oxford

Waddington, I. 1973 'The role of the hospital in the development of modern medicine' *Sociology* vol. 7, no. 2, pp. 211–24

World Health Organization 1986 *Ottawa Charter for Health Promotion* WHO, Ottawa

PART 4

Prevention matters

Prevention is a key area of concern in late twentieth-century health policy. Although the bulk of health spending continues to go towards hospital-based curative medicine, increasingly it is argued that 'prevention is better than cure' and is ultimately a more cost-effective approach. The question of what 'prevention' entails—what is to be prevented, who is to be the focus of preventive intervention, which preventive measures are to be adopted, and so on—is no straightforward matter. Policies reflect broader values and social priorities, such as respect for individual freedoms versus concerns for collective welfare, recognition of minority rights, and regard for equal opportunities. Our conceptions of these problems and how they should be dealt with are shaped by our images of society and the individual. For example, the idea that people need to be protected by society strongly evokes images of the 'nanny state'. If we believe that there is no such thing as 'society' (as former British Prime Minister, Margaret Thatcher, proclaimed), or that people are essentially 'selfish', 'greedy' and 'competitive', or that parts of society have some natural tendency to operate for 'the health of the whole', this will be reflected in our health and social policies. To simply accept the tenet that prevention is necessarily 'a good thing', without exploring the impact of these images, values and priorities on policies and practices, is to overlook some important influences on social action.

With the emergence of a new, postmodern or poststructural sensibility in sociology and other social sciences, scholars have begun to cast a critical gaze over the categories and concepts underlying and informing health promotion and public health. More and more it is recognised that just because something is deemed by the experts to be good for 'our health' it does not necessarily mean that it ultimately serves our individual or collective well-being. We are beginning to see the emergence of a new, critical sociology of health promotion and public health that interrogates the knowledges, values, and practices of the experts (Bunton, et al. 1995; Lupton 1995; Petersen & Lupton 1996). Sociologists are drawing on perspectives developed in the mainstream of their discipline, as well as from outside their discipline (e.g. feminism, philosophy, queer theory, and geography), to explore the normative biases and implications of public health policies and practices; for example, the implicit masculine and heterosexist biases of AIDS policy, explored by Cathy Waldby (Chapter 21). Developments such as those described earlier by Robin Bunton (Chapter 2)—changes in the welfare state, a transformation in the way we have come to understand 'the social', the questioning of the effectiveness of nation states, criticisms of singular definitions of need, and so on—call for an imaginative engagement with theory. Sociologists are taking up the challenge posed by this changing context, questioning rather than simply accepting the basic tenets of public health and its health promotion philosophies. The following chapters deal with a number of these questions.

In Chapter 19, Sarah Nettleton and Roger Burrows offer a novel perspective on the link between home ownership and health in the UK, drawing on Anthony Gidden's (1984) notion of ontological security. Recent work has underlined the importance of psychosocial factors in explaining health inequalities. While social class and material deprivation have an undoubted influence on the health status of individuals and groups, increasingly it is recognised that 'social cohesion' is a critical factor. Thus, policies which emphasise individualism, such as private provision of housing, are likely to be detrimental to the health and well-being of all individuals in a society. As Nettleton and Burrows indicate, in Britain owner occupation has become the norm as a result of housing policy over the last two decades. Whereas in the past, owner occupation was the prerogative of the well-paid and securely employed middle classes, a growing number of home owners are on low incomes and in less secure employment. Home ownership is widely seen as offering 'an island of security', providing people with a 'sense of belonging' in a society where a feeling of impermanence is common (Ignatieff, 1996). However, socioeconomic changes, including recession in the housing market and the restructuring of work, has made home buyers vulnerable to losing their homes. Nettleton and Burrows discuss the personal and public consequences and costs of unsustainable home ownership, particularly the generation of 'ontological insecurity', involving heightened individual consciousness of risks and uncertainties. They conclude that a policy which emphasises the expansion of owner occupation is likely to contribute to a 'cash and keys' society where people prioritise their own material well-being and security over the well-being of the 'community' as a whole.

In Chapter 20, Sherry Saggers and Dennis Gray examine two strategies employed by indigenous Australians to deal with harmful consumption of alcohol and associated risks: 'treatment' and legislative controls. They focus on the issue of how societies balance the 'rights' of the individual and the collectivity, as well as on the mechanisms through which non-indigenous people dominate indigenous people, and how the latter resist. The chapter questions the applicability of Western notions of 'rights' to the issue of indigenous alcohol misuse, emphasising as they do the good of the individual over the collectivity. According to the dominant liberal ideology of Anglo-Western societies, problems of alcohol misuse are attributed to the weakness or susceptibility of individuals, and the control of problems is seen as best solved through education, rather than state intervention. The applicability of liberal notions of individuality to indigenous communities, however, is complicated by the fact that some communities give precedence to the collectivity over the individual while others articulate a strong sense of individual autonomy. It is in light of these issues that Saggers and Gray describe and evaluate how 'treatment' and legislative approaches are applied in indigenous contexts. In their view, theories of both structure and action are needed to adequately understand the problems of, and potential solutions to, problems of alcohol abuse. Social scientists can offer an important contribution to resolving problems, they argue, by critiquing and evaluating models used to explain alcohol misuse and intervention programs and by challenging the notion that problems are a consequence of personal choice.

In Chapter 21, Catherine Waldby exposes some assumptions in AIDS discourse, which result in the exemption of the heterosexual male body from 'safe sex' education campaigns. More specifically, she focuses on the epidemiology of AIDS and its gender and sexual biases. Epidemiology plays a key role in public health campaigns in relation to AIDS, in identifying those categories 'at risk' of infection and those in need of surveillance and control. It operates as a means of delineating boundaries between the 'general population' and the 'risk group/s' and hence serves as a means of defining the norm. Waldby critically scrutinises the category, the 'general population', finding that, once all 'risk groups' have been excluded, all that is left is heterosexual men. While gay men are relatively easily excluded from the 'general population', 'as the exemplary "risk group"', it is not easy to disqualify women who constitute half the population. Women, Waldby argues, occupy an uneasy position within the 'general population'—a group that is simultaneously included and excluded. That is, while they may be included as married or at least monogamous or as virgins—as enforcers of 'safe sex' practices—they are vulnerable to exclusion as sex workers or simply heterosexually active, as pregnant, and as the partners of bisexual or IV-drug-using men. Waldby explores the logic of this displacement as it manifests in epidemiological discourse and, more broadly, within the body politic and acts in the protection of heterosexual male bodies. She then explores how epidemiology maps the topography of sexual infection, with particular reference to gay men and straight women, both of whom are conceptualised as fluid entities and as conduits of infection.

Finally, in Chapter 22, David Buchbinder also critically examines social constructions of gender and sexuality in his analysis of what constitutes 'a well-shaped man'. The study of men's health and illness has received much attention of late (see, e.g. Sabo & Gordon 1995); but few have been prompted to critically scrutinise the theories underpinning conceptions of the healthy, 'well-shaped' man. According to Buchbinder, essentialist models of gender and of health, which see the body and its well-being as determined by biology, has come to dominate contemporary understandings of men and masculinity. Essentialist theories neglect social relationships and dynamics, and the social and historical constructions of gender. Medical discourse is a paradigmatic example of essentialism in that it assumes that gender behaviour is encoded in the body of the appropriate sex, and leads inevitably to the view that if there is a conflict between sex and gender, then this is due to some fault in the individual. However, following Judith Butler, Buchbinder argues that gender is performative, implying that it is inherently fragile and that its enactment needs to be continually repeated. Men are always performing for other men in order to gain their approval and acceptance, with the ever-present threat of exclusion or of undergoing humiliation or physical abuse of some kind. Buchbinder is concerned with the ways in which the gender system operates so as to enable masculinity to maintain its dominance, leading to, among other things, health-threatening behaviours. The dominant masculinity is sustained through the exclusion of two other categories, the feminine and the male homosexual, he argues. However, a new queer theory offers a radical challenge to gendered structures and gender identifications, and offers strategies by which to alleviate the social pressures on men to perform a particular version of masculinity.

REFERENCES

Bunton, R., Nettleton, S. & Burrows, R. (eds) 1995 *The Sociology of Health Promotion: Critical Analyses of Consumption, Lifestyle and Risk* Routledge, London

Giddens, A. 1984 *The Constitution of Society* Polity, Cambridge

Ignatieff, M. 1996 'There's no place like home: The politics of belonging' in *The Age of Anxiety* eds S. Dunant & R. Porter, Virago, London

Lupton, D. 1995 *The Imperative of Health: Public Health and the Regulated Body* Sage, London

Petersen, A. & Lupton, D. 1996 *The New Public Health: Health and Self in the Age of Risk* Allen & Unwin, Sydney & Sage, London

Sabo, D. & Gordon, F. (eds) 1995 *Men's Health and Illness: Gender, Power and the Body* Sage, Thousand Oaks, CA

19 Home ownership and health in the United Kingdom

Sarah Nettleton & Roger Burrows

In his book *Unhealthy Societies: The Afflictions of Inequality* Richard Wilkinson (1996) explores a puzzle which emerged from his earlier work which found that wealthy nations are not necessarily always the most healthy nations. He concludes that it is inequalities in income and wealth that are the most important factors in determining health status. Those countries categorised as the most egalitarian (such as Japan, Norway and Italy) are those with the highest life expectancies, while those countries which have wider gaps between the rich and the poor (such as the US, Germany and the UK) have lower life expectancies. Drawing on the empirical research findings of anthropologists, physiologists and sociologists, Wilkinson argues that social cohesion is the critical variable in explaining these differences. That is, while social class membership and the experience of material deprivation undoubtedly impact upon the health status of individuals and groups, such effects are exacerbated in those environments which also have a damaged social fabric. According to Wilkinson, it is the *psychosocial mechanisms* that are associated with social cohesion which determine the nature of health inequalities. Societies which are socially cohesive are defined thus:

> They have a strong community life. Instead of social life stopping outside the front door, public space remains a social space. The individualism and the values of the market are restrained by a social morality. People are more likely to be involved in social and voluntary activities outside the home. The societies have more of what has been called 'social capital' which lubricates the workings of the whole society and economy. There are fewer signs of anti-social aggressiveness, and society appears more caring. In short, the social fabric is in better condition. (Wilkinson 1996, p. 4)

If this theory is correct it has significant implications for social and public policies which foreground individualism at the expense of social cohesion (Nettleton & Burrows 1998): social and public policies which tend to privilege individuals over social groups; market transactions over other forms of social exchange; and financial well-being over emotional security. Social policies which encourage members of society to 'watch out for themselves' may be detrimental to the health and well-being of all individuals in that society. This chapter attempts to briefly explore this thesis by examining one area of social policy in the UK—that of housing policy—which has most strongly come to represent the 'individualisation' of contemporary social policy.

THE GROWTH OF HOME OWNERSHIP IN THE UNITED KINGDOM

The key thrust of the British housing policy over the last two decades has been the expansion of owner occupation matched with a concomitant reduction in the provision of social housing and the deregulation of the private rented sector (PRS). Owner occupation refers to people buying their own home, usually by borrowing a sum of money which forms a large proportion of the value of the property being purchased, from a lender such as a bank or a building society, and paying it back over a long-term period of twenty-five years or so.

Some specific policies accelerated the long-term growth of the proportion of households living in owner occupation. Prime among these was the 1980 *Housing Act* which introduced the highly popular 'Right to Buy' (RTB) scheme which permitted people to buy homes which they had previously been renting from a local authority (known in the UK as 'council houses') at discounted rates. Between 1981 and 1995 some 1.57 million homes were bought under this scheme (Wilcox 1996, p. 106). Other policy changes which had an impact included the deregulation of the credit market. This resulted in new players coming onto the lending scene, expanding the market and offering mortgages to social groups who had hitherto been regarded as 'risky' customers.

While in the early post-war years only a minority of households were homeowners, this tenure has now come to dominate and now comprises some 68 per cent of all households in the UK. Since 1979, when the first Thatcher government came into office, 3.8 million more households are buying or own their homes—an increase of some 38 per cent (Department of the Environment 1995, p. 6). An important feature of this increase in owner occupation has been the significant increase in the number of homeowners on lower incomes and in more insecure employment (Ford & Wilcox 1998). Owner occupation is not now limited to members of the well-paid and securely employed middle classes.

In terms of policy implementation the rise of owner occupation provides a clear example of a policy being successfully translated into action. The government's aim was to increase home ownership and it succeeded. No doubt this was facilitated by the fact that it was what many people wanted (Kempson & Ford 1995). The sociological implications of this push and pull towards owner occupation throughout the 1980s was widely debated (Saunders 1990) as people rushed to buy properties. Not surprisingly house prices spiralled and there was a significant degree of confidence in the housing market (Doling & Ford 1996) leading some commentators to conclude that not only was home ownership a deep and natural desire, it was also a very sound financial investment—there was nothing more secure than 'bricks and mortar' (Saunders 1990).

THE COLLAPSE OF HOME OWNERSHIP?

As the 1980s ended, four processes combined to produce a dramatic increase in the unsustainability of home ownership. First, as a result of the financial deregulation noted above, a highly competitive market and rising property prices, high-loan-to-value mortgages became widely available. Secondly, mortgage rates rapidly increased from 9.5 per cent in 1988 to peak at 15.4 per cent in February 1990 before slowly decreasing throughout the 1990s. Thirdly, a deep economic recession led to job losses, under-employment and small business failure among substantial numbers of mortgagors. Fourthly, the housing market itself entered a deep and persistent recession. Consequently, many highly geared borrowers first faced rising mortgage costs and then often lost income. However, many were denied the possibility of selling their way out of problems due to the housing recession (Forrest & Murie 1994). Consequently the number of households with mortgage arrears increased as did the number of households who actually lost their homes through mortgage repossession (Ford et al. 1995). As Forrest and Murie (1994) point out, if the discourse of home ownership in the 1980s was littered with terms such as 'trading up', 'equity gain' and 'gentrification', the discourse of the 1990s has been dominated by terms such as 'negative equity', 'arrears', 'possessions' and 'debt overhang'. For many people the dream of owning their home went very sour indeed.

Although the situation has now stabilised, levels of mortgage arrears and mortgage possessions are still running at rates significantly higher than they were prior to the collapse of the housing market and are likely to remain at such levels for the foreseeable future. This is because unsustainable or problematic home ownership is but one element of a set of circumstances associated with what some commentators refer to as the 'new insecurity' of social and economic life (Hutton 1995). Unless social and public policy is dramatically altered, the historically high levels of mortgage indebtedness and possession (the forced or voluntary giving up of the home by the borrower to the lender (Ford 1993)) currently being witnessed, will remain enduring features of *social life* in the UK. This is due to a set of fundamental structural changes which are currently transforming economic life. These changes are numerous, but five factors in particular are interacting in order to produce increasing levels of insecurity among home-owners.

First, the restructuring or 'flexibilisation' of work is resulting in continuous and secure employment contracts being displaced by more insecure and short-term employment contracts and/or increasing rates of self-employment. Mortgages are premised on the assumption of stable employment over a long period of time. There is an increasingly clear disjuncture emerging between the supposed need for flexible labour markets and the ability of people to sustain mortgage costs over long periods (Burrows 1998; Ford & Wilcox 1998). Secondly, in a low inflation economy, the long-term (usually twenty-five years) nature of the credit contract that constitutes a mortgage means that the entry ratio of mortgage costs to earnings is prolonged, making a mortgage the largest component of household consumption for much longer than under conditions of high(er) inflation. Households are thus more vulnerable for a much longer period of time than hitherto. Thirdly, in a volatile global economy the costs of credit will continue to be highly variable and unpredictable—financial risks are thus increased. Fourthly, entry into home ownership has increasingly necessitated the formation of dual-earner families. As families break up due to the pressures of contemporary life this necessarily translates into increased rates of unsustainable home ownership. Fifthly, at the same time as these risks which are associated with home ownership have been increasing, the welfare state has been retreating from its 'safety net' provision for mortgagors (Oldman & Kemp 1996; Williams 1995) in order to encourage the take up of private insurance schemes, few of which have so far proved to be adequate (Ford & Kempson 1997).

In short, policies designed to increase owner occupation have been vigorously pursued within the context of a changing environment. The nature of the housing and lending markets has changed, the nature of work has changed, the nature of welfare has changed and the economic climate has changed. This means that home buyers have become more vulnerable. One tangible consequence of this is the growing popularity of mortgage protection plans. What appears to be happening is that money lenders are securing their loans less by the value of the property and more on the borrower's ability to pay. The risks fall squarely on the shoulders of individuals—risk has become increasingly privatised.

THE 'EPIDEMIOLOGY' OF PROBLEMATIC HOME OWNERSHIP

Problematic or unsustainable home ownership does not occur randomly to families, it is strongly socially patterned (Burrows 1998). Households with certain social characteristics are significantly more likely to experience home ownership which becomes unsustainable than are others. Table 1 shows some illustrative data derived from the Office of National Statistics and Data Archive's annual nationally representative *Survey of English Housing* which shows the proportion of mortgagor households in arrears and/or finding mortgage payments difficult during 1993/4.

Some clear patterns of relative disadvantage emerge from this data, few of which are surprising. First, households headed by younger people are at greatest risk. Secondly, households with dependent children, especially lone parents, are at greater risk than are couples with no children. Thirdly, single males are at greater risk than are single females. Fourthly, the divorced and separated are at greater risk than those who are not. Fifthly, the currently economically inactive are at greater risk than are the employed. Sixthly, there is a clear social class gradient, with those in the lower social classes being at greatest risk. Seventhly, among employees those in the private sector are at greater risk than are those in the public sector. However, the self-employed (especially sole traders) are at greater risk than employees. Finally, households headed by individuals who identify themselves as being from 'minority ethnic groups' are at greater risk than are households headed by individuals who identify themselves as 'white British'. Thus, although homeowners tend, on average, to be more

Table 1.   Proportions of mortgagor households in arrears and finding payments difficult by selected socioeconomic characteristics

Characteristics of household	% 3 or more months in arrears	% in arrears or finding payments difficult	N
Age of head of household			
16–29	3.4	19.4	1146
30–44	3.2	21.3	3890
45–54	2.4	19.0	2164
55–64	1.5	17.9	964
65–74	1.7	17.0	241
75+	1.8	10.9	57
Household structure			
Couples, no dependent children	1.8	14.3	3461
Couples, with dependent children	3.1	22.7	3250
Lone parents	6.4	37.6	295
Large adult household	4.5	29.0	401
Single male	4.8	22.4	564
Single female	1.6	19.3	491
Marital status of the head of household			
Not divorced or separated	2.5	18.6	7710
Divorced or separated	5.7	33.3	752
Economic status of head of household			
Employed full-time	1.8	16.2	6943
Employed part-time	4.9	34.7	344
Unemployed	15.1	56.2	397
Retired	1.9	13.9	377
Unable to work	6.0	40.3	400
Social class of head of household			
I Professional	0.8	10.1	888
II Intermediate	2.2	16.1	2857
IIIN Skilled non-manual	2.2	21.1	1038
IIIM Skilled manual	3.8	24.3	2442
IV Semi-skilled manual	4.1	24.3	827
V Unskilled manual	4.3	28.0	186
Self-employed or employee status			
Employee	2.4	17.2	67032
(Private sector)	(2.7)	(18.2)	(5031)
(Public sector)	(1.4)	(14.5)	(1669)
Self-employed	4.4	29.5	1598
(Small business owner)	(2.9)	(22.9)	(510)
(Sole trader)	(5.1)	(32.5)	(1088)
Ethnicity of head of household			
White	2.6	18.5	7978
Minority ethnic	5.8	41.9	484

Source: SEH 1993/94, author's analysis

advantaged than are households living in either the social housing or private rented sectors, within the tenure there are clear patterns of relative disadvantage.

THE PERSONAL AND PUBLIC CONSEQUENCES AND COSTS OF UNSUSTAINABLE HOME OWNERSHIP

We can see from the data discussed above that unsustainable home ownership is now, like divorce or unemployment, not just a 'personal trouble' but it is also a 'public issue' (to use C. Wright Mills' (1959) famous distinction). Currently some 820 homes a week are being repossessed in England, adding incrementally to the 388 000 households (containing over one million individuals) who have already lost their homes between 1990 and 1996. It is therefore a structural problem which has consequences not just for the individuals who experience it but also, we argue here, for everyone else in society.

Personal troubles

The evidence suggests that at the level of each household the main reasons for mortgage indebtedness (and then sometimes repossession) are a complex combination of factors such as job loss; reductions in household income; illness; relationship breakdown; small business failure; and the taking on of additional caring responsibilities (Ford et al. 1995). The experience of problematic home ownership will therefore be related to other biographical changes. Perhaps, like illness, it may be best conceptualised as a 'biographical disruption' (Bury 1982) which can have profound consequences for a person's self-identity and will involve the development of a series of complex coping strategies.

Hitherto, the literature on housing and health has tended to focus on the impact of the physical aspects of housing on health. The impact of the affordability of housing on health has been relatively unexplored and this is particularly so in relation to home ownership. However, a secondary data analysis of the *British Household Panel Survey* (BHPS) by the authors reveals that there are significant consequences for both mental health and the use of primary health care services for those who experience problematic home ownership. All mortgagors and their partners (if any) in the sample from the fourth wave of the BHPS carried out in 1994/95 were included in the analysis. Subjective well-being was measured using the standard General Health Questions

12 (GHQ12) measure of psychiatric morbidity (a commonly used series of twelve questions designed to produce a reliable scale able to measure variations in subjective mental health). Those mortgagors in arrears were significantly ($p < 0.001$) more likely to score in the top 20 per cent (i.e. to possess poor subjective well-being) of the scale than those not in arrears. Further, within a multivariate analysis, this relationship holds (sig. at $p < 0.001$ for men and $p < 0.05$ for women) even after controlling for employment status, income levels, age, measures of physical health, household structure and the presence or otherwise of dependent children in the household. This impact of arrears on mental health also translates into an increased use of primary health care services. Even after controlling for all of the other factors noted above, women in households with mortgage arrears were almost three times more likely, and men over two times more likely, to be in the top third of users of general practitioners (GPs).

Public issues

As well as the direct stress placed on individuals and households the growth of mortgage arrears and repossessions in the UK also has a much wider social importance (Ford & Burrows 1997). The majority of homeowners do manage to keep up with their mortgage repayments and do not have their homes repossessed. However, the *spectacle* of repossessions, especially when considered alongside growing job insecurity, impacts upon *everyone's* sense of security and well-being. The rise in mortgage arrears and repossession has invoked a wider sense of unease among homeowners especially at a time of substantial economic and employment restructuring. It can be argued that when we become aware of the insecurity of others this influences how we begin to think about ourselves which, in turn, can alter the nature of social relationships and of our capacity to provide social support or 'care' for others (Nettleton & Burrows 1998). The impact of this new problematic home ownership is as great as it is because owner occupation has hitherto been strongly articulated as a source of private stability and security in an otherwise increasingly chaotic public sphere.

HOME OWNERSHIP AND ONTOLOGICAL INSECURITY

This view of home ownership has been most clearly expressed by Saunders (1990) in his *A Nation of Home Owners*. For him, in a world characterised by change and instability home ownership provides a major source of 'ontological security, for a home of one's own offers both a physical (hence a spatially rooted) and permanent (hence temporally rooted) location in the world' (1990, p. 293). He even goes so far as to argue that home ownership is something to which people universally, even innately desire! He derives this notion of ontological security from the work of Giddens (1984). Essentially it refers to emotional security which in turn is contingent upon one's biographical continuity and freedom from perceived and real external threats. These factors are necessary for the formation of a stable sense of self and identity.

Home ownership, Saunders argues, facilitates a greater sense of ontological security:

> the privately owned home seems to represent a secure anchor point where the nerves can be rested and the senses allowed to relax . . . When ordinary people own their own homes, they seem more confident and self reliant. (1990, p. 311)

And certainly the idea that owning one's home can confer a basis for social status and enhance social identity has been argued by a number of authors (see Morgan (1996) for a summary) and has also been explored empirically (Richards 1990). However, as we have already argued, within the context of economic restructuring, globalisation, newly emerging household patterns, and so on, it is looking increasingly unlikely that home ownership will ensure permanence and security. In fact it will, for many, be a source of ontological *insecurity*.

The decisions and social processes associated with buying a home constitute very concrete examples of what Giddens (1992) calls 'lifestyle choices' and 'life planning' (for further discussion see Nettleton & Burrows 1998). When buying a home, the purchaser is sensitised to a whole series of potential risks and so has to make many calculated decisions. There are uncertainties about future levels of inflation and interest rates; about trends in the housing market and labour market conditions; about the condition of the property and the future desirability of its location; and about future government policies on housing, social security and employment. The buyer is forced to consider potential risks as they are being offered policies for life insurance, contents insurance, mortgage protection, building insurance, and endowments. Having bought the property those uncertainties will not diminish. Households with mortgages will be sensitive to changes in interest rates, levels of inflation, and the stability or otherwise of the housing market. If the earning capacity of the mortgagee is threatened so too is the possibility of keeping up with payments and so keeping one's home.

A nation of homeowners, such as the UK, may therefore be a nation wherein individuals are self-consciously facing an ever-increasing array of risks and uncertainties. A housing policy that is designed to maximise owner occupation and minimise other forms of social housing and state regulation is problematic within a global context which precipitates significant socioeconomic restructuring and profoundly alters the nature of work. Sustainable home ownership, in its present form, requires financial stability and, for the most part, the maintenance of secure and long-term incomes. The majority of home-owners do, of course, have such security, although as we have seen, a growing minority of households are losing their homes. While the likelihood of mortgage indebtedness is socially patterned, the growing numbers of household possessions may make other homeowners more nervous and insecure about their futures (Memery et al. 1995).

CONCLUSION

A housing policy which has at its core the expansion of owner occupation wholeheartedly privileges the ideologies of individualisation and marketisation and may facilitate a corresponding shift in social values. The awareness of potential risks and hazards which may threaten individual households may mean that people are propelled to prioritise the needs of themselves and their families over the well-being of the 'community' as a whole. Such a policy contributes to what Wilkinson calls a 'cash and keys' society.

> Increasingly we live in what might be called a cash and keys society. When ever we leave the confines of our own homes we face the world with two perfect symbols of the nature of social relations on the street. Cash equips us to take part in transactions mediated by the market, while keys protect our private gains from each other's envy and greed . . . Instead of being people with whom we have bonds and share common interests, others become rivals, competitors for jobs, for houses, for space, seats on the bus, parking places. (Wilkinson 1996, p. 226)

Specific social policies, broader socioeconomic transformations and the health and well-being of individuals are therefore inextricably interlinked. This has important implications both for the formation and evaluation of social policies in that those responsible for developing and assessing them must be sensitive to their health consequences and their impact on health inequalities.

ACKNOWLEDGEMENTS

Material from the *Survey of English Housing* was made available through the Office of National Statistics and the Data Archive with the permission of the Controller of Her Majesty's Stationery Office. Data from the *British Household Panel Survey* used in this paper were also made available through the ESRC Data Archive. The data were originally collected by the ESRC Research Centre on Micro-social Change at the University of Essex. Neither the original collectors of the data nor the archive bear any responsibility for the analyses or interpretations presented here.

REFERENCES

Burrows, R. 1998 'Mortgage indebtedness in England: An "epidemiology"' *Housing Studies* vol. 13, no. 5, pp. 5–22
Bury, M. 1982 'Chronic illness as a biographical disruption' *Sociology of Health and Illness* vol. 4, no. 2, pp. 167–82
Department of the Environment 1995 *Our Future Homes: Opportunity, Choice, Responsibility* HMSO, London
Doling, J. & Ford, J. 1996 'The new home ownership' *Environment and Planning* no. 28, pp. 157–72
Ford, J. 1993 'Mortgage possession' *Housing Studies* no. 8, p. 4
Ford, J. & Burrows, R. 1997 *The Costs of Unsustainable Home Ownership* Centre for Housing Policy, University of York, York
Ford, J. & Kempson, E. 1997 *Bridging the Gap? Private Insurance for Mortgagors* Centre for Housing Policy, York
Ford, J., Kempson, E. & Wilson, M. 1995 *Mortgage Arrears and Possessions: Perspectives from Borrowers, Lenders and the Courts* HMSO, London
Ford, J. & Wilcox, S. 1998 'Owner occupation, welfare and work' *Housing Studies* no.13
Forrest, R. & Murie, A. 1994 'Home ownership in recession' *Housing Studies* vol. 9, no. 1, pp. 55–74
Giddens, A. 1984 *The Constitution of Society* Polity, Cambridge
——1992 *Modernity and Self-Identity* Polity, Cambridge
Hutton, W. 1995 *The State We're In* Jonathan Cape, London
Kempson, E. & Ford, J. 1995 *Attitudes, Beliefs and Confidence: Consumer Views of the Housing Market in the 1990s* Council of Mortgage Lenders, London
Memery, C., Munro, M., Madigan, R. & Gibb, K. 1995 'Reacting to the housing market slump' in *Economic Beliefs and Behaviour Programme* Discussion Paper 10, University of Glasgow
Mills, C. Wright 1959 *The Sociological Imagination* Oxford University Press, New York
Morgan, D. 1996 *Family Connections* Polity, Cambridge
Nettleton, S. & Burrows, R. 1998 'Individualization processes and social policy: Insecurity, reflexivity and risk in the restructuring of contemporary British health and housing policies' in *Postmodernity and the Fragmentation of Welfare* ed. J. Carter, Routledge, London
Oldman, C. & Kemp, P. 1996 *Income Support Mortgage Interest: An Assessment of Current Issues and Future Prospects* Council of Mortgage Lenders, London
Richards, L. 1990 *Nobody's Home: Dreams and Realities in a New Suburb* Oxford University Press, Melbourne

Saunders, P. 1990 *A Nation of Home Owners* Unwin Hyman, London

Wilcox, S. 1996 *Housing Review 1996/97* Joseph Rowntree Foundation, York

Williams, P. 1995 'A shrinking safety net for a changing market' in *Housing Finance Review 1995/96* ed. S. Wilcox, Joseph Rowntree Foundation, York

Wilkinson, R. 1996 *Unhealthy Societies: The Afflictions of Inequality* Routledge, London

20   Alcohol in indigenous Australian communities

Sherry Saggers & Dennis Gray

This chapter examines two of the strategies employed by indigenous Australian communities to deal with harmful consumption of alcohol and the risks it poses to them. Such an examination highlights the balance that all societies must strike between the 'rights' of individuals and the collectivity; some of the processes by which non-indigenous people dominate indigenous Australians; and the resistance of indigenous people to those processes.

Available evidence indicates that the pattern of drinking among indigenous peoples differs significantly from that found in non-indigenous populations. In Australia, for example, while a greater proportion of the indigenous population does not consume alcohol, among the proportion that does, more people do so at harmful levels (Hunter et al. 1992; Knowles & Woods 1993; Perkins et al. 1994; Watson et al. 1988).

The deleterious health and social consequences of excessive indigenous alcohol consumption—that is, consumption at levels which causes harm to both individual drinkers and those around them—are well documented. Indigenous people in Australia experience significantly higher rates of alcohol-related illness such as alcoholic cardiomyopathy, alcoholic gastritis, and alcoholic liver cirrhosis, as well as traumatic injuries, road accidents, suicide, and violent death (Gray, A. 1990; Johnson 1991; Swensen & Unwin 1994; Veroni et al. 1993). Excessive alcohol consumption also contributes to unemployment, family breakdown, child neglect and school absenteeism (Johnson 1991). In addition, there is widespread concern about the association between excessive alcohol consumption and violence in the home and other forms of intra- and inter-personal violence (d'Abbs et al. 1994).

Indigenous communities themselves recognise the harmful health and social consequences of excessive drinking. For many Aboriginal Australians alcohol is unambiguously implicated in 'too much sorry business' (Langton 1991). Aboriginal people strongly expressed their concerns about the impact of excessive alcohol use to the Royal Commission into Aboriginal Deaths in Custody (Johnson 1991), and three-quarters of those interviewed for the 1994 National Aboriginal and Torres Strait Islander Survey (Madden 1995) identified it as a health problem. However, such a view is not universally held. For other indigenous people alcohol consumption is pleasurable, a means of social exchange, and a means of protest against the wider society in which they are encapsulated (Collman 1979; Sackett 1988; Sansom 1980).

There has been a broad range of responses by both indigenous and non-indigenous people to the problem of excessive alcohol consumption. These responses have been implemented at community, state, and national levels. Specific responses have included acute interventions, treatment, prevention, supply reduction, provision of alternatives to use, and broad based socioeconomic interventions (Gray & Morfitt 1996). These responses are not value free. Embedded in each are philosophical understandings and ideological constructions of the risks that alcohol poses to individuals and society, and the way in which a democratic society should 'properly' respond to those risks.

There is a longstanding tension between sociological theories which emphasise the institutional and structural constraints upon individual behaviour, and those in which individual agency is paramount (Giddens 1992). Over two decades, in most of our analyses of indigenous health, we have pursued what are often seen as unfashionable notions of political economy: not simply because they reflect our ideological predilections, but because they still appear to be powerfully valid (Gray & Saggers 1994; Saggers 1994; Saggers & Gray 1991a, 1991b). Like many contemporary observers, however, we see the need not simply to '. . . formulate the global systematic theory which holds everything in place, but to analyse the specificity of mechanisms of power, to locate the connections and extensions, to build little by little a strategic knowledge' (Foucault 1980, p. 83). For Foucault, social control 'operates less through a system of legal, state, or economic repression than through the application of technologies of discipline that spread from the military to prisons, factories, schools, hospitals, asylums, and virtually all organisations' (Seidman 1994, p. 227).

Interwoven throughout these technologies of discipline are medico-scientific discourses that control what people desire, how they express themselves and what they do, by establishing norms of belief and behaviour. Analysis of these discourses heightens our understanding of the links between the structural factors underlying much behaviour and micro-level psychosocial interactions.

In Australia, colonialism established widespread institutions of control that provided surveillance over most aspects of the lives of indigenous people—including missions, segregated schools, and prisons. The dominant discourses which rationalised this approach were imbued with racist notions of biological and social difference, cloaked in Christian goodwill. The way in which problems associated with alcohol misuse are conceived and the interventions proposed illustrate colonial legacies of control, indigenous resistance to them, and ongoing changes within indigenous societies and cultures. Managing the risks alcohol misuse poses within acceptable limits to individual and community liberty requires theoretical attention to both structure and agency. In the past we have stressed the need to focus on the structural determinants of alcohol use. However, it is also clear that these have to be linked to the shared understandings of individuals and communities, for it is upon these that successful interventions must be based.

RISK AND LIBERTY

In Western industrialised societies the 'rights' of individuals have been generally accorded greater priority than those of the collectivity. In those societies, among the key medico-scientific discourses which establish norms of belief and behaviour are those surrounding the autonomy of the individual and the liberal values arising from them. These values arose with the development of industrial capitalism and emphasised the 'right' of individuals to pursue their interests (particularly economic interests) unfettered by the intrusion of the state. This philosophy has been most clearly articulated by John Stuart Mill.

In his essay *On Liberty* (1859) Mill argued that mature people should neither be forced to do anything because it might be good for them, nor prohibited from doing anything because it might be bad for them. For Mill, drug use was simply the act of independent people rationally exercising their 'tastes and pursuits', and he argued that intervention in this exercise by the state was not warranted.

Against the argument that state intervention could be justified because the exercise of individual 'tastes and pursuits' might have consequences for others, Mill responded that such harm should have actually occurred or be at least a definite risk. It was not sufficient to posit indirect or possible harm in order to justify state intervention (Mill 1859, ch. 4). The only people requiring the paternalistic protection of the state, according to Mill, were children or immature adults; although, some whole societies—so-called 'savages' and 'barbarians'—were deemed to be immature, and required paternal intervention to realise their historical potential.

Such liberal discourse represents the dominant ideology in Anglo-Western societies. Liberal ideology attributes the misuse of alcohol and other drugs to the weakness or susceptibility of individuals—whether biological, psychological or moral—and denies or minimises the role of political and economic factors in such misuse. However, as with all ideologies it has been contested, and its dominance has not been exclusive. In addition to this ideology, assessment of the risks posed by alcohol and other drugs has been strongly influenced by cultural preference and economic interest—rather than objective appraisal. In Australia, non-medical use of opiates and stimulants such as cocaine—which have never been used by a majority of people and of which there is no significant domestic production industry—has been regarded as high-risk activity and generally has been proscribed. On the other hand, there has been a down-playing of the risks associated with use of alcohol—the most commonly used recreational drug, and one in which there is significant capital investment in production and distribution. Control of alcohol use has been viewed as more properly based on the education of individuals rather than on state intervention (Bakalar & Grinspoon 1988, pp. 32–34); and there has been considerable resistance—justified in terms of Mill's notion of individual liberty—by consumers, suppliers and producers to any but limited regulatory measures to control consumption.

In what follows, we examine the relationship of these liberal views to the ways in which alcohol-related problems are defined, and to the intervention strategies employed to deal with the risks and consequences of alcohol misuse. First, however, it is necessary to consider indigenous notions of individuality or selfhood and their implications for alcohol misuse and strategies to deal with it.

INDIGENOUS NOTIONS OF SELFHOOD AND COMMUNITY

As indicated previously, all societies must strike a balance between the rights of individuals and the collectivity (although this is often shifting). The level at which this balance is struck has important implications for patterns of alcohol consumption, and its resolution will determine whether interventions are most appropriately directed at individuals, groups of problem drinkers, or wider communities. However, in the case of indigenous Australian communities, the ethnographic literature provides no clear-cut answer to this problem.

There are several descriptions of indigenous communities in which drinking is the norm, and which suggest that the collectivity takes clear precedence over the individual (Bain 1974; O'Connor 1984; Sansom 1980). In such communities 'The choice is simple: drink and belong, or abstain and remain outside' (O'Connor 1984, p. 181). This style of drinking has been described as 'contingent drunkenness' (O'Connor 1984, p. 180), because it is intimately connected to a communal drinking lifestyle, rather than any particular individual susceptibility to alcohol. Such drinking defies conventional descriptions of alcohol addiction or dependence, as individuals seem able to control their drinking while apart from the collectivity.

On the basis of such studies, it is argued, interventions that target individuals are misdirected because they fail to differentiate between drinking in indigenous communities where heavy drinking is the norm, and drinking in other settings where the problem drinker is an alienated outsider. When individuals return to their communities, newly sober after having undergone treatment, the struggle to maintain a transformed way of life proves too difficult for most. Accordingly, it is suggested there is a need for intervention programs which identify and strengthen group processes which will control the level of alcohol consumption.

Tempering such optimism about the use of endogenous social control mechanisms to reduce alcohol misuse, however, are ethnographic descriptions which highlight the limits to the collectivity and articulate a strong sense of individual autonomy where people are 'bosses for themselves' (Bell 1983; Brady 1990, 1992; Myers 1986). Brady has documented the ability of individuals to give up the grog despite being members of drinking communities. However, she claims that traditional social controls may actually facilitate drunkenness and that individual autonomy more often than not allows individuals to maintain their drinking rather than enabling them to stay sober.

Rowse cautions against such generalisations, pointing to the places where non-drinking is normative—like the 'dry' communities where alcohol is prohibited and in places where mostly senior women choose not to drink. Diverse Aboriginal sub-cultures where drinking is not part of everyday life provide a possible place for hard-drinking individuals who want to give up the grog—a place where both individual autonomy and the strength of the collectivity can be expressed in mutually supportive ways (Rowse 1993, p. 397).

The differences described in the literature are probably a function of the perspectives of the anthropological observers, the diversity of indigenous communities, and the changes that have taken and are taking place in those communities. Nevertheless, this debate about notions of indigenous selfhood and the way in which they impact on drinking patterns and intervention options brings into question the simple applicability of liberal notions of individuality to indigenous societies.

STRATEGIES OF INTERVENTION

Indigenous people can access alcohol and other drug programs provided by state, territory and private agencies and some do so. Increasingly though, there has been recognition that these programs cannot provide the type of support that many indigenous people want. The first indigenous alcohol intervention program, an Aboriginal Alcoholics Anonymous program was established in Redfern in 1972, and currently about 120 community organisations conduct alcohol and other drug-related intervention programs (Gray & Morfitt 1996). In this section we review two of the intervention strategies—treatment, and use of liquor licensing-related legislation—employed by indigenous Australians to reduce excessive alcohol consumption and the risks it poses. It is our contention that these strategies reflect on the one hand, the colonial discourse of control of indigenous people and on the other, indigenous resistance to such control.

Treatment

Clearly, people who are using alcohol to such an extent that they are harming themselves and/or others require some kind of help, and the most common response is to advocate the provision of treatment. Application of the term 'treatment' to describe measures used to address alcohol misuse implies that the problem to be addressed is a biological or psychological disease or disorder—located in individuals—which is amenable to cure or amelioration.

Some treatments are pharmacologically based. For example use of the drug disulfiram inhibits the metabolism of acetaldehyde (a toxic metabolite of alcohol) thus inducing illness when alcohol is consumed. The purpose of this treatment is to induce aversion to alcohol and its consumption. However, most treatments are based on some form of 'counselling' in which individuals are encouraged to identify dysfunctional behaviours or psychological conflicts that are then addressed through behavioural modification, psychotherapy or some form of self-help. The aim in some of these treatment modes is abstinence, in others it is controlled drinking. Such treatment is provided on a non-residential basis, and/or in rehabilitation or treatment centres where access to alcohol is denied and where counselling activities can be conducted on an intensive basis.

When provided by mainstream agencies, such treatment programs have not been well utilised by indigenous people and dropout rates among participants have been high. Accordingly, there have been calls to acknowledge that program models developed for white, mostly middle-class males may not suit indigenous clients and there has been a push to make treatment more 'culturally appropriate' (National Clearinghouse for Alcohol Information 1985, p. 4).

All of the treatment services conducted by indigenous organisations are based on some form of counselling and in 1997, eighty-six programs provided such services. In contrast to our usage, many indigenous people reserve the term treatment for services conducted in a residential facility (of which there are thirty-eight across the country), and refer to non-residential services as counselling. The majority of non-residential programs are conducted in prisons or detention centres by indigenous organisations. Treatment in such latter settings is often conducted in fulfilment of court orders—a process which itself reflects the definition of indigenous alcohol misuse by non-indigenous society.

More than any other intervention strategy, the treatment programs conducted by indigenous organisations reflect either an explicit or implicit acceptance of liberal definitions of alcohol misuse. As indicated previously, the first indigenous Alcoholics Anonymous (AA) group was started in 1972 by Val Bryant (Anonymous 1978). Currently, of the eighty-six indigenous treatment programs, forty-nine are based exclusively on the AA model—a model which defines alcohol misuse or 'alcoholism' as an incurable disease against which an individual must struggle throughout their life.

In addition, the AA model provides the basis for another twenty-nine programs. In some of these programs, the AA approach to treatment is supplemented with strategies such as life-skills counselling. In others, while the liberal discourse of AA has been accepted, attempts have been made to modify it so that it is more congruent with indigenous cultural practice and/or includes some elements of indigenous healing.

Perhaps the most well known example of the latter type of program was that conducted by the Central Australian Aboriginal Alcohol Programs Unit (CAAAPU). CAAAPU was based on an indigenous Canadian program developed by Poundmaker's Lodge— itself based on the philosophy and guiding principles of the Nechi Training Research and Health Promotions Institute. The Nechi Institute's mission statement includes a list of beliefs which make clear its roots in the Alcoholics Anonymous approach to alcohol use, including the statement that: 'Alcoholism, drug, and gambling dependencies, like other addictive/dependency behaviours, are diseases which can be treated and from which recovery is possible' (1987, Annual Report, p. 3, cited in *Visions* 1996, p. 19).

In the Poundmaker's program this liberal philosophical approach underlies a treatment program which incorporates many indigenous Canadian healing symbols such as the sweatlodge, drum, sweetgrass, eaglefeather, and the natural elements of fire, rock, air and water. All staff are required to be abstinent, in their terms to not only 'talk the talk' but also 'walk the walk' and most staff are indigenous, many of them being previously alcohol or drug dependent.

Although not without its indigenous Canadian critics, Poundmaker's Lodge has attracted enthusiastic attention world-wide, and leading figures such as Eric Shirt have been brought to Australia to facilitate development of indigenous alcohol and drug programs. In 1991, using the message of 'Let's beat the grog together' CAAAPU launched an outreach program. Initially, Eric Shirt and other workers helped to train people from Central Australia to run an alcohol counsellor training program. This was followed by a twenty-eight-day treatment program, based on the Poundmaker model. Two years later in 1993, CAAAPU received funding from the Northern Territory Department of Health and Community Services to run a full-time alcohol treatment program, under their Territory-wide 'Living with Alcohol' program. Subsequent evaluation of the program found inadequacies in its staffing and the inappropriateness of some of the treatment curriculum but made no findings about its overall effectiveness (Miller & Rowse 1995). For a variety of reasons, the Centre ceased its activities.

It is not known how effective most of these treatment programs are, as very few have been subjected to systematic evaluation (Gray et al. 1995b). While most programs claim they are successful, the literature gives little cause for optimism. For instance, a review of several evaluations of alcohol treatments utilising a wide range of therapies (hypnosis, group therapy, drug therapy, aversion treatment, incarceration and probation) found, after controlling for treatment setting, no statistically significant differences in results, a finding confirmed by more recent studies (Mandell 1979; Weibel-Orlando 1989).

One of the reasons posited for the lack of success of AA programs among indigenous people is that such programs are not culturally appropriate, in that they ascribe to individuals greater autonomy and freedom of choice than they actually possess within indigenous societies. However, the heterogeneity of indigenous communities and variations of belief and behaviour within them necessitates caution in subscribing to such generalisation.

Although AA-based treatment programs have not generally been successful, through these types of programs or on their own, individuals have dramatically reduced or completely curtailed their use of alcohol and consequently transformed their lives (Brady 1995). Our argument highlights the limitations of liberal notions of individuality, but does not negate the importance of the actions that individuals can themselves take. It is clear that, when attempting to reduce the misuse of alcohol, individual motivations and actions are integral. However, they are not sufficient.

Legislation and regulation

As indicated previously, the libertarian position with regard to availability of alcohol has never had total ascendancy. From the time of colonisation, there have always been some legislative controls over the production, sale, supply and consumption of alcohol; both because taxes and levies on these have been a significant source of revenue for the state and because it has been perceived as a drug whose unfettered use poses some risks to society. These controls have included conditions under which licences to produce or sell alcohol are granted; restrictions on hours of trading; prohibitions on supply to minors and intoxicated persons; and, prohibitions against public drunkenness. Up until as late as the 1970s in some jurisdictions, they also included prohibitions on the supply of alcohol to indigenous persons. Nevertheless, the liquor industry has argued—and governments have generally agreed—that the misuse of alcohol is an individual problem, not to be addressed through restrictions on availability and individual liberty, but one to be dealt with by education and health agencies (Levine & Reineman 1993, p. 179).

In a review of state and territory liquor licensing legislation, Craze and Norberry identify four broad objectives: public order or public good; revenue raising or profitability; public health; and regulation of the industry. Summarising the thrust of legislative activities, they write:

> A noticeable development during the current century has been the shift by legislatures away from the social purposes of the restriction of liquor sale, supply and public consumption to the purposes of deregulation, the reduction of State interference [sic] within the liquor industry, the encouragement of diversity in services and facilities and the promotion of tourism and economic prosperity. (Craze & Norberry 1995, p. 35)

Even recent inclusion, or proposals for inclusion, of harm minimisation objectives in some jurisdictions has been accompanied by greater deregulation of the industry.

Despite the fact that liquor licensing legislation has generally favoured the interests of the industry, there are provisions in the various Acts to limit these interests, thereby supporting some indigenous groups who reject the notion that misuse of alcohol is wholly or largely the problem of the individual consumer. Either explicitly or implicitly, such groups have identified what much research demonstrates, that is, the availability of alcohol is a key factor in the level of alcohol-related harm (Saggers & Gray 1997), and they have taken various steps to reduce such availability.

Northern Territory legislation provides an option for discrete Aboriginal communities to declare themselves 'dry'—that is, to prohibit the distribution and consumption of alcohol within those communities. In Western Australia, similar provisions are contained within the *Aboriginal Communities Act*. Many indigenous communities have taken advantage of such legislation, affirming that the interests of the community as a whole have precedence over the rights of individual drinkers. The effect of such action has been mixed. Generally, community members comply with such prohibitions, which are sometimes backed up with local sanctions. However, some disaffected individuals have moved more-or-less permanently to nearby towns, while others often go to nearby towns on 'binges'—thus transferring the problems associated with excessive consumption from the home communities to nearby population centres.

Where restrictions on availability have been confined to discrete indigenous communities, they have tended either to have attracted little widespread attention or to have been applauded by paternalistic whites. They have been much more contentious where indigenous groups have successfully applied for restrictions on the sale of alcohol in communities consisting of both indigenous and non-indigenous people. One recent example is Tennant Creek in the Northern Territory where in July 1995 the Northern Territory Liquor Commission agreed to a trial restriction of the sale and supply of alcohol for a period of six months (d'Abbs et al. 1996, p. 8).

Trial restrictions, introduced in two thirteen-week periods, included restricted trading on Thursdays ('pension day'), variations to trading on days other than Thursdays, and restrictions on front bar sales and take-away sales (d'Abbs et al. 1996, p. 7). The restrictions provoked intense debate both before and during the twenty-six-week trial because of fears of the economic costs to local businesses, perceived infringements of individual rights, and heightening of racial tensions as some non-Aboriginal people perceived themselves to be disadvantaged because of the drinking excesses of Aboriginal people. While most people in the town acknowledged the social disruption caused by excessive drinking, some were unhappy with the proposed solution. An evaluation found that the trial had resulted in improvements in terms of fewer police incidents, reduced disturbance to public order, and improved health and welfare in terms of fewer alcohol-related hospital presentations and admissions to the women's refuge. The economic impact of the measures was varied with a downturn in alcohol sales in the town of Tennant Creek, offset to some extent by increases in sales at roadside inns (d'Abbs et al. 1996, pp. 1–4, 77). After reviewing the evidence the Liquor Commission found that although liquor controls could not solve alcohol problems in the town, there was general community support for limited restrictions (d'Abbs et al. 1996, p. 81).

Not all such actions by indigenous people have been successful. Indeed, as Gray et al. indicate with regard to Western Australia, the bureaucratic procedures entailed in actions such as objecting to the granting of new licences or extended trading permits, or lodging complaints against licensees, severely curtail their chances of success (1995a, p. 181). Difficulties with existing legislation in Western Australia led a number of indigenous organisations to make a detailed submission to a committee established to review existing liquor licensing legislation. In this submission, the groups actively sought to have legislation amended to give local communities much greater control over the availability of alcohol and made recommendations for the inclusion of a harm reduction objective in the Act and greater, non-discriminatory enforcement of existing provisions of legislation such as those dealing with sales to minors and intoxicated persons (Gray et al. 1995a). Unfortunately, to the extent that these recommendations conflict with the government's objective of increased deregulation of the liquor industry, it appears that their success will be limited.

In spite of the threat that such controls pose for individual liberty, many small indigenous communities are showing they are prepared to sacrifice some freedoms for a reduction in alcohol-related harm. Their position has recently been supported by the Race Discrimination Commissioner (1995) who favours amendments to the *Racial Discrimination Act 1975* recognising community rights and public health concerns.

CONCLUSION

For many people, indigenous and non-indigenous alike, alcohol is central to what Mill (1859) referred to as our 'tastes and pursuits', providing a pleasurable focus for much of social life. Among many indigenous communities, however, in the past twenty or thirty years, excessive consumption and related harm have become so great that concerned individuals and organisations are demanding that action be taken to address these problems.

Indigenous societies themselves are changing in response to the ongoing colonial process. Within some there has been an acceptance of aspects of the liberal model which have been accommodated within their world views. In some cases this has been facilitated by indigenous views on the nature of personal autonomy. This can be seen in the AA focused treatment programs which 'require the subordination of the particularities of the drinking self to the ideal universal, sober self which AA promotes and sustains' (Rowse 1993, pp. 397–98).

In other cases indigenous people have promoted interventions which theoretically confront Western ideals of individual liberty and autonomy. These have been most controversial where they include attempts to assert disciplined drinking regimes in communities of both indigenous and non-indigenous people. It is in these contexts where conflicting notions of risk and liberty are most problematic. But, on balance, it appears that there is general community support for local-level structural interventions which may reduce some of the health and social consequences of excess. Ideological justification for this includes the nineteenth-century notion espoused by Mill that indigenous people require paternal intervention to realise their historic potential. Indigenous justifications have been both philosophical and practical. For some regulating supply constitutes indigenous attempts to gain some control over a problem created by colonisation and maintained by unequal power relations. For others it is simply the most obvious and direct method to curb excessive drinking.

Structural interventions such as the regulation of supply have been more successful than attempts to treat alcohol-affected people. Our research indicates that indigenous alcohol programs have increased in number over the past several years, but they are patently too few to deal with a problem acknowledged as a primary contributor to Aboriginal ill health and social disruption.

It is these circumstances that reinforce our belief that theories of both structure and action are required to understand the problems of and potential solutions to indigenous alcohol abuse. Understanding the way in which the political economy of alcohol operates at the global and local level to influence the supply of alcohol is crucial, and indigenous communities have shown they are prepared to tackle this issue by lobbying liquor licensing authorities so that they will consider health and community concerns in their deliberations. They are demonstrating too their belief that local, indigenously controlled treatment programs and support services are necessary, but most are woefully under-resourced and there are simply too few to provide for the numbers of people requiring them.

Social scientists can contribute in two important ways to indigenous attempts to deal with alcohol and its consequences. We need to critique and evaluate the models used to explain alcohol misuse and the intervention programs either in place or planned, resisting monolithic solutions to what are very complex problems. More importantly, however, we have to use our knowledge of indigenous communities and the wider societies in which they are located to refute the current outrageous lie that indigenous health in general and problems with alcohol in particular, are the consequences of personal choice.

ACKNOWLEDGEMENTS

The research upon which this chapter is based was funded by Edith Cowan University, the National Centre for Research into the Prevention of Drug Abuse, Curtin University of Technology and the Department of Health and Family Services. The Albany Aboriginal Corporation and the Carnarvon Medical Service Aboriginal Corporation have provided strong support for our research on the supply and promotion of alcohol. Brooke Morfitt and Deirdre Bourbon have been valuable research associates on a number of alcohol- and other drug-related projects. Clive Linklater provided very helpful introductions to indigenous Canadian programs and important background on alcohol issues in Canada.

REFERENCES

Aboriginal Communities Act 1979 Western Australian Government Press, Perth

Anonymous 1978 'Bennelong's Haven' *Aboriginal News* vol. 3, no. 3, pp. 16–17

Bain, M.S. 1974 'Alcohol use and traditional social control in Aboriginal society' in *Better Health for Aborigines* eds B.S. Hetzel et al., University of Queensland Press, St Lucia

Bakalar, J.B. & Grinspoon, L. 1988 *Drug Control in a Free Society* Cambridge University Press, Cambridge

Bell, D. 1983 *Daughters of the Dreaming* McPhee Gribble, Melbourne & George Allen & Unwin, Sydney

Brady, M. 1990 'Indigenous and government attempts to control alcohol use among Australian Aborigines' *Contemporary Drug Problems* vol. 17, no. 2, pp. 195–220

——1992 'Ethnography and understandings of Aboriginal drinking' *Journal of Drug Issues* vol. 22, no. 3, pp. 699–712

——1995 *Giving Away the Grog: Aboriginal Accounts of Drinking and not Drinking* AGPS, Canberra

Collman, J. 1979 'Social order and the exchange of liquor: A theory of drinking among Australian Aborigines' *Journal of Anthropological Research* vol. 32, no. 2, pp. 208–24

Craze, L. & Norberry, J. 1995 'The objectives of liquor licensing laws in Australia' in *Alcohol Misuse and Violence: an Examination of the Appropriateness and Efficacy of Liquor Licensing Laws across Australia* Report 5 for the National Symposium on Alcohol Misuse and Violence ed. T. Stockwell, AGPS, Canberra

d'Abbs, P., Hunter, E., Reser, J. & Martin, D. 1994 *Alcohol-Related Violence in Aboriginal and Torres Strait Islander Communities: A Literature Review*, Report No. 8 for the National Symposium on Alcohol Misuse and Violence, AGPS, Canberra

d'Abbs, P., Togni, S. & Crundall, I. 1996 *The Tennant Creek Liquor Licensing trial, August 1995–February 1996: An Evaluation* Menzies Occasional Papers, Menzies School of Health Research and NT Living With Alcohol Program, Darwin

Foucault, M. 1980 *Power/Knowledge: Selected Writings and Other Interviews* Pantheon, New York

Giddens, A. 1992 *Sociology* Polity, New York

Gray, A. 1990 *A Matter of Life and Death: Contemporary Aboriginal Mortality* Aboriginal Studies Press, Canberra

Gray, D., Drandich, M., Moore, L., Wilkes, T., Riley, R. & Davies, S. 1995a 'Aboriginal well-being and liquor licensing legislation in Western Australia' *Australian Journal of Public Health* vol. 19, no. 2, pp. 177–85

Gray, D. & Morfitt, B. 1996 'Harm minimisation in an indigenous context (Australia)' in *Cultural Variations in the Meaning of Harm Minimisation: The Implications for Policy and Practice in the Drugs Arena* proceedings of a conference convened by the World Health Organization Collaborating Centre for Prevention and Control of Drug Abuse, National Centre for Research into the Prevention of Drug Abuse and National Drug and Alcohol Research Centre, Perth & Sydney

Gray, D. & Saggers, S. 1994 'Aboriginal health: The harvest of injustice' in *Just Health* eds C. Waddell & A. Petersen, Churchill Livingstone, Sydney

Gray, D., Saggers, S., Drandich, M., Wallam, D. & Plowright, P. 1995b 'Government health and substance abuse programs for indigenous peoples: A comparative review' *Australian Journal of Public Health* vol. 19, no. 6, pp. 567–72

Hunter, E.M., Hall, W.D. & Spargo, R.M. 1992 'Patterns of alcohol consumption in the Kimberley Aboriginal population' *Medical Journal of Australia* vol. 1156, pp. 764–68

Johnson, E. 1991 *Royal Commission into Aboriginal Deaths in Custody: National Report* 4 vols AGPS, Canberra

Knowles, S. & Woods, B. 1993 *The Health of Noongar People in the Great Southern Health Region* Health Department of Western Australia, Perth

Langton, M. 1991 'Too much sorry business' (Report of the Aboriginal Issues Unit of the Northern Territory) Appendix D (I), in *Royal Commission into Aboriginal Deaths in Custody: National Report* AGPS, Canberra

Levine, H.G. & Reineman, C. 1993 'From prohibition to regulation: Lessons from alcohol policy for drug policy' in *Confronting Drug Policy* eds R. Bayer & G.M. Oppenheimer, Cambridge University Press, Cambridge

Madden, R. 1995 *National Aboriginal and Torres Strait Islander Survey 1994* Australian Bureau of Statistics, Canberra

Mandell, W.A. 1979 'A critical overview of evaluations of alcoholism treatment' *Alcoholism: Clinical and Experimental Research* vol. 3, no. 4, pp. 315–23.

Mill, J.S. 1859 *On Liberty* J.W. Parker, London

Miller, K. & Rowse, T. 1995 *CAAAPU: An Evaluation* Menzies occasional paper 1/95, Menzies School of Health Research, Darwin

Myers, F. 1986 *Pintupi Country, Pintupi Self* Australian Institute of Aboriginal Studies, Canberra and Smithsonian Institute, Washington

National Clearinghouse for Alcohol Information 1985 *Alcohol and Native Americans* National Institute on Alcohol Abuse and Alcoholism, Maryland

O'Connor, R. 1984 'Alcohol and contingent drunkenness in Central Australia' *Journal of Social Issues* vol. 19, no. 3, pp. 173–83

Perkins, J.J., Sanson-Fisher, R.W., Blunden, S., Lunnay, D., Redman, S. & Hensley, M.J. 1994 'The prevalence of drug use in urban Aboriginal communities' *Addiction* vol. 89, no. 10, pp. 1319–31

Race Discrimination Commissioner 1995 *Alcohol Report. Racial Discrimination Act 1975. Race Discrimination, Human Rights and the Distribution of Alcohol* AGPS, Canberra

Rowse, T. 1993 'The relevance of ethnographic understanding to Aboriginal anti-grog initiatives' *Drug and Alcohol Review* vol. 12, pp. 393–99

Sackett, L. 1988 'Resisting arrests: drinking, development and discipline in a desert context' *Social Analysis* vol. 24 (December), pp. 66–77

Saggers, S. 1994 '"But that was all in the past": The relevance of history to contemporary Aboriginal health' *Australian Journal of Occupational Therapy* vol. 40, no. 4, pp. 153–56

Saggers, S. & Gray, D. 1991a *Aboriginal Health and Society* Allen & Unwin, Sydney

——1991b 'Policy and practice in Aboriginal health' in *The Health of Aboriginal Australia* eds J. Reid & P. Trompf, Harcourt, Brace, Jovanovich, Sydney

——1997 'Supplying and promoting "grog": The political economy of alcohol in Aboriginal Australia' *Australian Journal of Social Issues* vol. 32, no. 3, pp. 215–37

Sansom, B. 1980 *The Camp at Wallaby Cross: Aboriginal Fringe-Dwellers in Darwin* Australian Institute of Aboriginal Studies, Canberra

Seidman, S. 1994 *Contested Knowledge* Blackwell, Cambridge

Swensen, G. & Unwin, E. 1994 *A Study of Hospitalisation and Alcohol Use in the Kimberley Health Region of Western Australia* occasional paper 57, Health Department of Western Australia, Perth

Veroni, M., Swensen, G. & Thomson, N. 1993 *Hospital Admissions in Western Australia Wholly Attributable to Alcohol Use: 1981–1990* Health Department of Western Australia, Perth

Visions 1996 *Nechi Review 1996* Nechi Training, Research and Health Promotions Institute, Edmonton

Watson, C., Fleming, J. & Alexander, K. 1988 *A Survey of Drug Use Patterns in Northern Territory Aboriginal Communities: 1986–1987* Northern Territory Department of Health and Community Services, Darwin

Weibel-Orlando, J. 1989 'Hooked on healing: Anthropologists, alcohol and intervention' *Human Organisation* vol. 48, pp. 148–55

21 AIDS, women and the body politic

Catherine Waldby

The heterosexual male body is absent from AIDS discourse as a problematic object, a body in need of specific education and discipline.[1] Other sexual 'identities'—women, bisexual men and gay men—have been the 'targets' of extensive safe sex education campaigns in Australia, but heterosexual men as a category have remained largely exempt from these exhortations to transform sexual practice.[2] This exemption has direct and serious consequences. It is common for heterosexual women to feel sole responsibility for the enforcement of safe sex practice within a sexual encounter, and to meet with resistance to these attempts from their partners.[3] This exemption is also, it seems to me, an exemplary instance of heterosexual masculine sexual privilege and freedoms, maintained even in the age of epidemic.

My concern in this chapter is to investigate some of the discursive conditions under which this privilege is naturalised, that is, made to seem a normal and inevitable biological truth. In what follows, I will argue that the sexuality of heterosexual men is exempted from disciplinary scrutiny through the making of an implicit equation in AIDS discourse between the health of heterosexual male bodies and the public health as a whole. Heterosexual male bodies in this way come to be the bodies that the resources of public health institutions are dedicated to protect, through the disciplining of other kinds of bodies.

This displacement can be seen if we consider some of the permutations in the central binary that has historically organised AIDS rhetoric, that of the 'general population'/'risk group' division.[4] Its usage both in the media and in AIDS epidemiology suggests that the health of 'the general population' is understood as synonymous with the public health. Both terms present themselves as inclusive, designating the health of the greatest possible number of the social body. Risk groups in this model constitute residual categories of persons whose sexual and drug use practices associate them with HIV infection and thus position them as *threats* to the 'public health'. This kind of usage can be seen in the following excerpt from an epidemiological article.

> Owing to the longevity and fatality of HIV infection, the public requires protection against a protracted, virulent, and, often, sequestered hazard. But AIDS is also a social disease; its major risk groups are associated with lifestyle behaviours such as homosexuality and illegal intravenous drug use, about which the larger society has moral and ethical precon-ceptions. Public policy, therefore, has to weigh civil liberties against the healthy survival of society. (Chavigny et al. 1989, p. 60)

The 'public', the imaginary subject of the public health which health policy is designed to both address and protect, is here threatened by a 'hazard' both viral and social, a minority which threatens a uniformly clean 'public' majority.

An examination of the shifting borders between the 'general population'/'risk group' division in a spectrum of AIDS literature over the history of the epidemic throws the inclusive claims of the 'general population' into question pretty quickly however. The identities denominated as 'risk groups' have at one time or another included quite a lot of people. To take an example from one Australian government document, we find mentioned homosexual and bisexual men, needle-sharing drug users, Aboriginal and Islander people, people in prison, people in other closed institutions, adolescents, women, people who work as prostitutes, and blood product recipients, all said to be in need of special kinds of AIDS education (Commonwealth Department of Community Services and Health 1988, p. iv).

This list clearly includes a large number of people, and is so comprehensive as to make the category 'general population' begin to seem residual. Who is left after this series of exclusions? The idea of the 'general population' implied by this list can be designated by the negative of each of the groups nominated. The 'general population', the group designated not to require 'special education' would in this case include white people not Aboriginals, adults not adolescents, people who have not received blood products, and so on. Using this logic, the groups designated as 'priority groups' on the grounds of sex or sexuality mark the relevant blind spot in its taxonomy. They imply a general population which includes men but not women, and het-erosexual men, not gay and bisexual men.

So here the term 'general population' is one which functions to exclude rather than include, a movement which Grover bluntly argues is typical of its use in relation to AIDS. 'The general population' he writes, 'is the repository of everything you wish to claim for yourself and deny to others' (Grover 1988, p. 24). In the use described here it works to exclude everybody with the single exception of heterosexual men, a regression which the term performs very readily.[5]

This ultimate reservation of the category of 'general population' for heterosexual men is not consistently visible in AIDS discourse, but its most reliable symptom is the difficult and ambivalent relationship that women maintain to this category. While gay men are easily excluded from the general population as the exemplary 'risk group', and as a minority easily subtracted from the public health majority, women constitute half of the population and cannot be so readily dispatched. They tend rather to be simultaneously included and excluded, acting as markers of the tension between the 'general population's' inclusive claims and its excluding and regressive movement. In other words, women are positioned at the threshold of the 'general population' rather than securely within it. They may be included as married or at least monogamous women or as virgins, that is, to the extent that they conform to the notional borders of the family as a safe haven from HIV.[6] They may be included to the extent that they act as the guardians of the purity of the 'general population', the enforcers of safe sex practice.[7] Ironically, women may also be included as lesbians, although not in a positive sense. Lesbians remain an unmarked category within AIDS discourse, included by default in the general population because they are understood to pose no infectious threat to men.

On the other hand, women are vulnerable to exclusion, in the sense of becoming the subjects of special education and epidemiological surveillance, as 'sex workers' or simply heterosexually active, as pregnant, as the partners of bisexual or IV-drug using men or even as passive and unable to negotiate safe sex.[8] Their ambivalent position is further evident in the tendency for biomedical literature to use statistics about HIV prevalence in women not as significant in themselves but as displaced indicators of potential infection in other sectors of the 'general population', particularly children. Treichler points out in her survey of the AIDS literature that women's infection rates are sometimes subsumed under the category 'paediatric AIDS' (Treichler 1992, p. 32). One readily encounters observations like the following in the medical literature.

> The majority of cases [of AIDS] so far have occurred in male homosexuals with other groups at risk including intravenous drug users, haemophiliacs . . . and infants of sexually promiscuous or drug addicted mothers. None

the less, the number of infected heterosexuals is steadily increasing. (Roitt 1991)

Here the infection of the 'sexually promiscuous or drug addicted mother' is made redundant to that of her child, and she is simultaneously excluded from the category 'heterosexuals'.

Once the equivocal position of women as a category is taken into account, the term 'general population' can be seen to regress very readily to the point where it is only heterosexual men who it reliably denominates, although it still acts *as if* it denominates the public health in its most general sense. What I want to discuss here is the logic of this metonymic displacement as it works itself out in AIDS epidemiology. And more broadly, I want to consider it as an instance in which the health and the sex of the body politic work in complicity so that the protection of heterosexual masculine bodies may be expressed as the protection of the public health.

THE BODY POLITIC

What do I mean by the term 'the body politic'? Certainly in popular usage it is a term taken to simply designate the unity of the polity, or some other form of social organisation. Recent theoretical interest in the body as the privileged site of political forces has precipitated a more literal regard for the bodily aspect of the 'body politic'. This literature cannot, however, provide a definitional answer to my question, because the theoretical status of the body is itself subject to intense contestation. My development of the question here should be regarded as context bound and provisional; a treatment limited to the purposes of this chapter.

At its most straightforward the body politic is a term which implies imagining the nation or some other governmental unit, a city for example, along anthropomorphic or organic lines. As Benedict Anderson suggests, all national formations, all societies, must imagine their conditions of unity, their boundaries, internal structures and the relationship between parts (Anderson 1991). A considerable amount of historical and anthropological literature indicates that human bodies readily act as models for kinds of social unity and coordination in a number of different societies.[9]

Following Foucault (1980a) and Haraway (1991) I would argue that the form taken by the body politic in our own social formation is that of the 'population'. This 'population' is not simply an amassing of citizens but is imagined as a composite body, 'with its specific phenomena and its peculiar variables: birth and death rates, life expectancy, fertility, state of health, frequency of illnesses, patterns of diet and habitation' (Foucault 1980a, p. 25). The management of the health of this population, Foucault suggests, is a primary commitment and source of legitimacy for modern forms of governmentality, concerned to maximise a healthy and thus productive and reproductive citizenry. Commenting on the historical transition from a monarchical body politic to that of the social contract, he writes:

> It's the body of society which becomes the new principle [of the political system] in the nineteenth century. It is this social body which needs to be protected, in a quasi-medical sense. In place of the rituals that served to restore the corporeal integrity of the monarch, remedies and therapeutic devices are employed such as the segregation of the sick, the monitoring of contagions, the exclusion of delinquents. (Foucault 1980b, p. 55)

This commitment to the protection and promotion of the health of the population involves the elaboration of knowledges adequate to the task of analysing relationships between the health of particular bodies and the health of the composite body of the population. The science of epidemiology is an exemplary instance of such knowledges, which would also include demography, actuarial statistics and nutrition for example. The practice of epidemiology consists precisely of the amassing of a series of discreet clinical 'cases', medical knowledges of particular bodies, and considering their implications as mass phenomena at the level of the population.

As Foucault's words imply, the population, as a composite, can be imagined as itself an entity, a singular organism which has a health and is liable to disease. This implication of the notion of the population is evoked whenever the term 'the public health' is used, designating as it does a unified and singular state, the health of the public body. The appeal for governmental and biomedical institutions of the notion of the population as an entity with a health resides, I suggest, in its usefulness as a metaphor for social cohesion and for the forging of consensus about what counts as an appropriate social strategy. It provides a set of well disseminated metaphors for imagining a variety of social processes and problems in terms of health and illness, evident in notions about the 'growth' of economies, or the representation of social problems as 'cancers' for example.

The notion of the population as a composite body with a singular state of health has implications for the particular bodies that comprise it. If certain historically specific ideas of health work upwards as ways to organise the 'public health' they also work downwards to organise the health of individual bodies. At the risk of oversimplifying, the relationship between particular bodies and the body politic is homologous, the moving of the same image up and down through different levels of scale. This relationship is well demonstrated in Corbin's (1986) treatment of nineteenth-century French public health and its generalisation of the single medical discourse of hygiene to apply to both personal bodily protocols and the operation of the urban environment. Corbin argues that the medical notion that excrement was a vehicle for infection both determined the new regimes of private defecation and personal hygiene and the building of sewerage systems, for example. The hygiene of the self played out in miniature the new forms of public hygiene, and public health became a means of amplifying medical knowledge of the body out into a strategy for the reorganisation of society, conceived as itself an organism, a body. It is in this way that particular subjects are made responsible in the name of health, exhorted to embody a regularised idea of the 'public health' in the health of their own bodies.

The population with a singular state of health is an idea which also carries implications for the ways that bodies are positioned *vis-à-vis* one another. Public health is not simply a matter of a uniform replication of healthy discipline upon each body in simple repetition, but also the ways that bodies are ordered in relation to each other. Ideas of the normal body elaborated within biomedicine tend to be deployed in normalisation, in the creation of hierarchies of value out of differences, as Canguilhem's (1989) work demonstrates. Under certain circumstances the protection of the public health may require the hierarchisation of bodies into a sacrificial order, wherein some more valuable bodies are protected against less valuable bodies.

But if the population is imagined as a composite body with a health, it must, like all bodies, also have a sex. The sex of the body politic is a question taken up in some recent feminist writing, notably that of Moira Gatens (1988, 1991a, 1991b) who has addressed it not to medical discourse but to classical and contemporary political discourse, where an explicit or implicit idea of the body politic has been articulated. In reading some of the classical texts of liberal political philosophy, Gatens points out that the body politic created by the social contract is indeed a sexed body, an implicitly masculine body presented as a sex-neutral, ideal body.

The purpose of the social contract is to represent its members, but the implicit masculinity of the body politic introduces a series of systematic displacements into this process of representation. The image of the body that it employs as the principle of unity and order works also to determine whose bodies incarnate this order and are deemed compatible with its interests, that is, whose interests can be fully represented without threatening its order. Gatens argues that the social contract only creates 'political representation' for those whose bodies are 'represented' as the image of the body politic, its masculine citizens. The body politic functions to exclude from political privilege, 'those whose corporeal specificity marks them as inappropriate analogues to the body politic' (Gatens 1991a, p. 82).

Hence the body politic is a means of naturalising women's exclusion from public participation, but more importantly for this argument, it is a means of effecting a slippage between masculine bodily interests and an idea of general social interests. Insofar as the body politic is an implicitly masculine body which presents itself as a sex-neutral 'human' body, then masculine bodies can claim to 'represent' the interests of all other bodies. Male bodies can thus claim to literally incorporate other bodily interests within their own, including the interests of health, because they are the bodies which are seen to incarnate the desirable social order. Hence the health of the heterosexual male body can be made to stand for the health of the body politic in its entirety. Conversely, a threat to the health of this body can seem like a comprehensive threat to the public health.

So if the body politic can be said to have both a health and a masculine sex, what is the relationship between these two attributes? This, I suggest, is an historical question in the sense that their relationship is contingent and mutable. They may operate independently from each other under circumstances where the public health is threatened by conditions that have little bearing on sexual difference, an influenza epidemic for example. On the other hand, the conditions of sexual epidemic constitute the kind of crisis in the body politic where it seems likely that the protection of its health and its sex become isomorphic. As I will demonstrate, this isomorphism is effected through the anatomies of the normal and the pathological elaborated in AIDS biomedicine, wherein the capacity of a body to infect is conceptualised according to its departure from phallic integrity and singularity. In this way heterosexual masculine bodily interests can find legitimate expression within the discourse of health.

THE TOPOGRAPHY OF SEXUAL INFECTION

I have argued that the morphology of the body politic is significant because of its power to order bodies in its own image and to naturalise their hierarchisation. The discourse of epidemiology seems to me to occupy a privileged position in articulating such orderings because it is the biomedical sub-discipline specifically concerned with the monitoring and maintenance of the public health. It is the study of disease not in the individual body as in clinical medicine, but of its incidence and distribution in the composite body of the population. Epidemiology interprets the vital signs and symptoms of the health of the body politic, and orders bodies according to its diagnoses.

Epidemiology attempts to establish reasons for the concentration of particular diseases within particular parts of a population in order to provide a map for clinical and public health intervention and prevention. The envisioning of patterns of disease distribution is the first step towards establishing possible social or environmental predisposing factors.

> The main objectives of surveillance are to evaluate the extent of disease in a population, and to indicate crudely which groups are most affected. It can also be used to suggest determinants of disease. Once surveillance has established the pattern of disease, more detailed epidemiological surveys may be required to identify the determinants of disease . . . The identification of disease determinants should lead to the establishment of prevention programs, designed to limit the occurrence of disease by eliminating or reducing exposure to these determinants. (Commonwealth AIDS Research Grants Epidemiology Advisory Committee 1990, p. 1)

Epidemiology differs from clinical medicine in its subscription to the notion of multiple determinants of disease. Clinical medicine tends to locate causal power in the 'aetiological agent', the specific organism which has a one-to-one relationship with a specific disease. Epidemiology as social medicine is committed to the consideration of disease as caused by a nexus of interactions between 'specific agent' (virus) and 'host'. It seeks to tip the balance of medical attention away from 'germ theory' (agent) and towards what it refers to as 'host factors'. Hence epidemiology brings to bear its more intensive forms of study on these 'host–agent interactions'. Detailed surveys are mounted in order to discover what characteristics of the 'host' population interact with the causative agent to intensify disease in that group, compared to the rest of the population.

This conceptualisation of disease aetiology means that epidemiological science can only proceed through the specification and classification of sub-populations. If the social topography of disease is taken to indicate a pattern of disease aetiology constituted at least in part through host factors, then hosts must be categorised according to these factors. They must be designated as a group because of the factors which place them at higher risk of infection, compared to other groups who are relatively free of infection.

In the field of AIDS this comparative method led, at the beginning of the epidemic in the industrialised democracies, to the designation of the general population/risk group binary as the principle of surveillance. Most notable of the risk groups were homosexual and bisexual men, and IV-drug users, whose sexual and/or drug use practices were identified as behaviours which spread the HIV virus, in comparison to the benign sexual practices and non-drug use of the notional 'general population'. While women have never been formally nominated as a 'risk group' by epidemiology, they have, as I indicated earlier, been nevertheless denied a secure position within the general population and subjected to surveillance and disciplinary intervention of various kinds. In what follows I will examine what epidemiology considers that gay men and heterosexual women have in common.

In epidemiological terms, homosexual men act as an infectious *reservoir* for HIV. 'The reservoir is the location in which the organism is normally found, that is, where it becomes established, metabolises, and multiplies' (Brachman 1990, p. 156). Homosexuality is an habitual reservoir of HIV because it forms a naturalised locus of the determinants of viral transmission. In epidemiology's imagination, sexual practices which are said to be the exclusive domain of homosexuality are taken to be both the behaviours which generate and spread HIV and the acts which delimit gay identity.

The sexual practice most closely associated with both viral transmission and gay identity in epidemiology is that of receptive anal intercourse, which is widely cited as the major means of contracting HIV infection. One study states for example, 'In all the major cohort studies of prevalent HIV-1 infection, receptive anal intercourse has been the major mode of transmission when other risk factors . . . were controlled' (Winklestein et al. 1989, p. 125). The active/passive distinction in anal intercourse is conceptualised in epidemiology to form a self-enclosed infectious circuit within gay populations, where active penetration is understood to 'give' infection and receptivity to 'take' infection. For this reason HIV infection among homosexual men is generally imagined by epidemiology as endogenous, wherein the nature of the risk group is established through its putative capacity to generate and intensify infection within its own borders. This concentration of infection is further enhanced by the repetition of sex, the tendency to 'increased numbers of sex partners' which epidemiology attributes to gay sexuality (Chamberland & Curran 1990).[10]

Women, on the other hand, pose an exogamous danger for AIDS epidemiology: they carry infection across specified borders. As this excerpt states, it is the feminine capacity to act as a transmission point between high- and low-risk males, and between high-risk male and foetus that presents their problem to epidemiology.

> Because women have the possibility of sexual contact with groups at high risk of HIV infection, such as bisexual males, they are viewed as the interface between homosexual/bisexual groups and the heterosexual population, where seepage of the infection to non-high-risk groups may take place. Following the progress of the epidemic through analysis of the frequency of cases in women may be a method of categorising the spread of the infection into the heterosexual population . . . It is also obvious that infected women are the source of the transplacental transmission that takes place from mother to infant, increasing the threat of AIDS to the unborn. (Chavigny et al. 1989, pp. 66–67)

This conceptualisation of women's bodies as mediums of boundary transgression is evident too in the tendency described at the beginning of this chapter to regard infectious prevalence in women as primarily indicators of infection elsewhere, rather than as indicative of the state of health of women as such. Guinan and Hardy (1987), for example, state blandly that the rate of HIV infection in women is 'of special interest' to epidemiological surveillance because they are the 'major source of infection of infants with AIDS' and because the rate may act as a 'surrogate for monitoring heterosexual transmission of infection'. Lesbian bodies are not addressed as a category within AIDS discourse because, in addition to lesbian sexual practices being conceptualised as low risk, any circulation of infection in lesbian encounters will remain, it is imagined, confined to feminine bodies. In other words lesbian women are unmarked because they refuse to act as conduits between men.

THE CONTROL OF INFECTIOUS FLOW

So what do gay men and straight women have in common, in the epidemiological imagination? In both cases they are conceptualised as fluid entities, in one case as reservoirs, with ominous connotations of potential spillage, and in the other case as tributaries or *conduits*. In both cases they lack proper boundaries, permitting infectious 'seepage' from one body to another, as the quote above expresses it. In the case of gay men, a lack of boundary renders them sites of viral replication, *reservoirs* which both harbour and intensify infection. The endogenous

nature of gay sexuality tends to intensify this reservoir image, a chan-
nelling of infectious flow within particular social borders. For women,
a lack of boundary renders them as *carriers*, whose epidemiological
significance relates to their ability to transmit infection between other
bodies.

In both cases too, this lack of boundary is imagined in the first
instance as a capacity for sexual receptivity, for the accommodation
of phallic breach of their body boundaries. Hence the importance
attached to the passive position in gay sexuality and the coy reference
in the quote stating that 'women have the possibility of sexual contact'
with both high- and low-risk men. And in both cases this is immediately equated with a capacity for receptive accommodation of a series
of such bodies, with 'anonymous multiple partners' among gay men,
and with a mixture of high- and low-risk men, or men and foetus in
the case of women. Their bodily capacities for repeated, receptive sex
are considered by epidemiology to implicate such bodies in the circulation of viral infection.

The following excerpt from an epidemiological essay provides a
highly schematic hydraulic model for characterising the bodies of 'risk
groups'.

> The transmission of an infective agent requires a reservoir that harbours
> the infective source; a route of transmission or vehicle for spreading the
> organism; a susceptible host; a portal of exit from the infected reservoir;
> and a portal of entry into the susceptible host. (Chavigny et al. 1989,
> p. 67)

For epidemiology the bodies of women and gay men furnish the virus
with precisely this kind of fluid pathway, *conduits* which carry the virus
throughout the corporeal matrix of the 'public health'. Just as these
bodies individually facilitate the spread of virus within themselves, so
too do they facilitate its circulation throughout the social milieu. And
just as the virus seeks to colonise the body it has entered, so too does
it seek to colonise the entire social field, through its propagation in
the maximum number of bodies. The bodies of 'risk group' members
are the means of the virus moving both from cell to cell and from
body to body because the ambiguity of their boundaries and their fluid
nature implies their promiscuous mingling with other bodies, either
sexual or uterine.

So it is the putative capacity for forming fluid relations of contagion specific to the sexually receptive body that epidemiology is
committed to control. Why, however, is this capacity considered
specific to sexually receptive bodies? I am addressing this question to

epidemiological discourse, but as Grosz observes, a fluid absence of boundary is associated with the feminine body, not only in biomedicine but in a number of cultural discourses. She writes:

> Can it be that in the West, in our time, the female body has been constructed not only as a lack or absence, but with more complexity, as a leaking, uncontrollable, seeping fluid . . . My claim is that women's corporeality is inscribed as a mode of seepage . . . The metaphorics of uncontrollability . . . the deep-seated fear of absorption, the association of femininity with contagion and disorder, the undecidability of the limits of the female body . . . are all common themes in literary and cultural representations of women. (Grosz 1994, p. 203)

Grosz adds: 'But these may be a function of the projection outwards of their corporealities, the liquidities that men seem to want to cast out of their own self-representations.' In other words, men are able to secure a collective self-image as stable, self-enclosed, individuated bodies, untroubled by fragmentation and confusion, only through projection of these qualities onto women, and in the contexts of AIDS, gay men. This projection is not simply an intra-psychic matter, I would argue, but one that is shored up and guaranteed by a number of institutional practices and discourses. It may be possible to claim that the securing of this projection, its stabilisation in various orders of knowledge, is one of the most important effects of the masculine imago of the body politic.

AIDS epidemiology betrays precisely the same kind of projective logic in its organisation of infection, an indication of the extent to which it shares or more precisely constitutes the point of view of a strictly phallic body. It represents infection as carried by fluid unstable bodies along pathways which converge upon heterosexual masculine bodies, which are themselves conceptualised as bounded, non-receptive and endowed with a phallic sexuality.[11] This point of view can be discerned in the following ways.

First, the equation made in AIDS epidemiology between sexually receptive bodies and contagious capacities only makes sense from the point of view of a phallic body. Bodies which are understood as strictly receptive, that is women's bodies, can only pose an infection threat to a strictly phallic body. For women, it is of course phallic bodies which are the 'source' of infectious threat, but epidemiology only recognises this when the phallic body is not strictly phallic, that is, when it is also receptive, a bisexual male body. If epidemiology was to be elaborated from a feminine point of view, this distinction would be redundant.

Secondly, an implicit economy of bodily value underpins the

epidemiologic of cause and effect and its representation of women's bodies. Women are considered important in AIDS epidemiology not because they are themselves infected, but because they are infecting. They have the status of vectors or carriers in AIDS epidemiology. The first is an animal which carries a virus from one group of humans to another; the second is a person who is infected and may transmit infection but remains themselves unaffected by illness (Brachman 1990). In both cases they are simply the medium of infection, its means of getting from somewhere important to somewhere else important. Women's bodies are relay points rather than the end point of infection. The point of infectious origin is provided by the gay male *reservoir*, where infection is siphoned off by bisexual men and transferred to heterosexual women. They in turn carry it to its end point, which is always imagined as either a phallic body or its progeny, a foetus or infant. It is this status which explains the logic of women's conditions of inclusion and exclusion from the 'general population' that I described in the introduction. Women who are married, monogamous, lesbian or virginal and not pregnant can be included in the general population because they do not act as a transmission point between one male body and another: they keep the borders of the 'general population'/'risk group' division intact.

Thirdly, the epidemiological anxiety about 'promiscuity' is, as Bersani (1988) points out, an implicitly phallic anxiety. It is directed against the at least potential ability of receptive bodies to repeat sex, an ability which strictly phallic bodies so plainly lack. In AIDS epidemiology sexually receptive bodies act as *conduits* in an *a priori* fashion, but they are also the bodies which can, in the phallic imagination, repeat sex indefinitely with an uncountable number of phallic bodies. The promiscuous capacities of sexually receptive bodies hence intensify their contagious dangers, both in the sense that they multiply the number of phallic bodies they come into contact with, and in that each previous contact increases their virulence for each subsequent man.

So what I am suggesting here is that within AIDS epidemiology heterosexual male bodies do not appear as problematic objects because they are not implicated in the circulation of the virus within the social matrix. They are not transmission points, but rather the ultimate end point of infection. It is this end point which epidemiology equates with the absolute decline of the public health and which the interventions of public health institutions are designed to avert. Heterosexual male bodies are threatened by the virus, but only insofar as the contagious circulation of other bodies is not controlled. The control of circulation is precisely what epidemiology and public health set out to do in the field of AIDS, but because heterosexual male bodies are not con-ceptualised as being implicated in this flow they form the privileged 'general population' which is implicitly protected by the control or responsiblisation of other bodies. Heterosexual men remain the masters of contagious circulation because they are not implicated in that circulation.

CONCLUSION

In summary then, heterosexual male bodily interests are made to coincide with the interests of the 'public health', as it is conceived in the age of AIDS, through their resemblance to an ideal bodily order which remains outside the circuits of AIDS contagion. They are the bodies which are held within biomedicine to enact within their morphology the protocols of individuation which Foucault tells us are the strategies undertaken by public health institutions to control infectious spread.[12] They are bodies which are considered to be *already* controlled, to *already* conform to an order proper to the public health.

This public health, the health of the body politic, is, however, lethally threatened by bodies with unstable boundaries and fluid tendencies, bodies which seep beyond the borders dictated by individ-uation. These bodies are considered to form contagious circuits within the body politic, to act as weak points in its corporeal matrix which enables the propagation of the virus. Epidemiology imagines its task to be the control of infectious flow, but in making flow an effect of difference from phallic integrity it addresses its strategies to the disciplining of feminine and gay sexualities in order to protect the true denizens of the 'general population', heterosexual men.

ACKNOWLEDGEMENTS

Versions of this chapter were presented at the Sex/Gender in Techno-Science Worlds Conference, University of Melbourne, 26 June–1 July 1993 and the Regimes of Sexuality Conference, Australian National University, Canberra, 5–8 July 1993. The author would like to thank Mark Berger, Bob Connell, Rosanne Kennedy, David McMaster, Carol Vance and the research staff at the Australian National Centre for HIV Social Research, Macquarie Unit, for their helpful comments on previous drafts of this chapter. I would also like to thank Moira Gatens for several discussions about the body politic, and John Kaldor for discussions about epidemiological practice.

NOTES

1   I have written about this absence in a number of articles and in my book. See
     Waldby (1996) and Waldby et al. (1990, 1991, 1993a, 1993b).
2   In response to this observation it is often pointed out to me that heterosexual
     men are included in those safe sex campaigns addressed to the 'general' or
     'heterosexual' population, as are heterosexual women. Nevertheless, heterosexual
     women have also been the object of specific campaigns, while to the best of my
     knowledge there has only been one campaign addressed specifically to heterosex-
     ual men in Australia. In late 1992 the New South Wales Family Planning
     Association received a small grant to run a safe sex campaign specifically for
     heterosexual men. This grant was the result of several years of lobbying on the
     part of feminist AIDS activists, including the author.
3   For documentation of these dynamics see Waldby et al. (1993a, 1993b); Holland
     et al. (1990a, 1990b); and Holland et al. (1990).
4   The binary general population/risk group is no longer in official use in epidemi-
     ological practice in Australia, the UK or the USA, although it is still current in
     popular media and some other more politically naive biomedical discourse. In
     epidemiological surveillance the idea of 'risk groups' has been replaced with that
     of 'transmission' or 'exposure' categories, which include heterosexuals as well as
     the previous risk categories. Nevertheless the idea of 'risk groups' still permeates
     this new terminology. While the categories of 'homosexual/bisexual men' and
     'IV-drug users' are used to simply designate rates of infection, a recording of HIV
     positivity for a heterosexual person must be further designated according to the
     'risk category' of the person who 'gave' them HIV—IV-drug user, bisexual man,
     person from a pattern-two country etc.
5   Patton (1991) also makes the point that the terms 'general population' or
     'heterosexual population' are often used to designate heterosexual men.
6   See Watney (1987) for discussion of the 'imaginary national family unit' as the
     subject to be addressed by the media's discourse about AIDS and the subject to
     be protected by public health policy.
7   In Australia women have been regularly appealed to in this way. The national
     'Tell him if it's not on, it's not on' campaign, designed to encourage women to
     ask their partners to use condoms, made quite explicit the assumption that it was
     up to women to enforce safe sex. Similarly a television campaign depicting a
     couple in bed has the woman saying 'well, no condom means no sex'.
8   See Waldby (1996) and Waldby et al. (1991) for a discussion of the significance
     of women's alleged sexual passivity in AIDS discourse.
9   See, for example, Douglas (1984), Kantorowicz (1957), Le Goff (1989), Mont-
     gomery (1991).
10   The epidemiological literature which links receptive anal intercourse and high
     numbers of sexual partners to both gay sexuality and HIV transmission is vast.
     For a comprehensive survey of this literature see Bolton (1992).
11   See Waldby et al. (1993b) for a documentation and discussion of this point of
     view as it is experienced by young heterosexual men in everyday life.
12   In *Discipline and Punish*, Foucault demonstrates that the strategies of individuation,
     which he nominates as the central feature of modern disciplinary subjectivity,
     receive their most detailed elaboration in the discourses of epidemic control. See
     particularly his account of the control of the plague town, pp. 195–99.

REFERENCES

Anderson, B. 1991 *Imagined Communities: Reflections on the Origin and Spread of Nationalism* rev. edn, Verso, London & New York

Bersani, L. 1988 'Is the rectum a grave?' in *AIDS: Cultural Analysis, Cultural Activism* ed. D. Crimp, Massachusetts Institute of Technology Press, Cambridge, MA

Bolton, R. 1992 'AIDS and promiscuity' *Medical Anthropology* no. 14, pp. 144–223

Brachman, P. 1990 'Epidemiology of infectious disease: Principles and methods' in *Principles and Practice of Infectious Diseases* eds G. Mandell, R. Douglas & J. Bennett, 3rd edn, Churchill Livingstone, New York

Canguilhem, G. 1989 *The Normal and the Pathological* first published 1966 Zone Books, New York

Chamberland, M. & Curran, J. 1990 'Epidemiology and prevention of AIDS and HIV' in *Principles and Practice of Infectious Diseases* eds G. Mandell, R. Douglas & J. Bennett, 3rd edn, Churchill Livingstone, New York

Chavigny, K., Turner, S. & Kibrick, A. 1989 'Epidemiology and health policy imperatives for AIDS' in *The AIDS Epidemic: Private Rights and Public Interest* ed. P. O'Malley, Beacon Press, Boston

Commonwealth AIDS Research Grants Epidemiology Advisory Committee 1990 'The role of epidemiology in controlling HIV disease in Australia' National Centre in HIV Epidemiology and Clinical Research, Sydney, Australia

Commonwealth Department of Community Services and Health 1988 *A Time to Care, a Time to Act: Towards a Strategy for All Australians* Policy Discussion Paper, AGPS, Canberra

Corbin, A. 1986 *The Foul and the Fragrant: Odour and the French Social Imagination* Berg Publishers, New York

Douglas, M. 1984 *Purity and Danger: An Analysis of the Concepts of Pollution and Taboo* first published 1966, Ark Paperbacks, London

Foucault, M. 1979 *Discipline and Punish: The Birth of the Prison* Peregrine Books, Harmondsworth, UK

——1980a *The History of Sexuality, Volume I: An Introduction* Vintage Books, New York

——1980b 'The politics of health in the eighteenth century' in *Power/Knowledge: Selected Interviews and Other Writings 1972–1977 by Michel Foucault* ed. C. Gordon, Pantheon Books, New York

Gatens, M. 1988 'Towards a feminist philosophy of the body' in *Crossing Boundaries: Feminisms and the Critique of Knowledges* eds B. Caine, E. Grosz & M. de Lepervanche, Allen & Unwin, Sydney

——1991a 'Corporeal representation in/and the body politic' in *Cartographies: Poststructuralism and the Mapping of Bodies and Spaces* eds R. Diprose & R. Ferrell, Allen & Unwin, Sydney

——1991b *Feminism and Philosophy: Perspectives on Difference and Equality* Polity, Cambridge

Grosz, E. 1994 *Volatile Bodies: Towards a Corporeal Feminism* Allen & Unwin, Sydney

Grover, J. 1988 'AIDS: Keywords' in *AIDS: Cultural Analysis, Cultural Activism* ed. D. Crimp, Massachusetts Institute of Technology Press, Cambridge, MA

Guinan, M. & Hardy, A. 1987 'Epidemiology of AIDS in women in the United States: 1981 through 1986' *Journal of the American Medical Association* vol. 257, no. 15, pp. 2039–42

Haraway, D. 1991 *Simians, Cyborgs and Women: The Reinvention of Nature* Routledge, London & New York

Holland, J., Ramazanoglue, C. & Scott, S. 1990a 'AIDS: From panic stations to power relations. Sociological perspectives and problems' *Sociology* vol. 25, no. 3, pp. 499–518

——1990b 'Managing risk and experiencing danger: Tensions between government AIDS education policy and young women's sexuality' *Gender and Education* vol. 2, no. 2, pp. 125–46

Holland, J., Ramazanoglue, C., Scott, S., Sharpe, S. & Thomson, R. 1990 'Sex, gender and power: Young women's sexuality in the shadow of AIDS' *Sociology of Health and Illness* vol. 12, no. 3, pp. 336–50

Kantorowicz, E. 1957 *The Kings Two Bodies* Princeton University Press, Princeton

Le Goff, J. 1989 'Head or heart? The political use of body metaphors in the Middle Ages' in *Fragments for a History of the Human Body* ed. M. Feher, vol. 3, Zone Books, New York

Montgomery, S. 1991 'Codes and combat in bio-medical discourse' *Science as Culture* vol. 2, part 3 (no. 12), pp. 341–91

Patton, C. 1990 *Inventing AIDS* Routledge, London & New York

Roitt, I. 1991 *Essential Immunology* 7th edn, Blackwell Scientific Publications, Oxford

Treichler, P. 1992 'Beyond *Cosmo*: AIDS, identity, and inscriptions of gender' *Camera Obscura* 28, pp. 21–77

Waldby, C. 1996 *Aids and the Body Politic* Routledge, London & New York

Waldby, C., Kippax, S. & Crawford, J. 1990 'Theory in the bedroom' *Australian Journal of Social Issues* vol. 25, no. 3, pp. 177–86

——1991 'Equality and eroticism: AIDS and the active/passive distinction' *Social Semiotics* vol. 1, no. 2, pp. 39–50

——1993a 'Heterosexual men and safe sex practice' *The Sociology of Health and Illness* vol. 15, no. 2, pp. 246–56

——1993b '*Cordon sanitaire*: Clean and unclean women in the AIDS discourse of young men' in *AIDS: The Second Decade* eds P. Aggleton, P. Davies & G. Hart, Falmer Press, London

Watney, S. 1987 *Policing Desire: Pornography, AIDS and the Media* Methuen, London

Winkelstein, W., Padian, N., Rutherford, G. & Jaffe, H. 1989 'Homosexual men' in *The Epidemiology of AIDS: Expression, Occurrence, and Control of Human Immunodeficiency Virus Type 1 Infection* eds R. Kaslow & D. Francis, Oxford University Press, New York & Oxford

22 A well-shaped man

David Buchbinder

> Saliva, chyle, bile
> Pancreatic juice, serum, and phlegm,
> There Adam lay supine—a well-shaped man.
>
> William Boyce, 'Man's First Estate on Earth'

As poetry, these lines might be deemed pretty ghastly. Indeed, I found them in a collection of bad verse (Wyndham Lewis & Lee 1948, p. 18). My concern, however, is less with the quality of Boyce's verse-making than with the epistemological paradigm that his lines imply, with reference to masculinity in particular, and to health. This description of the newly-created Adam has its origins in scientific epistem- ology as it arose—in England, at any rate—in the early seventeenth century. That way of knowing humans and the physical world they inhabit has been a continuing influence on our own ways of seeing and knowing, and has been especially powerful in medical discourse, strengthened as it was by nineteenth-century positivist beliefs that the material world can be entirely known, and explained through material causes alone.

Boyce's catalogue of juices and secretions suggests that the shape-liness (or otherwise) of man[1] is to be judged according to a certain set of criteria and a certain notion of knowing the world. But there have been other criteria and ways of knowing. The classical Greeks, for instance, foregrounded the ability to reason correctly and to behave morally. For a thinker of Plato's temperament, the comeliness of the individual's exterior was the material reflection of the right balance and harmony of that person's thought, desires and behaviour, while Aristotle's famous dictum, in his *Politics*, that man is a political creature suggests still another way of conceiving 'a well-shaped man'. Mediaeval thought about what made for the appropriate, harmonious individual tended to combine notions of morality with politics in the belief that the individual should be obedient, first, to the laws of God and, second, to those of the socio-political hierarchy, itself ostensibly modelled on the divinely ordained structure of the universe. Hamlet's ironic and sad tribute takes account of Renaissance man's capacity to reason, his creativity, his physical attributes and other factors; but ultimately the melancholy prince sees all individuals, however well- or badly-shaped, arriving at the same end, so that well-shapedness is ultimately characterised as futile:

> What piece of work is a man, how noble in reason, how infinite in faculties, in form and moving how express and admirable, in action how like an angel, in apprehension how like a god: the beauty of the world, the paragon of animals—and yet, to me, what is this quintessence of dust? (Shakespeare 1982, act II, scene ii, lines 303–08)

In Boyce's formulation, however, the judgement is to be made on the basis of whether man is composed of necessary bits and pieces, and has the appropriate fluids flowing through the various parts of his body and its organs. If all is present and correct, then the individual may be pronounced healthy, 'well-shaped'. The epithet therefore signifies here not comeliness or beauty, as it might in our own culture, but rather 'so put together as to function well, in conformity with a predetermined design'.

A mechanistic, hydraulic model like this of the body and its state of well-being, however, tends to background social relationships and dynamics; and it is on this issue of the degree of influence of social factors on gender behaviour that essentialist and constructionist (also called constructivist) theories of gender converge and—frequently— disagree. Essentialist models of gender (and of bodily health) argue that gender behaviour is innate within the sexed human body. Thus, for example, hormones are judged as important influences on social behaviour: testosterone, by this light, *predisposes* males to aggressive and competitive behaviour. This way of seeing the relationship of gender to the body may lead to a behaviourist perspective which points in turn towards a notion of human history that reaches back to archaic origins paralleling the ontogenic development of other species.

If I may oversimplify, this argument makes connections among the sexed body, human and animal, and behaviour, allowing people to arrive at conclusions like the notion—so popular in the culture now that it has taken on the guise of fact—that the entrepreneurial businessman is simply the contemporary version of Man the Hunter. The prehistoric plains teeming with game, by a similar transposition, become the real meaning to which the contemporary urban setting, itself now apparently merely illusory or at any rate metaphorical, points. Such a hypothesis often puts into abeyance or discreetly backgrounds those arguments that are often made precisely to *distinguish* the human from the animal, such as the capacity to reason, to invent and radically to alter the natural environment. A well-shaped man, according to essentialist theories, therefore, is one whose gender behaviour accords well with the sexing of his body, and thence with the physiological constitution of that body—a position not so very distant from Boyce's, it would seem, but also one that comes very close to being tautologous: a man is masculine because he is male. 'Man', 'masculine' and 'male' thus become virtual synonyms.

What is less frequently asked, in essentialist views of gender and gender behaviour, is how we *know* which behaviours are appropriate to each sex.[2] One consequence of this is the imposition of a fairly narrow repertoire of acceptable and approved behaviours for the members of either sex. Deviations from these or failures to meet an assumed norm often result in the submission of the individual to a regimen of therapy, whether pharmaceutical, surgical or psychiatric. An obvious example of this, as Michel Foucault points out, is the normativisation of heterosexuality, and the concomitant pathologisation of other sexualities by medicine in the nineteenth century (Foucault 1980, pp. 36–49). Such categorisations are not merely theoretical: they have real social consequences for individuals in the culture, consequences which may make a person the focus of medical, psychiatric, juridical and other sorts of attention, as well as threatening a quarantine of the individual from society by isolating them in a hospital, psychiatric ward or prison.

The constructionist approach, by contrast, advances the idea that while *sex*, as biological difference, might be a given, and hence natural (though here there are large questions concerning such matters as anatomical hermaphroditism and gender dysphoria), *gender*, as a systemic expectation of behaviours appropriate to either sex, is produced and reproduced socially. It might be described, therefore, as an *ideology* which encodes what sorts of behaviours are deemed appropriate for men and women *in that culture, at that time*—for gender constructions can change historically: in eighteenth-century England, for instance, men were encouraged, under the influence of the philosophy of sentimentalism, to express their emotions openly. This would sit at odds with today's ideology of masculinity, which has rather tended to

foreground stoicism and emotional blankness as appropriate to masculine behaviour. Thus, constructionist notions of gender allow a
distinction to be made between a man's sex—male—and his gender—
masculine. A well-shaped man, according to this approach, is therefore
one who conforms to the expectations of his culture's ideology of
masculinity.

Medical discourse tends towards essentialism—unsurprisingly,
given its roots in the paradigm of scientific epistemology and in
positivism. It frequently assumes, therefore, that gender behaviour *is
encoded in the body* of the appropriate sex. Where there is a conflict—
for instance, an effeminate man, a woman engaging in masculine
behaviour—it is inferred that there is something wrong with the
individual concerned, not with the definition of gender and its deployment, in our culture, between only two sexes: other cultures may make
provision for 'intersexes', by which term I include not only physical
hermaphrodites but also gender-dysphoric individuals (see, e.g.
Greenberg 1988, on berdaches and shamans, pp. 40–62).

It is not my intention here to unfold the essentialist/constructionist
controversy: much has already been written on the topic (see, for
instance, Rubin 1975, an important article which sets up the idea of a
culture's sex-gender system; Berger, Wallis et al. 1995; Fuss 1989; Stein
1992). Rather, I wish to suggest that issues of men's health may not be
merely bodily ones. However, while many health professionals may
willingly and eagerly concede that there are social factors contributory
to men's health, often these are seen as specific to individual patients,
in the first place, and, in the second, their clinical significance is often
dependent upon a particular magnitude of importance. For instance,
while most will accept that a man diagnosed as suffering from testicular
cancer will no doubt undergo traumatic anxiety about his sexual abili-
ties and, importantly, about his masculine subjectivity (i.e. his sense of
himself as a man), it is unlikely that the same level of professional
concern will be generated by a man who presents with the symptoms of
a bad cold—yet the business executive with a red nose, a continual
sniffle and impaired speech who must attend an important meeting may
also feel himself to be disempowered and less than masculine, though
doubtless not to the same extent or in the same way.

It is important to understand that constructionist theory does not
assert that gender and gender behaviours can be simply determined
by individuals: as Judith Butler observes about sexuality,

> constructivism needs to take account of the domain of constraints
> without which a certain living and desiring being cannot make its way.

And every such being is constrained by not only what is difficult to imagine, but what remains radically unthinkable . . . (Butler 1993, p. 94)

Those constraints are social and cultural, and not only *precede* the individual, who is born into them, but also therefore *determine* the range and acceptability of that infant individual's future behaviour. Thus, biological difference constitutes maleness or femaleness in the individual body, and all that this might imply in terms of hormonal differences and influences, the impact of anatomical difference on behaviour, and so on—one cannot, of course, completely exclude or discount the body, together with its structures and secretions. However, the culture determines which, of all these factors, will constellate with social behaviours and patterns of speech, gesture and so on to signify 'masculinity' or 'femininity' for members of that culture, at that time. In this respect, there is more to buying blue for a baby boy and pink for a baby girl than being able simply to tell their sexes apart.

An important element informing Butler's argument is the notion that gender behaviour is not merely *performance*—that is, something that an individual of either sex can 'do'—but is also *performative*: that is, its enactment announces the individual's gender to others in the culture. Butler suggests that this enactment must continually be repeated, since gender identifications remain fragile and apparently ephemeral (Butler 1993, pp. 12–16). This implies, in turn, that gender is less an innate characteristic than ideological: that is, the distribution of gender traits and behaviours between the two sexes serves the interests of a particular group in the culture. In a patriarchal culture like our own, that group is made up of men. In order to retain male ascendancy in the politics of the culture, therefore, it is important that what counts as masculinity and what as femininity appear stable and permanent to the members of the culture.

Such a gender ideology necessarily establishes a system of inclusions and exclusions. Thus, submissive women obedient to their menfolk have traditionally been included; as the various protests and political interventions by women over the past couple of decades have demonstrated, a woman who refuses such a posture with regard to men will tend to be excluded as pushy, ambitious, power-hungry—traits, we might note, that are often lauded and applauded in men.

Intrinsic to this system of inclusions and exclusions, with regard specifically to men, is a system of surveillance by which each individual male's credentials for entry into the patriarchal structure are continually examined and judged. In practical terms, this means that men constantly keep other men under observation, ready to accord the status of masculinity to other individual males or to withhold it from them. Thus, men are always performing masculinity *for other men*, in order to gain their approval and acceptance. As a consequence, men find themselves under a tremendous strain for much of their lives, because the penalty for *not* performing masculinity for other males is to find oneself excluded and, in many cases, forced to undergo humiliation or even physical abuse of some kind, sometimes even unto death, as the many cases of gay-bashing—unfortunately all too amply—make clear.

By what criteria does the inclusion/exclusion process operate under patriarchy? I am here less concerned with the actual mechanics or instances of the process than with the ways that the gender system enables masculinity structurally and systemically to maintain its dominance. The ideological self-positioning of masculinity proposes that it is the ground-zero of gender, so that femininity appears as a deviation from that defining term. This can be seen from many fairly common instances, commencing with the way in which the masculine is often used as the generic grammatical gender—'the common man', 'mankind', the use of 'he' to signify both genders—to the still common favouring of men over women in business and industry (except, of course, where a policy of reverse discrimination has been put in place—usually over the objections and complaints of male employees). And it is discernible, too, in the way that men and men's health have traditionally been seen as the norm, against which women and women's health have been compared and judged. In this regard, then, until quite recently many issues affecting men's health—risky behaviours, including smoking and drinking; physically and/or psychologically stressful work conditions; difficulties dealing with emotional matters; and so on—have historically been overlooked or ignored as simply the way men 'are'. The effect of such factors on men's health has been viewed, according to this logic, therefore, as perfectly normal, as part of being a man.

However, if instead of accepting the masculine at its own valuation as the defining term of gender, we viewed it rather as a term in a system of gender positions which includes not only anatomical sexing but also the orientation of sexual desire, a somewhat different picture emerges. The masculine now appears to rely for its own definition *on the simultaneous presence and refusal of two other categories*, the feminine and the (male) homosexual. It is, in other words, a definition by negative in terms of sex, on the one hand, and, on the other, of sexuality: men are *not* feminine and they are *not* homosexual. Again, ordinary examples show us that this may be the case. After all, the two deadliest insults that one male, young or old, may offer another is to call him either a woman (often in terms metonymically reducing the allusion to the anatomical difference between the sexes, for instance, 'cunt') or a homosexual (the latter often in pejorative terms, for instance, not 'gay' but rather something like 'poof' or 'faggot').[3]

The feminine and the homosexual thus function not only as the categories which help to define the masculine, they are also the categories of exclusion, to which the deviant, intransigent or otherwise disobedient male may be relegated by way of humiliation and punishment.[4] This is, then, a structural analysis of the culture's gender system, and therefore also of how gender identifications may be policed under patriarchy. Such an analysis, however, runs the risk of hypostasising the reality, leading one as a result to imagine that it is a stable, static system. It is for this reason that Butler's argument (a constant theme in her book *Bodies That Matter*) about the iteration of gender is important: the culture repeatedly requires one to enunciate one's gender through gesture and behaviour, lest the very provisionality and contingency of the patriarchal gender system itself be exposed (Butler 1993).

Men, of course, and especially heterosexual men, have much to lose in any such exposure, for it would then become more difficult to justify the privileges and power which patriarchy makes available to men. We should note, however, that though as a generality men are advantaged under patriarchy, in reality individual men do not share power equally. In addition to differences in sexual orientation, so that same-sex male desire is disparaged along with the individual who manifests such desire, differences of physical size and strength, class, age or race also create lines of division which function as relays of power and opportunity. Likewise, exhibitions of individual ability or courage (often characterised as 'having balls', an interesting idiom which suggests that, by comparison, other men are emasculated) establish other differences of privilege and position in the hierarchies set up by patriarchal ideology. The apparent egalitarianism and co-operative nature of group efforts, for instance, those of a sports team or the workers in an office or business, are often undermined by the singling out of an individual for the award of 'Man of the Match' or 'Employee of the Month'. Men are thus encouraged ideologically to compete with one another for supremacy, a situation which often creates a particular strain on the individual, for he is directed, by patriarchal imperatives, to vie with those from whom he also seeks approval as a man, namely, other men.

It is a sign of the efficacy of patriarchal ideology that it works so well, so that most men not only do not contest its terms, they fail even to see that their lives are governed by ideological, not natural and therefore not inevitable, directives; and that, as a result, they may choose other possible patterns. In this respect, we may say that this gender ideology is a form of rhetoric. I borrow a particular use of this term from Stanley Fish's study of the ways the language of seventeenth-century literature positions and manipulates its readers. Fish defines the rhetorical work thus:

> A presentation is rhetorical if it satisfies the needs of its readers. The word 'satisfies' is meant literally here; for it is characteristic of a rhetorical form to mirror and present for approval the opinions its readers already hold. It follows then that the experience of such a form will be flattering, for it tells the reader that what he has always thought about the world is true and that the *ways* of his thinking are sufficient. This is not to say that in the course of a rhetorical experience one is never told anything unpleasant, but that whatever one is told can be placed and contained within the categories and assumptions of received systems of knowledge. (Fish 1972, p. 1)

If we apply this to the structures and directives of patriarchy, it allows us to see that the naturalising tendencies of ideology function here to normalise masculinity and its required behaviours, so that to 'think' masculinity 'other-wise' or to perform it differently seem both eccentric and dangerous. Of course, those who are principally excluded by the patriarchal ideology of gender, namely, women and gay men, are enabled, precisely by that marginalisation, to see how patriarchal masculinity is only *one* possibility for men that has been elevated to the status of the *only* possibility.

To the rhetorical presentation Fish opposes what he calls a dialectical presentation, which he describes as

> disturbing, for it requires of its readers a searching and rigorous scrutiny of everything they believe in and live by. It is didactic in a special sense; it does not preach the truth, but asks that its readers discover the truth for themselves, and this discovery is often made at the expense not only of a reader's opinions and values, but of his self-esteem. If the experience of a rhetorical form is flattering, the experience of a dialectical form is humiliating. (Fish 1972, pp. 1–2)

In the light of this, we may characterise as dialectical presentations the various feminist analyses of gender, as well as those undertaken by gay political activist writers and, more recently, by men dissatisfied with the inequities and injustices distributed and imposed by the power differentials by which patriarchy sustains itself. However, much of this work has, even if only implicitly, subscribed to the two-sex/two-gender/one-sexuality view imposed by patriarchal ideology, dissent being voiced more and more loudly by gay and lesbian theorists; some feminist theorists, too, have considered the notion of androgyny as a possible solution to the politics of gender produced by patriarchy (see, for instance, the succinct summary of feminist androgynist and anti-androgynist positions in Tong 1989, p. 4, and *passim*).

Within the past decade a new theory of gender and sexuality has emerged within the excluded fields of the non-normative and non-heterosexual in the culture; a body of theoretical work and analysis called queer theory. It presents a radical challenge to familiar gendered structures and gender identification, and therefore may be thought of as a powerful instance of the dialectical, in Fish's sense. This is because 'queer' encompasses not merely the male and female homosexual, but also the male and female bisexual, the transgendered, the transsexual, the transvestite, the gender dysphoric, and many other identifications or subject positions which have hitherto been either ignored or relegated to some form of therapeutic 'cure' or 'correction'. 'Queer' embraces also the normative male and female heterosexual, insofar as individuals falling into these categories may choose to violate the category boundaries from time to time, or may find themselves positioned at times in ways that demonstrate the constructedness of the categories with which they normally identify and which may have hitherto seemed beyond question or doubt.

Queer theory, then, by its very nature is a complex, difficult and elusive approach to issues of gender and sexuality. (For a fuller account of queer theory, see Jagose (1996).) Nonetheless, it may offer many the sort of experience which Fish attributes to the dialectical form of argument:

> Obviously the risk, on the part of the dialectician, of so proceeding, is considerable. A reader who is asked to judge himself may very well decline, but should he accept the challenge, the reward that awaits him . . . will be more than commensurate with his efforts. For the end of a dialectical experience is (or should be) nothing less than a *conversion*, not only a changing, but an exchanging of minds. It is necessarily a painful process (like sloughing off a second skin) in the course of which both parties forfeit a great deal; on the one side the applause of a pleased audience, and on the other, the satisfaction of listening to the public affirmation of our values and prejudices. The relationship is finally less one of speaker to hearer, or author to reader than of physician to patient, and it is as the 'good physician' that the dialectician is traditionally known. (Fish 1972, p. 2)

The advantage, in the context of a concern regarding men's health, is that queer theory offers strategies by which to alleviate the

social pressures on men to perform a particular notion of masculinity:
it broadens notions of gender, and expands the possible repertoires of
behaviour, desire and subjectivity available to individuals in the
culture.

We have come some distance from Boyce's complacent assertion
quoted at the outset of this chapter. I hope, however, that what has
emerged is that gender patterns and behaviours are not natural, and
even less transhistorical or transcultural, but, rather, are responsive to
requirements made of men and women by the culture which they
inhabit. The tendency of medical—indeed, of much scientific—discourse to assume a stable, unchanging notion of gender serves certain
purposes to which medicine is committed; but this is only one perception of the nature and function of gender. Others not only produce
different readings of gender, but also throw into relief problems actually
or potentially related to the health of individuals, problems which may
require solutions other than medication, surgery or being told to pull
oneself together. The solutions will often lie where the problems
themselves are located, namely, in the social structure and in the
culture's requirements of the sexes. It is unlikely that the patriarchal
gender system will be dismantled overnight. But dialectical explorations
of that system, such as queer theory offers, help to create ruptures in it
and open spaces that permit individuals *to play* with gender/desire/sex-
uality. And, in that play, why might one not produce new notions of
what it is to be a well-shaped man?

NOTES

1   I am, of course, aware that 'man' is here being used in part as a generic term for
     'humanity'. However, it is also true that the male has traditionally been considered
     the norm or template according to which the female has corresponded or from
     which she has varied. Moreover, since this chapter is about men, masculinity and
     health, it has seemed appropriate to allow the masculine generic to stand, in
     order to signify 'man' specifically.
2   Arguments made on the basis of animal experimentation often seem, on the face
     of it, conclusive; however, since the social organisation of various species is often
     radically different from human societies, and since many species function
     instinctually and reflexively (they do not seem, for instance, to be able to predict
     future events on the basis of present circumstances in the same way that humans
     can), we probably need to be circumspect about what the behaviour of male rats
     or pigs, for instance, can tell us about the behaviour of male humans.
3   There is, of course, in this system a fourth category, that of the female homosexual,
     which lies outside the scope of this chapter. We might note, however, that the
     patriarchal masculine does not require this category for its self-definition: it may

be subsumed under that of the feminine proper, as indeed it often is when the lesbian body becomes the object of the desiring heterosexual male gaze, and when lesbian desire is thought to be merely wayward heterosexual female desire (hence the oft-heard maxim that all a lesbian needs is a good fuck with a man in order to transfer her desire to its proper object, the penis/phallus).

4 The lesbian, by contrast, may become the category by which the heterosexual feminine is excluded, and to which the woman who refuses a man's advances may be relegated, by way both of humiliation and of explanation for her refusal of sexual access or the failure of the man's (presumed) sexual attractiveness.

REFERENCES

Berger, M., Wallis, B. et al. (eds) 1995 *Constructing Masculinity* Routledge, New York & London

Butler, J. 1993 *Bodies That Matter: On the Discursive Limits of 'Sex'* Routledge, New York & London

Fish, S.E. 1972 *Self-Consuming Artifacts: The Experience of Seventeenth-Century Literature* University of California Press, Berkeley, Los Angeles & London

Foucault, M. 1980 *The History of Sexuality, Volume 1: An Introduction* trans. R. Hurley, Random House, New York

Fuss, D. 1989 *Essentially Speaking: Feminism, Nature and Difference* Routledge, New York & London

Greenberg, D.F. 1988 *The Construction of Homosexuality* University of Chicago Press, Chicago & London

Jagose, A. 1996 *Queer Theory* Melbourne University Press, Carlton

Rubin, G. 1975 'The traffic in women: Notes on the "political economy" of sex' in *Towards an Anthropology of Women* ed. R.R. Reiter, Monthly Review Press, New York & London, pp. 157–210

Shakespeare, W. 1982 *The Arden Edition of the Works of William Shakespeare: Hamlet* (original work published c. 1601) ed. H. Jenkins, Methuen, London & New York

Stein, E. (ed.) 1992 *Forms of Desire: Sexual Orientation and the Social Constructionist Controversy* Routledge, New York & London

Tong, R. 1989 *Feminist Thought: A Comprehensive Introduction* Routledge, London

Wyndham Lewis, D.B. & Lee, C. (eds) 1948 *The Stuffed Owl: An Anthology of Bad Verse* Dent Everyman's Library, London

Index